If it's APRIL 2006
and you are still using this Directory,
it's time to order the NEW Edition.

Please visit our website

www.cabells.com

or contact us at

Box 5428, Beaumont, Texas 77726-5428
(409) 898-0575
Fax (409) 866-9554
Email: publish@cabells.com

Cabell's Directory Of Publishing Opportunities In Economics and Finance

VOLUME II   J
NINTH EDITION 2004-05

David W. E. Cabell, Editor
McNeese State University
Lake Charles, Louisiana

Deborah L. English, Editor
Twyla J. George, Assistant Editor

To order additional copies
visit our web site
www.cabells.com

or contact us at

Box 5428 Beaumont, Texas 77726-5428
(409) 898-0575 Fax (409) 866-9554

$119.95 U.S. for addresses in United States
Price includes shipping and handling for U.S.
Add $50 for surface mail to countries outside U.S.
Add $100 for air mail to countries outside U.S.

ISBN # 0-911753-23-0

Japanese Economic Review (The)

ADDRESS FOR SUBMISSION:

M. Yano and N. Kiyotaki, Co-Editors
Japanese Economic Review (The)
The Institute of Statistical Research
1-18-16 Shinbashi
Minato-Ku
Tokyo, 105-0004
Japan
Phone: 81 3 3453 4511
Fax: 81 3 3798 7480
E-Mail: makoto@ml.cet.co.jp
Web: www.blackwellpublishing.co.uk
Address May Change:

PUBLICATION GUIDELINES:

Manuscript Length: 21-25
Copies Required: Four
Computer Submission: No
Format: N/A
Fees to Review: 0.00 US$

Manuscript Style:
See Manuscript Guidelines

CIRCULATION DATA:

Reader: Academics
Frequency of Issue: Quarterly
Copies per Issue: 3,001 - 4,000
Sponsor/Publisher: Blackwell Publishing
Subscribe Price: 51.00 US$ N. America
117.00 US$ N. America Institution
37.00 Pounds Rest of World

REVIEW INFORMATION:

Type of Review: Editorial Review
No. of External Reviewers: 2
No. of In House Reviewers: 0
Acceptance Rate: 21-30%
Time to Review: 2 - 3 Months
Reviewers Comments: Yes
Invited Articles: 0-5%
Fees to Publish: 0.00 US$

MANUSCRIPT TOPICS:

Analysis of the Japanese Economy; Econometrics; Economic Development; Economic Dynamics; Game Theory; Industrial Organization; International Economics & Trade; International Finance; Macro Economics; Micro Economics; Public Policy Economics

MANUSCRIPT GUIDELINES/COMMENTS:

Aims and Scope
Started in 1950 by a group of leading Japanese economists under the title *The Economic Studies Quarterly*, the journal became the official English language publication of the Japanese Economic Association in 1959.

As its successor, *The Japanese Economic Review* aims to become the Japanese counterpart of *The American Economic Review*, publishing substantial economic analysis of the highest quality across the whole field of economics from the researchers both within and outside Japan. It also welcomes innovative and thought-provoking contributions with strong relevance to real economic issues, whether political, theoretical or policy-oriented.

Instructions to Contributors

1. Manuscripts and editorial communications should be sent in quadruplicate to The Editors, The Japanese Economic Review, The Institute of Statistical Research, 1-18-16 Shimbashi, Minato-ku, Tokyo, Japan 105.

Manuscripts should be written in English, and should be accompanied by a letter of submission stating that they are original unpublished work, not submitted for consideration elsewhere. Authors should supply an English abstract not exceeding 100 words and the JEL classification number(s).

Upon acceptance of an article, author(s) will be asked to transfer copyright of the article to the Japanese Economic Association. This transfer will ensure the widest possible dissemination of information.

2. Manuscripts should be typed on one side of the paper only, using double spacing throughout and leaving adequate margins on all sides. All pages should be numbered consecutively, and references, tables and legends for figures should be prepared on separate pages.

3. The first page of manuscripts should contain the following information:
   a. the title;
   b. the name(s) and affiliation(s) of the author(s); and
   c. the address for editorial correspondence, including phone and fax numbers and an e-mail address.

4. Footnotes should be kept to a minimum and be numbered consecutively. Acknowledgements can be given before the list of references.

5. Where mathematical derivations are abbreviated, the full workings necessary for justifying each step of the argument should accompany all manuscripts of a mathematical nature in order to assist referees. These workings will not be published.

6. In choosing mathematical notation, the rules should be observed in order to avoid unnecessary delays and reduce printing expenses. Visit www.blackwellpublishing.com for rules.

7. Statistical tables and diagrams should be neatly prepared with clear explanations, so that the reader can understand their meaning without hunting in the text for explanations.

8. Bibliographical references should be accurate, and follow the style and punctuation in the following examples:

References
Aitchison, J. and J. A. C. Brown (1957) The Lognormal Distribution, Cambridge: Cambridge University Press.

Arrow, K.J. (1951) "An Extension of the Basic Theorems of Classical Welfare Economics", in J. Neyman, ed., Proceedings of the Second Berkeley Symposium on Mathematical Statistics and Probability, Berkeley: University of California Press, pp. 507-32.

Panzer, J.C. and R.D. Willig (1977a) "Free Entry and the Sustainability of Natural Monopoly", Bell Journal of Economics, Vol. 8, No. 1, pp. 1-22.

— and — (1977b) "Economies of Scale in Multi-Output Production", Quarterly Journal of Economics, Vol. 91, No. 3, pp. 481-93.

Citation of references in the text should be by author(s) followed by parenthesized Arabic numerals denoting the year of publication, as Aitchison and Brown (1957), Arrow (1951, Theorem 1), Panzer and Willig (1977b, p. 488), etc.

9. Manuscripts that do not conform to these requirements may cause unnecessary delay in processing and may have to be returned to the authors.

Journal for Economics Educators (Journal of the Tennessee Economics Association)

ADDRESS FOR SUBMISSION:

David A. Penn, Editor
Journal for Economics Educators (Journal
  of the Tennessee Economics
  Association)
Middle Tennessee State University
Economics and Finance Department
PO Box 102
Murfreesboro, TN 37132
USA
Phone: 615-904-8571
Fax: 815-898-5045
E-Mail: dpenn@mtsu.edu
Web: www.ntsu.edu
Address May Change:

PUBLICATION GUIDELINES:

Manuscript Length: 6-10
Copies Required: Three
Computer Submission: Yes
Format: MS Word
Fees to Review: 20.00 US$

Manuscript Style:
  See Manuscript Guidelines

CIRCULATION DATA:

Reader: Academics, Highschool Teachers
Frequency of Issue: 2 Times/Year
Copies per Issue: Online Only
Sponsor/Publisher: Tennesee Economics
  Association and Middle Tennesee State
  University
Subscribe Price: 0.00 US$

REVIEW INFORMATION:

Type of Review: Blind Review
No. of External Reviewers: 2
No. of In House Reviewers: 1
Acceptance Rate: 50%
Time to Review: 1 Month
Reviewers Comments: Varies
Invited Articles: 0-5%
Fees to Publish: 20.00 US$

MANUSCRIPT TOPICS:

Economic Development; Economic Education; International Economics & Trade; Macro
Economics; Micro Economics; Public Policy Economics; Regional Economics

MANUSCRIPT GUIDELINES/COMMENTS:

The *Journal for Economics Educators* was previously titled Journal of the Tennessee
Ecoromics Association.

Length of Articles. Ordinarily, articles should not exceed eight single-spaced, typewritten
pages, references and tables inclusive.

Mathematics. The use of mathematics and graphics should be kept at a minimum. Avoid technical jargon. Number the equations. In identifying variables in formulas, capitalize only the initial letter of abbreviations—except where common usage indicated otherwise.

Submission of Articles. Submission by Word attachment is preferred. Otherwise, send four copies of all articles, a 3.5" data diskette with article in a Word file, and a US$20 submission fee to the Editor.

Make checks payable to the Tennessee Economics Association. We regret that we are unable to return or store manuscripts or diskettes.

Review. Manuscripts are first reviewed to determine if a good fit exists between the author's work and the journal. Manuscripts that fit the purpose of the journal are then reviewed by the Review Board. Reviewed manuscripts are then:
- Accepted as is, or
- Accepted with modifications (second review), or
- Rejected.

Typing. The manuscript should be single-spaced throughout, approximating journal format. This applies to text footnotes, references, and figure legends. Use standard 8½" x 11" white paper. The following fonts and sizes should be used: Title—G.C. Times 18pt., bold; by—G.C. Times 10pt.; author—G.C. Times 12pt.; abstract body—G.C. Times 10pt., italics; introduction—G.C. Times 12pt, bold; text—Times Roman 10pt. Submit four copies and keep another for your own use. Type on one side only. Leave a 1-inch margin on all four sides of the text. Mathematical symbols must be clearly represented—typed if at all possible. Submit by diskette or word attachment by e-mail.

Title Page and Summary. Use a cover page, which shows the title of the paper, the name of the author(s) with their titles, institutional affiliations, telephone numbers, and e-mail addresses.

Abstract. Include on the top of page one an abstract of the article in 150 words or less. If appropriate, add as footnote material about previous publications or other information that can be used to identify the author(s). Conclude the abstract with the appropriate JEL classification numbers in parenthesis as (JEL-A22, 121).

Footnotes. Use footnotes sparingly. Number sequentially. Type footnotes double-spaced on a separate page at the end of the article. In general, avoid lengthy explanatory footnotes. This material can usually be incorporated in the text.

Section Headings. If sparingly used, section headings and subheadings enhance the readability of an article. Do not try to indicate typographical style, but show the relative weights by using all capital letters for the main headings (i.e., CONCLUSIONS) and initial capital letters (only) for words in the subheadings (i.e., Test Results).

Tables and Charts. Avoid excessively long tables. Type tables and charts on pages separate from the text. Captions of all figures should be consistent. Capitalize the first letter in all words in main headings (i.e., Text Results). For captions of lesser importance in the column headings or subs, capitalize only the first letter of the initial word (i.e., Goodness of fit).

References. Type single-spaced with each item being flush left. For entries requiring more than one line, run-over lines should be indented. Authors in the references should be listed alphabetically: do not number the entries. Citations for books should contain author's last name, first name and middle initials followed by full title of the book, place of publication, publisher, and publication (copyright) date. The following example illustrates the desired form and punctuation:

Smith, Arthur G., Economics, New York: Goodwin 1999.

Journal articles should include (in addition to author and title, as above) the name of the journal, date, volume, and page. For example:

Smith, Arthur G., "Teaching Economics," Journal of Economic Education, Spring 1976, 7, 4-12.
Vibhakar, Ashvin P., and Kennedy, Robert E. "Alternate Estimates of the Cost of Equity Capital: Electric Utilities Revisited," Journal of Business and Economic Perspectives, Fall 1982, 8, 1-22.

In referring to references in the text of the article, use the author's name, publication date, and page number (if needed). For example, "...as the date indicates (Smith, 1978, p.456)" or, "...as Smith (1978) has stated..."

Copyright. The *JEE* is an online journal with open access to any viewer. Therefore, publication in the journal places the author's work in the public domain and there is no express or implied ownership.

Journal of Academy of Business and Economics

ADDRESS FOR SUBMISSION:

Alan S. Khade, Editor
Journal of Academy of Business and
    Economics
California State University, Stanislaus
College of Business Administration
983 Woodland Drive
Turlock, CA 95382-7281
USA
Phone: 209-667-3074
Fax: 209-667-3210
E-Mail: akhade@csustan.edu
Web: www.iab-e.org
Address May Change: 10/10/2010

PUBLICATION GUIDELINES:

Manuscript Length: 10-20
Copies Required: Two
Computer Submission: Yes Disk or Email
Format: MS Word
Fees to Review: 0.00 US$

Manuscript Style:
    Chicago Manual of Style

CIRCULATION DATA:

Reader: Academics, Business Persons
Frequency of Issue: 2 Times/Year
Copies per Issue: Less than 1,000
Sponsor/Publisher: IABE, AABE
Subscribe Price: 50.00 US$ Individual

REVIEW INFORMATION:

Type of Review: Blind Review
No. of External Reviewers: 2
No. of In House Reviewers: 1
Acceptance Rate: 21-30%
Time to Review: 2 - 3 Months
Reviewers Comments: Yes
Invited Articles: 21-30%
Fees to Publish: 0.00 US$

MANUSCRIPT TOPICS:

Corporate Finance; Econometrics; Economic Development; Economics; Financial Institutions
& Markets; Financial Services; Fiscal Policy; Industrial Organization; Insurance; International
Economics & Trade; International Finance; Macro Economics; Monetary Policy; Portfolio &
Security Analysis; Public Policy Economics; Regional Economics

MANUSCRIPT GUIDELINES/COMMENTS:

Please follow the following Manuscript Guidelines for *Journal of Academy of Business and
Economics (JABE)*.

The original, high-quality research papers and articles (not currently under review or
published in other publications) on all topics related to business and economics will be
considered for publication in *Journal of Academy of Business and Economics (JABE)*.

1. **Copyright**. Articles, papers, abstracts or cases submitted for publication should be original
contributions and should not be under consideration for any other publication at the same

time. Authors submitting articles/papers/abstracts/cases for publication warrant that the work is not an infringement of any existing copyright, infringement of proprietary right, invasion of privacy, or libel and will indemnify, defend, and hold IABE harmless from any damages, expenses, and costs against any breach of such warranty. For ease of dissemination and to ensure proper policing of use, papers/articles/abstracts/cases and contributions become the legal copyright of the IABE unless otherwise agreed in writing.

2. **Typing**. Paper must be laser printed on 8.5" x 11" white sheets in **Arial 10-point font, single-spaced lines, justify style in MS Word**. All four margins must be 1" each.

3. **First Page**. Paper title, not exceeding two lines, **must be capitalized and centered in bold letters**. Author name and university/organizational affiliation of each author must be printed on one line each. Do NOT include titles such as, Dr., Professor, Ph.D., department, address, email address etc. Please print the word "**ABSTRACT**" in capitalized bold letters, left justified, and double-spaced from last author's name/affiliation. Abstract should be in italic. Please see the sample manuscript.

4. **All Other Headings**. All other section headings starting with INTRODUCTION must be numbered, in capitalized bold letters, left justified, and double-spaced from last line above them.

5. **Tables, Figures, and Charts**. All tables, figures or charts must be inserted in the body of the manuscripts within the margins with headings/titles in centered **capitalized bold** letters.

6. **References and Bibliography**. All references listed in this section must be cited in the article and vice-versa. The reference citations in the text must be inserted in parentheses within sentences with author name followed by a comma and year of publication. Please follow the following formats:

Journal Articles
Khade, Alan S. and Metlen, Scott K., "An Application of Benchmarking in Dairy Industry", *International Journal of Benchmarking*, Vol. III (4), 1996, 17-27.

Books
Harrison, Norma and Samson, D., Technology Management: Text and Cases, McGraw-Hill Publishing, New York, 2002.

Internet
Hesterbrink, C., E-Business and ERP: Bringing two Paradigms together, October 1999; PricewaterhouseCoopers, www.pwc.com.

6. **Author Profile(s)**. At the end of paper, include author profile(s), not exceeding five lines for each author, including name, highest degree/university/year, current position/ university, and major achievements. For example:

Dr. Andrew J. Wagner earned his Ph.D. at Texas A and M University in 1997. Currently he is an associate professor of finance at California State University, Stanislaus, and Program Chair of the IABE.

7. **Manuscript**. Absolutely **no** footnotes allowed! Please do not forget to run spelling and grammar check for the completed paper. **Save the manuscript on a diskette** and label the diskette with title of your paper, your name, and email address.

8. **Submission**
Submissions By Mail
   Please mail the following items in a 9" x 12" envelope:
   1. Two camera-ready laser-printed copies of the manuscript.
   2. Diskette containing your manuscript.

Submissions by Email
   Send your paper as an attachment to the email to: AKhade@csustan.edu

Journal of Accounting and Finance Research

ADDRESS FOR SUBMISSION:

Roger Calcote, Editor
Journal of Accounting and Finance
    Research
JAFR
220 Oliver Drive
Brookhaven, MS 39601
USA
Phone: 601-833-9741
Fax: 601-823-3666
E-Mail: calcote@telepak.net
Web: www.aaafonline.org
Address May Change:

PUBLICATION GUIDELINES:

Manuscript Length: 21-25
Copies Required: Three + Disk
Computer Submission: Yes - Disk Required
Format: MS Word, WordPerfect
Fees to Review: 90.00 US$
    25.00 US$ Per Co-Author

Manuscript Style:
    , Accounting Horizons

CIRCULATION DATA:

Reader: Academics
Frequency of Issue: Quarterly
Copies per Issue: Less than 1,000
Sponsor/Publisher: American Academy of
    Accounting and Finance
Subscribe Price: 150.00 US$

REVIEW INFORMATION:

Type of Review: Blind Review
No. of External Reviewers: 2
No. of In House Reviewers: 2
Acceptance Rate: 21-30%
Time to Review: 2 - 3 Months
Reviewers Comments: Yes
Invited Articles: 0-5%
Fees to Publish: 0.00 US$

MANUSCRIPT TOPICS:

Accounting Education; Accounting History; Accounting Information Systems; Accounting Theory & Practice; Auditing; Corporate Finance; Cost Accounting; Finance Education; Financial Institutions & Markets; Financial Services; Government & Non-Profit Accounting; Insurance; International Economics & Trade; International Finance; Portfolio & Security Analysis; Real Estate; Tax Accounting

MANUSCRIPT GUIDELINES/COMMENTS:

The *Journal of Accounting and Finance Research* is the official publication of the American Academy of Accounting and Finance.

To be eligible for submission to the *Journal*, manuscripts must have completed a documented process of public scrutiny by academic peers or practitioners. Papers presented at the Academy's annual meeting meet this eligibility requirement. Under certain circumstances the Academy may allow this requirement to be met by posting the manuscript on the Academy's discussion forum website. Such manuscripts must, in the editor's opinion, receive sufficient, relevant feedback from academic peers and/or practitioners via the discussion forum to be eligible for submission to the *Journal*.

The Academy's annual meeting is held in New Orleans, Louisiana during the first or second week of December. Information about the Academy, the *Journal*, and the annual meeting can be obtained from our website: www.aaafonline.org. Written requests for information on the Academy and the annual meeting should be addressed to: John Gill, AAAF Program Director, P.O. Box 1399, Clinton, MS 39060, USA. Written requests for information on the *Journal* should be addressed to Roger Calcote, Editor, *Journal of Accounting and Finance Research*, 220 Oliver Dr., Brookhaven, MS 39601, USA. The email addresses are jwgill@bellsouth.net and calcote@telepak.net, respectively.

Format Instructions

The *Journal of Accounting and Finance Research* follows the style of *Issues in Accounting Education*. Papers submitted in an alternate format will be returned.

Title

The title should be in CG Times (Scalable) size 16 font, all capital letters, centered at the top of the first page, and beginning on or near the 1.50" line. Titles of more than one line should be single spaced.

Authors

The author(s), name(s) and affiliation(s) should be centered and single spaced, beginning on the second line below the title. Do not use titles such as Dr. or Assistant Professor, etc. Use CG Times (Scalable) size 14 font. The rest of the paper should be in CG Times (Scalable) size 12 font.

Headings

All headings should be in bold type. First-level headings should be centered and set in all caps. Second-level headings should be set flush left with initial caps. Do not use headings other than these two. Separate headings from preceding and succeeding text by one line space.

Abstract

Introduce the paper with an abstract of approximately 150-200 words. Begin the left column with the first-level heading, **"ABSTRACT."**

Body

The body of the paper should be single spaced and should follow the abstract. Use a first-level heading of some type after the abstract and before the first paragraph of the body of the paper to separate the two.

Figures and Tables

Figures and tables should be placed either "in-column" across the page as close as possible to where they are cited. First-level headings state the table or figure number and may be followed by a second-level heading. Scalable fonts smaller than CG 12 may be used to fit a table "in-column" provided, in the author's opinion, the data is still legible.

Footnotes
The use of footnotes is strongly discouraged.

Equations
All equations should be placed on a separate line and numbered consecutively, with the equation numbers placed within parentheses and aligned against the right margin.

$$R_1 = f(X_1) \tag{1}$$

References (Bibliography)
Since the bibliography should only include those references cited in the paper, it should be referred to as **"REFERENCES"**, a first-level heading. References should be listed at the end of the paper and follow *Issues in Accounting Education* style.

Appendices
An appendix should immediately follow the body of the paper, precede the references, and should be referred to as **"APPENDIX"**, a first-level heading. If there is more than one appendix, number each consecutively.

Word Processing Software and Type Size
Papers are to be prepared using Corel WordPerfect or Microsoft Word. Submit the final version of your paper on a 3.5" disk. Also, submit three (3) laser printed hard-copies of the final version of the paper.

Layout and Margins
Except for the title and author(s) information, papers are to be laid out using the Balanced Newspaper Columns. Set the column margins as follows:

Column	Left	Right
1	1.00	4.00
2	4.50	7.50

All paragraphs should be indented 0.3". Set the top and bottom margins of the paper at 0.700". Use "Full Justification" and hyphenation. Do not skip a line between paragraphs.

Spacing
Single space the body of the paper. Double space before and after all headings. Triple space after the last authors' name preceding the abstract heading.

Page Numbers
Don't type in page numbers. Keep pages in sequence and lightly pencil in the page number on the back of each page.

Submission Deadline
Papers must be submitted to the *Journal* by May 1, of the year following presentation at the December annual meeting or when otherwise deemed eligible for submission by the editor.

Journal of Agricultural and Applied Economics

ADDRESS FOR SUBMISSION:

John B. Penson, Jr. Editor
Journal of Agricultural and Applied
  Economics
Texas A & M University
352 Blocker Building
College Station, TX 77843-2124
USA
Phone: 979-845-2335
Fax: 979-862-1563
E-Mail: JAAE@tamu.edu
Web: www.agecon.uga.edu/~jaae/
Address May Change:

PUBLICATION GUIDELINES:

Manuscript Length: 21-30
Copies Required: Four
Computer Submission: No
Format: N/A
Fees to Review: 0.00 US$

Manuscript Style:
  Chicago Manual of Style

CIRCULATION DATA:

Reader: Academics
Frequency of Issue: 3 Times/Year
Copies per Issue: 1,001 - 2,000
Sponsor/Publisher: Professional Assoc.
Subscribe Price: 30.00 US$

REVIEW INFORMATION:

Type of Review: Blind Review
No. of External Reviewers: 2
No. of In House Reviewers: 0
Acceptance Rate: 28%
Time to Review: 8 - 10 Weeks
Reviewers Comments: Yes
Invited Articles: 21-30%
Fees to Publish: 75.00 US$

MANUSCRIPT TOPICS:
Agricultural Economics; Economic Development; International Finance

MANUSCRIPT GUIDELINES/COMMENTS:

Contributors of manuscripts who closely adhere to the following guidelines will receive prompt and efficient consideration.

1. **Copyright**. The *JAAE* is copyrighted. Authors are required to sign a release form, which will prohibit publication of material contained in the article elsewhere unless specific permission is granted by the editors.

2. **Publication costs**. Authors submitting manuscripts are expected to assume obligation for payment of page charges. Page charges currently are $75 per page.

3. **Format**. Manuscripts should be typed on good quality 3½" x 11" paper with 1" margins. Use 12-point Times New Roman for manuscripts. Double-space all material throughout the manuscript, including the abstract, acknowledgments, footnotes, references, and tables. Type

only on one side of the paper and do not use right-margin or full-margin justification. Use a separate cover page that lists authors and affiliations.

4. **Abstract**. On a separate page, include an abstract not to exceed 100 words, followed by no more than eight key words or short phrases, listed in alphabetical order and appropriate JEL codes.

5. **Footnotes**. Number footnotes consecutively throughout the manuscript. Type the content of the footnotes on separate pages placed immediately after the main text. Footnotes should not be used solely for citations or directives to other literature. Reference citations should be incorporated into the main text or into the text of the footnotes.

6. **References**. Place all references cited in the text alphabetized by author's last name on separate pages immediately after the footnotes. Citations may appear parenthetically or as part of the text. Within the text use parentheses rather than brackets for citations. Spell out up to three authors' last names; for works with four or more authors, include only the first author followed by "et al." When citing a direct quote, include page number(s). Do not specify the publication year unless there is mote than one reference by the same author(s).

7. **Tables**. Place each table on a separate page immediately after the references.

8. **Figures**. Place each figure, chart, or graph on a separate page immediately after the tables.

9. **Mathematical formulations**. Use Arabic numbers enclosed in parentheses placed flush left on the first line of the equation. Number equations consecutively throughout the manuscript. Indent the equation after the equation number. Punctuate all mathematical material.

10. **Copies**. Send four clean copies to the Editor along with cover letter clearing stating that the manuscript is not being considered for publication by another journal.

Journal of Alternative Investments (The)

ADDRESS FOR SUBMISSION:

Thomas Schneeweis, Editor
Journal of Alternative Investments (The)
University of Massachusetts
CISDM/SOM
Amherst, MA 01003
USA
Phone: 413-545-5641
Fax: 413-545-3858
E-Mail: jai@som.umass.edu
Web: www.iijai.com
Address May Change:

PUBLICATION GUIDELINES:

Manuscript Length: 21-25
Copies Required: Two
Computer Submission: Yes
Format: MS Word
Fees to Review: 0.00 US$

Manuscript Style:

CIRCULATION DATA:

Reader: Academics, Business Persons
Frequency of Issue: Quarterly
Copies per Issue: Less than 1,000
Sponsor/Publisher: Institutional Investor,
   Inc.
Subscribe Price: 540.00 US$

REVIEW INFORMATION:

Type of Review: Editorial Review
No. of External Reviewers: 2-3
No. of In House Reviewers: 0
Acceptance Rate: 11-20%
Time to Review: 2 - 3 Months
Reviewers Comments: Yes
Invited Articles: 6-10%
Fees to Publish: 0.00 US$

MANUSCRIPT TOPICS:

Alternative Investments; Financial Institutions & Markets; Financial Services; Hedge Funds; International Finance; Portfolio & Security Analysis; Real Estate; Tax Accounting

MANUSCRIPT GUIDELINES/COMMENTS:

Please follow the guidelines below when you prepare a manuscript for submission. The editors will edit and copyedit articles for clarity and consistency. *Please note that we reserve the right to return to an author any paper accepted for publication that is not prepared according to these instructions.*

1. **Article Submission**. Please submit 2 copies double-spaced sized on an 8.5"x11" page with 1.5"-2" margins and numbered pages. Include on the title page the authors' names and titles as they are to appear, including affiliation, mailing address, telephone and fax numbers, and e-mail address. Also submit an electronic file. Text should be formatted in 12 point type. If submitting a PDF file, please prepare with all fonts embedded and, if possible, include an accompanying Word file which would include the running text. We do not support articles submitted in WordPerfect. Please save any WordPerfect files as a text document and please provide separate eps files for any graphic elements. **All manuscripts are expected to be**

submitted in final form. We reserve the right to limit any changes following article formatting based upon content, not style.

2. **Abstract**. On the page after the title page, please provide a brief article summary or abstract suitable for the table of contents. Do not begin the paper with a heading such as "introduction." Do not number section or subsection headings.

3. Do not asterisk or footnote any authors' names listed as bylines. Footnoting should only begin in the body of the article.

4. **Exhibits**. Please put tables and graphs on separate individual pages at the end of the paper. Do not integrate them with the text; do not call them table 1 and figure 1. Please call any tabular or graphical material Exhibits, numbered in Arabic numbers consecutively in order of appearance in the text. We reserve the right to return to an author for reformatting any paper accepted for publication that does not conform to this style.

5. **Exhibit Presentation**. Please organize and present tables consistently throughout a paper, because we will print them the way they are presented to us. **Exhibits should be created as grayscale, as opposed to color, since the journal is printed in black and white. Please make sure that all categories in an exhibit can be distinguished from each other.** Align numbers correctly by decimal points; use the same number of decimal points for the same sorts of numbers; center headings, columns, and numbers correctly; use the exact same language in successive appearances; identify any bold-faced or italicized entries in exhibits; and provide any source notes necessary.

6. **Graphs**. Please submit graphs for accepted papers in electronic form. We cannot produce graphs for authors. Graphs will appear the way you submit them. Please be consistent as to fonts, capitalization, and abbreviations in graphs throughout the paper, and label all axes and lines in graphs clearly and absolutely consistently. When pasting graphs into Word, paste as an object, not as a picture, so we will be able to have access to original graph.

7. **Equations**. Please display called-out equations on separate lines, aligned on the exact same indents as the text paragraphs and with no punctuation following. Number equations consecutively throughout the paper in Arabic numbers at the right-hand margin. Clarify in handwriting any operations signs or Greek letters or any notation that may be unclear. Leave space around operations signs like plus and minus everywhere. We reserve the right to return for resubmission any accepted article that prepares equations in any other way. It would be preferable if manuscripts containing mathematical equations be submitted in Microsoft Word using either Equation Editor or MathType.

8. **Reference Citations**. In the text, please refer to authors and works as: Smith [2000]. Use brackets for the year, not parentheses. The same is true for references within parentheses, such as: "(see also Smith [2000])."

566

9. **Reference Styles**

Brokerage house internal publications	Askin, D.J., and S.D. Meyer. "Dollar Rolls: A Low-Cost Financing Technique." Mortgage-Backed Securities Research, Drexel Burnham Lambert, 1986.
Journal articles	Batlin, C.A. "Hedging Mortgage-Backed Securities with Treasury Bond Futures." *Journal of Futures Markets,* 7 (1987), pp. 675-693.
———. "Trading Mortgage-Backed Securities with Treasury Bond Futures." Journal of Futures Markets, 7 (1987), pp. 675-693.	Same author, alphabetized by title, two em-dashes instead of repeating name
Working papers	Boudoukh, J., M. Richardson, R. Stanton, and R.F. Whitelaw. "Pricing Mortgage-Backed Securities in a Multifactor Interest Rate Environment: A Multivariate Density Estimation Approach." Working Paper, New York University, 1995.
Sections of books	Breeden, D.T., and M.J. Giarla. "Hedging Interest Rate Risk with Futures, Swaps, and Options." In F. Fabozzi, ed., *The Handbook of Mortgage-Backed Securities.* Chicago: Probus Publishing, 1992, 3rd edition, pp. 847-960.
Books	Hull, J., ed. *Options, Futures and Other Derivative Securities.* Englewood Cliffs, NJ: Prentice-Hall, 1993, 2nd edition.

10. **Endnotes**. Please put in endnotes only material that is not essential to the understanding of an article. If it is essential, it belongs in the text. Do not place a footnote by the authors' names. Any biographical information can be indicated in a separate section and will not be footnoted. Authors' bio information appearing in the article will be limited to their titles, current affiliations, and locations. Do not include in endnotes full reference details; these belong in a separate references list; see below. We will delete non-essential endnotes in the interest of minimizing distraction and enhancing clarity. We also reserve the right to return to an author any article accepted for publication that includes endnotes with embedded reference detail and no separate references list in exchange for preparation of a paper with the appropriate endnotes and a separate references list.

11. **References lists**. Please list only those articles cited in a separate alphabetical references list at the end of the paper. Please follow absolutely the style you see in this journal. We reserve the right to return any accepted article for preparation of a references list according to this style.

12. **Electronic Files**. Word documents are preferred for the articles themselves. Excel can be used for the preparation of graphic elements, making sure that they are embedded in the Word document prior to submission. For those working with .tek or LaTeX files: *pdf files of the*

articles must be submitted, making sure to embed all fonts when the pdf file is prepared. Please also include a Word file which contains the text of the article.

13. **Copyright Agreement**: Institutional Investor Inc.'s copyright agreement form - giving us non-exclusive rights to publish the material in all media - must be signed prior to publication.

14. Upon acceptance of the article, no further changes are allowed, except with the permission of the editor. If the article has already been forwarded to our production department, any changes must be made on the hard copy of the original submitted manuscript and faxed to them.

Journal of American Academy of Business, Cambridge (The)

ADDRESS FOR SUBMISSION:

Turan Senguder, Jean Gordon, Co-Editors
Journal of American Academy of Business,
  Cambridge (The)
995 Weeping Willow Way
Hollywood, FL 33019
USA
Phone: 954-923-2404
Fax: 954-923-4057
E-Mail: drsenguder@aol.com
Web: www.jaabc.com/journal.htm
Address May Change:

PUBLICATION GUIDELINES:

Manuscript Length: 8 Pages Maximum
Copies Required: Two
Computer Submission: Yes Preferred
Format: MS Word, English
Fees to Review: 0.00 US$

Manuscript Style:
    See Manuscript Guidelines

CIRCULATION DATA:

Reader: Academics, Business Persons
Frequency of Issue: 2 Times/Year
Copies per Issue: Less than 1,000
Sponsor/Publisher:
Subscribe Price: 78.00 US$ Individual

REVIEW INFORMATION:

Type of Review: Blind Review
No. of External Reviewers: 2
No. of In House Reviewers: 2
Acceptance Rate: 38-42%
Time to Review: 1 - 2 Months
Reviewers Comments: Yes
Invited Articles: 31-50%
Fees to Publish: 495.00 US$
    55.00 US$ Each page over maximum

MANUSCRIPT TOPICS:
Accounting Information Systems; Auditing; Economic Development; Government & Non-Profit Accounting; International Economics & Trade; International Finance; Macro Economics; Regional Economics

MANUSCRIPT GUIDELINES/COMMENTS:

How To Submit A Paper For The Journal (JAAB)
Submissions may be made electronically via e-mail to: drsenguder@aol.com. Electronic submissions are preferred. Submissions will be acknowledged within 48 hours. If submissions are mailed, please submit a paper or an abstract/proposal for a paper (follow the submission guidelines) to the attention of Dr. Turan Senguder and Dr. Jean Gordon, JAAB, 995 Weeping Willow Way, Hollywood, FL 33019. The cover letter should include each author's name, institutional affiliation, complete mailing and e-mail addresses. Please also submit a résumé. See Website for submission deadline.

General Information
The *Journal of American Academy of Business* (*JAAB*) invites you to participate in the journal. The *Journal of American Academy of Business* (*JAAB*) publishes articles of interest to

members of the Business Community and will provide leadership in introducing new concepts to its readership. Because business is a diverse field, articles should address questions utilizing a variety of methods and theoretical perspectives.

The *Journal of American Academy of Business*, Cambridge has been accepted by ABI/INFORM (ProQuest) for inclusion in their internationally acclaimed business database, ABI/INFORM (ProQuest). Also, The *Journal of American Academy of Business*, Cambridge is listed in the Ninth Edition of Cabell's Directory. The primary goal of the journal will be to provide opportunities for business related academicians and professionals from various business related fields in a global realm to publish their paper in one source. The *Journal of American Academy of Business*, Cambridge will bring together academicians and professionals from all areas related business fields and related fields to interact with members inside and outside their own particular disciplines. The journal will provide opportunities for publishing researcher's paper as well as providing opportunities to view other's work. Doctoral students are highly encouraged to submit papers to *JAAB* for competitive review. All submissions are subject to a two-person, blind-peer-review process.

JAAB reserves the rights to amend, modify, add to, or delete its rules, policies, and procedures affecting its institutional relationship with authors (contributors) as deemed necessary by the administration. Any such amendment, modification, addition, or deletion shall not be considered a violation of the relationship between JAAB and authors (contributors). The final paper and registration fee must be submitted prior to submission deadline. When the paper is accepted, each author must pay the registration fee.

Submission Guidelines
Submissions may be made electronically via e-mail to: drsenguder@aol.com. Electronic submissions are preferred. The manuscript should be in one file entirely in Microsoft Word. No other software may be used. The paper should be a maximum of eight pages including appendices, references, figures and tables. The paper must be singled-spaced, printed at 10-point with 1-inch margins in any Times font. Page numbers should begin with 1 and the paper should not exceed eight pages in length. In general, the paper must be the way you want it to look in the publication. Hence tables must be placed where you want them to appear. There will be a $55 charge for each published page exceeding the page limit. Papers are to be prepared in English and totally edited to avoid grammatical and typographical errors. Papers must be written in a clear, concise manner for ease of reading and interpretation.

Each submission should include the paper's title and the name, address and telephone number of the contact person for the paper.

Manuscript Format
Page number should begin with the number 1 and be centered at the bottom of the page in a Times font at 10-point. The manuscript must be single-spaced with 1-inch margins on all four sides and not exceed eight pages in length. The entire paper must be in any Times font at 10-point with the exception of the title, which must be at 16-point and bold. The paper should begin with title, author's information (10-point font and lower case), and the word "abstract" (10-point font, bold and capitalized), each of which must be centered. The balance of the paper should be fully justified.

As for line spacing, it should be title on the first line or lines and then author's information with one line per author and no blank lines between the title and author's information. The author's information line should contain first name, last name and institutional affiliation. Leave two blank lines between author's information and the word abstract. Leave one blank line between the word abstract and the abstract itself. Leave two blank lines between the abstract and the body of the manuscript. There must be a blank line between paragraphs with the first line each paragraph indented. Please do not use columns. Please omit headers and footers. References need to be consistent and in a generally accepted format. Every sub-heading should be bold and capitalized. The manuscript should be in one file entirely in Microsoft Word. No other software may be used. View website for manuscript deadline.

2. Each submission should include the paper's title and the name, address and telephone number of the contact person for the paper. However, papers submitted earlier will be reviewed immediately and participants will be notified as soon as possible.

Journal of Applied Corporate Finance

ADDRESS FOR SUBMISSION:

Don Chew, Editor
Journal of Applied Corporate Finance
Stern Stewart and Co.
135 East 57th Street
New York, NY 10022
USA
Phone: 212-261-0714
Fax: 212-581-6420
E-Mail: dchew@sternstewart.com
Web:
Address May Change:

CIRCULATION DATA:

Reader: Business Persons
Frequency of Issue: Quarterly
Copies per Issue: 10,001 - 25,000
Sponsor/Publisher: Profit Oriented Corp.
Subscribe Price: 95.00 US$
          35.00 US$ Academic/Library

PUBLICATION GUIDELINES:

Manuscript Length: 11-20
Copies Required: One
Computer Submission: Yes
Format: N/A
Fees to Review: 0.00 US$

Manuscript Style:
      See Manuscript Guidelines

REVIEW INFORMATION:

Type of Review: N/A
No. of External Reviewers: No Reply
No. of In House Reviewers: No Reply
Acceptance Rate: No Reply
Time to Review: No Reply
Reviewers Comments: No Reply
Invited Articles: 50% +
Fees to Publish: 0.00 US$

MANUSCRIPT TOPICS:

Capital Structure; Corporate Performance Measurement; Cost Accounting; Incentive Compensation; International Finance; Portfolio & Security Analysis; Risk Management (Derivatives)

MANUSCRIPT GUIDELINES/COMMENTS:

The *Journal of Applied Corporate Finance* is a quarterly journal co-published by Accenture and Stern Stewart & Company, the company that pioneered the measurement of shareholder wealth and developed EVA® (Economic Value Added) framework. The *Journal of Applied Corporate Finance* offers fresh thinking on corporate finance, business strategy and corporate governance.

Journal of Applied Econometrics

ADDRESS FOR SUBMISSION:

M. Hashem Pesaran, Editor
Journal of Applied Econometrics
University of Cambridge
Faculty of Economics and Politics
Sidgwick Avenue
Cambridge, CB3 9DD
UK
Phone: 44 (0) 12 23 335 291
Fax: 44 (0) 12 23 335 471
E-Mail: mhpl@econ.cam.ac.uk
Web: jae.wiley.com/jae
Address May Change:

PUBLICATION GUIDELINES:

Manuscript Length: 16-20
Copies Required: Four
Computer Submission: Yes
Format: N/A
Fees to Review: 0.00 US$

Manuscript Style:
See Manuscript Guidelines

CIRCULATION DATA:

Reader: Academics
Frequency of Issue: Bi-Monthly
Copies per Issue: Less than 1,000
Sponsor/Publisher: University/ John Wiley
& Sons
Subscribe Price: 1050.00 US$

REVIEW INFORMATION:

Type of Review: Editorial Review
No. of External Reviewers: 3
No. of In House Reviewers: 0
Acceptance Rate: 11-20%
Time to Review: 4 - 6 Months
Reviewers Comments: Yes
Invited Articles: 0-5%
Fees to Publish: 0.00 US$

MANUSCRIPT TOPICS:
Econometrics

MANUSCRIPT GUIDELINES/COMMENTS:

Co-Editors
Steven Durlauf, Department of Economics, University of Wisconsin, 1180 Observatory Drive, Madison, WI 53706, USA. +1 608-263-6269; Email: sdurlauf@ssc.wisc.edu
Tim Bollerslev, Department of Economics, Duke University, Durhan, NC 27708, USA; Email: boller@econ.duke.edu
John Rust, Department of Economics, Yale University, PO Box 208264 Yale Station, New Haven, CT 06520-8264 USA; Tel: +1 203-432-3569; Email: jrust@gemini.econ.yale.edu
Herman K. van Dijk, Econometric Institute, Erasmus University Rotterdam, Burg Oudlaan 50, PO Box 1738, NL-3000 DR Rotterdam, The Netherlands; Email: hkvandijk@few.eur.nl

Book Review Editor
Melvyn Weeks, Faculty of Economics and Politics. University of Cambridge, Sidgwick Avenue, Cambridge CB3 9DD, UK; Email: Melvyn.weeks@econ.cam.ac.uk

Software Review Editor and Coordinator of the Data Archive

James MacKinnon, Department of Economics, Queen's University, Kingston, Ontario, K7l 3N6, Canada. Tel: +613-545-2293; Email: jgm@qed.econ.queensu.ca

Aims and Scope

The *Journal of Applied Econometrics* is a bi-monthly international journal which aims to publish articles of high quality dealing with the application of existing as well as new econometric techniques to a wide variety of problems in economics and related subjects, covering topics in measurement, estimation, testing, forecasting, and policy analysis. The emphasis is on the careful and rigorous application of econometric techniques and the appropriate interpretation of the results. The economic content of the articles is stressed.

A special feature of the Journal is its emphasis on the replicability of results by other researchers. To achieve this aim, authors are expected to make available a complete set of the data used as well as any specialized computer programs employed through a readily accessible medium, preferably in a machine-readable form. The use of microcomputers in applied research and transferability of data is emphasized. The Journal also features occasional sections of short papers re-evaluating previously published papers.

The intention of the *Journal of Applied Econometrics* is to provide an outlet for innovative, quantitative research in economics, which cuts across areas of specialization, involves transferable techniques, and is easily replicable by other researchers. Contributions that introduce statistical methods that are applicable to a variety of economic problems are actively encouraged. The Journal also aims to publish review and survey articles that make recent developments in the field of theoretical and applied econometrics more readily accessible to applied economists in general.

Notes For Contributors

1. Four copies of each manuscript should be submitted to the Editor.

2. To speed up the review process, authors can submit articles electronically. This is a two-stage process; in the first instance, title, author names, author affiliations, article abstract and references of the article should be sent via email to the Editorial Office at: sc387@econ.cam.ac.uk. An editor will be assigned and instructions given on submission of the whole manuscripts direct to the assigned editor. Full details of the procedure will be published in the Journal from time to time, or may be obtained via email on request from the Editorial Office.

3. Only original papers will be accepted, and copyright in published papers will be vested in the publisher. Papers are accepted for review only on the condition that they are not under review by another journal. Papers of special interest delivered at conferences may be accepted if copyright has not been previously surrendered. Copyright laws require that the transfer of copyright from authors to publisher must be explicit to enable the publisher to ensure maximum dissemination of the author's work. A copy of the Copyright Transfer Agreement to be used for the Journal of Applied Econometrics is reproduced in each volume. Additional copies are available from the Journal editors or from the publishers, or contributors may

photocopy the agreement from this journal. A copy of this agreement signed by the author, must accompany every article submitted for publication.

4. The language of the Journal is English.

5. Twenty-five offprints of each paper will be provided free of charge. Additional copies may be purchased on offprint order form, which will accompany the proofs.

6. Proofs will be sent to authors so they can correct printer's errors only.

7. Manuscripts should be typed double-spaced with wide margins, on one side of the paper only and submitted in quadruplicate. Illustrations should be submitted with the manuscript on separate sheets. There is no maximum length for contributions, but authors should write concisely.

8. The title should be brief, typed on a separate sheet and the author's name should be typed on the line below the title; the affiliation and address should follow on the next line. In the case of co-authors, respective addresses and affiliations should be clearly indicated. Authors should also give telephone, fax and electronic mail contact details. Correspondence, proofs and reprints will be sent to the first-named author, unless otherwise indicated.

9. The body of the manuscript should be preceded by a Summary (maximum length 100 words), which should be a summary of the entire paper, not of the conclusions alone. The summary will appear at the head of the article when published.

10. The paper should be reasonably subdivided into sections and, if necessary, subsections.

11. Mathematical symbols should be typewritten. Greek letters and unusual symbols should be identified separately in the margin. Distinction should be made between capital and lower case letters; between the letter O and zero; between the letter l, the number one and prime; between k and kappa. Superscripts and subscripts should be displayed clearly above and below the line respectively. All equations should be numbered consecutively, and the numbers should be placed in parentheses in the right hand margin.

12. Half-tone illustrations are to be restricted in number to the minimum necessary. Good, glossy bromide prints should accompany the manuscripts and should not be attached to manuscript pages. Photographs should be enlarged sufficiently to permit clear reproduction in half tone after reduction. If words or numbers are to appear on a photograph two prints should be sent, the lettering being clearly indicated on the print only. All should be clearly identified on the back with the figure number and author's name.

Color illustrations will be accepted if the Editor considers them necessary and if the costs are borne by the author(s).

13. Line drawings should be supplied on a separate sheet at the same size as the intended printed version (so no enlargement or reduction is required), maximum width 140 mm. Lettering on the artwork should be set in 8pt type. Computer-generated artwork must be

submitted as laser printed output at a resolution of 600 dots per inch on high quality paper. Dot matrix printer output is unacceptable. Tints are to be avoided; hatching should be used instead. Drawn artwork should be carefully lettered and drawn in black ink. Provide copies as well as the originals, all of which should be clearly identified on the back with the figure number and the author's name.

Artwork on disk is preferred on 3.5 inch PC or Macintosh format disk in a dedicated drawing package, such as Adobe Illustrator/Corel Draw/Macromedia Freehand not presentation, spreadsheet or database packages. Each graphic should be in a separate file, should conform to the information above and be supplied as a source (original) file as well as .EPS file, if different. Provide a hard copy print out of each figure, clearly identified.

14. **Figure** legends should be typed on a separate sheet and placed at the end of the manuscript. The amount of lettering on a drawing should be reduced as far as possible by transferring it to the legend.

15. **Provision of Final Accepted Manuscripts on Disk**. If authors wish to supply their accepted paper on disk, then the following guidelines should be observed. **In addition to the hard copy print out**, please supply two disks containing the **final, accepted** version of your paper to the Editor. The disks should be clearly labeled with the title of the paper, author names, date, hardware type, software package used and the file name. An example of the file name would be JAEMHP—the first three letters represent the Wiley journal code and the next three letters the first name author's initials (if an author only has two initials the middle letter should be X) The preferred medium is a 3.5- or 5.25-inch disk for PC (MS-DOS or Window) or Macintosh. Our preferences are WordPerfect, Word or TeX (and/or one of its derivatives). If the disk and the hard copy print out differ, the hard copy will be treated as the definitive version. Disks, which are not accompanied by a hard copy, cannot be accepted.

16. It is the author's responsibility to obtain written permission to quote material that has appeared in another publication.

17. Tables should be numbered consecutively and titled. All table columns should have an explanatory heading. Tables should not repeat data that are available elsewhere in the paper, e.g., in a line diagram.

18. References to published literature should be quoted in the text by giving the author's name, year of publication, and, where needed for a quote, the page number, e.g., Stone (1954, p. 511). References should be listed alphabetically in a section labeled 'References' at the end of the paper. [Underline titles of journal and books.]

Journal references should be arranged thus, giving journal titles in full:
Mellander, E.,A. Vredin and A. Warne (1992), 'Stochastic trends and economic fluctuations in a small open economy', Journal of Applied Econometrics, 7, 369-394.

Book references should be given as follows:
Amemiya, T. (1985), Advanced Econometrics, Blackwell, Oxford. Hansen, B.E. (1993), 'The likelihood ratio test under nonstandard conditions: testing the Markov switching model of

GNP', in M.H. Pesaran and S.M. Potter (eds.), Nonlinear Dynamics, Dhaos and Econometrics, Wiley, Chichester.

19. No manuscript or figures will be returned following publication unless a request for return is made when the manuscript is originally submitted.

20. The publisher will do everything possible to ensure prompt publication. It will therefore be appreciated if manuscripts and illustrations conform from the outset to the style of the journal. Corrected proofs must be returned to the publishers within ten days to minimize the risk of the author's contribution having to be held over to a later issue.

21. Authors will be expected to make available a complete set of data used as well as any specialized computer programs employed, preferably in a machine-readable form. In cases where there are restrictions on the dissemination of the data the responsibility of obtaining the required permission to use the data rests with the interested investigator and not with the author. The condition of making available the specialized computer programs can be met either by providing a program listing or by allowing other investigators to use the program on an installation to which public access is possible. Authors of accepted papers are expected to deposit their data in electronic form onto the journal's data archive. Copies of the Guidelines for Users of the *Journal of Applied Econometrics* Data Archive can be obtained from the journal editors or the publishers. The Guidelines will also be published in the journal from time to time.

Journal of Applied Finance

ADDRESS FOR SUBMISSION:

Ali Fatemi & Keith Howe, Co-Editors
Journal of Applied Finance
DePaul University
College of Commerce
1 E. Jackson Boulevard, Suite 6100
Chicago, IL 60604
USA
Phone: 312-362-8826 & 312-362-5126
Fax: 312-362-6566
E-Mail: jaf@depaul.edu
Web: www.fma.org
Address May Change:

PUBLICATION GUIDELINES:

Manuscript Length: 16-20
Copies Required: Four
Computer Submission: No Reply
Format: N/A
Fees to Review: 70.00 US$ Member FMA
170.00 US$ Non-Member FMA

Manuscript Style:
See Manuscript Guidelines

CIRCULATION DATA:

Reader: Academics, Practitioners
Frequency of Issue: 2 Times/Year
Copies per Issue: 5,001 - 10,000
Sponsor/Publisher: Financial Management
Association
Subscribe Price: 125.00 US$ Library

REVIEW INFORMATION:

Type of Review: Blind Review
No. of External Reviewers: 1
No. of In House Reviewers:
Acceptance Rate: 15%
Time to Review: 2 - 3 Months
Reviewers Comments: Yes
Invited Articles: 0-8%
Fees to Publish: 0.00 US$

MANUSCRIPT TOPICS:
Corporate Finance; Education; Financial Institutions & Markets; Financial Practice;
Investments; Portfolio Analysis

MANUSCRIPT GUIDELINES/COMMENTS:

Editors' Emails   Ali M. Fatemi,   afatemi@depaul.edu
Keith M. Howe,   khowe@depaul.edu

Journal of Applied Finance promotes scientific debate on the theory, practice, and education of finance. The Journal is devoted to the publication of original manuscripts falling into one of the following broad categories:

- Articles: theoretical, empirical, practical, survey, and synthesis.
- Clinical Studies: characterizations of real world situations using unique sources of data.
- Education: well-motivated, scientifically sound manuscripts that represent major contributions to the field of financial education, and
- Financial Practitioner Forum Proceedings.

Submit four copies of manuscripts to: Ali Fatemi and Keith Howe, Co-Editors.

A submission fee is required for evaluation of each manuscript; $170 for non-FMA members, $100 for doctoral students who are not members, and $70 for FMA members.

Manuscripts are evaluated anonymously. Names of authors should not appear on the article itself. Attach a separate cover page that includes the title, authors, and title and affiliations of each author to one copy of the article. Double space the text with ample margins.

Attach a short, one-paragraph (approximately 100 words) **abstract** of the article. The abstract should provide a brief overview of the article.

Avoid tedious mathematical expressions. When algebraic terms do appear in the text, accompany them with a clear explanation. Each equation should be numbered consecutively, with the number in parentheses and flush with the right margin. Place derivations and proofs in the appendix. When submitting a paper for review, please provide supplemental sheets showing all steps in algebraic derivations so that the reviewers do not have to re-create them.

Tables and figures should appear on separate pages labeled in numerical order and grouped at the end of the text. Label tables at the top and follow the heading with a description of the table in sufficient detail so that it is capable of standing alone. Label figures at the bottom. Include marginal notation in the article for the approximate placement of all tables and figures.

Minimize extensive content footnotes. When preparing accepted papers, place all footnotes, double-spaced, at the end of the manuscript.

Place references in an unnumbered, alphabetic list at the end of the manuscript. Provide all relevant publication information available (i.e., season/month, year, city and state, author(s), etc.) Examples of references are provided below:

References

Baldwin, C., 1991, "The Impact of Asset Stripping on the Cost of Deposit Insurance," Harvard Business School Working Paper 92-053 (December).

Commerce Clearing House, 1993, *1993 U.S. Master Tax Guide* , Chicago, IL.

Brick, L.E. and O. Palmon, 1993, "The Tax Advantages of Refunding Debt by Calling, Repurchasing, and Putting," *Financial Management* (Winter), 96-105.

Myers, S.C., 1993, "Finance Theory and Financial Strategy," in D.H. Chew, Jr., Ed., *The New Corporate Finance* , New York, NY, McGraw-Hill, 90-97.

Smith, C.W., Jr. and C.W. Smithson, 1990, *The Handbook of Financial Engineering* , New York, NY, Harper Business.

Cite references in the text by citing the author(s) name(s) and then the year of publication in parenthesis.

Authors of accepted articles must supply camera-ready artwork for all charts and graphs. Camera-ready means a professional drawing on white paper in India ink or a clean, laser-printed copy of computer-generated charts and/or graphs.

Authors of accepted papers must supply a word-processed copy of their article on an IBM-formatted disk. (Macintosh disks may cause significant delays in publication.) Any questions regarding disk preparation should be directed to the Managing Editor, Financial Management Association, University of South Florida, College of Business Administration, Tampa, FL 33620-5500, Voice: 1 813 974 2084, Fax: 1 813 974 3318, E mail: publications@fma.org

Journal of Asian Economics

ADDRESS FOR SUBMISSION:

M. Dutta, Editor
Journal of Asian Economics
Rutgers University
Faculty of Economics
New Brunswick, NJ 08901-1248
USA
Phone: 732-932-7054
Fax: 732-932-1558
E-Mail: mdutta@rci.rutgers.edu
Web: http://economics.rutgers.edu
Address May Change:

PUBLICATION GUIDELINES:

Manuscript Length: 40 Pages Maximum
Copies Required: Three
Computer Submission: Yes Email
Format: WordPerfect
Fees to Review: 50.00 US$ ACAES
          60.00 US$ Non-ACAES member

Manuscript Style:
    Chicago Manual of Style

CIRCULATION DATA:

Reader: Academics, Policy Makers
Frequency of Issue: Bi-Monthly
Copies per Issue:
Sponsor/Publisher: American Committee on
    Asian Economic Studies / Elsevier
    Science Publishing Co.
Subscribe Price: 95.00 US$ Individual
    420.00 US$ Institution
    376.00 Euro Institution

REVIEW INFORMATION:

Type of Review: Editorial Review
No. of External Reviewers: 3
No. of In House Reviewers: 1
Acceptance Rate: 40%
Time to Review: 2 - 3 Months
Reviewers Comments: Yes
Invited Articles: 0-5%
Fees to Publish: 0.00 US$

MANUSCRIPT TOPICS:

Econometrics; Economic Development; Economic History; Economic Regionalization; Fiscal Policy; Industrial Organization; International Economics & Trade; International Finance; Macro Economics; Micro Economics; Monetary Policy; Public Policy Economics; Regional Economics

MANUSCRIPT GUIDELINES/COMMENTS:

1. Papers must be in English.

2. Papers for publication should be sent in quadruplicate along with a submission fee of US$ 60 (US$50 for ACAES members) checks payable to Journal of Asian Economics to: Professor M. Dutta, Faculty of Economics, Rutgers – The State University of New Jersey, New Jersey Hall, 75 Hamilton Street, New Brunswick, New Jersey 08901-1248, U.S.A.

Submission of a paper will be held to imply that it contains original unpublished work and is not being submitted for publication elsewhere. The Editor does not accept responsibility for damage or loss of papers submitted. Upon acceptance of an article, author(s) will be asked to transfer copyright of the article to the publisher. This transfer will ensure the widest possible dissemination of information.

3. Submission of accepted papers as electronic manuscripts, i.e., on disk with accompanying manuscript, is encouraged. Electronic manuscripts have the advantage that there is no need for rekeying of text, thereby avoiding the possibility of introducing errors and resulting in reliable and fast delivery of proofs. The preferred storage medium is a 5.25- or 3.5-inch disk in MS-DOS format, although other systems are welcome, e.g., Macintosh (in this case, save your file in the usual manner; do not use the option "save in MS-DOS format"). Do not submit your original paper as electronic manuscript, but hold on to disk until asked for this by the Editor (in case your paper is accepted without revisions). Do submit the accepted version of your paper as electronic manuscript. Make absolutely sure that the file on the disk and the printout are identical. Please use a new and correctly formatted disk, and label this with your name; also, specify the software and hardware used as well as the title of the file to be processed. Do not convert the file to plain ASCII. Ensure that the letter 'l' and digit '1', and also the letter 'O' and digit '0' are used properly, and format your article (tabs, indents, etc.) consistently. Characters not available on your word processor (Greek letters mathematical symbols, etc.) should not be left open but indicated by a unique code (e.g., gralpha, <alpha>, etc., for the Greek letter α). Such codes should be used consistently throughout the entire text; a list of codes used should accompany the electronic manuscript. Do not allow your word processor to introduce word breaks, and do not use a justified layout. Please adhere strictly to the general instructions below on style, arrangement, and in particular, the reference style of the *Journal*.

4. Manuscripts should be double-spaced, with wide margins, and printed on one side of the paper only. All pages should be numbered consecutively. Titles and subtitles should be short. References, tables, and legends for the figures should be printed on separate pages.

5. The first page of the manuscript should contain the following information: (i) the title; (ii) the name(s) and institutional affiliation(s) of the author(s); (iii) an abstract of not more than 100 words; and (iv) at least one classification code according to the Classification System for Journal Articles as used by the *Journal of Economic Literature*. In addition, up to five key words should be supplied.

A footnote on the same sheet should give the name, address, and telephone and fax numbers of the corresponding author as well as an e-mail address.

6. Acknowledgements and information on grants received can be given in a first footnote, which should not be included in the consecutive numbering of footnotes.

7. Footnotes should be kept to a minimum and numbered consecutively throughout the text with superscript Arabic numerals. They should be double-spaced and not include displayed formulae or tables.

8. Displayed formulae should be numbered consecutively throughout the manuscript as (1), (2), etc., against the right-hand margin of the page. In cases where the derivation of formulae has been abbreviated, it is of great help to the referees if the full derivation can be presented on a separate sheet (not to be published).

9. References to publications should be as follows:
'Smith (1992) reported that...' or 'This problem has been studied previously (e.g., Smith et al., 1969)'.

The author should make sure that there is a strict one-to-one correspondence between the names and years in the text and those on the list. The list of references should appear at the end of the main text (after any appendices, but before tables and legends for figures). It should be double-spaced and listed in alphabetical order by author's name.

References should appear as follows:
For monographs
Hawawini, G., Swary, I., 1990. Mergers and Acquisitions in the U.S. Banking Industry: Evidence from the Capital Markets. North-Holland, Amsterdam.
For contributions to collective works
Brunner, K., Meltzer, A.H., 1990. Money supply, in: Friedman, B.M., Hahn, F.H. (Eds.), Handbook of Monetary Economics, Vol. 1. North-Holland, Amsterdam, pp. 357--396.
For periodicals
Griffiths, W., Judge, G., 1992. Testing and estimating location vectors when the error covariance matrix is unknown. Journal of Econometrics 54, 121-138.

Note that journal titles should not be abbreviated.

10. Illustrations will be reproduced photographically from originals supplied by the author— they will not be redrawn by the publisher. Please provide all illustrations in quadruplicate (one high-contrast original and three photocopies). Care should be taken that lettering and symbols are of a comparable size. The illustrations should not be inserted in the text, and should be marked on the back with figure number, title of paper, and author's name. All graphs and diagrams should be referred to as figures, and should be numbered consecutively in the text in Arabic numerals. Illustration for papers submitted as electronic manuscripts should be in traditional form.

11. Tables should be numbered consecutively in the text in Arabic numerals and printed on separate sheets. Any manuscript, which does not conform to the above instructions, may be returned for the necessary revision before publication.

12. Page proofs will be sent to the corresponding author. Proofs should be corrected carefully; the responsibility for detecting errors lies with the author. Corrections should be restricted to instances in which the proof is at variance with the manuscript. Extensive alterations will be charged. Fifty reprints of each paper are supplied free of charge to the corresponding author; additional reprints are available at cost if they are ordered when the proof is returned.

Journal of Asset Management

ADDRESS FOR SUBMISSION:

Susan Marshall, Publishing Editor
Journal of Asset Management
Henry Stewart Publications
Museum House
25 Museum Street
London, WC1A 1JT
UK
Phone: 44 20 7323 2916
Fax: 44 20 7323 2918
E-Mail: susan@hspublications.co.uk
Web: www.henrystewart.co.uk
Address May Change:

PUBLICATION GUIDELINES:

Manuscript Length: 2,000-5,000 Words
Copies Required: Two
Computer Submission: Yes
Format: MS Word 97
Fees to Review: 0.00 US$

Manuscript Style:
    See Manuscript Guidelines

CIRCULATION DATA:

Reader: Academics, Business Persons
Frequency of Issue: Bi-Monthly
Copies per Issue: Less than 1,000
Sponsor/Publisher: Henry Stewart
    Publications
Subscribe Price: 360.00 US$ Provisional

REVIEW INFORMATION:

Type of Review: Blind Review
No. of External Reviewers: 2
No. of In House Reviewers: 1
Acceptance Rate: 60%
Time to Review: 1 - 2 Months
Reviewers Comments: No
Invited Articles: 21-30%
Fees to Publish: 0.00 US$

MANUSCRIPT TOPICS:
Asset Management; International Finance; Portfolio & Security Analysis

MANUSCRIPT GUIDELINES/COMMENTS:

About the *Journal*
An international forum for latest thinking, techniques and developments in the industry, *Journal of Asset Management* provides a bridge between academic work, commercial best practice and regulatory interests, globally. It encompasses:

- New investment techniques, methodologies and strategies;
- New products, models and technologies;
- Empirical studies with implications for practice;
- Important regulatory and legal developments;
- Best practice;
- Emerging trends in asset management.

The quality of the articles that appear in *Journal of Asset Management* are assured—every submission is subjected to peer review by members of the eminent Editorial Board, who strive to ensure content is of the highest calibre.

Notes for Contributors

1. Contributions should be between 2,000 and 5,000 words in length. All submissions should be typewritten and double spaced.

2. The *Journal*'s Editors and Editorial Board particularly welcome submissions which present case study material, new approaches, techniques, empirical research or conceptual papers.

3. All articles should be accompanied by a short abstract outlining the paper's aims and subject matter.

4. All articles should be accompanied by up to six keywords.

5. Articles should be accompanied by a short (about 80 words) description of the author(s) and, if appropriate, the organization of which he or she is a member.

6. Authors should not seek to use the *Journal* as a vehicle for marketing any specific product or service.

7. Authors should avoid the use of language or slang which is not in keeping with the professional and academic style of the *Journal*.

8. Titles of organizations etc should be written out first in full and thereafter in initials.

9. Papers should be supported by references. References should be set out in accordance with the Harvard style—that is, they should be indicated in the text by the author's surname followed by the year of publication, both in brackets (eg Boyle, 1992) and then set out in full in a corresponding alphabetical list at the end of the text in the following form: [for journal articles] Author (year) 'Title of article', Journal name, Vol., No., pp,; [for books] Author (year) 'Title of chapter' in 'Editor' (ed), 'Book title', Publisher, place of publication.

10. Photographs and illustrations supporting articles should be submitted where appropriate. Photographs should be good quality positives, printed from the original negatives and preferably in black and white only. Figures and other line illustrations should be submitted in good quality originals and a copy of the data should also be included.

11. Authors must ensure that references to named people and/or organizations are accurate, not racist or sexist and without libellous implications.

12. All contributions sent to the Publisher, whether invited or not, will be submitted to the *Journal*'s Editors and Editorial Board. Any such contribution must bear the author's full name and address, even if this is not for publication. Contributions, whether published pseudonymously or not, are accepted on the strict understanding that the author is responsible for the accuracy of all opinion, technical comment, factual report, data, figures, illustrations

and photographs. Publication does not necessarily imply that these are the opinions of the Editorial Board, Editors or the Publisher, nor does the Board, Editors or Publisher accept any liability for the accuracy of such comment, report and other technical and factual information. The Publisher will, however, strive to ensure that all opinion, comments, reports, data, figures, illustrations and photographs are accurate, insofar as it is within its abilities to do so. The Publisher reserves the right to edit, abridge or omit material submitted for publication.

13. All Articles submitted for publication will be subject to a double-blind refereeing procedure.

14. The author bears the responsibility for checking whether material submitted is subject to copyright or ownership rights, eg photographs, illustrations, trade literature and data. Where use is so restricted, the Publisher must be informed with the submission of the material.

15. No contribution will be accepted which has been published elsewhere, unless it is expressly invited or agreed by the Publisher. Articles and contributions published become the copyright of the Publisher, unless otherwise agreed.

16. All reasonable efforts are made to ensure accurate reproduction of text, photographs and illustrations. The Publisher does not accept responsibility for mistakes, be they editorial or typographical, nor for consequences resulting from them.

17. Submissions should be sent to Henry Stewart Publications, Museum House, 25 Museum Street, London WC1A 1JT, email: submissions@hspublications.co.uk. Please clearly state for which journal you are contributing.

Journal of Bank Cost & Management Accounting

ADDRESS FOR SUBMISSION:

Journal Editor
Journal of Bank Cost & Management
  Accounting
Association for Management Information
 in Financial Services (AMI)
3895 Fairfax Court
Atlanta, GA 30339
USA
Phone: 770-444-3557
Fax: 770-444-9084
E-Mail: ami@amifs.org
Web: www.amifs.org
Address May Change:

PUBLICATION GUIDELINES:

Manuscript Length: 3,000 words
Copies Required:
Computer Submission: Yes
Format: Almost any WP
Fees to Review: 0.00 US$

Manuscript Style:
    , Contact AMIF's for details

CIRCULATION DATA:

Reader: Business Persons
Frequency of Issue: 3 Times/Year
Copies per Issue: Less than 1,000
Sponsor/Publisher: Assn. For Management
  Information in Financial Services
Subscribe Price: 200.00 US$
    210.00 US$ International

REVIEW INFORMATION:

Type of Review: Editorial Review
No. of External Reviewers: 1
No. of In House Reviewers: 1
Acceptance Rate: 80%
Time to Review: 1 - 2 Months
Reviewers Comments: Yes
Invited Articles: 50%
Fees to Publish: 0.00 US$

MANUSCRIPT TOPICS:
Accounting Information Systems; Accounting Theory & Practice; Auditing; Cost Accounting

MANUSCRIPT GUIDELINES/COMMENTS:

The Journal of Bank Cost and Management Accounting - published by the Association for Management Information in Financial Services seeks articles on issues relevant to the management accounting profession. Articles should be on a subject of interest to practitioners in the field of bank cost and management accounting and should reflect the views of the author. Authors should not hesitate to submit articles that present a minority or unusual view as long as that view is effectively presented. A sample copy of the *Journal* can be viewed from our website www.amifs.org.

The *Journal* is published three times a year and distributed to 700 subscribers worldwide. The *Journal* publishes articles that have not appeared or been accepted for publications elsewhere. Exceptions to this policy may be approved of the author obtains a release from the copyright holder. Likewise, all contributing authors will be required to complete an AMIfs Copyright Agreement.

Although no direct sponsors or advertising is accepted for this publication, sponsors or practitioners can gain visibility by authoring relevant articles. Articles published in the *Journal* entitle the author to any one of the following benefits:

- One-year subscription to the *Journal*
- One-year AMI membership
- $250 Discount on AMI workshop on the Institute
- One issue advertisement in the AMI Bulletin
- 20 copies of the *Journal*

Guidelines for Preparation of Manuscripts

Format. The entire manuscript, including test, footnotes, charts, and quotations, must be provided in an electronic format as follows:

- Documents accepted in Microsoft Word or compatible program.
- The document should be prepared in Times New Roman, font size 12, and single spaced.
- Supporting files, charts, graphs may be sent in Excel or PowerPoint.
- All charts, tables or non-text elements must be in black and white. No color submissions of any kind will be accepted.
- Maximum height and width of any graphic is 7" high and 4.25" wide.
- Any articles submitted with mathematical equations or special characters should also be supplied as a PDF file, as some of these special characters may not translate in a Word Document.

All contributing authors will be expected to proof their articles on two occasions prior to final print.

Length. The preferred length of manuscripts is between 2000 and 5000 words. Manuscripts of any length will be considered. The final determinant of an acceptable length is the subject matter of the article. The Editor reserves the right to edit manuscripts for length.

Style. Punctuation should be kept simple, adding to the readability of the article. Tables and exhibits should be numbered. Footnotes should include author's name, title of reference, publisher, and date. Unless a direct quote is used, no page or volume numbers are required in footnotes. References or bibliographies should be included at the end of the document.

Review and Editing

Submission. All manuscripts should be e-mailed to AMIfs at ami@amifs.org or sent on a diskette/CD to the address above. Please include an Adobe PDF as an illustration of the preferred final view if possible. If manuscripts include copyright material other than quotes, a letter of permission to reprint from the copyright holder must accompany submissions.

Review/Editing. Articles are screened by the Editor and may be sent to other reviewers for comment. Manuscripts are evaluated based on coverage of the subject matter and whether it will be of interest to readers. Each manuscript is edited for grammar, punctuation, and structure, and may be returned to the author for suggested changes.

The review process generally takes 2-4 months. If a manuscript is accepted for publication, the Copyright Agreement must be signed and returned within 10 days for final approval. Published articles become the property of AMI and may not be reprinted without permission of the publisher.

Journal of Banking & Finance

ADDRESS FOR SUBMISSION:

Giorgio P. Szego, Editor
Journal of Banking & Finance
c/o Associazione Bancaria Italiana
Piazza Del Gesú 49
00186 Roma,
Italy
Phone: +39 06 86 32 4395
Fax: +39 06 86 21 4805
E-Mail: giorgio.szego@fastwebnet.it
Web: www.elsevier.nl/locate/econbase
Address May Change:

PUBLICATION GUIDELINES:

Manuscript Length: 16-30
Copies Required: Four
Computer Submission: Yes Disk, Email
Format: MS Word, WordPerfect, PDF
Fees to Review: 180.00 US$

Manuscript Style:
    See Manuscript Guidelines

CIRCULATION DATA:

Reader: , Entrepreneurs, Practioners
Frequency of Issue: Monthly
Copies per Issue:
Sponsor/Publisher: North-Holland, Elsevier
    Science Publishing
Subscribe Price: 135.00 US$ Individual
    2331.00 US$ Institution
    129.00 Euro Ind, 2,084 Euro Institution

REVIEW INFORMATION:

Type of Review:
No. of External Reviewers: 2
No. of In House Reviewers: 0
Acceptance Rate: 6-10%
Time to Review: 2 - 3 Months
Reviewers Comments: Yes 2 Reports
Invited Articles: 0%
Fees to Publish: 0.00 US$

MANUSCRIPT TOPICS:
Banking & Finance; Corporate Finance

MANUSCRIPT GUIDELINES/COMMENTS:

Description
The aim of this international journal is to provide an outlet for the increasing flow of scholarly research concerning financial institutions and the money and capital markets within which they function.

It includes studies, which investigate the interaction of individuals and non-financial enterprises with financial intermediaries and markets. The emphasis is primarily on applied and policy oriented research. The *Journal* thus intends to improve communications between, and within, the academic and other research communities and those members of financial institutions, both private and public, national and international, who are responsible for operational and policy decisions.

The *Journal* encourages contributions in quantitative methods and the application of management science techniques to financial problems; analysis of monetary and fiscal theoretic applications to domestic and international situations; and the application of recent advances in financial theory to practical problems such as bank asset management.

Since 1989, the *Studies in Banking & Finance* have been incorporated with the Journal.

Audience
Financial Economists, Policy Makers in both private and public institutions.

Guide for Authors
1. Papers must be in English.

2. Papers for publication should be sent both as a hardcopy (in triplicate) and on diskette (more instructions under 3) to:
Professor Giorgio P. Szegö
Journal of Banking and Finance
c/o A.B.I. Piazza del Gesú 49
00186 Roma, ITALY
Tel: + 39 06 8632 4395; E-mail: e.jbf@tiscalinet.it or e.jbf@fastwebnet.it

Unsolicited manuscripts must be accompanied by a submission fee of US$ 200.00. Any additional manuscript submitted within the same year, as well as all revised and resubmitted manuscripts, must include a fee of US$ 180.00. The price of a regular personal subscription is available upon request. Checks shall be drawn to the Journal of Banking and Finance and can be in any convertible currency. Submission of a paper will be held to imply that it contains original unpublished work and is not being submitted for publication elsewhere. The Editor does not accept responsibility for damage or loss of papers submitted. Upon acceptance of an article, author(s) will be asked to transfer copyright of the article to the publisher. This transfer will ensure the widest possible dissemination of information.

3. In order to guarantee quicker turnaround times in the review process submission of papers should also be submitted electronically. The preferred storage medium is a 3.5-inch disk in MS-DOS format, although other systems are welcome, e.g., Macintosh (in this case, save your file in the usual manner; do not use the option "save in MS-DOS format"). Make absolutely sure that the file on the disk and the printout are identical. Please use a new and correctly formatted disk and label this with your name; also specify the software and hardware used as well as the title of the file to be processed. Do not convert the file to plain ASCII. Ensure that the letter 'l' and digit '1', and also the letter 'O' and digit '0' are used properly, and format your article (tabs, indents, etc.) consistently. Characters not available on your word processor (Greek letters mathematical symbols, etc.) should not be left open but indicated by a unique code (e.g. gralpha, <alpha>, etc., for the Greek letter α). Such codes should be used consistently throughout the entire text; a list of codes used should accompany the electronic manuscript. Do not allow your word processor to introduce word breaks and do not use a justified layout. Please adhere strictly to the general instructions below on style, arrangement and, in particular, the reference style of the journal.

4. Once your paper has been accepted you will be asked by the Editor to resubmit the accepted version of your paper both on diskette and as a hardcopy.

5. Manuscripts should be double spaced, with wide margins, and printed on one side of the paper only. All pages should be numbered consequently. Titles and subtitles should be short. References, tables, and legends for the figures should be printed on separate pages.

6. The first page of the manuscript should contain the following information: (i) the title; (ii) the name(s) and institutional affiliation(s) of the author(s); (iii) an abstract of not more than 100 words; (iv) at least one classification code according to the Classification System for Journal Articles as used by the *Journal of Economic Literature*; in addition, up to five key words should be supplied.

A footnote on the same sheet should give the name, address, and telephone and fax numbers of the corresponding author [as well as an e-mail address].

7. Acknowledgements and information on grants received can be given in a first footnote, which should not be included in the consecutive numbering of footnotes.

8. Footnotes should be kept to a minimum and numbered consecutively throughout the text with superscript Arabic numerals. They should be double spaced and not include displayed formulae or tables.

9. Displayed formulae should be numbered consecutively throughout the manuscript as (1), (2), etc. against the right-hand margin of the page. In cases where the derivation of formulae has been abbreviated, it is of great help to the referees if the full derivation can be presented on a separate sheet (not to be published).

10. References to publications should be as follows:
'Smith (1992) reported that...' or 'This problem has been studied previously (e.g., Smith et al., 1969)'.

The author should make sure that there is a strict one-to-one correspondence between the names and years in the text and those on the list. The list of references should appear at the end of the main text (after any appendices, but before tables and legends for figures). It should be double spaced and listed in alphabetical order by author's name.

References should appear as follows:
For monographs
Hawawini, G., Swary, I., 1990. Mergers and Acquisitions in the U.S. Banking Industry: Evidence from the Capital Markets. North-Holland, Amsterdam.

For contributions to collective works
Brunner, K., Meltzer, A.H., 1990. Money supply, in: Friedman, B.M., Hahn, F.H. (Eds.), Handbook of Monetary Economics, Vol. 1. North-Holland, Amsterdam, pp. 357--396.

For periodicals
Griffiths, W., Judge, G., 1992. Testing and estimating location vectors when the error covariance matrix is unknown. Journal of Econometrics 54, 121--138.

Note that journal titles should not be abbreviated.

11. Illustrations will be reproduced photographically from originals supplied by the author; they will not be redrawn by the publisher. Please provide all illustrations in quadruplicate (one high-contrast original and three photocopies). Care should be taken that lettering and symbols are of a comparable size. The illustrations should not be inserted in the text, and should be marked on the back with figure number, title of paper, and author's name. All graphs and diagrams should be referred to as figures, and should be numbered consecutively in the text in Arabic numerals. Illustration for papers submitted as electronic manuscripts should be in traditional form.

12. Tables should be numbered consecutively in the text in Arabic numerals and printed on separate sheets.

Any manuscript which does not conform to the above instructions may be returned for the necessary revision before publication.

13. Page proofs will be sent to the corresponding author. Proofs should be corrected carefully; the responsibility for detecting errors lies with the author. Corrections should be restricted to instances in which the proof is at variance with the manuscript. Extensive alterations will be charged. Fifty reprints of each paper are supplied free of charge to the corresponding author; additional reprints are available at cost if they are ordered when the proof is returned.

Journal of Behavioral Finance (The)

ADDRESS FOR SUBMISSION:

Deborah Trask, Managing Editor
Journal of Behavioral Finance (The)
Center for Investment Research
PMB 310
1900 Preston Road #267
Plano, TX 75093
USA
Phone: 817-442-5404
Fax: 817-442-5404
E-Mail: dtrask@investmentresearch.org
Web: www.psychologyandmarkets.org
Address May Change:

PUBLICATION GUIDELINES:

Manuscript Length: 21-25
Copies Required: No Reply
Computer Submission: Yes
Format: MS Word
Fees to Review: 0.00 US$

Manuscript Style:
American Psychological Association

CIRCULATION DATA:

Reader: Academics, Business Persons
Frequency of Issue: Quarterly
Copies per Issue: 1,001 - 2,000
Sponsor/Publisher: Institute of Psychology
and Markets/Lawrence Erlbaum
Associates, Inc.
Subscribe Price: 80.00 US$ Individual
295.00 US$ Institution
US/Canada - Print/Online

REVIEW INFORMATION:

Type of Review: Blind Review
No. of External Reviewers: 2
No. of In House Reviewers: 1
Acceptance Rate: 21-30%
Time to Review: 1 - 2 Months
Reviewers Comments: Yes
Invited Articles: 0-5%
Fees to Publish: 0.00 US$

MANUSCRIPT TOPICS:
Behavioral Economics; Behavioral Patterns/Influences on Markets; Financial Institutions & Markets; Financial Services; Portfolio & Security Analysis

MANUSCRIPT GUIDELINES/COMMENTS:

Content
The Journal of Psychology & Financial Markets is intended to foster debate among groups who have keen insights into the behavioral patterns of markets but have not historically published in the more traditional financial and economic journals. Further, it is designed to stimulate new interdisciplinary research and theory that will build a body of knowledge about the psychological influences on market fluctuations. The most obvious benefit is a new understanding of markets that can greatly improve investment decision making. Another benefit is the opportunity for behavioral scientists to expand the scope of their studies via the use of the enormous databases that document behavior in markets. Offering penetrating insights into the impact of psychological forces on economic performance, *The Journal of Behavioral Finance* is an indispensable resource for academics and practitioners alike.

Audience
Practitioners and investment professionals; personality, social, and organizational psychologists; clinical and cognitive psychologists, psychiatrists, and other mental health professionals; specialists in consumer behavior and marketing; specialists in the multidisciplinary study of judgment and decision making; researchers in finance and accounting; specialists in behavioral economics; and economic sociologists and anthropologists.

Submissions
Please follow these guidelines when preparing and submitting an article. Keep in mind you are writing for readers with a variety of backgrounds not necessarily the same as your own. Write to express, not to impress, and write the way you talk. Keep it simple; brevity and conciseness are valued, but be sure to create interest. Colorful language and examples are encouraged. Equations and formulas are discouraged, except in appendixes.

The publication agreement must be signed and returned before an accepted article can be published.

Formatting Style
Manuscripts should be prepared according to the guidelines in the *Publication Manual of the American Psychological Association* (4th ed.; the manual is available from the APA Book Order Department, Dept. KK, P.O. Box 92984, Washington, DC 20090-2984; 800-374-2721; http://www.apa.org).

Length
Manuscripts should generally be no more than 30 pages and should be double spaced with wide margins and numbered pages.

Cover Page
The front page should include the authors' full name(s), title(s), address(es), zip code(s), phone number(s), e-mail address(es), and type of software used.

References and Citations
References, endnotes, tables, and figures should appear on separate pages at the end of the text.

Limit references to works cited in the text and list them alphabetically. Citations in the text should appear as "Smith [1990] suggests that..." Use page numbers for quotes. Use periods instead of commas between authors' names and titles of references.

Endnotes
Minimize the number of endnotes. Use superscript Arabic numbers in the text and on the endnote page.

Figures and Tables
Number and title all exhibits, with one to a page. Write out the column heads and legends; they should be understandable figures and graphs in camera-ready form as we cannot draw them for you.

Equations
Center any equations on a separate line, numbered consecutively with Arabic numbers placed in parenthesis in the right margin.

Special Characters
Identify Greek letters in the margin for the typesetter. Please make clear markings, in a color other than black, when inserting Greek letters or equations into the text.

Summary
Include a brief article summary. The summary should include five key words that can be used in searches for the article.

Address
Authors should submit three (3) hard copies of the manuscript, along with a copy on disk (in Microsoft Word if possible), and should be sent to Deborah Trask, Managing Editor.

Reprints
Authors may order reprints of their articles when they receive page proofs. Printing considerations do not permit the ordering of reprints after authors have returned proofs.

Journal of Business

ADDRESS FOR SUBMISSION:

Albert Madansky, Editor
Journal of Business
University of Chicago
Graduate School of Business
1101 East 58th Street
Chicago, IL 60637
USA
Phone: 773-702-7140
Fax: 773-834-7002
E-Mail: job@gsb.uchicago.edu
Web: www.journals.uchicago.edu/JB/
Address May Change:

PUBLICATION GUIDELINES:

Manuscript Length: No Reply
Copies Required: Two
Computer Submission: No
Format: N/A
Fees to Review: 50.00 US$

Manuscript Style:
Chicago Manual of Style

CIRCULATION DATA:

Reader: Academics
Frequency of Issue: Quarterly
Copies per Issue: 2,001 - 3,000
Sponsor/Publisher: University of Chicago
Press
Subscribe Price: 30.00 US$

REVIEW INFORMATION:

Type of Review: Blind Review
No. of External Reviewers: 1-2
No. of In House Reviewers: 1
Acceptance Rate: 11-20%
Time to Review: 2 - 3 Months
Reviewers Comments: Yes
Invited Articles: 0-5%
Fees to Publish: 0.00 US$

MANUSCRIPT TOPICS:
Accounting Theory & Practice; Econometrics; Industrial Organization; Insurance;
International Economics & Trade; International Finance; Macro Economics; Micro
Economics; Monetary Policy; Portfolio & Security Analysis; Real Estate

MANUSCRIPT GUIDELINES/COMMENTS:

Journal of Business & Economic Studies

ADDRESS FOR SUBMISSION:

Luis E. Rivera-Solis, Editor
Journal of Business & Economic Studies
Dowling College
School of Business
Rm 406
Oakdale, NY 11769
USA
Phone: 631-244-3214
Fax: 631-244-5098
E-Mail: riveral@dowling.edu
Web: www.dowling.edu
Address May Change:

PUBLICATION GUIDELINES:

Manuscript Length: 21-25
Copies Required: Three
Computer Submission: No
Format: N/A
Fees to Review: 0.00 US$

Manuscript Style:
       American Psychological Association

CIRCULATION DATA:

Reader: Academics
Frequency of Issue: 2 Times/Year
Copies per Issue: 600-1,000
Sponsor/Publisher: Dowling College
   Northeast Business and Economics
   Assoc.
Subscribe Price: 25.00 US$ Individual

REVIEW INFORMATION:

Type of Review: Blind Review
No. of External Reviewers: 2
No. of In House Reviewers: 1
Acceptance Rate: 11-20%
Time to Review: 4 - 6 Months
Reviewers Comments: Yes
Invited Articles: 0-5%
Fees to Publish: 300.00 US$

MANUSCRIPT TOPICS:

Corporate Finance; Econometrics; Economic Development; Financial Institutions & Markets;
Financial Services; Fiscal Policy; Industrial Organization; International Economics & Trade;
International Finance; Macro Economics; Micro Economics; Monetary Policy; Portfolio &
Security Analysis; Public Policy Economics; Regional Economics

MANUSCRIPT GUIDELINES/COMMENTS:

Submissions
Initial submissions must be made in triplicate with a cover letter stating that the manuscript is
not currently being considered at another publication. Send submission to Editor-in-Chief,
Luis Eduardo Rivera-Solis.

Manuscripts should have a cover page with the author's name, address, and affiliation. No
other pages should contain information about the author. A fifty to one hundred word abstract
should appear on the second page. The paper itself should appear on the third page. All
manuscripts accepted by *JBES* for publication must be submitted in Microsoft Word on a

floppy disk accompanied by a printout of the article. Complete guidelines for accepted manuscripts will be sent upon acceptance. Some basic guidelines include:

1. **Equations**. Default settings should be used. Set point size at 10 points, use Arabic numbers flush left in parenthesis.

2. **References** in the text should be parenthetical references with the author's last name and date of publication. Alphabetical list of reference should be included.

3. **Tables** should be numbered in Arabic numbers, e.g., Table 1. Columns of the tables should be set using tab stops, not spaces, to align. Tables should be placed at the end of your article and their appropriate placement in the text noted.

4. **Figures** are numbered similarly to tables, e.g., Figure 1. The author will provide the figures on a disk in a Microsoft Word compatible program.

5. If you need to use footnotes, DO NOT use the endnote or footnote setting in Word. Use superscript numbers to refer to your endnote, which should appear at the end of the article.

6. Sections of the paper, such as INTRODUCTION, should be flush left in all capital letters with one extra line between section thread and text. For example:

Introduction
Subheads should be in upper and lower case letters, flush left with one extra line above and no extra line below the subhead. For subheads below the first level subhead, indent on tab for the second level subhead. Please limit subheads to no more than two.

7. Do not use headers or footers or page breaks in your paper.

8. *JBES* reserves the right to edit all accepted papers.

Journal of Business and Behavioral Sciences

ADDRESS FOR SUBMISSION:

Wali I. Mondal, Editor
Journal of Business and Behavioral
   Sciences
ASBBS
Box 10367
San Bernadino, CA 92423-0367
USA
Phone: 909-748-6287
Fax: 909-335-9279
E-Mail: mondal@asbbs.org
Web: www.asbbs.org
Address May Change:

PUBLICATION GUIDELINES:

Manuscript Length: 11-15
Copies Required: Four
Computer Submission: No
Format: N/A
Fees to Review: 20.00 US$

Manuscript Style:
   American Psychological Association

CIRCULATION DATA:

Reader: Academics
Frequency of Issue: 2 Times/Year
Copies per Issue: 1,001 - 2,000
Sponsor/Publisher: American Society of
   Business and Bevioral Sciences
Subscribe Price: 50.00 US$

REVIEW INFORMATION:

Type of Review: Blind Review
No. of External Reviewers: 3
No. of In House Reviewers: 1
Acceptance Rate: 11-20%
Time to Review: 4 - 6 Months
Reviewers Comments: Yes
Invited Articles: 0-5%
Fees to Publish: 0.00 US$

MANUSCRIPT TOPICS:

Accounting Information Systems; Accounting Theory & Practice; Auditing; Behavioral Economics; Corporate Finance; Cost Accounting; Econometrics; Economic Development; Economic History; Financial Institutions & Markets; Financial Services; Fiscal Policy; Government & Non-Profit Accounting; Industrial Organization; Insurance; International Economics & Trade; International Finance; Macro Economics; Micro Economics; Monetary Policy; Portfolio & Security Analysis; Psychology; Public Policy Economics; Real Estate; Regional Economics; Tax Accounting

MANUSCRIPT GUIDELINES/COMMENTS:

Manuscripts in any area of Accounting, Economics, and Finance will be considered for publication. Papers must be prepared in double-space and must accompany an abstract not to exceed 250 words. Authors should follow the *APA* guidelines in preparing their manuscripts. Guidelines for final submission to the *Journal* will be sent only if a paper is accepted after review.

Journal of Business and Economic Perspectives

ADDRESS FOR SUBMISSION:

Bob Figgins, Editor
Journal of Business and Economic
    Perspectives
University of Tennessee at Martin
College of Business and Public Affairs
Martin, TN 38238
USA
Phone: 731-587-7226
Fax: 731-587-7241
E-Mail: bfiggins@utm.edu
Web:
Address May Change:

PUBLICATION GUIDELINES:

Manuscript Length: 16
Copies Required: Three
Computer Submission: Yes
Format: Request Style Sheet
Fees to Review: 15.00 US$

Manuscript Style:
    Chicago Manual of Style

CIRCULATION DATA:

Reader: Academics
Frequency of Issue: 2 Times/Year
Copies per Issue: Less than 1,000
Sponsor/Publisher: University
Subscribe Price: 15.00 US$ Individual
    26.00 US$ Institution
    $20/$36 - 2 Yrs

REVIEW INFORMATION:

Type of Review: Blind Review
No. of External Reviewers: 2
No. of In House Reviewers: 1
Acceptance Rate: 30-35%
Time to Review: 4 - 6 Months
Reviewers Comments: No
Invited Articles: 0-5%
Fees to Publish: 0.00 US$

MANUSCRIPT TOPICS:

Accounting Information Systems; Accounting Theory & Practice; Auditing; Capital Budgeting; Cost Accounting; Econometrics; Economic Development; Economic History; Fiscal Policy; Government & Non-Profit Accounting; Industrial Organization; Insurance; International Economics & Trade; International Finance; Macro Economics; Micro Economics; Monetary Policy; Portfolio & Security Analysis; Public Policy Economics; Real Estate; Regional Economics; Tax Accounting

MANUSCRIPT GUIDELINES/COMMENTS:

Manuscripts related to popular aspects of Business and Economics are solicited. All articles of interest to both practitioners and academics in business will be considered. Topics such as ethical and international aspects of business, which cut across disciplines, are encouraged.

Length of Articles. Ordinarily, articles should not exceed sixteen, double-spaced, typewritten pages, references and tables inclusive.

Mathematics. The use of mathematics and graphics should be kept at a minimum. Avoid technical jargon. Number equations. In identifying variables in formulas, capitalize only the initial letter of abbreviations—except where common usage indicates otherwise.

Submission of Articles. Send four copies of all articles and US$15 submission fee to Editor. We regret that we are unable to return or store manuscripts.

Review. Before publication, manuscripts are reviewed by the Editor and one or more reviewers from other institutions to be sure the material is appropriate for the Journal. On occasion, revisions may be suggested to the author to make the material of the greatest possible use to Journal readers.

Typing. The manuscript should be double-spaced throughout. This applies to text, footnotes, references, and figure legends. Use standard 8½" x 11" white paper. Submit four copies and keep another for your own use. Type on one side of page only. Leave a 1-inch margin on all four sides of the text. Mathematical symbols must be clearly represented—typed if at all possible. Make sure that final changes are made on all four copies.

Title Page and Summary. Use a cover page that shows the title of the paper, the name of the author(s) with their titles, institutional affiliations, and telephone numbers. Include on this page a summary of the article in 150 words or less. If appropriate, add as a footnote material about previous publications or other information, which can be used to identify the author(s).

Corrections and Insertions. Keep corrections in the manuscript to a minimum. Retype any page on which more than a few changes are necessary. Do not write in the margins. Type lengthy insertions on a separate page, and mark the place in the text where the insertion is to appear. This page should also indicate that the insertion follows. (For example, number the insertion 12a. Page 12 should be marked, "Followed by p. 12a.")

Footnotes. Use footnotes sparingly. Number sequentially. Type footnotes double-spaced on a separate page at the end of the article. In general, avoid lengthy explanatory footnotes. This material can usually be incorporated in the text.

Section Headings. If sparingly used, section headings and subheadings enhance the readability of an article. Do not try to indicate typographical style, but show the relative weights by using all capital letters for the main headings (i.e., CONCLUSIONS) and initial capital letters (only) for words in the subheadings (i.e., Test Results).

Tables and Charts. Avoid excessively long tables. Type tables and charts on pages separate from the text. Captions of all figures should be consistent. Capitalize the first letter in all words in main headings (i.e., Test Results). For captions of lesser importance in the column headings or subs, capitalize only the first letter of the initial word (i.e., Goodness of fit.)

References. Type double-spaced with each item beginning flush left. For entries requiring more than one line, run-over lines should be indented. Authors in the references should be listed alphabetically; do not number the entries. Citations for books should contain author's last name, first name and middle initials followed by full title of the book, place of publication, publisher, and publication (copyright) date. The following example illustrates the desired form and punctuation.

Smith, Arthur G., Economics, New York: Godwin, 1978.

Journal articles should include (in addition to author and title, as above) the name of the journal, date, volume, and page. For example:

Smith, Arthur G., "Teaching Economics," Journal of Economic Education, Spring 1976, 7, 4-12.
Vibhakar, Ashvin P., and Kennedy, Robert E., "Alternate Estimates of the Cost of Equity Capital: Electric Utilities Revisited," Journal of Business and Economic Perspectives, Fall 1982, 8, 1-22.

In referring to references in the text of the article, use the author's name, publication date, and page number (if needed). For example: "... as the date indicates (Smith, 1978, p. 456)" or "...as Smith (1978) has stated..."

Journal of Business and Economics

ADDRESS FOR SUBMISSION:

Alan S. Khade, Editor
Journal of Business and Economics
California State University, Stanislaus
College of Business Administration
983 Woodland Drive
Turlock, CA 95382-7281
USA
Phone: 209-667-3074
Fax: 209-667-3210
E-Mail: akhade@csustan.edu
Web: www.aibe.org
Address May Change: 10/10/2010

PUBLICATION GUIDELINES:

Manuscript Length: 10-20
Copies Required: Two
Computer Submission: Yes Disk or Email
Format: MS Word
Fees to Review: 0.00 US$

Manuscript Style:
    Chicago Manual of Style

CIRCULATION DATA:

Reader: Academics, Business Persons
Frequency of Issue: 2 Times/Year
Copies per Issue: Less than 1,000
Sponsor/Publisher: IABE and AABE
Subscribe Price: 50.00 US$ Individual

REVIEW INFORMATION:

Type of Review: Blind Review
No. of External Reviewers: 2
No. of In House Reviewers: 1
Acceptance Rate: 21-30%
Time to Review: 2 - 3 Months
Reviewers Comments: Yes
Invited Articles: 21-30%
Fees to Publish: 0.00 US$

MANUSCRIPT TOPICS:
Corporate Finance; Econometrics; Economic Development; Economics; Financial Institutions & Markets; Financial Services; Fiscal Policy; Industrial Organization; Insurance; International Economics & Trade; International Finance; Macro Economics; Monetary Policy; Portfolio & Security Analysis; Public Policy Economics; Regional Economics

MANUSCRIPT GUIDELINES/COMMENTS:

Please follow the following Manuscript Guidelines for *Journal of Business and Economics* (*JBE*).

The original, high quality research papers and articles (not currently under review or published in other publications) on all topics related to business and economics will be considered for publication in *Journal of Business and Economics* (*JBE*).

I. **Copyright**. Articles, papers, abstracts or cases submitted for publication should be original contributions and should not be under consideration for any other publication at the same time. Authors submitting articles/papers/abstracts/cases for publication warrant that the work

604

is not an infringement of any existing copyright, infringement of proprietary right, invasion of privacy, or libel and will indemnify, defend, and hold IABE/AIBE harmless from any damages, expenses, and costs against any breach of such warranty. For ease of dissemination and to ensure proper policing of use, papers/articles/abstracts/cases and contributions become the legal copyright of the IABE/AIBE unless otherwise agreed in writing.

II. **Typing**. Paper must be laser printed on 8.5" x 11" white sheets in <u>Arial 10-point font, single-spaced lines, justify style in MS Word.</u> All four margins must be 1" each.

III. **First Page**. Paper title, not exceeding two lines, must be CAPITALIZED AND CENTERED IN BOLD LETTERS. Author name and university/organizational affiliation of each author must be printed on one line each. Do NOT include titles such as, Dr., Professor, Ph.D., department, address, email address etc. Please print the word "ABSTRACT" in capitalized bold letters, left justified, and double-spaced from last author's name/affiliation. Abstract should be in italic. Please see the sample manuscript.

IV. **All Other Headings**. All other section headings starting with INTRODUCTION must be numbered, in capitalized bold letters, left justified, and double-spaced from last line above them.

V. **Tables, Figures, and Charts**. All tables, figures or charts must be inserted in the body of the manuscripts within the margins with headings/titles in centered CAPITALIZED BOLD letters.

VI. **References and Bibliography**. All references listed in this section must be cited in the article and vice-versa. The reference citations in the text must be inserted in parentheses within sentences with author name followed by a comma and year of publication. Please follow the following formats:

Journal Articles:	Khade, Alan S. and Metlen, Scott K., "An Application of Benchmarking in Dairy Industry", *International Journal of Benchmarking*, Vol. III (4), 1996, 17-27.
Books:	Harrison, Norma and Samson, D., <u>Technology Management: Text and Cases</u>, McGraw-Hill Publishing, New York, 2002.
Internet:	Hesterbrink, C., E-Business and ERP: Bringing two Paradigms together, October 1999; PricewaterhouseCoopers, *www.pwc.com*.

VII. **Author Profile(s)**. At the end of paper, include author profile(s), not exceeding <u>five</u> lines each author, including name, highest degree/university/year, current position/university, and major achievements. For example:

Dr. Andrew J. Wagner earned his Ph.D. at Texas A and M University in 1997. Currently he is an associate professor of finance at California State University, Stanislaus, and Program Chair of the IABE.

VIII. **Manuscript**. Absolutely <u>no</u> footnotes allowed! Please do not forget to run spelling and grammar check for the completed paper. <u>Save the manuscript on a diskette</u> and label the diskette with title of your paper, your name, and email address.

IX. Submission
Submissions by Mail:
Please mail the following items in a 9" x 12" envelope:
1. Two camera-ready laser-printed copies of the manuscript
2. Diskette containing your manuscript

Submissions by Email:
Send your paper as an attachment to the email to: AKhade@csustan.edu

Journal of Business and Economics Research

ADDRESS FOR SUBMISSION:

Ronald C. Clute, Editor
Journal of Business and Economics
   Research
P O Box 620760
Littleton, CO 80162
USA
Phone: 303-904-4750
Fax: 303-978-0413
E-Mail: cluter@wapress.com
Web: www.wapress.com
Address May Change:

PUBLICATION GUIDELINES:

Manuscript Length: 6-10
Copies Required: One
Computer Submission: Yes Email prefrd,
   disk
Format: MS Word
Fees to Review: 0.00 US$

Manuscript Style:
   Other

CIRCULATION DATA:

Reader: Academics
Frequency of Issue: Monthly
Copies per Issue: Less than 1,000
Sponsor/Publisher: International Applied
  Business Research Conference / Western
  Academic Press, Inc.
Subscribe Price: 150.00 US$ Individual
  495.00 US$ Library

REVIEW INFORMATION:

Type of Review: Blind Review
No. of External Reviewers: 1
No. of In House Reviewers: 1
Acceptance Rate: 11-20%
Time to Review: 2 - 3 Months
Reviewers Comments: Yes Sometimes
Invited Articles: 0-5%
Fees to Publish: 25.00 US$ Per page
  single-spaced

MANUSCRIPT TOPICS:

Accounting Information Systems; Accounting Theory & Practice; Auditing; Cost Accounting; Econometrics; Economic Development; Economic History; Fiscal Policy; Government & Non-Profit Accounting; Industrial Organization; Insurance; International Economics & Trade; International Finance; Macro Economics; Micro Economics; Monetary Policy; Portfolio & Security Analysis; Public Policy Economics; Real Estate; Regional Economics; Tax Accounting

MANUSCRIPT GUIDELINES/COMMENTS:

The *Journal of Business & Economics Research* welcomes articles in all areas of business and economics. Both theoretical and applied manuscripts will be considered for publication. Theoretical manuscripts must provide a clear link to important and interesting business and economics applications.

Authors desiring to submit a paper for publication need only inform our conference chair. This is normally accomplished by checking the appropriate box on the conference registration form. The *JBER* publishes the "Best Paper" manuscripts from our conferences for the preceding year in addition to other manuscripts. All papers to be considered for publication in the *JBER* for next year are selected from the papers presented at one of our conferences for the current year. Prospective authors should comply with the conference submission requirements. The *JBER* imposes a page fee on all accepted manuscripts. These fees are necessary to offset the very substantial cost of putting a manuscript into print. The page fee is $25.00 per author's single-spaced page (with one-inch margins) and is due only if the manuscript is accepted for publication.

Further information about our conferences and journals is available at www.wapress.com.

Journal of Business and Finance Librarianship

ADDRESS FOR SUBMISSION:

Charles Popovich, Editor
Journal of Business and Finance
   Librarianship
The Ohio State University
Business Library
Raymond E. Mason Hall
250 West Woodruff Avenue
Columbus, OH 43210
USA
Phone: 614-292-2136
Fax: 614-292-7859
E-Mail: popovich.1@osu.edu
Web: www.haworthpressinc.com
Address May Change:

PUBLICATION GUIDELINES:

Manuscript Length: 10-50
Copies Required: Four
Computer Submission: Yes Disk
Format: WordPerfect 6.0/5.1
Fees to Review: 0.00 US$

Manuscript Style:
   Uniform System of Citation (Harvard
   Blue Book)

CIRCULATION DATA:

Reader: Academics
Frequency of Issue: Quarterly
Copies per Issue: 1,001 - 2,000
Sponsor/Publisher: Haworth Press, Inc.
Subscribe Price: 36.00 US$ Individual
   76.50 US$ Institution

REVIEW INFORMATION:

Type of Review: Blind Review
No. of External Reviewers: 2
No. of In House Reviewers: 1
Acceptance Rate: 50%
Time to Review: 2 - 3 Months
Reviewers Comments: Yes
Invited Articles: 21-30%
Fees to Publish: 0.00 US$

MANUSCRIPT TOPICS:

Accounting Information Systems; Accounting Theory & Practice; Auditing; Business &
Finance; Capital Budgeting; Cost Accounting; Econometrics; Economic History; Government
& Non-Profit Accounting; Insurance; International Economics & Trade; International
Finance; Library Related Topics; Portfolio & Security Analysis; Public Policy Economics;
Real Estate; Tax Accounting

MANUSCRIPT GUIDELINES/COMMENTS:

Note. All manuscript topics must discuss some relationship to Libraries.

JBFL is a peer-reviewed journal, which is published quarterly by the Haworth Press. It is
devoted to publishing articles of importance to information professionals who are involved
with, or have an interest in, the creation, organization, dissemination, retrieval, and use of
business and finance information. Articles generally pertain to the needs of information
professionals in business and finance libraries and information centers or services outside of

the traditional library setting. *JBFL* is not only and outlet for practice-oriented articles, but also a forum for new empirical studies on librarianship related to business and finance information. Also, many of the articles reflect the multinational and international scope of today's business community.

For an informational "Instructions for Authors" brochure, contact the Editor.

1. **Original Articles Only**. Submission of a manuscript to this *Journal* represents a certification on the part of the author(s) that it is an original work, and that neither this manuscript nor a version of it has been published elsewhere nor is being considered for publication elsewhere.

2. **Manuscript Length**—5 to 50 typed pages

3. **Manuscript Style**—*Chicago Manual of Style*

4. **Manuscript Preparation**
Margins. Leave at least one-inch margins on all four sides
Paper. Use clean, white, 8½" x 11" bond paper
Number of Copies. 4 (the original plus 3 photocopies)
Cover Page. *Important*—Staple a cover page to the manuscript, indicating only the article title (this is used for anonymous refereeing)
Second "Title Page". Enclose a regular title page but do not staple it to the manuscript. Include the title again, plus:
- Full authorship
- An ABSTRACT of about 100 words (below the abstract, provide 3-10 key words for index purposes)
- An introductory footnote with authors' academic degrees, professional titles, affiliations, mailing addresses, and any desired acknowledgment of research support or other credit

5. **Return Envelopes**. When you submit your four manuscript copies, also include:
- A regular envelope, stamped and self-addressed—this is for the Editor to send you an "Acknowledgement of Receipt" letter.
- Manuscripts will not be returned.

6. **Spelling, Grammar, and Punctuation**. You are responsible for preparing manuscript copy which is clearly written in acceptable scholarly English, and which contains no errors of spelling, grammar, or punctuation. Neither the Editor nor the Publisher is responsible for correcting errors of spelling and grammar: the manuscript, after acceptance by the Editor, must be immediately ready for typesetting as it is finally submitted by the author(s). Check your paper for the following common errors.
- Dangling modifiers
- Misplaced modifiers
- Unclear antecedents
- Incorrect or inconsistent abbreviations

Also, check the accuracy of all arithmetic calculations, statistics, numerical data, text citations, and references.

7. **Inconsistencies** must be avoided. Be sure you are consistent in your use of abbreviations, terminology, and in citing references, from one part of your paper to another.

8. **Preparation of Tables, Figures, and Illustrations**. All tables, figures, illustrations, etc., must be "camera-ready." That is, they must be cleanly typed or artistically prepared so that they can be used either exactly as they are or else used after a photographic reduction in size. Figures, tables, and illustrations must be prepared on separate sheets of paper. Always use black ink and professional drawing instruments. On the back of these items, write your article title and the journal title lightly in pencil, so they do not get misplaced. In text, skip extra lines and indicate where these figures and tables are to be placed (please do not write on face of art). Photographs are considered part of the acceptable manuscript and remain with Publisher for use in additional printings. If submitted art cannot be used, the Publisher reserves the right to redo the art and to charge the author a fee of $35.00 per hour for this service.

9. **Alterations Required by Referees and Reviewers**. Many times a paper is accepted by the Editor contingent upon changes that are mandated by anonymous specialist referees and members of the Editorial Board. If the Editor returns your manuscript for revisions, you are responsible for retyping any sections of the paper to incorporate these revisions (if applicable, revisions should also be put on disk).

10. **Typesetting**. You will not be receiving galley proofs of your article. Editorial revisions, if any, must therefore be made while your article is still in manuscript. The final version of the manuscript will be the version you see published. Typesetter's errors will be corrected by the production staff of The Haworth Press. Authors are expected to submit manuscripts, disks, and art that are free from error.

11. **Electronic Media**. Haworth's in-house typesetting unit is able to utilize your final manuscript material as prepared on most personal computers and word processors. This will minimize typographical errors and decrease overall production time lag. Please send the first draft and final draft copies of your manuscript to the *Journal* Editor in print format for his/her final review and approval. **After approval** of your final manuscript, please submit the final, approved version both on printed format ("hard copy") and floppy diskette. On the outside of the diskette package write:
A. The brand name of your computer or word processor;
B. The word-processing program that you used;
C. The title of your article; and
D. File name.

NOTE: Disk and hard copy must agree. In case of discrepancies, it is The Haworth Press's policy to follow hard copy. Authors are advised that no revisions of the manuscript can be made after acceptance by the Editor for publication. The benefits of this procedure are many with speed and accuracy being the most obvious. We look forward to working with you on this, knowing we will be able to serve you more efficiently in the future.

12. **Reprints**. The senior author will receive two copies of the *Journal* issue and 25 complimentary reprints of his or her article. The junior author will receive two copies of the *Journal* issue. These are sent several weeks after the *Journal* issue is published and in circulation. An order form for the purchase of additional reprints will also be sent to all authors at this time. (Approximately 4-6 weeks is necessary for the preparation of reprints.) Please do not query the *Journal*'s Editor about reprints. All such questions should be sent directly to The Haworth Press, Inc., Production Department, 21 East Broad Street, West Hazleton, PA 18201.

To order additional reprints (minimum: 50 copies), please contact The Haworth Document Delivery Center, 10 Alice Street, Binghamton, NY 13904-1580; Tel: 1-800-342-9678 or Fax (607) 722-6362.

13. **Copyright** ownership of your manuscript must be transferred officially to The Haworth Press, Inc., before we can begin the peer-review process. The Editor's letter, acknowledging receipt of the manuscript, will be accompanied by a form fully explaining this. All authors must sign the form and return the original to the Editor as soon as possible. Failure to return the copyright form in a timely fashion will result in delay in review and subsequent publication.

Journal of Business Disciplines

ADDRESS FOR SUBMISSION:

Douglas Barney / Tom Keefe, Co-Editors
Journal of Business Disciplines
Indiana University, SE
School of Business
Hillside Hall
4201 Grant Line Road
New Albany, IN 47150
USA
Phone: 812-941-2628
Fax: 812-941-2672
E-Mail: tkeefe@ius.edu; dbarney@ius.edu
Web: abdwebsite.com
Address May Change:

PUBLICATION GUIDELINES:

Manuscript Length: 11-20
Copies Required: Four
Computer Submission: No
Format: N/A
Fees to Review: 25.00 US$

Manuscript Style:
    American Psychological Association

CIRCULATION DATA:

Reader: Academics
Frequency of Issue: 2 Times/Year
Copies per Issue: Less than 1,000
Sponsor/Publisher: Academy of Business
    Disciplines, Indiana University SE
    School of Business, Shippensburg Univ.
Subscribe Price: 25.00 US$ Individual
    50.00 US$ Library

REVIEW INFORMATION:

Type of Review: Blind Review
No. of External Reviewers: 3
No. of In House Reviewers: 2
Acceptance Rate: 11-20%
Time to Review: 1-3 Months
Reviewers Comments: Yes
Invited Articles: 11-20%
Fees to Publish: 0.00 US$

MANUSCRIPT TOPICS:

Accounting Information Systems; Auditing; Behavioral Economics; Corporate Finance; Cost Accounting; Econometrics; Economic Development; Economic History; Financial Institutions & Markets; Financial Services; Fiscal Policy; Government & Non-Profit Accounting; Industrial Organization; Insurance; International Economics & Trade; International Finance; Macro Economics; Micro Economics; Monetary Policy; Portfolio & Security Analysis; Public Policy Economics; Real Estate; Regional Economics; Tax Accounting

MANUSCRIPT GUIDELINES/COMMENTS:

Goal
To increase and share business knowledge.

Aim and Scope
The *Journal* is dedicated to publishing quality applied business articles designed to inform business practitioners and business academics. Articles should be of current importance and can be either empirical or theoretical in approach. General readability of the articles is of

critical importance. (Manuscripts submitted should not be so technical or specialized that they are of interest only to specialists in that area. Manuscripts should be free of technical jargon or should define terms used. Also, manuscripts should not be focused on, or overly dwell on, an issue that is not of practical importance.) Possible application areas include:

Accounting	Finance
Applied Business Economics	Information Systems
Business History	International Business
Business Education	Management
E-Commerce	Marketing
Entrepreneurship	Small Business
Ethics	

Manuscripts will be subjected to external blind reviews.

Submit only original, unpublished manuscripts that are not under review elsewhere:

Manuscript Guidelines
Submit four copies of the manuscript on 8½ x 11-inch paper and a check for $25 payable to the *Journal of Business Disciplines*. If you are submitting an article or if your article has been accepted for publication, please adhere to the following guidelines.

- Title page listing all authors and contact information for corresponding author (for submission purposes only)
- Title page includes no personal titles for authors (for submission purposes only)
- Title should be limited to 8 words
- Body of the text starts on new page with title and no author identification (for accepted manuscripts, authors are listed below the title and the first footnote(s) should provide information about the author(s))
- Margins of 1 inch and full justification
- First level headings (title) centered, initial capitalization, bold, 16-point font
- Second-level headings (major captions, e.g., Introduction) centered, initial capitalization, bold, 14-point font
- Third level headings, left justified, initial capitalization, bold, 12-point font
- Fourth level headings, indented, initial capitalization, bold, 10-point font
- The text should be in 10-point font
- Single space text (double space for submission purposes only)
- Bullet points—consistency within each group of bullet points, italicize opening phrases of lengthy bullets, no bold
- Use footnotes
- Number tables sequentially, label, and describe
- In-text references include (author, year, page) notation
- Reference section at the end of the text:
  o Reference only works cited in the text
  o Reference multiple works by the same author(s) using a, b, c

- o Reference as follows: Author, Date, Title, Publisher (or if no identifiable authors) Title, Date, Publisher
  - Journal: Platt, ILD., Platt, M.B., 1991. A note on the use of industry-relative ratios in bankruptcy prediction. *Journal of Banking and Finance* 15 (6), 1183-1194.
  - Book: Wasserman, P.D., 1989. Neural Computing: Theory and Practice. Van Nostrand Reinhold, New York.
  - Institute Publication: US Congress, 1985. Public Law 99-198. 99 United States Statutes as Large 1325. US Government Printing Office, Washington, DC.

If your work is accepted to the *Journal*, submit the manuscript in MS Word.

Journal of Business Economics Research

ADDRESS FOR SUBMISSION:

Shyam L. Bhatia, Editor
Journal of Business Economics Research
Indiana University Northwest
School of Business Economics
Gary, IN 46408
USA
Phone: 219-980-6634 / 773-667-5063
Fax: 219-980-6916
E-Mail: sbhatia@iun.edu
Web:
Address May Change:

PUBLICATION GUIDELINES:

Manuscript Length: 20
Copies Required: Three
Computer Submission: No
Format: N/A
Fees to Review: 50.00 US$

Manuscript Style:
, American Economic Review
footnoting and referencing style

CIRCULATION DATA:

Reader: Academics, Professional
Frequency of Issue: 2 Times/Year
Copies per Issue: 300
Sponsor/Publisher: Midwest Business
  Economics Assn. / Indiana University
  Northwest
Subscribe Price: 50.00 US$

REVIEW INFORMATION:

Type of Review: Blind Review
No. of External Reviewers: 2
No. of In House Reviewers: 2
Acceptance Rate: 25-30%
Time to Review: 2 - 3 Months
Reviewers Comments: Yes
Invited Articles: 0-5%
Fees to Publish: 0.00 US$

MANUSCRIPT TOPICS:

All Aspects of Business Economics; Econometrics; Economic Development; Fiscal Policy; Industrial Organization; International Economics & Trade; Macro Economics; Micro Economics; Public Policy Economics; Regional Economics

MANUSCRIPT GUIDELINES/COMMENTS:

Statement of Purpose: The *Journal of Business Economics Research* is a refereed journal that publishes the results of significant basic and applied research in international and comparative business economics. It also publishes significant conceptual and theoretical contributions that augment the knowledge in the field. More specifically, the Journal aims to encourage cross-fertilization of ideas among the fields of business economics; to offer readers an accessible source for state-of-the-art economic thinking; to provide insights and readings for classroom use; and to address issues pertaining to the economics profession.

Its principal audience consists of scholars, researchers, teachers, officials in government and international organizations as well as executives of international enterprises.

Journal of Business Finance and Accounting

ADDRESS FOR SUBMISSION:

Andrew Stark, Managing Editor
Journal of Business Finance and Accounting
Manchester Business School
Booth Street West
Manchester, M15 6PB
UK
Phone: +44 0 161 275 6425
Fax: +44 0 161 275 6340
E-Mail: astark@man.mbs.ac.uk
Web: www.blackwellpublishing.co.uk
Address May Change:

CIRCULATION DATA:

Reader: Academics
Frequency of Issue: 5 Times/Year
Copies per Issue: 1,001 - 2,000
Sponsor/Publisher: Basil Blackwell Ltd.
Subscribe Price: 175.00 US$ Ind Prt+Oln
    1015.00 US$ Inst. Prm. Online Only
    1175.00 US$ Inst. Prt + Prm. Online

PUBLICATION GUIDELINES:

Manuscript Length: 11-30
Copies Required: Four
Computer Submission: No
Format: N/A
Fees to Review: 75.00 US$ USA Address
    36.00 Pounds UK Addresses

Manuscript Style:
    See Manuscript Guidelines

REVIEW INFORMATION:

Type of Review: Blind Review
No. of External Reviewers: 2
No. of In House Reviewers: 1
Acceptance Rate: 11-20%
Time to Review: 3-4 Months
Reviewers Comments: Yes
Invited Articles: 0-5% 0%
Fees to Publish: 0.00 US$

MANUSCRIPT TOPICS:
Accounting Theory & Practice; Econometrics; Portfolio & Security Analysis

MANUSCRIPT GUIDELINES/COMMENTS:

Aims and Scope
The *Journal of Business Finance & Accounting* exists to publish high quality research papers in Finance and economic aspects of Accounting. The scope of the *Journal* is broad. It includes studies of the functioning of security and exchange markets through to the economics of internal organisation and management control. It also includes research papers relating to market microstructure, asset pricing, and corporate financial decision making. A distinctive feature of the *Journal* is that it recognises that adverse selection and moral hazard issues are pervasive in financial markets and business organisations, and that Accounting (both financial and managerial) plays a part in ameliorating the problems arising from such informational problems. Thus the editors see Accounting and Finance as being conceptually inter-linked. These linkages are especially apparent in the areas of corporate governance, financial communication, financial performance measurement, and managerial reward and control structures.

The *Journal* welcomes both theoretical and empirical contributions, especially theoretical papers that yield novel testable implications, and empirical papers that are theoretically well motivated. The *Journal* is not a suitable outlet for highly abstract mathematical papers, or purely descriptive papers with limited theoretical motivation. The editors view Finance and Accounting as being closely related to Economics, and look for theoretical contributions and theoretical motivations that are based in economics. This includes mainstream neo-classical economics, as well as game theory and transaction costs economics. The *Journal* also welcomes papers in behavioural finance, which seek to advance our understanding of how the limits to human information processing ability influence financial decisions, and the framing and completeness of financial contracts.

The majority of papers in the *Journal* employ econometric or related empirical methods as a central feature of their research design. However, the editors welcome contributions that employ alternative empirical research methods, such as case studies. The journal also publishes survey articles which present the current state of the art in Accounting and Finance. One issue each year is a special issue containing selected papers from the annual Capital Market Based Accounting Research conference.

Author Guidelines

All manuscripts should be submitted to:
> The Editors
> *Journal of Business Finance & Accounting*
> Manchester Business School
> Booth Street West, Manchester M15 6PB, UK

Manuscripts are considered on the understanding that they are original, unpublished works not concurrently under consideration for publication elsewhere. The receipt of manuscripts will be acknowledged, but the editors and publishers can accept no responsibility for any loss or non-return of manuscripts. Suitable manuscripts will be given anonymous review, following which a copy of any review report will be supplied together with the editor's decision. As regards papers accepted for publication, the author(s) will be asked to transfer copyright to the publishers. Authors are requested to follow *JBFA*'s manuscript and style requirements closely, to minimise later delay or redrafting. In particular, authors should draft their papers and footnotes etc. to avoid identifying themselves directly or indirectly, to help ensure a fair review.

Submission Fee. Each manuscript submitted for possible publication in *JBFA* (including rewritten and resubmitted manuscripts which had previously been rejected with advice that a rewritten paper could be reconsidered) must be accompanied by a submission fee. The fee is currently £36 for submission from UK addresses, and $75 USA (or the equivalent exchange value in other currencies) for submissions from all other addresses. However, please note that for designated authors who are paid-up personal subscribers to *JBFA* the submission fee is reduced to only one-half of the above rates. The rates of submission fees may alter with inflation: the latest rates are always printed on the inside front cover of the current issue of the journal. Submission fees should accompany the relevant manuscript, in the form of a cheque or draft made payable to the University of Manchester. If only the half-rate fee is sent, a cover note should give definite confirmation that the author is currently a paid-up subscriber.

618

Authors who wish to take out a subscription at the same time as submitting a manuscript must send a separate cheque for the subscription made payable to Blackwell Publishing Ltd.

Manuscript Requirements. Submit four photocopies of the manuscript (together with any submission fee) typed double-spaced (preferably on international-size A4 paper). On the title page include the names, titles and institutional affiliations of (all) the author(s) (if any), and also the complete address of the designated author to whom decisions, proofs and reprint requests should be sent. Also provide a running title of fewer than 50 characters and spaces, which will appear on alternate pages in the journal. If the paper is to include any acknowledgements these should be typed as a footnote on the title page. The second page should repeat the full title of the paper (but not the author(s) names) and contain the Abstract of the paper, not exceeding 100 words for full-length papers, or 60 words for shorter Notes, Comments, Replies or Rejoinders. The third page may repeat the full title of the paper (but not the author(s)' names) and here the text proper begins. The main text should be followed by any appendices, by any footnotes (which should be kept to the essential minimum identified in the text by superscript numerals and listed together at the end, not separately at the bottom of each page), and by the list of source references (see below). Tables and figures should be numbered in order of their appearance with Arabic numerals, and each should have a concise descriptive title (and source, where relevant).

References. citation in the text is by name(s) of author(s), followed by year of publication (and page numbers where relevant) in parentheses. For references authored by more than two contributors use the first author's name and 'et al'. For multiple citations in the same year use a, b, c immediately following the year of publication. The source reference list should be typed in alphabetic order, and in accordance with the following examples of style: Amey, L. R. (1979), Budget Planning and Control Systems (Pitman, 1979) Budget Planning: a Dynamic Reformulation', Accounting and Business Research (Winter 1979), pp. 17-24. Lee, T. A. (1981), 'Cash Flow Accounting and Corporate Financial Reporting' in Essays in British Accounting Research, M. Bromwich and A. Hopwood, eds. (Pitman, 1981), pp. 63-78. Peasnell, K. V. , L. C. L. Skerratt and P. A. Taylor (1979), 'An Arbitrage Rationale for Tests of Mutual fund Performance', Journal of Business Finance & Accounting (Autumn 1979), pp. 373-400.

Mathematical and Statistical Material. Mathematical notation should be used only when its rigour and precision are essential to comprehension, and authors should explain in narrative format the principal operations performed. Preferably detailed mathematical proofs and statistical support should be relegated to appendices. Any equations used should be numbered sequentially in parentheses positioned flush with the right-hand margin. Whilst the journal does not wish to publish unnecessary mathematical or statistical detail, or specimen questionnaires, supplementary information of these kinds may be of assistance to the editors and reviewers in assessing papers, and authors are invited to submit such supporting evidence as separate documents clearly marked as being for information rather than publication.

Illustrations: All graphs, charts etc. submitted with papers must be referred to in the text, and be fully legible and clearly related to scales on the axes. If illustrations are numerous, a proportion may have to be deleted unless the author is able to supply artwork of camera-ready quality or to reimburse the journal for the cost of art-work.

Proofs, Offprints and Prices. The designated author will receive proofs, which should be corrected and returned within ten days of receipt. This author is responsible for proof-reading the manuscript: the editors/publishers are not responsible for any error not marked by the author on the proofs. Corrections to proofs are limited to rectifying errors: no substantial author's changes can be allowed at this stage unless agreement to pay full costs is communicated with the return of proofs. Similarly, offprints in excess of the twenty-five free copies automatically supplied to the designated author (for sharing among any co-authors) must be ordered at the time of return of proofs, in accord with the instructions and price list accompanying the proofs.

Comments and Replies. The journal welcomes non-trivial Comments on papers previously published in *JBFA*. To avoid publishing Comments based on misunderstandings, and to obtain Replies quickly so that they can be published simultaneously with the Comments, it is required that draft comments should be sent to the original authors for their reactions, prior to any formal submission to the editors for publication.

Journal of Business Forecasting Methods & Systems

ADDRESS FOR SUBMISSION:

C.L. Jain, Editor
Journal of Business Forecasting Methods &
   Systems
St. John's University
College of Business Administration
Department of Economics and Finance
Jamaica, NY 11432
USA
Phone: 718-990-7314
Fax: 718-544-9086
E-Mail: jainc@stjohns.edu
Web: www.ibf.org
Address May Change:

PUBLICATION GUIDELINES:

Manuscript Length: 6-10
Copies Required: Three
Computer Submission: Yes
Format: MS Word
Fees to Review: 0.00 US$

Manuscript Style:
   Chicago Manual of Style

CIRCULATION DATA:

Reader: Academics, Business Persons
Frequency of Issue: Quarterly
Copies per Issue: 3,001 - 4,000
Sponsor/Publisher: Graceway Publishing
   Co.
Subscribe Price: 85.00 US$ Domestic
   110.00 US$ Foreign
   55.00 US$ PDF file (domestic/foreign)

REVIEW INFORMATION:

Type of Review: Blind Review
No. of External Reviewers: 2
No. of In House Reviewers: 1
Acceptance Rate: 21-30%
Time to Review: 2 - 3 Months
Reviewers Comments: Yes
Invited Articles: 0-5%
Fees to Publish: 0.00 US$

MANUSCRIPT TOPICS:
Business Forecasting; Econometrics; Financial Services; Industrial Organization; Insurance;
Micro Economics

MANUSCRIPT GUIDELINES/COMMENTS:

The *Journal of Business Forecasting Methods & Systems* is published by Graceway
Publishing Company, P.O. Box 159, Station C, Flushing, NY 11367. The editor is C.L. Jain,
Ph.D., Professor, College of Business Administration, St. John's University, Jamaica, NY
11432, to whom articles should be submitted.

The *Journal* is designed to keep business managers abreast of developments in forecasting
methods and systems and to help them gain a better understanding of, and appreciation for, the
forecasting function. Articles dealing with forecasting methods applicable to manufacturing,
processing, wholesaling, retailing, and service industries and financial institutions are invited.

Both descriptive and prescriptive methods may be discussed in such areas as finance, sales, marketing, production, inventory management, labor force leveling, new product introduction, technology, etc.

There is no restriction on the professional disciplines of those whose articles may be published; articles receive equal consideration.

The criteria are that:
1. The author demonstrate professional competence in the subject
2. The contents of the paper indicate that the author has taken existing knowledge into account
3. The methods described can be replicated by others in the same or different industry
4. The subject is handled in such a manner that it is understandable to business managers whose backgrounds may not include an advanced degree in mathematics

The last-mentioned criterion places the onus upon those in the forecasting profession for communicating their concepts to users who constitute the largest segment of the *Journal*'s readership. While the editors do not underestimate the need for, or importance of, mathematical models, or wish to discourage their use, contributors should recognize that unless the business manager understands the material he/she cannot put it to use.

We suggest, therefore that, wherever possible, authors divide articles into two parts: the first should describe the method of system in common business language to capture the interest of the non-technical business manager; the second part should present the mathematical formulations required by the technician, whose help may be solicited by the business manager in adopting the system.

In those instances where the material does not lend itself to the structure described above, authors may incorporate the models within the body of the text. However, when this method is adopted the models should be explained in common business language in a brief paragraph within brackets; examples of business oriented situations represented by the symbolic language of the model are effective in achieving the objective.

When either of the above suggestions is adopted (or some other of the author's choosing), the author should strive for reader comprehension, keeping in mind that the reader of the *Journal*, as pointed out earlier, is not an academician. He/she is, nevertheless, willing and able to learn what the technician has to offer.

Articles dealing with any subject on a purely theoretical level should not be submitted; pragmatism is the guide by which papers are judged.

Articles are subject to a blind review by an Editorial Advisory Board composed of technicians and business users. The latter determine the value of the material to a business enterprise and judge the method of presentation on the basis of the ease of comprehension by business users; the technicians judge the technical adequacy of the method or system presented, with emphasis on the extent to which the author has used existing knowledge.

There is no limitation on length; however, authors should be mindful of:
1. The limited time available to an executive and
2. The executive propensity to devote time to those subjects that capture and hold his/her interest and promise to help him/her achieve personal and company goals.

The editors insist on clear and concise writing. The multi-disciplinary composition of the *Journal*'s readership dictates that authors eschew professional jargon. Care should be exercised to avoid ambiguity, which arises from loose sentence construction, poor punctuation and careless choice of words. Clarity is enhanced by limiting the number of thoughts in one sentence to two; one is better. Contrary to warnings you may have received from instructors in creative writing courses, repetition of a word or phrase in the same paragraph contributes to clarity in technical literature. Avoid pompous language.

Articles should be typewritten double-spaced with no more than 40 characters and spaces per line. Submit papers in triplicate to the editor at the above address. Computer printouts of tables, graphs or other material are acceptable, provided they are legible. Line drawings should be clear and ready-for-camera. Do not submit photographs clipped from printed material; only original black/white glossy photos are acceptable. After article is accepted, it has to be furnished on a disk in Word format. Type tables and graphs on separate sheets.

Avoid footnotes; place explanatory material in the body of the text within brackets. Where footnotes cannot be avoided, type them on a separate sheet(s) of paper. References should always appear on a separate sheet(s).

Type the title and the name(s) of the author(s) on one sheet of paper, give the affiliation of each author, the address(es), telephone number(s), and fax number(s). Type the abstract on a second sheet; identify the abstract by repeating the first three or four words of the title. Start the manuscript on the third page; repeat the first three or four words of the title in the upper left corner of each page of the manuscript.

The author is responsible for obtaining permission to use copyrighted material. Permission to use data obtained while employed by an organization shall be obtained by the author from a responsible officer of the organization, if its identity is disclosed in the article. Such permission shall be in writing and a copy submitted to the editor. At his discretion, the editor may ask a responsible officer of an identified organization to reply to any critical comments of the organization appearing in an article.

Copyright of articles published in the *Journal* is the property of the *Journal*. It is our intention to publish original works only.

Journal of Business in Developing Nations

ADDRESS FOR SUBMISSION:

Peter Schroth, Editor
Journal of Business in Developing Nations
Lally School of Management
 and Technology
Rensselaer Polytechnic Institute
275 Windsor Street
Hartford, CT 06120-2991
USA
Phone: 860-548-7845
Fax: 860-547-0866
E-Mail: dkent@ggu.edu
Web: www.rh.edu/jbdn
Address May Change:

PUBLICATION GUIDELINES:

Manuscript Length: 15-40 pages
Copies Required: Three
Computer Submission: Yes Preferred
Format: MS Word, WordPerfect
Fees to Review: 0.00 US$

Manuscript Style:
 , Academy of Management Journal

CIRCULATION DATA:

Reader: Academics
Frequency of Issue: As Received
Copies per Issue: Electronic
Sponsor/Publisher: Rensselaer Polytechnic
 Institute
Subscribe Price: Free/Web

REVIEW INFORMATION:

Type of Review: Blind Review
No. of External Reviewers: 2-3
No. of In House Reviewers: 1
Acceptance Rate: 11-20%
Time to Review: 2 - 3 Months
Reviewers Comments: Yes
Invited Articles: 0-5%
Fees to Publish: 0.00 US$

MANUSCRIPT TOPICS:
Economic Development; Economic History; Industrial Organization; International Economics & Trade; International Finance; Regional Economics

MANUSCRIPT GUIDELINES/COMMENTS:

The journal is a combined effort of Rensselaer Polytechnic Institute and dedicated researchers throughout the world. The journal publishes the results of quality research of current interest to developing nations with an emphasis on its application to general managers. The Editor welcomes conceptual and empirical contributions from researchers in both academic and business organizations in all functional areas of business.

Philosophy of the Journal
The Editorial Review Board is committed to balancing a supportive environment for prospective authors with the desire to publish research that meets rigorous standards. The journal seeks to accommodate alternative perspectives and research methods, especially as they relate to less-researched areas of interest. Indeed, there is also a desire to expand the size

and scope of the journal in the coming years. However, this goal will not be met by relaxing the quality standards on which the journal was founded.

The views of the authors do not necessarily reflect those of the Editor, the Editorial Review Board, or Rensselaer Polytechnic Institute.

Submission Guidelines

The journal welcomes submissions in areas including, but not limited to, the following:
- Successes and failures in businesses in developing nations
- Comparisons of organizational processes in developing nations to those in developed countries
- Appropriate economic development strategies, including privatization, in developing nations
- Case studies and industry notes

Although the domain of developing nations is broadly defined, the journal especially welcomes studies addressing issues in less-researched regions of the developing world, including Africa and the Middle East.

Papers are blind-refereed and judged on the following criteria:
- Interest to a broad scholarly audience representing all functional areas of business.
- Timeliness of subject matter and integration with recently published work in the field.
- For conceptual papers, extent to which models are complete and free from logical flaws. For empirical papers, application of appropriate statistical tools.
- Clarity and writing style.
- The presentation of clear and supported practical implications and recommendations.

Manuscripts should be prepared in APA format with several notable exceptions:

Author(s) should be identified only on the title page. The title page should include the names, addresses, telephone and fax numbers, and e-mail addresses of all authors. The second page should include the title and a 50-100 word abstract which clearly argues why the general manager should read the article. The body of the paper should begin on the third page, followed by figures and tables. Short papers will be considered as research notes.

Implications for practitioners should be maximized and highlighted.

The number of tables and figures should be kept to a minimum and placed on separate pages with the corresponding number and title.

Manuscripts should be submitted electronically if possible. Doing so substantially expedites the review and publication processes. See below for details. If you are unable to send your manuscript by e-mail, please send a diskette.

Every effort is made to complete the first blind review phase and provide detailed reviewer comments within 6 to 8 weeks., but authors are cautioned that the Editor is at the mercy of slow reviewers. Correspondence should be by e-mail, if possible, to: Schroth@rh.edu. Correspondence by snail mail should be addressed to Professor Peter W. Schroth, Editor, The Journal of Business in Developing Nations, Lally School of Management and Technology, Rensselaer Polytechnic Institute, 275 Windsor Street, Hartford, Connecticut 06120-2991, U.S.A.

Electronic Submission of Manuscripts

Papers should be submitted to the Journal of Business in Developing Nations electronically, if possible. Please include the following *submission information for manuscripts* in an e-mail and send your manuscript as an attachment to: Schroth@rh.edu.

Submission Information for Manuscripts

Name:
Mailing Address:
Telephone Number:
Fax Number:
E-mail address:
Title of paper:
Name of attached file (WordPerfect or MS-Word preferred; contact the Editor about other formats, if necessary):
Is this the first submission of this manuscript or a revision?
Comments to the Editor:

Notes: For revised manuscripts, please make any comments to reviewers on the first pages of your manuscript, followed by the title page, abstract, etc.

Journal of Business, Industry & Economics

ADDRESS FOR SUBMISSION:

Jim Couch, Editor
Journal of Business, Industry & Economics
University of North Alabama
Department of Economics and Finance
Box 5141
Florence, AL 35632
USA
Phone: 256-765-4412
Fax: 256-765-4930
E-Mail: jcouch@unanov.una.edu
Web:
Address May Change:

PUBLICATION GUIDELINES:

Manuscript Length: 6-10
Copies Required: Three
Computer Submission: No
Format: No Reply
Fees to Review: 50.00 US$
    25.00 US$ SOBIE Conf attendee

Manuscript Style:
    Chicago Manual of Style

CIRCULATION DATA:

Reader: Academics
Frequency of Issue: 2 Times/Year
Copies per Issue: Less than 1,000
Sponsor/Publisher: University of North
  Alabama/Society of Business, Industry &
  Economics
Subscribe Price: 35.00 US$

REVIEW INFORMATION:

Type of Review: Blind Review
No. of External Reviewers: 2
No. of In House Reviewers: 1
Acceptance Rate: 11-20%
Time to Review: 4 - 6 Months
Reviewers Comments: Yes
Invited Articles: 0-5%
Fees to Publish: 0.00 US$

MANUSCRIPT TOPICS:

Accounting Information Systems; Accounting Theory & Practice; Auditing; Behavioral Economics; Corporate Finance; Cost Accounting; Econometrics; Economic Development; Economic History; Financial Institutions & Markets; Financial Services; Fiscal Policy; Government & Non-Profit Accounting; Industrial Organization; Insurance; International Economics & Trade; International Finance; Macro Economics; Micro Economics; Monetary Policy; Portfolio & Security Analysis; Public Policy Economics; Real Estate; Regional Economics; Tax Accounting

MANUSCRIPT GUIDELINES/COMMENTS:

Journal of Commercial Banking and Finance

ADDRESS FOR SUBMISSION:

Current Editor's Name/Check Web Site
Journal of Commercial Banking and
   Finance
Digital Submission Through Web Site
Please address other questions to:
  Jim or JoAnn Carland at #s below
USA
Phone: 828-293-9151
Fax: 828-293-9407
E-Mail: info@alliedacademies.org
Web: www.alliedacademies.org
Address May Change:

PUBLICATION GUIDELINES:

Manuscript Length: 16-20
Copies Required: Submit through website
Computer Submission: Yes
Format: MS Word, WordPerfect
Fees to Review: 0.00 US$

Manuscript Style:
   American Psychological Association

CIRCULATION DATA:

Reader: Academics
Frequency of Issue: 2 Times/Year
Copies per Issue: Less than 1,000
Sponsor/Publisher: Allied Academies, Inc.
Subscribe Price: 75.00 US$ Individual
      150.00 US$ Foreign

REVIEW INFORMATION:

Type of Review: Blind Review
No. of External Reviewers: 3
No. of In House Reviewers: 2
Acceptance Rate: 21-30%
Time to Review: 3 - 4 Months
Reviewers Comments: Yes
Invited Articles: 0-5%
Fees to Publish: 75.00 US$ Membership

MANUSCRIPT TOPICS:
Banking; Financial Services; Institutional Finance

MANUSCRIPT GUIDELINES/COMMENTS:

The journal publishes theoretical or empirical research on any of the Manuscript Topics.

Comments. All authors of published manuscripts must be members of the appropriate academy affiliate of Allied Academies. The current membership fee is $75.00 U.S.

Editorial Policy Guidelines
The primary criterion upon which manuscripts are judged is whether the research advances the discipline. Key points include currency, interest and relevancy.

In order for a theoretical manuscript to advance the discipline, it must address the literature to support conclusions or models which extend knowledge and understanding. Consequently, referees pay particular attention to completeness of literature review and appropriateness of conclusions drawn from that review.

In order for an empirical manuscript to advance the discipline, it must employ appropriate and effective sampling and statistical analysis techniques, and must be grounded by a thorough literature review. Consequently, referees pay particular attention to the research methodology and to the conclusions drawn from statistical analyses and their consistency with the literature.

Journal of Common Market Studies

ADDRESS FOR SUBMISSION:

Jim Rollo & William Paterson, Co-Editors
Journal of Common Market Studies
University of Sussex
Sussex European Institute
Arts Building A
Falmer
Brighton, BN1 9SH
UK
Phone: +44 (0) 1273 678 713
Fax: +44 (0) 1273 678 571
E-Mail: jcms@sussex.ac.uk
Web: www.blackwellpublishing.com
Address May Change:

PUBLICATION GUIDELINES:

Manuscript Length: 8,000 Wds. Max.
Copies Required: Three
Computer Submission: No
Format: N/A
Fees to Review: 0.00 US$

Manuscript Style:
    See Manuscript Guidelines

CIRCULATION DATA:

Reader: Academics
Frequency of Issue: Quarterly
Copies per Issue: 1,001 - 2,000
Sponsor/Publisher: Basil Blackwell Ltd.
Subscribe Price: 166.00 US$ Individual
    403.00 US$ Institution
    38.00 US$ Indv. Members, UACES,
    ECS

REVIEW INFORMATION:

Type of Review: Blind Review
No. of External Reviewers: 2
No. of In House Reviewers: 1
Acceptance Rate: 11-20%
Time to Review: 2 - 3 Months
Reviewers Comments: Yes
Invited Articles: 6-10%
Fees to Publish: 0.00 US$

MANUSCRIPT TOPICS:

Behavioral Economics; Financial Institutions & Markets; Financial Services; Fiscal Policy;
Industrial Organization; International Economics & Trade; International Finance; Macro
Economics; Micro Economics; Monetary Policy; Public Policy Economics; Regional
Economics; Regional Integration

MANUSCRIPT GUIDELINES/COMMENTS:

Co-Editors

Professor William Paterson
Institute for German Studies
European Research Institute
Edgbaston
Birmingham B15 2TT, UK
Phone: 0121 414 7185
Fax: 0121 414 7329
Email: w.e.paterson@bham.ac.uk

Professor Jim Rollo
Sussex European Institute
University of Sussex
Arts Building A
Falmer, Brighton BN1 9SH, UK
Phone: 1273 678578
Fax: 1273 678571
Email: j.rollo@sussex.ac.uk

Aims and Scope

Journal of Common Market Studies is a leading journal in the field, publishing high quality, and accessible articles on the latest EU issues. For more than 30 years *Journal of Common Market Studies* has been the forum for the development and evaluation of theoretical and empirical issues in the politics and economics of integration, focusing principally on developments within the European Union.

Journal of Common Market Studies aims to achieve a disciplinary balance between political science and economics, including the various sub-disciplines such as monetary economics, fiscal policy, political economy, public policy studies, public administration and international relations. In addition to mainstream theoretical and empirical articles, *Journal of Common Market Studies* publishes shorter pieces which focus on specific policy areas or which report the results of specialized research projects. Each year a special issue is devoted to a comprehensive review of the activities of the European Union in the previous year. *Journal of Common Market Studies* is committed to deepening the theoretical understanding of European integration. It will continue to develop as the primary forum for the analysis of all aspects relating to the process of European integration.

Coverage

- A forum for theoretical debate
- Comparative studies of international integration
- Interdisciplinary in scope
- Comprehensive analysis of the European Union
- Covers political forces, institutions and public policy of the EU
- A key resource for academics and policy-makers
- Examines economic dynamics of integration
- Occasional thematic special issues
- Regular analysis of policy areas
- Book reviews covering all relevant publications

Manuscripts

1. Manuscripts of mainstream articles, shorter manuscripts for *European Agenda* and correspondence relating to the Journal should be sent to the Editors of the *Journal of Common Market Studies*.

2. Manuscripts are welcome on all areas covered by the *Journal* as set out in the policy statement on the inside front cover.

3. Three copies of any manuscript should be submitted. Each copy must be typed on one side of the paper only, using double-spacing throughout (including any footnotes and references). Authors should indicate the length of the article and the inclusion of any diagrams. Articles should be accompanied by a note of the author's name and affiliation and by an abstract not exceeding 100 words. The abstract should summarize the main argument of the article.

4. Please include a standard, formatted diskette, with all relevant documentation stored as either Word documents or Excel spreadsheets, or any other format. Any figures to be included should be in black and white.

5. Mainstream articles should not exceed 8,000 words.

6. Shorter research notes, short notes raising matters for scientific debate, and occasional reviews of important policy developments are published in *European Agenda*. These should not exceed 4000 words.

7. Bibliographical references should be incorporated into the text using the author-date system, with page numbers where necessary. All references should be listed alphabetically at the end of the article. For journal articles, the volume and issue number, month and year of publication and inclusive page numbers should be provided. Bibliographical references should follow the style used in this issue.

8. Footnotes should be numbered consecutively, and should not solely comprise references.

9. Manuscripts, which do not conform to this format, if accepted, may be subject to delay, since it is not possible to have them typeset until suitable copy has been supplied.

10. The *Journal* is indexed in the *Journal of Economic Literature* and in *ABC POLSCI: A Bibliography of Contents: Political Science and Government*.

11. Each article contributor receives 20 free offprints of his or her article, together with a copy of the issue in which it appears. Each review contributor receives four free offprints of the review section together with a copy of the issue in which his or her review appears.

The European Union: The Annual Review of Activities, published each autumn, is included in the annual subscription to *Journal of Common Market Studies*.

The purpose of *The European Union: The Annual Review of Activities* is to provide an information resource, which can be used as a reference tool for teaching and research by all who are interested in European Union Affairs.

Each edition of *The European Union: The Annual Review of Activities* includes a useful chronology of key events during the preceding year and an evaluation of key issues and developments, which provide a succinct yet comprehensive guide to the progress of EU policy and plans.

Regular features include:
- Governance and Institutional Developments
- Internal Policy Developments
- External Policy Developments
- Developments in the Economies of the European Union
- Developments in European Law

- Developments in the Member States
- A Guide to the Documentation of the European Community/Union
- Chronology of Key Events
- Books on European Integration.

The *Journal* is published by Blackwell Publishers, 238 Main Street, Cambridge, MA, 02142, USA. Tel 617-547-7110, Fax 617-547-0789.

Journal of Comparative Economics

ADDRESS FOR SUBMISSION:

John P. Bonin, Editor
Journal of Comparative Economics
Wesleyan University
Department of Economics
238 Church Street
Middletown, CT 06459-0007
USA
Phone: 860-685-2313
Fax: 860-685-2301
E-Mail: jce@weslayan.edu
Web: http://jce.web.weslayan.edu
Address May Change:

PUBLICATION GUIDELINES:

Manuscript Length: 26-30
Copies Required: Three
Computer Submission: No
Format: N/A
Fees to Review: 0.00 US$

Manuscript Style:
    See Manuscript Guidelines

CIRCULATION DATA:

Reader: Academics
Frequency of Issue: Quarterly
Copies per Issue: 1,001 - 2,000
Sponsor/Publisher: Academic Press, Inc.,
    Elsevier Science Publishing Co.
Subscribe Price: 95.00 US$ Individual
    520.00 US$ Institution
    75.00 US$ Student

REVIEW INFORMATION:

Type of Review: Blind Review
No. of External Reviewers: 2
No. of In House Reviewers: 0
Acceptance Rate: 20%
Time to Review: 2 - 3 Months
Reviewers Comments: Yes
Invited Articles: 0-5%
Fees to Publish: 0.00 US$

MANUSCRIPT TOPICS:

Comparative Economics; Econometrics; Economic Development; Financial Institutions &
Markets; Industrial Organization; International Economics & Trade; International Finance;
Macro Economics; Micro Economics; Monetary Policy

MANUSCRIPT GUIDELINES/COMMENTS:

The *Journal of Comparative Economics* is devoted to the analysis and study of contemporary,
historical, and hypothetical economic systems. Such analyses may involve comparisons of the
performance of different economic systems or subsystems, studies linking outcomes to system
characteristics in one economy or investigations of the origin and evolution of one or more
economic systems. Empirical, theoretical, and institutional approaches are equally welcome.
Empirical analyses should display appropriate sensitivity to the problems of comparing data
generated by different economic systems and seek to employ methodologies that permit the
researcher to distinguish between the effects of the system and of other causal variables on
observed outcomes. Theoretical work that develops new ways of viewing economic systems
and their operation or explains the behavior of systems or of agents within a system will also
be considered for publication. Authors of technical papers are requested to provide a verbal

explanation of their results as part of their conclusions. Although papers limited to the description of institutions will generally not be published by the *Journal*, such descriptions accompanied by the analysis of the interaction of the institution with the system are also welcome. The *Journal* is open to all viewpoints and ideologies. Nevertheless, authors should recognize that the Editor would not publish material that, in his opinion, cannot be expected to command the assent of the readership due to deficient or inadequate methodology.

It is the policy of the *Journal* to provide authors with an editorial decision within three months of the receipt of submissions.

Manuscripts should be submitted in triplicate to the Editor.

It is the policy of the *Journal* to send manuscripts to referees without authorial identification. Please refrain from identifying the author(s) in the manuscript, footnotes, or references. Please prepare a cover page for the Editor that includes the title of the manuscript, the names and affiliations of all authors, the complete mailing address, and the e-mail address of the author to whom correspondence should be sent. Please include on this cover page the acknowledgment footnote if one exists and delete this footnote from the manuscript. The first page of the manuscript, i.e., the page following the cover page, should repeat the title and include a short abstract. Failure to conform to these directions may result in a delay in the reviewing process.

Manuscripts are accepted for review with the understanding that the same work will not be nor is presently submitted elsewhere; that its submission for publication has been approved by all of the authors; and that any person cited as a source of personal communications has approved such citation.

Authors submitting a manuscript do so on the understanding that if it is accepted for publication, copyright in the article, including the right to reproduce the article in all forms and media, shall be assigned exclusively to the Publisher. The Copyright Transfer Agreement, which may be copied from the pages following the Information for Authors or found on the *Journal* home page, should be signed by the appropriate person(s) and should accompany the original submission of a manuscript to this *Journal*. The transfer of copyright does not take effect until the manuscript is accepted for publication.

Any statements in the article – once the Editor accepts it – remain the sole responsibility of the author(s), including personal communications from other scholars. They represent only the opinions of the author(s) and should not be construed to reflect the opinions of the Editors, the Association, or the Publisher.

Manuscripts should be prepared according to the style rules outlined below. Deviation from these rules may cause publication delays.

Form of Manuscript. Manuscripts must be typed, double-spaced on one side of 8½ x 11" white paper. All pages, including title page, should be numbered. **Page 1** should contain the article's title, author(s) name(s) and affiliations) (name of institution, city, state and zip code); the complete mailing address of the author to whom proofs should be sent; and a suggested running head (abbreviated form of the title) of less than 35 characters. **Page 2** should contain a short abstract of approximately 100 words. The abstract will appear at the beginning of the article in the *Journal*; use the abstract format and classification numbers, which are required by the *Journal of Economic Literature*. **Key words** should be listed immediately after the abstract. The text of the article begins with **page 3**.

List of Symbols. A complete list of symbols used in the manuscript must be included. All symbols should be identified typographically, not mathematically. This list will not appear in print, but it is essential to avoid costly author's corrections in proof. Distinguish between "oh" and "zero", "ell" and "one", "kappa" and "kay", etc. All letters used as symbols should be set in italics unless a special type (e.g., Greek, boldface, script) is specified. Note that *if the equations are handwritten in the text, then the list of symbols should also be handwritten.*

Equations. All displayed equations should conform to the author's list of symbols and be typewritten, if possible, or neatly handwritten. All equations to which reference is made in the text should be numbered consecutively, with optional subdivision by sections; equation numbers should be placed in parentheses against the right margin.

Footnotes. Number footnotes consecutively, with superscript Arabic numerals, beginning with the acknowledgment note to the article title. Footnotes should be typed double-spaced on separate pages at the end of the text.

Tables. Number all tables consecutively with Arabic numerals. Each table should be typed double-spaced on a separate page. All tables should have titles. If footnotes to the table are necessary they should be indicated by superscript italic letters, a, 6, c, and should be typed immediately below the table. Indicate in the margins where you would prefer to have the table inserted.

Figures. All illustrations are to be considered as figures and should be provided as camera-ready copy. Number the figures consecutively; type their legends double-spaced on a separate page, not on the figures themselves. Plan figures to fit the proportions of the printed page (approximately 5 x 7" or 8 x 10" originals). Figures should be professionally drawn, and lettering should be planned so that it will be legible after a reduction of 50 to 60%. Indicate in the margins where you would prefer to have the figures inserted. Illustrations in color can be accepted only if the authors defray the cost.

References. All references should be cited in the text by the author's surname and date of publication, e.g., Smith and Jones (1984) or (Smith, 1984) and typed double-spaced. All references should be listed at the end of the article in alphabetical order by authors' surnames. All authors should be listed by last name first, first name last. Abbreviations of journal titles should conform to general usage in economics. The following reference styles should be used in the reference list.

References that are books
Montias, John M. *The Structure of Economic Systems*. New Haven, CT: Yale University Press, 1976.

636

References that are government documents
Ericson, Paul G., and Miller, Ronald S., "Soviet Foreign Economic Behavior: A Balance of Payments Perspective." In *Soviet Economy in a Time of Change*, Vol. 2, pp. 208-244. Comp. of Papers, Joint Econ. Comm., U.S. Congress. Washington, D.C.: U.S. Govt. Printing Office, 1979.

References that are journal articles
Slay, Ben, "Polish Banks on the Road to Recovery." *Post-Soviet Geog. and Econ.* 37, 8: 511-522, Oct. 1996.

References that are chapters in edited volumes
van Brabant, Jozef M., "The New East and Old Trade and Payment Problems." In Kazimierz A. Poznanski, Ed., *Stabilization and Privatization in Poland: An Economic Evaluation of the Shock Therapy Program*. International Studies in Economic and Econometrics, Vol. 29, pp. 105-123. Norwell, MA and Dordrecht: Kluwer Academic Press, 1993.

References that are reports
Organisation for Economic Co-operation and Development, OECD *Economic Surveys 1995-1996: The Slovak Republic*. Paris: OECD, 1996.

Proofs will be sent to the Author. Authors are responsible for correcting the proofs of their article. Authors will be charged for changes (other than corrections of printing errors) in excess of 10% of the cost of composition.

Reprints. Reprint order forms will accompany the proofs. Fifty reprints without covers will be provided free of charge. Additional reprints may be purchased from the Publisher.

Journal of Conflict Resolution

ADDRESS FOR SUBMISSION:

Bruce M. Russet, Editor
Journal of Conflict Resolution
Yale University
Department of Political Science
P O Box 208301
New Haven, CT 06520-8301
USA
Phone: 203-432-5235
Fax: 203-432-6196
E-Mail: jcr28@pantheon.yale.edu
Web: www.sagepub.com
Address May Change:

PUBLICATION GUIDELINES:

Manuscript Length: 20+
Copies Required: Three
Computer Submission: No
Format: N/A
Fees to Review: 0.00 US$

Manuscript Style:
    Chicago Manual of Style

CIRCULATION DATA:

Reader: Academics
Frequency of Issue: Bi-Monthly
Copies per Issue: 2,001 - 3,000
Sponsor/Publisher: Sage Publications
Subscribe Price: 107.00 US$ Individual
    649.00 US$ Institution

REVIEW INFORMATION:

Type of Review: Blind Review
No. of External Reviewers: 2
No. of In House Reviewers: 0
Acceptance Rate: 20-25%
Time to Review: 2 - 3 Months
Reviewers Comments: Yes
Invited Articles: 6-10%
Fees to Publish: 0.00 US$

MANUSCRIPT TOPICS:
Economic Development; International Economics & Trade

MANUSCRIPT GUIDELINES/COMMENTS:

ABOUT THE JOURNAL
Social Science Citation Index
The most recent Journal Citation Reports published by the Social Science Citation Index rank the *Journal of Conflict Resolution* at number 13 in International Relations, and at number 8 in Political Science.

The Interdisciplinary Journal of Social Scientific Research and Theory on Human Conflict...

The journal focuses largely on international conflict, but also explores a variety of national, intergroup and interpersonal conflicts.

Comprehensive

For over forty years, the *Journal of Conflict Resolution* has provided scholars and researchers with the latest studies and theories on the causes of and solutions to the full range of human conflict, serving as a leading international forum for the systematic study of war and peace.

Incisive

The *Journal of Conflict Resolution* cuts through the controversies and emotions that often surround conflict, and focuses instead on solid measurable facts and carefully reasoned arguments. *JCR* provides you with the latest ideas, approaches and processes in conflict resolution.

Interdisciplinary

Committed to the belief that a thorough study of conflict resolution requires the concepts and theories from a variety of disciplines, the *Journal of Conflict Resolution* regularly features papers from the following areas: Political Science, Law, Economics, Sociology, International Relations, History, Psychology, Anthropology, and Methodology.

Published Six Times a Year!

The *Journal of Conflict Resolution* publishes the latest theory and research as it develops. Published bimonthly, the journal promises readers research at the very forefront of the field. You'll receive comprehensive coverage of all the key issues in conflict resolution, including: Alliance Stability, Negotiation, Foreign Policy, Disarmament/Arms Control, Crisis Decision-Making, Modelling Deterrence, Military Spending, Mediation/Arbitration, National Security.

Notes for Authors

Manuscripts should be submitted in triplicate to the Editor.

Articles should be typewritten double-spaced, with footnotes, references, tables, and chat, on separate pages, and should follow the Chicago Manual of Style. Manuscripts will be sent out anonymously for editorial evaluation, so the author's name and affiliation should appear only on a separate cover page. Each article should begin with an abstract of about 150 words. A statement of our evaluation procedures appears in the March 1978 issue. Manuscripts will be returned only if they are accompanied, on submission, by a stamped self-addressed envelope. A copy of the final revised manuscript saved on an IBM-compatible disk should be included with the final revised hard copy.

Submission of a manuscript implies commitment to publish in the journal. Authors submitting manuscripts to the journal should not simultaneously submit them to another journal, nor should manuscripts have been published elsewhere in substantially similar form or with substantially similar content. Authors in doubt about what constitutes prior publication should consult the editor.

Journal of Consumer Affairs

ADDRESS FOR SUBMISSION:

Herbert Jack Rotfeld, Editor
Journal of Consumer Affairs
201 Business Building
Department of Marketing
415 W. Magnolia Avenue
Auburn University, AL 36849-5246
USA
Phone: 334-844-2459
Fax:
E-Mail: rotfeld@business.auburn.edu
Web: See Guidelines
Address May Change:

PUBLICATION GUIDELINES:

Manuscript Length: 10-25
Copies Required: Five
Computer Submission: Yes Require
   disk+paper
Format: MS Word
Fees to Review: 0.00 US$

Manuscript Style:
   Chicago Manual of Style

CIRCULATION DATA:

Reader: Academics, Government
Frequency of Issue: 2 Times/Year
Copies per Issue: 2,000
Sponsor/Publisher: American Council on
   Consumer Interests
Subscribe Price: Included
      In ACCI
      Membership

REVIEW INFORMATION:

Type of Review: Blind Review
No. of External Reviewers: 2-4
No. of In House Reviewers: Editors
Acceptance Rate: 15-19%
Time to Review: 6-12 Weeks
Reviewers Comments: Yes
Invited Articles: None
Fees to Publish: 0.00 US$

MANUSCRIPT TOPICS:

Advertising & Promotion; Behavioral Economics; Business Law; Consumer Education;
Consumer Interests; Consumer Psychology & Communications; Direct Marketing;
Economics; Global Business; Marketing Theory & Application; Non-Profit Organizations;
Nutrition; Public Choice; Public Policy Economics; Public Responsibility & Ethics

MANUSCRIPT GUIDELINES/COMMENTS:

Web   http://www.consumerinterests.org
   or   http://www.consumerinterests.org/public/articles/index.html/cat=13

Associate Editor. Marla Royne Stafford, University of Memphis, College of Business and
Economics, 300 Fogelman Administration Building, Memphis, TN 38152 USA

Subscription price is included with membership in ACCI. Single copies of back issues
US$30 each.

The *Journal of Consumer Affairs* contains scholarly research and professionally informed opinions that involve analysis of individual, business, and/or government decisions and actions that can impact upon the interests of consumers in the marketplace. Topics that can be addressed from the consumer's point of view include consumer education, business law and ethics, economics, nutrition, public policy, consumer psychology, communications and marketing. The "Bits, Briefs and Applications" section contains short research notes, applications, theoretical briefs, and individual commentary that are designed to assist the consumer interest professionals, public policy decision makers or consumer affairs researchers and educators. Appropriate topics for this section must have pragmatic implications for consumers, public policy or consumer affairs professionals and may include: (1) Practical applications based on new or existing theories/models of economics, consumer behavior and other areas of consumer affairs; (2) Brief research findings related to consumer rights, education, policy and regulation; (3) Research reports that contribute to an understanding of consumer behavior and its implications for consumer policy makers and consumer educators; (4) Comments and position papers on key issues in consumer rights, education, policy and regulation.

The focus for papers in terms of both research questions and implications must involve the consumer's interests. *JCA* is not a journal of marketing management, broad economic theory or general consumer psychology. Our origins are with the consumer movement and consumer protection concerns.

Manuscript Preparation
- Submit five (5) copies of the manuscript. Double-space throughout, including footnotes and quoted material. Additionally, manuscripts must include, with the original submission, an electronic copy of the manuscript on disk in Word 95 or Word 97 that removes the author names from the title page and all other parts of the file.
- A separate title page should be attached to ONE copy of the manuscript. This page will include the title of the paper, author's title and affiliation, address, phone and fax numbers, e-mail address, summer contact information (e.g., phone fax, and e-mail), and any acknowledgments. The authors should not be identified anywhere else in the manuscript.
- All manuscripts must be submitted using the Chicago Style (*The Chicago Manual of Style*, 15th ed. (2003), Chicago: The University of Chicago Press). *JCA* uses the author-date system of documentation, and the headline style of capitalization for titles of books and articles. For details, consult these sections of the *Chicago Manual*: "The Author-Date System: Reference Lists and Text Citations," sections 16.90-16.120 (pp. 616-624), and "Headline-Style Capitalization," section 8.167 (pp. 336-367). Authors should check a current issue of the *Journal* for specific examples on reference lists and citations.
- Manuscripts should include an abstract not exceeding 75 words. Abstracts are not necessary for papers submitted to the Bits, Briefs and Applications section.
- Manuscripts submitted to the Bits, Briefs and Applications section should not exceed 3,500 words and should be sent directly to the associate editor.
- Endnotes should be numbered consecutively throughout the paper and included on a separate page entitled Endnotes. The Endnotes page should be placed at the end of the main text, preceding the References page.

- Each table, graph, figure, or chart should be placed on a separate page and included at the end of the manuscript. Omit all vertical lines. Use letters for footnotes and tables, and asterisks for statistical significance levels.

Other Information

1. In a cover letter indicate: that the material in the manuscript will not infringe upon any statutory copyright; that the paper will not be submitted elsewhere while under *JCA* review; and the consumer interest topic areas addressed in the manuscript.
2. All research papers are double-blind reviewed by members of the editorial board and ad hoc reviewers selected by the editor or associate editor. Most authors receive notice of a decision in less than 8 weeks from the date the paper is received by the editor.
3. Manuscripts cannot be returned
4. There is no submission fee. There is no page charge for published papers.
5. Acceptance of a manuscript for *JCA* publication gives ACCI the right to publish and copyright the material. Republication elsewhere is contingent upon written approval from the Editor.

Journal of Corporate Finance

ADDRESS FOR SUBMISSION:

Jeffry Netter / Annette Poulsen
Journal of Corporate Finance
University of Georgia
Terry College of Business
Athens, GA 30602
USA
Phone: 706-542-3654
Fax: 706-542-9434
E-Mail: jcf@terry.uga.edu
Web: www.elsevier.com
Address May Change:

PUBLICATION GUIDELINES:

Manuscript Length: No Reply
Copies Required: Four
Computer Submission: Yes if accepted
Format: MS-DOS
Fees to Review: 85.00 US$
    50.00 US$ Subscriber

Manuscript Style:
    American Psychological Association

CIRCULATION DATA:

Reader: Academics, Legal Practitioners,
   Economists
Frequency of Issue: Quarterly
Copies per Issue: Less than 1,000
Sponsor/Publisher: Elsevier Publishing,
   North-Holland
Subscribe Price: 50.00 US$ Individual
   380.00 US$ Institution
   339.00 Euro Institution

REVIEW INFORMATION:

Type of Review: Blind Review
No. of External Reviewers: 2
No. of In House Reviewers: 1
Acceptance Rate: 21-30%
Time to Review: 4 - 6 Months
Reviewers Comments: Yes
Invited Articles: 0-5%
Fees to Publish: 0.00 US$

MANUSCRIPT TOPICS:

Capital Budgeting; Corporate Control; Corporate Finance; Corporate Governance; Cost Accounting; International Finance; Regional Economics

MANUSCRIPT GUIDELINES/COMMENTS:

Description

The *Journal of Corporate Finance* publishes only original quality manuscripts (theoretical and empirical) on the contractual arrangements that govern firms, including financial contracts, corporate governance structures, and business contracts. The *Journal* differs from any existing journal in economics and finance by concentrating solely on issues concerning financial contracts, corporate governance and business contracting that are important to the functioning of the modern corporation. Additionally, the *Journal* will combine the disciplines of industrial organization, financial economics, corporate finance, corporate law, econometrics, and accounting into the analysis of the modern corporation in an international context.

Possible topics include, but are not limited to:
- Incentive structures contained in business contracts
- Executive compensation, the structure of equity and debt ownership

- The role of boards of directors
- Corporate voting rights, the effect of financial distress on the governance of firms
- Franchising
- Corporate restructuring
- Corporate takeovers and proxy contests
- The design of securities
- How legal differences in the rights of creditors affect the complexity of debt contracts across countries
- The ways in which multinational companies organize the production of similar products in countries with different contracting environments
- The effects of regulation on corporate governance and business contracts
- Factors affecting the structures of vertical contracts and the degree of vertical integration
- Comparative studies of vertical contracts across countries
- Joint ventures and strategic alliances
- Accounting issues related to corporate governance and business contracting
- The application of option pricing to corporate contracting issues
- Factors affecting the degree of decentralization in firms
- Financial sector reform and corporate contracting issues in Eastern European and the developing countries.

All manuscripts submitted for consideration for publication will be promptly reviewed and processed.

Guide for Authors
1. Papers must be in English.

2. Papers for publication should be sent in triplicate to:
   Jeffry Netter / Annette Poulsen,
   Terry College of Business, University of Georgia
   Athens, GA 30602, USA
   Tel: +1 706 542-3654; Fax: +1 706 542-9434
   E-mail: jcf@terry.uga.edu

Accompanied by a submission fee of US$50. Payments are by credit card by printing and completing the manuscript transmittal form online. Submission fees will not be refunded. Submission of a paper will be held to imply that it contains original unpublished work and is not being submitted for publication elsewhere. The Editor does not accept responsibility for damage or loss of papers submitted. Upon acceptance of an article, author(s) will be asked to transfer copyright of the article to the publisher. This transfer will ensure the widest possible dissemination of information.

3. Submission of accepted papers as electronic manuscripts, i.e., on disk with accompanying manuscript, is encouraged. Electronic manuscripts have the advantage that there is no need for rekeying of text, thereby avoiding the possibility of introducing errors and resulting in reliable and fast delivery of proofs. The preferred storage medium is a 3.5-inch disk in MS-DOS format, although other systems are welcome, e.g., Macintosh (in this case, save your file in the

usual manner; do not use the option 'save in MS-DOS format'). Do not submit your original paper as electronic manuscript but hold on to disk until asked for this by the Editor (in case your paper is accepted without revisions). Do submit the accepted version of your paper as electronic manuscript. Make absolutely sure that the file on the disk and the printout are identical. Please use a new and correctly formatted disk and label this with your name; also specify the software and hardware used as well as the title of the file to be processed. Do not convert the file to plain ASCII. Ensure that the letter 'l' and digit '1', and also the letter 'O' and digit '0' are used properly, and format your article (tabs, indents, etc.) consistently. Characters not available on your word processor (Greek letters mathematical symbols, etc.) should not be left open but indicated by a unique code (e.g., gralpha, alpha, etc., for the Greek letter α). Such codes should be used consistently throughout the entire text; a list of codes used should accompany the electronic manuscript. Do not allow your word processor to introduce word breaks and do not use a justified layout. Please adhere strictly to the general instructions below on style, arrangement and, in particular, the reference style of the *Journal*.

4. Manuscripts should be double spaced, with wide margins, and printed on one side of the paper only. All pages should be numbered consequently. Titles and subtitles should be short. References, tables, and legends for the figures should be printed on separate pages.

5. The first page of the manuscript should contain the following information: (i) the title; (ii) the name(s) and institutional affiliation(s) of the author(s); (iii) an abstract of not more than 100 words. A footnote on the same sheet should give the name, address, and telephone and fax numbers of the corresponding author [as well as an e-mail address].

6. The first page of the manuscript should also contain at least one classification code according to the Classification System for Journal Articles as used by the *Journal of Economic Literature*; in addition, up to five key words should be supplied.

7. Acknowledgements and information on grants received can be given in a first footnote, which should not be included in the consecutive numbering of footnotes.

8. Footnotes should be kept to a minimum and numbered consecutively throughout the text with superscript Arabic numerals. They should be double-spaced and not include displayed formulae or tables.

9. Displayed formulae should be numbered consecutively throughout the manuscript as (1), (2), etc. against the right-hand margin of the page. In cases where the derivation of formulae has been abbreviated, it is of great help to the referees if the full derivation can be presented on a separate sheet (not to be published).

10. References to publications should be as follows: 'Smith (1992) reported that...' or 'This problem has been studied previously (e.g., Smith et al., 1969)'. The author should make sure that there is a strict one-to-one correspondence between the names and years in the text and those on the list. The list of references should appear at the end of the main text (after any appendices, but before tables and legends for figures). It should be double spaced and listed in alphabetical order by author's name. References should appear as follows:

For Monographs
Hawawini, G. and I. Swary, 1990, Mergers and acquisitions in the U.S. banking industry: Evidence from the capital markets (North-Holland, Amsterdam).

For Contributions to Collective Works
Brunner, K. and A.H. Meltzer, 1990, Money supply, in: B.M. Friedman and F.H. Hahn, Handbook of monetary economics, Vol. 1 (North-Holland, Amsterdam) 357-396.

For Periodicals
Griffiths, W. and G. Judge, 1992, Testing and estimating location vectors when the error covariance matrix is unknown, Journal of Econometrics 54, 121-138.

Note that journal titles should not be abbreviated.

11. Illustrations will be reproduced photographically from originals supplied by the author; they will not be redrawn by the publisher. Please provide all illustrations in quadruplicate (one high-contrast original and three photocopies). Care should be taken that lettering and symbols are of a comparable size. The illustrations should not be inserted in the text, and should be marked on the back with figure number, title of paper, and author's name. All graphs and diagrams should be referred to as figures, and should be numbered consecutively in the text in Arabic numerals. Illustration for papers submitted as electronic manuscripts should be in traditional form.

Papers that were received by Elsevier after mid January 2004 for this journal will appear in colour on Science Direct in this new programme. For those papers which contain a mixture of colour and black & white illustrations, some of the figures that appear in black and white in the printed version of the *Journal* will appear in colour, online, in Science Direct. There is no extra charge for authors who participate in this new facility. Further information on electronic artwork can be found at http://authors.elsevier.com/artwork

12. Tables should be numbered consecutively in the text in Arabic numerals and printed on separate sheets.

Empirical studies must include a short appendix describing the data and computational procedures. Likewise articles that contain simulation results must include a brief appendix describing the random number generator used and any other relevant computational aspects of the study. The editor will decide whether the appendix itself is to be published along with the final version of an accepted manuscript.

Any manuscript which does not conform to the above instructions may be returned for the necessary revision before publication. Page proofs will be sent to the corresponding author. Proofs should be corrected carefully; the responsibility for detecting errors lies with the author. Corrections should be restricted to instances in which the proof is at variance with the manuscript. Extensive alterations will be charged. Fifty reprints of each paper are supplied free of charge to the corresponding author; additional reprints are available at cost if they are ordered when the proof is returned.

Journal of Corporate Real Estate

ADDRESS FOR SUBMISSION:

Simon Beckett, Editor
Journal of Corporate Real Estate
Henry Stewart Publications
Museum House
25 Museum Street
WC1A 1JT London,
UK
Phone: +44 (0) 20 7323 2916
Fax: +44 (0) 20 7323 2918
E-Mail: simon@hspublications.co.uk
Web: www.henrystewart.co.uk
Address May Change:

PUBLICATION GUIDELINES:

Manuscript Length: 11-30
Copies Required: Three
Computer Submission: Yes
Format: MS Word
Fees to Review: 0.00 US$

Manuscript Style:
    Uniform System of Citation (Harvard
    Blue Book), Vancouver

CIRCULATION DATA:

Reader: Academics, Business Persons
Frequency of Issue: Quarterly
Copies per Issue: 1,001 - 2,000
Sponsor/Publisher: Henry Stewart
    Publications
Subscribe Price: 130.00 US$ Individual
    280.00 US$ Institution

REVIEW INFORMATION:

Type of Review: Blind Review
No. of External Reviewers: 2-3
No. of In House Reviewers: 1-2
Acceptance Rate: 40%
Time to Review: 1 - 2 Months
Reviewers Comments: Yes
Invited Articles: 31-50%
Fees to Publish: 0.00 US$

MANUSCRIPT TOPICS:
Accounting Theory & Practice; Corporate Finance; Financial Institutions & Markets;
Insurance; International Finance; Real Estate

MANUSCRIPT GUIDELINES/COMMENTS:

About the Journal
Making the key strategic decisions on real estate occupancy for our major corporate users is a
critical function. It is estimated that major corporations, either as owners or long-term lessees,
control 60-70% of the global value of commercial real estate.

It's hardly surprising therefore that CRE functions are coming under intense, and increasing,
pressure both to improve their real estate assets' performance and, crucially, convince key
players in their corporations of the real value leading-edge use of CRE can unlock.

Journal of Corporate Real Estate is the solution, providing a valuable fund of ideas,
techniques, best practice examples and high quality research to support the work and develop
the careers of senior CRE managers and consultants. At the same time it seeks to help CRE

professionals demonstrate—to CEOs, CFOs and other key players—the real value the best CRE functions can yield.

- Original, in-depth, refereed articles on the latest thinking, techniques, and developments in CRE by some of the world's leading CRE practitioners, advisors and academics
- High quality research from leading academic institutions
- Major player interviews with executives from some of the worlds largest corporate.
- CRE and capital markets prepared by Rick Pederson of Ross Consulting, giving you a regular update on the types of real estate financing vehicles, analytic tools and transactions completed by companies worldwide
- Management Digest, edited and prepared by Virginia Gibson of University of Reading, reviews important management ideas coming from some of the world's most prestigious journals and, crucially, their value to CRE professionals
- Guided by an international Editorial Board of leading practitioners, consultants, and academics
- Each article is subjected to peer review to ensure that the *Journal* is authoritative, accessible and relevant

Notes for Contributors

1. Contributions should be between 2,000 and 5,000 words in length. All submissions should be typewritten and double-spaced.

2. The *Journal*'s Editors and Editorial Board particularly welcome submissions, which present case study material, new approaches, techniques, empirical research or conceptual papers.

3. All articles should be accompanied by a short abstract outlining the paper's aims and subject matter.

4. All articles should be accompanied by up to six keywords.

5. Articles should be accompanied by a short (about 80 words) description of the author(s) and, if appropriate, the organization of which he or she is a member.

6. Authors should not seek to use the *Journal* as a vehicle for marketing any specific product or service.

7. Authors should avoid the use of language or slang which is not in keeping with the professional and academic style of the *Journal*.

8. Titles of organizations etc should be written out first in full and thereafter in initials.

9. Articles should be supported by references. For all Henry Stewart journals excluding *Corporate Reputation Review, Tourism and Hospitality Research, Journal of Fashion Marketing and Management, Journal of Small Business and Enterprise Development, Journal of Asset Management* and *International Journal of Police Science Management*, these should be set out in accordance with the Vancouver referencing system. References for the *Journals* listed above should be set out in accordance with the Harvard referencing system.

10. Photographs and illustrations supporting articles should be submitted where appropriate. Photographs should be good quality positives, printed from the original negatives and preferably in black and white only. Figures and other line illustrations should be submitted in good quality originals and a copy of the data should also be included.

11. Authors must ensure that references to named people and/or organizations are accurate, not racist or sexist and without libelous implications.

12. All contributions sent to the Publisher, whether invited or not, will be submitted to the *Journal*'s Editors and Editorial Board. Any such contribution must bear the author's full name and address, even if this is not for publication. Contributions, whether published pseudonymously or not, are accepted on the strict understanding that the author is responsible for the accuracy of all opinion, technical comment, factual report, data, figures, illustrations and photographs. Publication does not necessarily imply that these are the opinions of the Editorial Board, Editors or the Publisher, nor does the Board, Editors or Publisher accept any liability for the accuracy of such comment, report and other technical and factual information. The Publisher will, however, strive to ensure that all opinion, comments, reports, data, figures, illustrations and photographs are accurate, insofar as it is within its abilities to do so. The Publisher reserves the right to edit, abridge or omit material submitted for publication.

13. All articles submitted for publication will be subject to a double-blind refereeing procedure.

14. The author bears the responsibility for checking whether material submitted is subject to copyright or ownership rights, e.g., photographs, illustrations, trade literature, and data. Where use is so restricted, the Publisher must be informed with the submission of the material.

15. No contribution will be accepted which has been published elsewhere, unless it is expressly invited or agreed by the Publisher. Articles and contributions published become the copyright of the Publisher, unless otherwise agreed.

16. All reasonable efforts are made to ensure accurate reproduction of text, photographs and illustrations. The Publisher does not accept responsibility for mistakes, be they editorial or typographical, nor for consequences resulting from them.

17. Submissions should be sent to Henry Stewart Publications, Museum House, 25 Museum Street, London WC1A 1JT, email: submissions@hspublications.co.uk. **Please clearly state for which *Journal* you are contributing**.

Journal of Cultural Economics (The)

ADDRESS FOR SUBMISSION:

Chris Wilby
Journal of Cultural Economics (The)
Editorial Journals Office
Kluwer Academic Publishers
PO Box 990
3300 AZ Dordrecht
Dordrecht, 3300 AZ
The Netherlands
Phone: +31 (0) 78 639.2392
Fax: +31 (0) 78 657-6350
E-Mail: cathelijne.vanherwaarden@wkap.nl
Web: www.kluweronline.com
Address May Change:

PUBLICATION GUIDELINES:

Manuscript Length: 16-20
Copies Required: Three
Computer Submission: Yes
Format: MS Word, WordPerfect, etc.
Fees to Review: 0.00 US$

Manuscript Style:
  Chicago Manual of Style

CIRCULATION DATA:

Reader: Academics, Practitioners
Frequency of Issue: Quarterly
Copies per Issue: Less than 1,000
Sponsor/Publisher: Association of Cultural
  Economics International/Kluwer
  Academic Publishers
Subscribe Price: 371.00 US$
  371.00 Euro

REVIEW INFORMATION:

Type of Review: Peer Review
No. of External Reviewers: 2
No. of In House Reviewers: 1
Acceptance Rate: 11-20%
Time to Review: 4 - 6 Months
Reviewers Comments: Yes
Invited Articles: 6-10%
Fees to Publish: 0.00 US$

MANUSCRIPT TOPICS:
Cultural Economics; Industrial Organization; Micro Economics

MANUSCRIPT GUIDELINES/COMMENTS:

Joint Editors
Gunther Schulze, Department of Economics, University of Freiburg, Germany

J. Mark Schuster, Department of Urban Studies and Planning, Massachusetts Institute of Technology, USA.

Book Review Editor
Michael Rushton, Department of Public Administration and Urban Studies, Georgia State University, USA

For questions related to any aspect of this journal, please contact Ms Cathelijne van Herwaarden, Publishing Editor, Kluwer Academic Publishers, Van Godewijckstraat 30, PO

Box 17, 3300 AA Dordrecht, The Netherlands; Tel +31-78 657-6157, Fax +31-78 657-6350, E-mail Marie.Sheldon@wkap.com.

The *Journal* is sponsored by the Association of Cultural Economics International.

Aims and Scope. Cultural Economics is the application of economic analysis to the area of all the creative and performing arts, the heritage and cultural industries, whether publicly or privately owned. It is concerned with the economic organization of the cultural sector and with the behavior of producers, consumers and governments in that sector. The subject includes a range of approaches, mainstream and radical, neoclassical, welfare economics, public policy and institutional economics.

The perspective of the cultural economic field is open to a range of approaches, mainstream and radical, neoclassical, welfare economics, public policy and institutional. It has attracted contributions from some of the most eminent economists of our time, and it is steadily growing as an area of economic inquiry; it is increasingly accepted by policy-makers as an important aspect of cultural decision-making.

The editors and editorial board of the *Journal of Cultural Economics* seek to attract the attention of the whole economics profession to this branch of economics, as well as those in related disciplines and practitioners with an interest in economic issues. The *Journal* publishes original papers that deal with the theoretical development of cultural economics as a subject, the application of economic analysis and econometrics to the field of culture, and with the economic aspects of policy. Besides full-length papers, research notes and short communications are also published.

Submission of Manuscripts. Articles should be submitted in quadruplicate to Chris Wilby, Editorial Journals Office.

The *Journal of Cultural Economics* is a double-blind, peer-reviewed journal.

Kluwer Academic Publishers prefer the submission of manuscripts and figures in electronic form in addition to a hard-copy printout. The preferred storage medium for your electronic manuscript is a 3½-inch diskette. Please label your diskette properly, giving exact details on the name(s) of the file(s), and the operating system and software used. Always save your electronic manuscript in the word processor format that you use—conversions to other formats and versions tend to be imperfect. In general, use as few formatting codes as possible. For safety's sake, you should always retain a backup copy of your file(s). After acceptance, please make absolutely sure that you send the latest (i.e., revised) version of your manuscript, both as hard-copy printout and on diskette (submission in electronic form of the final version of your article is compulsory).

Kluwer Academic Publishers prefer articles submitted in word processing packages such as MS Word, WordPerfect, etc., running under operating systems MS-DOS, Windows, and Apple Macintosh, or in the file format LaTeX. Articles submitted in other software programs can also be accepted.

For submission in LaTeX, Kluwer Academic Publishers have developed a Kluwer LaTeX class file, which can be downloaded from http://www.wkap.nl/authors/jrnlstylefiles/. Use of this class file is highly recommended. Do not use versions downloaded from other sites. Technical support is available at texhelp@wkap.nl. If you are not familiar with TeX/LaTeX, the class file will be of no use to you. In that case, submit your article in a common word processor format.

For purposes of reviewing (the *Journal* is maintaining a double-blind review system), articles for publication should be submitted as hard-copy printout (four-fold) and on diskette to the Editorial Journals Office.

For more information on submission of papers, view the journals website at:
  http://www .kluweronline.com/issn/0885-2545.

Manuscript Preparation. Final versions of accepted papers should be all double-spaced with 1-inch margins. Include:

1. **A title page**, with the article's title, the author's name(s) and permanent affiliation(s), and the author's current address, telephone and fax numbers, for sending proofs and offprints.

2. **A second page** containing an abstract of not more than 100 words, plus two to six key words.

3. **The text of the article.** The location of tables and figures should be indicated in the text. Equation numbers should be placed flush right. References to sources should be in the form: Smith (1989, pp. 14-17) or (Smith, 1989, pp. 14-17) as appropriate.

4. **Notes**. Notes are to be typed double-spaced in a separate section beginning on a new page following the text. An acknowledgement note should be keyed with an asterisk at the author's name on the title page. Other notes should be keyed to superscript Arabic numbers at the end of sentences in the text.

5. **References** are to be typed double-spaced in a separate section. Underline or italicize book and journal titles. Examples:
For monographs
  Throsby, C.D. and Withers, G.A. (1979) *The Economics of the Performing Arts*. Edward Arnold, London.
For contributions to collective works
  Peacock, Alan (1992) "Economics, Cultural Values and Cultural Policies", in Ruth Towse and Abdul Khakee, eds. *Cultural Economics*. Springer, Heidelberg.
For periodicals
  Pommerchoe, Werner W. and Frey, Bruno S. (1990) "Public Promotion of the Arts; A Survey of Means". *Journal of Cultural Economics* 14: 73-95.

Note that the journal titles should not be abbreviated.

6. **Tables** come after the References. They should be numbered consecutively in the text in roman numerals. Each should be titled and typed double-spaced, beginning on a separate page. Tables should be typed on separate pages. The legends and titles on tables must be sufficiently descriptive such that they are understandable without reference to the text. The body of tables must be clearly labelled in English. Explain all abbreviations. Notes to tables are designated by superscript letters a, b, c, ...

7. **Figures** for accepted manuscripts are to be in professional-quality, camera- ready form; i.e. drawn in India ink on drafting paper on high-quality white paper. Lettering should be legible after reduction to size. Provide the original plus two copies. The drawings should not be inserted in the text and should be legible after reduction to size. Provide the original plus two copies. The drawings should not be inserted in the text and should be marked on the back with figure numbers, title of paper, and name of author. All graphs and diagrams should be referred to as figures and should be numbered consecutively in the text in Arabic numerals. Legends for figures should be typed on separate pages. The legends and titles of figures must be sufficiently descriptive such that they are understandable without reference to the text. The dimensions of figure axes must be clearly labeled in English.

8. Units

- Any numerical results in dimensional form should be presented in SI units.
- Important formulae (displayed) should be numbered consecutively throughout the manuscript as (1), (2) etc. on the right-hand side of the page.
- Please indicate clearly the differences between 0 (zero) and O, o (the letters), between the numeral 1 and the letter l, between a and alpha, k and kappa, p and rho, u and mu, v and nu, n and eta, epsilon and ϵ, zeta and xi, delta and theta, alpha and ∞, X and $\times$ etc.
- The use of the exponent $1/2$ is preferred to the sign $\sqrt{}$.
- The author should also see to it that the level of subscripts, subscripts to subscripts, exponents as well as exponents in exponents, cannot be misunderstood.
- Fractions to be printed in the body of the text (not in display formulae) should make use of the solidus (e.g. a/b instead of a/b).
- The use of negative exponents (e.g. u^{-1} instead of $1/u$) will save both space and typesetting costs.
- Attention should be paid to the consistent use of braces, brackets, and parentheses.
- Any manuscript that does not conform to the above instructions may be returned for the necessary revision before publication. Compliance with *Journal of Cultural Economics* Information for Authors will be required before a manuscript is accepted.

9. Important formulae (displayed) should be numbered consecutively throughout the manuscript as (1), (2) etc., on the right-hand side of the page.

Proofs and Offprints. Authors will be sent page proofs and should return the corrected proofs within three days of receipt. Alterations other than typesetting errors may be charged to the author. The first-mentioned author will receive 25 free copies. Further copies can be ordered when returning page proofs.

Journal of Deferred Compensation

ADDRESS FOR SUBMISSION:

Bruce J. McNeil, Editor
Journal of Deferred Compensation
Dorsey & Whitney, LLP
Suite 1500
50 South Sixth Street
Minneapolis, MN 55402-1498
USA
Phone: 612-340-5640
Fax: 612-340-2777
E-Mail: mcneil.bruce@dorsey.com
Web: www.dorseylaw.com
Address May Change:

PUBLICATION GUIDELINES:

Manuscript Length: Any
Copies Required: Two
Computer Submission: No
Format: N/A
Fees to Review: 0.00 US$

Manuscript Style:
    See Manuscript Guidelines

CIRCULATION DATA:

Reader: Business Persons
Frequency of Issue: Quarterly
Copies per Issue: 1,001 - 2,000
Sponsor/Publisher: Panel Publishers, Aspen
    Law Publishing Co.
Subscribe Price: 0.00 US$

REVIEW INFORMATION:

Type of Review: Editorial Review
No. of External Reviewers: 2
No. of In House Reviewers: No Reply
Acceptance Rate: 65%
Time to Review: 1 Month or Less
Reviewers Comments: Yes
Invited Articles: 21-30%
Fees to Publish: 0.00 US$

MANUSCRIPT TOPICS:

Accounting Theory & Practice; Employee Benefits; Executive Compensation; Government &
Non-Profit Accounting; Insurance; Options; Stock-Based Benefits; Tax Accounting

MANUSCRIPT GUIDELINES/COMMENTS:

Journal of Deferred Compensation (*JDC*) is devoted to providing practical information and
ideas to professionals who deal with the tax, legal, and business planning aspects of
nonqualified plans and executive compensation.

JDC emphasizes quality and clarity of exposition. Reviewers consider the following criteria in
assessing submissions: value of the information to the *Journal*'s audience, substantive
contribution to the broadly defined field of nonqualified plans and executive compensation,
and overall quality of manuscript. The decision to publish a given manuscript is made by the
Editor-in-Chief, relying on the recommendations of the reviewers.

Submission of a manuscript clearly implies commitment to publish in the *Journal*. Papers
previously published or under review by other journals are unacceptable. Articles adapted

from book-length works-in-progress will be considered under acceptable copyright arrangements.

Manuscript Specifications: All textual material-including notes and references-must be double-spaced in a full-size nonproportional typeface (e.g., 12 pt. Courier), on one side only of 8½" x 11" good-quality paper, with 1½" margins all around. All pages must be numbered. References should be double-spaced and placed at the end of the text on a separate page headed "References." Notes must not be embedded in the text; they should be printed as double-spaced endnotes rather than footnotes. Improperly prepared manuscripts will be returned for repreparation.

Within the article, use short subheadings for organization and emphasis. Include a cover sheet with title, author's address and affiliations, mailing and e-mail addresses, and phone and fax numbers.

Artwork, including tables, charts, and graphs, must be of camera-ready quality. Each should be on a separate page placed at the end of the text, with proper placement indicated within text (e.g., "Insert Table 2 here").

Three high-quality copies of the manuscript should be submitted to the Editor-in-Chief. Include a biographical statement of 20 words or less.

Acceptance: Once an article has been formally accepted, the author must submit the article to the publisher in two formats: three high-quality manuscript copies and a Word 6.0 computer file on 3½" floppy diskette labeled with file type and name, soft ware version, article title, and author's name. No other software is acceptable.

Copyright is retained by the publisher, and articles are subject to editorial revision. There is no payment for articles; authors receive five copies of the issue in which the article is published. Manuscripts not accepted for publication are not returned. Authors should keep a copy of any submission for their files.

Manuscript submissions and inquiries should be directed to the Editor-in-Chief. For business and production matters, contact Melissa A. Green, Editor, Journal of Deferred Compensation, Aspen Publishers, 125 Eugene O'Neill Drive, Suite 103, New London, CT 06320
800-876-9105 Ext. 251   melissa.green@aspenpubl.com

Journal of Derivatives (The)

ADDRESS FOR SUBMISSION:

Stephen Figlewski, Editor
Journal of Derivatives (The)
New York University
Stern School of Business
44 West 4th Street, Suite 9-160
New York, NY 10012-1126
USA
Phone: 212-998-0712
Fax: 212-998-4220
E-Mail: sfiglews@stern.nyu.edu
Web: www.iijod.com
Address May Change:

PUBLICATION GUIDELINES:

Manuscript Length: 16-20
Copies Required: Three
Computer Submission: Yes
Format: MS Word, Adobe Acrobat
Fees to Review: 0.00 US$

Manuscript Style:
    See Manuscript Guidelines

CIRCULATION DATA:

Reader: Business Persons
Frequency of Issue: Quarterly
Copies per Issue: 1,001 - 2,000
Sponsor/Publisher: Institutional Investor,
Inc.
Subscribe Price: 365.00 US$
    Academics 50% Discount

REVIEW INFORMATION:

Type of Review: Editorial Review
No. of External Reviewers: 2
No. of In House Reviewers: 0
Acceptance Rate: 11-20%
Time to Review: 4 - 6 Months
Reviewers Comments: No Reply
Invited Articles: 0-5%
Fees to Publish: 0.00 US$

MANUSCRIPT TOPICS:
Corporate Finance; Financial Institutions & Markets; Portfolio & Security Analysis; Risk
Management

MANUSCRIPT GUIDELINES/COMMENTS:

Additional Topics
- Risk Management applications of derivatives.
- Theory and practice of trading in any exchange-traded or OTC derivative product.
- Valuation and risk assessment models for derivative instruments and securities with derivative features.

The *Journal of Derivatives* is the leading analytical, practical journal on the latest derivatives theories used in industry today. Readers include financial engineers, professionals who structure these products, senior portfolio managers, strategists, analysts and traders in derivatives.

Submission Guidelines

1. Submit three copies of the manuscript double-spaced with wide margins and pages numbered. The front page should include the authors' full names, titles, affiliations, addresses, zip codes, phone/fax numbers, and email addresses. The authors should also supply an electronic file. If submitting a PDF file, the Word file must accompany it. Please note to which journal you are submitting your article.

2. Supply an abstract that describes the article succinctly for the editor and referees.

3. References, endnotes, tables, and figures should appear on separate pages at the end of the text.

4. Limit references to works cited in the text and list them alphabetically. Citations in the text should appear as "Smith [1990] suggests that..." Include page numbers in works cited.

5. Minimize the number of endnotes. Use periods instead of commas between authors' names and titles of references. Use superscript Arabic numbers in the text and on the endnote page.

6. Number and title all exhibits. Write out the column heads and legends; they should be understandable without reference to the text. Submit graphs in electronic form. Please avoid embedding pictures in Word files. Note: we cannot draw graphs for you.

7. Center each equation on a separate line, numbered consecutively with Arabic numbers, in parentheses in the right margin. Identify Greek letters in the margin for the typesetter. Please make clear markings when inserting Greek letters or equations into the text. It would be preferable if manuscripts containing mathematical equations be submitted in Microsoft Word using either Equation Editor or MathType. If files have to be submitted in .Tex or LaTeX form, please supply PDF files as well.

8. Institutional Investor Inc.'s copyright agreement form—giving us non-exclusive rights to publish the material in all media—must be signed prior to publication.

9. Upon acceptance of the article, no further changes are allowed, except with the permission of the editor. If the article has already been submitted for copyediting, any changes must be made on the hard copy of the original submitted manuscript.

10. We may return any paper to the author for revisions that do not follow these guidelines.

Journal of Developing Areas

ADDRESS FOR SUBMISSION:

Abu Wahid, Editor
Journal of Developing Areas
Tennessee State University
College of Business
330 10th Avenue North
Nashville, TN 37203-3401
USA
Phone: 615-963-7121
Fax: 615-963-7139
E-Mail: jda@tnstate.edu
Web:
Address May Change:

PUBLICATION GUIDELINES:

Manuscript Length: 20-35
Copies Required: Three
Computer Submission: Yes
Format: N/A
Fees to Review: 0.00 US$

Manuscript Style:
    Chicago Manual of Style

CIRCULATION DATA:

Reader: Academics
Frequency of Issue: Quarterly
Copies per Issue: 1,001 - 2,000
Sponsor/Publisher: Tennessee State
    Universtiy
Subscribe Price: 25.00 US$ Individual
    30.00 US$ Institution

REVIEW INFORMATION:

Type of Review: Blind Review
No. of External Reviewers: 3
No. of In House Reviewers: 1
Acceptance Rate: 11-20%
Time to Review: 4 - 6 Months
Reviewers Comments: Yes
Invited Articles: 0-5%
Fees to Publish: 0.00 US$

MANUSCRIPT TOPICS:

Behavioral Economics; Econometrics; Economic Development; Financial Institutions & Markets; Financial Services; Fiscal Policy; International Economics & Trade; Macro Economics; Micro Economics; Monetary Policy; Portfolio & Security Analysis; Public Policy Economics; Regional Economics

MANUSCRIPT GUIDELINES/COMMENTS:

Purpose

The *Journal of Developing Areas (JDA)* aims to stimulate in-depth and rigorous empirical and theoretical research on all issues pertaining to the process of economic development. It also intends to encourage research on economic, social, urban/regional, and inner city problems of the United States and other developed countries.

General Policy

1. The *Journal of Developing Areas* shall be published in English language twice per academic year – in fall and in spring – by the College of Business at Tennessee State University.

658

2. In addition to original research articles, the *JDA* will publish book reviews appropriate for the journal.

3. Advertisements shall be carried in the journal @per page (per issue) - US$500.00

4. The *JDA* will acknowledge the receipt of all books sent by publishers for book reviews.

5. From time to time, the *JDA* will also publish special issues by order from various professional groups and international agencies at the following rates: a) Fifteen thousand dollars per 1,000 copies and ten thousand dollars per 500 copies; b) In each case, camera-ready copy must be provided.

6. Subscriptions of the *JDA* shall be at a) $30.00 per year;   b) Shipping and handling $4.00 per year for the U.S. and Canada and $10.00 per year for all other countries. c) Regular subscribers will be charged extra for special issues. d) These rates are subject to change at any time, depending on the printing costs and postal rates.

7. For subscription and advertisement, all checks or money orders shall be made payable to *the Journal of Developing Areas.*

8. Awards shall be given every year for the best article, book review and manuscript review report. The author(s) of the best article shall receive (a) certificate(s) of recognition and a cash benefit of US$250.00. The best book reviewer and the best manuscript reviewer shall receive certificates of recognition and a cash benefit of US$125.00 each.

9. The *JDA* will recognize the contributions of all referees by mentioning their names in the relevant issue of the journal.

10. The *JDA* adopts the policy of fast reference and decision-making process for all submissions.

11. The editor reserves the right to make minor changes on the final manuscript without prior approval of respective authors.

12. The *JDA* reserves the right to change its policy any time without prior notice.

Abstracting and Indexing. The *JDA* is included in the *Social Science Citation Index, Bacon's Information Inc., International Political Science Abstracts,* and *Cambridge Scientific Abstracts.* Articles appearing in the *JDA* are abstracted and indexed in the *Historical Abstracts and America: History and Life.* The *JDA* articles are also indexed by the *Journal of Economic Literature.*

Online Availability. From Spring 2004, the *JDA* will be available online at the Johns Hopkins University Press Project MUSE Website.

Submission Guidelines

1. All manuscript submissions shall preferably be made electronically to: JDA@tnstate.edu.

2. All submitted papers shall be original, employing rigorous research methodology and appropriate statistical tests.

3. No submitted paper shall be under simultaneous consideration by any other journal or publication outlet.

4. The length of the article, including abstract, figures, illustrations, tables, mathematical expressions and equations, endnotes and references shall be in the neighborhood of 7,000 words.

5. Authors' name shall be followed by their affiliation and the text of the paper shall be preceded by an abstract of around 150 words. The abstract shall clearly highlight the problem(s) dealt with, the methodology, the findings and the policy implications.

6. All figures, illustrations, tables, mathematical expressions and equations shall be embodied in the text in a single file.

7. References shall adhere to the following style.
a) **Journal article**: White, Halbert (1980), A Heteroscadasticity Consistent Covariance Matrix Estimator and a Direct Test for Heteroscadasticity, *Econometrica,* Vol. 48, No. 2, pp. 203-23.
b) **Book chapter:** Balkin, Steven, (1993) "A Grameen Bank Replication: The Full Circle Fund of the Women's Self Employment Project of Chicago", in Abu Wahid (ed.) *The Grameen Bank: Poverty Relief in Bangladesh*, Westview Press, pp. 235-266.
c) **Book**: Keynes, John M. (1936) *General Theory of Employment, Interest and Money,* Macmillan.

8. All manuscripts shall use endnotes instead of footnotes. All endnotes shall be numbered consecutively throughout the manuscript and be presented at the end.

9. All spellings shall follow American style, not British.

Manuscript Review And Publication Process. 1. Our reference and decision making process is fast. We endeavor to make a final decision within four to eight weeks of submission.

2. On preliminary review, the author shall be notified within a week or so if his/her paper is accepted for further consideration.

3. Once the reference process begins, we expect to respond to the author within four to eight weeks with the review report.

4. Once the review report is available and the paper requires corrections, revised version of the paper in line with reviewers' comments shall be turned in by the author electronically within 30 days.

5. Depending on the extent of revision, a final decision shall be made within one to four weeks.

6. Should the paper be accepted the authors shall be asked to pay a processing fee at the rate of $15.00 per 1,000 words, payable to *the Journal of Developing Areas.*

7. At this stage, the author shall be required to sign a copyright agreement with the *JDA*.

8. The final version of the *JDA* manuscript will be copy edited by our professional staff.

9. On publication, the author shall receive five copies of the offprint. A copy of the whole journal containing the article may be obtained at a payment of $17.00 for the U.S. and Canada and $23.50 for all other countries.

10. Book reviewers shall receive the book free and on publication, they will receive a copy of the published review. Copies of the whole journal containing the book review may be obtained at the rates mentioned above.

Journal of Development Economics

ADDRESS FOR SUBMISSION:

Pranab Bardhan, Editor
Journal of Development Economics
University of California at Berkeley
Department of Economics
Berkeley, CA 94720
USA
Phone: 510-642-0823
Fax: 510-642-0563
E-Mail: jde@econ.berkeley.edu
Web: www.elsevier.com
Address May Change:

CIRCULATION DATA:

Reader: Academics
Frequency of Issue: Bi-Monthly
Copies per Issue: No Reply
Sponsor/Publisher: Elsevier Science
   Publishing Co.
Subscribe Price: 135.00 US$ Individual
   1491.00 US$ Institution
   129.00 Euro Indv. & 1,333 Euro Inst.

PUBLICATION GUIDELINES:

Manuscript Length: 26-30
Copies Required: Three
Computer Submission: No
Format:
Fees to Review: 60.00 US$ Manuscript
   30.00 US$ Comments

Manuscript Style:
   See Manuscript Guidelines

REVIEW INFORMATION:

Type of Review: Editorial Review
No. of External Reviewers: 2
No. of In House Reviewers: No Reply
Acceptance Rate: 20%
Time to Review: 4 - 6 Months
Reviewers Comments: Yes
Invited Articles: 0-5%
Fees to Publish: 0.00 US$

MANUSCRIPT TOPICS:
Economic Development

MANUSCRIPT GUIDELINES/COMMENTS:

Aims and Scope
The *Journal of Development Economics* publishes papers relating to all aspects of economic development—from immediate policy concerns to structural problems of underdevelopment. The emphasis is on quantitative or analytical work, which is relevant as well as intellectually stimulating.

Book Reviews
The *Journal of Development Economics* will include book reviews, which will be in greater depth and longer than usual. Books for review should be addressed to Clive Bell, Suedasien Institut der Universitaet Heidelberg, Fachbereich Wirtschaftswissenschaften, Im Neuenheimer Feld 330, D-69120 Heidelberg, Germany.

Guide for Authors
1. Papers must be in English.

2. Papers for publication should be sent in triplicate to the Editor. There is a submission fee of US$60 for all unsolicited manuscripts submitted for publication, US$30 for manuscripts of comments on an article already published in this journal. Personal checks or money orders should accompany the manuscripts and be made payable to the *Journal of Development Economics*. In some cases, submissions from authors from developing countries may be exempted from the submission fee by the Editor. Submission of a paper will be held to imply that it contains original unpublished work and is not being submitted for publication elsewhere. The Editor does not accept responsibility for damage or loss of papers submitted. Upon acceptance of an article, author(s) will be asked to transfer copyright of the article to the publisher. This transfer will ensure the widest possible dissemination of information.

3. **Submission of accepted papers** as electronic manuscripts, i.e., on disk with accompanying manuscript, is encouraged. Electronic manuscripts have the advantage that there is no need for rekeying of text, thereby avoiding the possibility of introducing errors and resulting in reliable and fast delivery of proofs. The preferred storage medium is a 5.25-inch or 3.5-inch disk in MS-DOS format, although other systems are welcome, e.g., Macintosh (in this case, save your file in the usual manner; do not use the option 'save in MS-DOS format'). Do not submit your original paper as electronic manuscript, but hold on to disk until asked for it by the Editor (in case your paper is accepted without revisions). Do submit the accepted version of your paper as electronic manuscript. Make absolutely sure that the file on the disk and the printout are identical. Please use a new and correctly formatted disk and label this with your name; also specify the software and hardware used as well as the title of the file to be processed. Do not convert the file to plain ASCII. Ensure that the letter 'l' and digit '1', and also the letter 'O' and digit '0', are used properly, and format your article (tabs, indents, etc.) consistently. Characters not available on your word processor (Greek letters, mathematical symbols, etc.) should not be left open but indicated by a unique code (e.g., gralpha, [alpha], @, etc., for the Greek letter α.) Such codes should be used consistently throughout the entire text; a list of codes used should accompany the electronic manuscript. Do not allow your word processor to introduce word breaks and do not use a justified layout. Please adhere strictly to the general instructions below on style, arrangement and, in particular, the reference style of the journal.

4. **Manuscripts** should be double-spaced, with wide margins, and printed on one side of the paper only. All pages should be numbered consecutively. Titles and subtitles should be short. References, tables, and legends for figures should be printed on separate pages.

5. The **first page** of the manuscript should contain the following information: (i) the title; (ii) the name(s) and institutional affiliation(s) of the author(s); and (iii) an abstract of not more than 100 words. A footnote on the same sheet should give the name, address, and telephone and fax numbers of the corresponding author as well as an e-mail address.

6. The **first page** of the manuscript should also contain at least one classification code according to the Classification System for Journal Articles as used by the *Journal of Economic Literature*; in addition, up to five key words should be supplied.

7. **Acknowledgements** and information on grants received can be given in a first footnote, which should not be included in the consecutive numbering of footnotes.

8. **Footnotes** should be kept to a minimum and numbered consecutively throughout the text with superscript Arabic numerals.

9. **Displayed formulae** should be numbered consecutively throughout the manuscript as (1), (2), etc., against the right-hand margin of the page. In cases where the derivation of formulae has been abbreviated, it is of great help to the referees if the full derivation can be presented on a separate sheet (not to be published).

10. **References** to publications should be as follows:
'Smith (1992) reported that...' or 'This problem has been studied previously (e.g., Smith et al., 1969)'.

The author should make sure that there is a strict one-to-one correspondence between the names and years in the text and those on the list.

The list of references should appear at the end of the main text (after any appendices, but before tables and legends for figures). It should be double-spaced and listed in alphabetical order by author's name. References should appear as follows:

For monographs
Hawawini, G., Swary, I., 1990, Mergers and acquisitions in the U. S. banking industry: Evidence from the capital markets. North-Holland, Amsterdam.

For contributions to collective works
Brunner, K. and A.H. Meltzer, 1990, Money supply, in : B.M. Friedman and F.H. Hahn, eds., Handbook of monetary economics, Vol. 1. North-Holland, Amsterdam, 357-396.

For periodicals
Griffiths, W., Judge, G., 1992, Testing and estimating location vectors when the error covariance matrix is unknown. Journal of Econometrics 54, 121-138.

Note that journal titles should not be abbreviated.

11. **Illustrations** will be reproduced photographically from originals supplied by the author; the publisher will not redraw them. Please provide all illustrations in quadruplicate (one high-contrast original and three photocopies). Care should be taken that lettering and symbols are of a comparable size. The illustrations should not be inserted in the text, and should be marked on the back with figure number, title of paper, and author's name. All graphs and diagrams should be referred to as figures, and should be numbered consecutively in the text in Arabic numerals. Illustrations for papers submitted as electronic manuscripts should be in traditional form.

12. **Tables** should be numbered consecutively in the text in Arabic numerals and printed on separate sheets.

Any manuscript, which does not conform to the above instructions, may be returned for the necessary revision before publication.

Page proofs will be sent to the corresponding author. Proofs should be corrected carefully; the responsibility for detecting errors lies with the author. Corrections should be restricted to instances in which the proof is at variance with the manuscript. Extensive alterations will be charged. Twenty-fine reprints of each paper are supplied free of charge to the corresponding author; additional reprints are available at cost if they are ordered when the proof is returned.

Journal of Development Studies (The)

ADDRESS FOR SUBMISSION:

Christopher Colclough, Managing Editor
Journal of Development Studies (The)
Frank Cass & Co. Ltd.
Crown House 47 Chase Side
Southgate London, N14 5BP
UK
Phone: +44 (0) 20 8920 2100
Fax: +44 (0) 20 8447 8548
E-Mail: info@frankcass.com
Web: www.frankcass.com
Address May Change:

PUBLICATION GUIDELINES:

Manuscript Length: 16-20
Copies Required: Three
Computer Submission: Yes
Format: Any
Fees to Review: 0.00 US$

Manuscript Style:
    See Manuscript Guidelines

CIRCULATION DATA:

Reader: Academics
Frequency of Issue: Bi-Monthly
Copies per Issue: 1,001 - 2,000
Sponsor/Publisher: Frank Cass Publishers
Subscribe Price: 103.00 US$ Individual
    490.00 US$ Institution

REVIEW INFORMATION:

Type of Review: Editorial Review
No. of External Reviewers: 2
No. of In House Reviewers: 2
Acceptance Rate: 6-10%
Time to Review: 1 - 2 Months
Reviewers Comments: Yes
Invited Articles: 0-5%
Fees to Publish: 0.00 US$

MANUSCRIPT TOPICS:
Economic Development; Industrial Organization; International Finance

MANUSCRIPT GUIDELINES/COMMENTS:

The Journal of Development Studies (*JDS*) is a refereed journal. Articles submitted to *JDS* should be original contributions and should not be under consideration for any other publication at the same time. If another version of the article is under consideration by another publication, or has been, or will be published elsewhere, authors should clearly indicate this at the time of submission.

Each manuscript should be submitted in triplicate. Articles should be typewritten on A4/Letter paper, on one side only, double-spaced and with ample margins. All pages (including those containing only diagrams and tables) should be numbered consecutively.

There is no standard length for articles, but 5,000-6,000 words (including notes and references) is a useful target. The article should begin with an indented and italicized summary of around 100 words, which should describe the main arguments and conclusions of the article.

Details of the author's institutional affiliation, full address and other contact information should be included on a separate cover sheet. Any acknowledgements should be included on the cover sheet, as should a note of the exact length of the article.

All diagrams, charts and graphs should be referred to as figures and consecutively numbered. Tables should be kept to a minimum and contain only essential data. Each figure and table must be given an Arabic numeral, followed by a heading, and be referred to in the text.

Following acceptance for publication, articles should be submitted on high-density 3½-inch **virus-free** disks (IBM PC or Macintosh compatible) in rich text format (.RTF) together with a hard copy. To facilitate typesetting, notes should be grouped together at the end of the file. Tables should also be placed at the end of the file and prepared using tabs. Any diagrams or maps should be copied to a separate disk in uncompressed .TIF or .JPG formats in individual files. These should be prepared in black and white. Tints should be avoided; use open patterns instead. If maps and diagrams cannot be prepared electronically, they should be presented on good quality white paper. If mathematics are included, $1/2$ is preferred over ½.

Each disk should be labeled with the journal's name, article title, lead author's name, and software used. It is the author's responsibility to ensure that where copyright materials are included within an article, the permission of the copyright holder has been obtained. Confirmation of this should be included on a separate sheet included with the disk.

Authors are entitled to 25 free offprints and a copy of the issue in which their article appears.

Copyright in articles published in *JDS* rests with the publisher.

Style
Authors are responsible for ensuring that their manuscripts conform to the journal style.

The Editors will not undertake retyping of manuscripts before publication. A guide to style and presentation is obtainable from the Editors, or from the publisher, Frank Cass & Co. Ltd., Newbury House, 900 Eastern Avenue, Newbury House, London IG2 7HH, England; Fax: +44(0)181 599 0984; Email: editors@frankcass.com.

Notes
• Simple references without accompanying comments: to be inserted at appropriate place in text, underlined and in squared brackets stating author's surname, publication date of work referred to, and relevant pages, e.g., [Brown, 1979: 33-711].

• References with comments to appear as Notes, indicated consecutively throughout the article, by raised numerals corresponding to the list of notes placed at the end.

• Book titles and names of journals should be underlined; titles of articles should be in inverted commas.

A Reference List should appear after the list of notes. It should contain all the works referred to, listed alphabetically by author's surname (or name of sponsoring body where there is no identifiable author). Style should follow: author's surname, forename and/or initials, date of publication, title of publication, place of publication, and publisher. Thus:

Brown, A.E., 1968a, <u>Development Economics</u>. London: MacRoutledge.

Brown, A.E., 1968b, 'Agricultural Policy in India', <u>Journal of Development Studies</u>. Vol.2, No.3.

House style: British spelling throughout; NB: -ise endings NOT -ize; Dates: 28 January 1968; Single quotes; double within single.

Journal of Developmental Entrepreneurship

ADDRESS FOR SUBMISSION:

Michael H. Morris, Editor
Journal of Developmental Entrepreneurship
Syracuse University
Department of Entrepreneurship
 and Emerging Enterprises
School of Management
Syracuse, NY 13244
USA
Phone: 315-443-3164
Fax: 315-529-2654
E-Mail: mhmorris@syr.edu
Web: www.som.syr.edu/eee/JDE/
Address May Change:

PUBLICATION GUIDELINES:

Manuscript Length: 25 Maximum
Copies Required: Four
Computer Submission: No
Format: N/A
Fees to Review: 0.00 US$

Manuscript Style:
 American Psychological Association

CIRCULATION DATA:

Reader: Academics, Agencies Supporting
 Microenterprise Development
Frequency of Issue: 3 Times/Year
Copies per Issue: 1,001 - 2,000
Sponsor/Publisher: Norfolk State University
 and Syracuse University
Subscribe Price: 35.00 US$ Individual
 125.00 US$ Institution
 15.00 US$ Add for Foreign

REVIEW INFORMATION:

Type of Review: Blind Review
No. of External Reviewers: 3
No. of In House Reviewers: 1
Acceptance Rate: 21-25%
Time to Review: 3 Months
Reviewers Comments: Yes
Invited Articles: 0%
Fees to Publish: 0.00 US$

MANUSCRIPT TOPICS:
Developmental Entrepreneurship; Economic Development

MANUSCRIPT GUIDELINES/COMMENTS:

The *Journal of Developmental Entrepreneurship* is soliciting the submission of high-quality, original manuscripts in the area of developmental entrepreneurship. Please send all submissions to the editor.

Purpose
The *Journal of Developmental Entrepreneurship* (*JDE*) provides a forum for the dissemination of descriptive, empirical and theoretical research that focuses on issues concerning entrepreneurship and microenterprise development under conditions of adversity. Special focus is placed on issues affecting women and minorities. In developed economies, the economically disadvantaged are often minorities and women, while in less developed nations the economically disadvantaged can be the majority of the population. Microenterprise

development entails preparing prospective entrepreneurs in business skills and providing access to start-up capital as well as facilitating the growth of early stage ventures.

The intended audiences for the *Journal* are scholars who study issues of developmental entrepreneurship and professionals involved in governmental or private efforts of facilitating entrepreneurship among the economically disadvantaged. Articles will cover a broad range of topics, including:

- Challenges and opportunities unique to minority and female entrepreneurs
- Microcredit funds and other sources of finance
- Marketing issues surrounding creation and growth of successful ventures.
- Resource strategies in emerging enterprises.
- Personal values, skills and behaviors associated with success in microenterprise development.
- Legislation that encourages entrepreneurship and community development.
- Governmental and corporate set-aside programs for minorities and women.
- CRA and other legislation that encourages community development and small business lending in disadvantaged neighborhoods.
- Private-sector small business lending practices.
- Education and training for aspiring entrepreneurs.
- International programs in developmental entrepreneurship

Editorial Policy

The *JDE* is a double-blind refereed journal that will publish quality articles on issues and topics concerning developmental entrepreneurship. We especially welcome articles that critically address specific programs and efforts to increase entrepreneurship among women and minorities. Program successes as well as failures provide valuable lessons for researchers and program managers. Given the broad range of readership, we value readability and practicality.

Only unpublished, non-copyrighted manuscripts should be submitted. Revised versions of papers previously published in Proceedings are acceptable if the author has retained the copyright. Submission of a paper will imply that it contains original unpublished work and is not submitted for publication elsewhere.

The editors will rigorously pursue a policy of timely and meaningful reviews. One goal is to provide an editorial decision within two months of receipt of a submission. The editor will notify the author concerning any delay if we cannot meet this goal. After initial screening, the editor will send papers for review to reviewers who are familiar with the main topic of the work. Upon receiving the reviewers' evaluations, the editor makes the final decision, based on this material.

After a manuscript is accepted, we require the corresponding author to mail back to *JDE*, a signed and binding copyright agreement. The author of an accepted manuscript is also responsible for obtaining permission to quote from copyrighted work cited in the manuscript. The author must also provide the manuscript's final version in an electronic file on a diskette.

We will publish the *Journal* in the spring and fall each year. Address subscription inquires and orders to the editor.

Subscription Address. Allan Unseth, Managing Editor, *JDE*, School of Business and Entrepreneurship, Norfolk State University, 2401 Corprew Avenue, Norfolk, VA 23504. Tel: 757-683-2563, Fax: 757-683-2506.

Please remit by check or money order in US$ made out to the Norfolk State University Foundation.)

Manuscript Guidelines
The *JDE* solicits unpublished manuscripts not currently under consideration by another publication. Submission of a paper will imply that it contains original unpublished work and is not submitted for publication elsewhere.

Authors must submit four copies of their manuscript; clearly typed with double spacing. Use only one side of the paper and one inch margins to facilitate editing. Manuscript text should be no longer than twenty double-spaced pages.

Arrange the pages of the manuscript as follows:
- The title page with title, author's name, institutional affiliation, running head for publication and name, mailing address, phone and fax numbers of the corresponding author
- Second page; repeat title then the abstract of 100 to 200 words, followed by a list of 4-5 keys used for indexing purposes
- Third page and following; text
- References (start on a separate page)
- Author note (start on a separate page)
- Footnotes (start on a separate page)
- Tables (start on a separate page)
- Figures (place each on a separate page)

The article should end with a non-technical summary statement of the main conclusions. Place lengthy mathematical proofs and very extensive detailed tables in an appendix or omit entirely. Attempt to eliminate all content footnotes. The *Journal* follows the *Publication Manual of The American Psychological Association*.

Journal of E-Business

ADDRESS FOR SUBMISSION:

Rajendar k. Garg, Editor
Journal of E-Business
Indiana University of Pennsylvania
Eberly College of Business
Department of Marketing
Indiana, PA 15705
USA
Phone: 724-357-4547
Fax: 724-357-6232
E-Mail: garg@iup.edu
Web: www.journalofe-business.org
Address May Change:

PUBLICATION GUIDELINES:

Manuscript Length: 21-25
Copies Required: Three
Computer Submission: Yes Disk or Email
Format: MS Word
Fees to Review: 0.00 US$

Manuscript Style:
, Journal of Marketing

CIRCULATION DATA:

Reader: Academics
Frequency of Issue: 2 Times/Year
Copies per Issue: Electronic Journal
Sponsor/Publisher: International Academy
  of E-Business
Subscribe Price: Electronic

REVIEW INFORMATION:

Type of Review: Blind Review
No. of External Reviewers: 3
No. of In House Reviewers: 1
Acceptance Rate: 11-20%
Time to Review: 2 - 3 Months
Reviewers Comments: Yes
Invited Articles: 0-5%
Fees to Publish: 0.00 US$

MANUSCRIPT TOPICS:

Accounting Theory & Practice; E-Business; E-Management; E-Marketing; Industrial
Organization; International Economics & Trade; International Finance; Tax Accounting

MANUSCRIPT GUIDELINES/COMMENTS:

Journal of E-Business invited manuscripts from authors relating to theory and practical
aspects of electronic business. The *Journal of E-Business* will be published twice a year in
June and December. The *Journal* will utilize a double blind review process.

Purposes/Objectives

- To enhance knowledge, understanding, training and scholarship in e-business/e-commerce
  that individuals must have to succeed in rapidly changing global, competitive environment
- To share and stimulate research in a variety of electronic commerce areas and topics
- To explore pedagogical/training approaches and issues
- To provide a dialogue between and among academicians, practitioners, and policy-makers
- To identify dynamic technological trends and their social, political and economic
  implications worldwide

- To create cross or interdisciplinary, integrated forums to benefit individuals in different business disciplines—marketing, finance, accounting, computer & information systems, production & operations management, purchasing & procurement, human resource management, R & D, etc.

Your paper may include topics listed below or any other relevant topic.
- E-Business Models/Theories/Conceptual Frameworks
- New & Old Economy—Similarities & Differences
- E-Commerce Strategies & Tactics
- E-Commerce Infrastructure & Technologies
- C2C (Consumer to Consumer)
- C2B (Consumer to Business)
- Nonprofit E-Commerce
- Intranet/Intra-Organizational E-Commerce
- Online Consumer & Business Behavior & Decision-Making
- Online Market Research/Data-Mining
- E-Communications and Advertising
- Relationship Marketing/One-2-One Marketing
- Web Design & Management
- Electronic Funds Transfer & Payment Systems
- E-Commerce Security
- Product/Service—Specific E-Business/Case Studies
- E-Commerce in Developed 16 Nations
- E-Commerce in Underdeveloped/Developing Nations
- Legal, Political, Ethical, Privacy Issues
- History of E-Commerce
- Future of E-Business—Trends, Forecasts, Prediction

Please submit 3 (three) copies of your manuscript on paper and an electronic version of the paper to the Editor. Please review the instructions to the authors prior to the submission of your paper.

Guidelines to Authors
The following instructions must be followed by authors for submitting their manuscripts to the *Journal of E-Business*.

Original Articles Only. Submission of a manuscript by authors to the *Journal of E-Business* represents a certification by them that the work contained in the manuscript is original, and that neither the manuscript nor any version of it has been previously published or under consideration by any other publication simultaneously.

Manuscript Length. Your manuscript may be no longer than 20-25 pages typed double-spaced. The limit of 25 pages includes figures, tables, references and abstract. More lengthy manuscripts may be considered, but only at the discretion of the Editor. The Editor will carefully assess the value and contribution of the article to the overall dissemination of knowledge in the field in making such a decision. Sometimes lengthier manuscripts may be considered if they can be divided into sections which may be submitted for publication under different titles in successive *Journal* issues.

Manuscript Style. References, citations, and general style of manuscripts submitted to the *Journal of E-Business* should follow the style used by *American Marketing Association* for its many journals such as, *Journal of Marketing*. References should be placed in alphabetical order at the end of the article.

Manuscript Preparation

- Margins: Leave at least a 1-inch margins on all four sides.
- Paper and/or Electronic Version: Authors are required to submit at least 3 copies of the manuscript on paper, and an electronic version via an email attachment using Microsoft Windows Word software (rtf format) and send it to JEB@iup.edu.
- Cover Page: <u>Important</u> Staple a cover page to the manuscript indicating only the article title (used for anonymous refereeing).
- Second "Title Page", which should not be stapled to the manuscript, should include full authorship information.
- ABSTRACT page should follow the second "Title Page" and should have 100-150 words abstract.
- The manuscript should be free of all spelling, grammar and punctuation errors.
- Inconsistencies: Please be sure that you are consistent in the use of abbreviations, terminology, and reference citations throughout your paper. When you use an abbreviation for the first time, please write it in full within brackets. For example, BEM (Big Emerging Markets).

Tables, Figures and Drawings. All tables, figures, illustrations, etc. should be embedded in the electronic version at the appropriate place within the text of the article. In the paper version, they should be appended to the article at the end.

Alterations. Often, a manuscript may be accepted by the Editor contingent upon satisfactory inclusion of changes mandated by anonymous referees and members of the Editorial Review Board. If the Editor returns your manuscript for such revisions, you are responsible for having the appropriate sections of the paper revised and altered.

Examples of References to Periods:
1. Journal Article: One Author
   Garg, Rajendar K. (1996), "The Influence of positive and negative wording and issue involvement on responses to liker scales in Marketing Research", *Journal of the Market Research Society*, Vol. 38, No. 3, 235-246.

2. Journal Article: Multiple Authors
   Kaynak, Erdner and Vinay Kothari (1984), "Export Behavior of small and medium sized manufacturers: Some policy guidelines for international marketers", *Management International Review*, Vol. 24, No. 2, 61-69.

Reprints. Upon publication, the senior author will receive one complimentary copy of the *Journal of E-Business* in the paper format. It would take approximately 10-12 weeks for the preparation of the reprints. For more copies, the authors would be able to download articles from the electronic version.

Copyright. If your manuscript is accepted for publication, copyright ownership must be officially transferred to the International Academy of E-Business. International Academy of E-Business retains all copyrights over all content published in the *Journal of E-Business*. The Editor's acceptance letter will include a form fully explaining this. This form must be signed by all authors and returned to the author at this time. Failure to return the copyright form in a timely fashion will result in delay of your manuscript in the *Journal*.

Journal of Economic and Administrative Science

ADDRESS FOR SUBMISSION:

Mohamed Yahia El-Bassiouni, Editor
Journal of Economic and Administrative
 Science
UAE University
College of Business & Economics
Department of Statistics
P O Box 17555
Al-Ain,
UAE
Phone: +9713 705.13.86
Fax: +9713 762.43.85
E-Mail: y.bassiouni@uaeu.ac.ae
Web: jeas.cbe.uaeu.ac.ae
Address May Change:

PUBLICATION GUIDELINES:

Manuscript Length: 26-30
Copies Required: Three
Computer Submission: Yes Disk, Email
Format: MS Word
Fees to Review: 0.00 US$

Manuscript Style:
 American Psychological Association

CIRCULATION DATA:

Reader: Academics, Professionals,
 Practitioners
Frequency of Issue: 2 Times/Year
Copies per Issue: Less than 1,000
Sponsor/Publisher: College of Business &
 Economics, UAE University
Subscribe Price: 17.00 US$ Individual
 41.00 US$ Institution
 28.00 US$ UAE Institution

REVIEW INFORMATION:

Type of Review: Blind Review
No. of External Reviewers: 1+
No. of In House Reviewers: 0-1
Acceptance Rate: 11-20%
Time to Review: Over 6 Months
Reviewers Comments: Yes
Invited Articles: 0-5%
Fees to Publish: 0.00 US$

MANUSCRIPT TOPICS:

Accounting Education; Accounting Theory & Practice; Cost Accounting; Econometrics;
Economic Development; Industrial Organization; International Economics & Trade;
International Finance; Management; Marketing; Portfolio & Security Analysis; Public Policy
Economics; Regional Economics

MANUSCRIPT GUIDELINES/COMMENTS:

The *Journal of Economic and Administrative Sciences* (*JEAS*) is a peer reviewed journal
published by the College of Business and Economics at the United Arab Emirates University,
for the purpose of promoting scholarly research in the areas of business administration,
accounting, economics, quantitative methods, and related subjects.

The *JEAS* addresses readers interested in both analytical and empirical research studies. The
audience consists of academicians, professionals, and/or practitioners who are concerned with
the latest developments in economic and administrative sciences.

In order to fulfill such goals, the *JEAS* adopts the following policy:

- Papers submitted for publication in the *JEAS*, should be original, innovative and addressing key areas of economic and administrative sciences.
- In order for a research paper to be accepted for publication, it should deal with an issue that represents a matter of paramount interest to the *JEAS* readership. In particular, priorities are given to applied research related to the UAE, Gulf, and Arab countries. Accepted papers should also be well designed and properly presented.
- The *JEAS* also publishes contributions related to business education aiming at enhancing methods of instruction and improving the quality and standards of business education.

Manuscripts submitted to the *JEAS* are first screened by the editorial board. Those that are considered inappropriate are returned to the submitting author. Manuscripts that pass the initial screening are sent to two referees for blind review. Usually, both referees are external reviewers. This is especially true for manuscripts submitted from the UAE. However, at times, one in-house reviewer might be selected for manuscripts submitted from outside the UAE. In case of a split decision, the manuscript is sent to a third referee.

MANUSCRIPT GUIDELINES

- Manuscripts submitted for publication in the *JEAS* should neither be under concurrent consideration by another journal, nor have been published elsewhere.
- Manuscripts should not disclose the author/authors' identity, in order to insure the integrity of the refereeing process.
- Manuscripts may be submitted either in Arabic or English.
- Manuscripts should follow the style of the American Psychological Association.
- Original manuscripts, along with two copies, should be submitted, typewritten, double-spaced on A4-size paper, on one side only. Copies of instruments used in field surveys and experiments, e.g., questionnaires, interview plans, etc., should be submitted as well. Where possible, the text must be submitted on a computer diskette or CD or via e-mail in Microsoft Word for Windows.
- Manuscripts should be as concise as possible and should not exceed 30 pages including tables, graphs, footnotes, references and appendices.
- All pages should be serially numbered, including tables, graphs, references and appendices.
- Abstracts in both Arabic and English should be provided on separate pages. Such abstracts should not exceed 150 words and should contain a summary of the research problem, methodology and key results.
- Manuscripts should include a cover page indicating: title of the paper; author/authors' full name, title and affiliation; corresponding author's mailing address, phone & fax numbers and e-mail address; acknowledgments (if any).
- Manuscripts should be mailed to Editor, address above. Alternatively, the *JEAS* can be contacted via the e-mail address jeas@uaeu.ac.ae.

Tables and Figures
Each table and figure should appear on a separate page and bear an Arabic number and a title. Each table and figure should be referenced in the text. The author should indicate on the manuscript where each table or figure should be inserted in the text.

Literature Citations
The name of the author and the year of publication of work cited should appear in parentheses in the body of the text, e.g., (Ashton, 1982); (Demski and Feltham, 1978); (Kanodia et al, 1989). All direct quotes must have a page citation. If the name of the author is mentioned in the text, it need not be repeated in the citation, e.g., Bazeman (1994: p.1220).

Reference List
All references cited in the text (and only those cited in the text) should appear in the list of references. The references should be alphabetized by author. Multiple works by the same author(s) should be listed in the chronological order of publication. Titles of journals should not be abbreviated.

Footnotes
Textual footnotes should be used for digressions whose inclusion in the text might disrupt the continuity. Footnotes should be numbered consecutively throughout the manuscript and follow the text of the manuscript. Footnotes should be avoided as much as possible.

Journal of Economic Behavior and Organization

ADDRESS FOR SUBMISSION:

J. Barkley Rosser, Jr., Editor
Journal of Economic Behavior and
    Organization
James Madison University
MSC 5505
1598 South Main Street
Harrisonburg, VA 22807
USA
Phone: 540-568-6821
Fax: 540-801-8650
E-Mail: jebo@jmu.edu
Web: www.elsevier.com
Address May Change:

PUBLICATION GUIDELINES:

Manuscript Length: 25 Average
Copies Required: Three
Computer Submission: Yes - Disk
Format: MS-DOS
Fees to Review: 35.00 US$

Manuscript Style:
    See Manuscript Guidelines

CIRCULATION DATA:

Reader: Academics, Business Researchers,
    Economists, Social Scientists
Frequency of Issue: Monthly
Copies per Issue: Less than 1,000
Sponsor/Publisher: Elsevier Science
    Publishing Co.
Subscribe Price: 96.00 US$ Individual
    1607.00 US$ Institution
    92.00 Euro Indv., 1,437 Euro Inst.

REVIEW INFORMATION:

Type of Review: Editorial Review
No. of External Reviewers: 2
No. of In House Reviewers: No Reply
Acceptance Rate: No Reply
Time to Review: 2 - 3 Months
Reviewers Comments: Yes
Invited Articles: 0-5%
Fees to Publish: 0.00 US$

MANUSCRIPT TOPICS:
Behavioral Economics; Corporate Finance; Econometrics; Economic Development;
Evolutionary Economics; Financial Institutions & Markets; Industrial Organization;
International Finance; Macro Economics; Micro Economics; Public Policy Economics

MANUSCRIPT GUIDELINES/COMMENTS:

Aims and Scope
The *Journal of Economic Behavior and Organization* is devoted to theoretical and empirical
research concerning economic decision, organization and behavior. Its specific purpose is to
foster an improved understanding of how human cognitive, computational and informational
characteristics influence the working of economic organizations and market economies.
Research with this purpose that explores the interrelations of economics with other disciplines
such as biology, psychology and law is particularly welcome. The *Journal* is eclectic as to
research method; systematic observation and careful description, experimental and ethological
study, simulation modeling and mathematical analysis are all within its purview. Empirical
work that probes close to the core of the issues in theoretical dispute is encouraged.

Instructions to Authors

1 Papers must be in English.

2. Papers for publication should be sent in triplicate to Professor Richard D. Day, Editor

Unsolicited manuscripts must be accompanied by a submission fee of US$35. Payment can be made by VISA, American Express, MasterCard or check. For credit card payments, please specify which card, card number, and expiration date. Checks should be made payable to the *Journal of Economic Behavior and Organization*.

Submission of a paper will be held to imply that it contains original unpublished work and is not being submitted for publication elsewhere. The Editor does not accept responsibility for damage or loss of papers submitted. Upon acceptance of an article, author(s) will be asked to transfer copyright of the article to the publisher. This transfer will ensure the widest possible dissemination of information.

3. **Submission of accepted papers** as electronic manuscripts, i.e., on disk with accompanying manuscript, is encouraged. Electronic manuscripts have the advantage that there is no need for rekeying of text, thereby avoiding the possibility of introducing errors and resulting in reliable and fast delivery of proofs. The preferred storage medium is a 5.25 or 3.5-inch disk in MS-DOS format, although other systems are welcome, e.g., Macintosh (in this case, save your file in the usual manner; do not use the option 'save in MS-DOS format'). Do not submit your original paper as electronic manuscript but hold on to the disk until asked for this by the Editor (in case your paper is accepted without revisions). Do submit the accepted version of your paper as electronic manuscript. Make absolutely sure that the file on the disk and the printout are identical. Please use a new correctly formatted disk and label this with your name; also specify the software and hardware used as well as the title of the file to be processed. Do not convert the file to plain ASCII. Ensure that the letter "l" and digit "1", and also the letter "O" and digit "0" are used properly, and format your article (tabs, indents, etc.) consistently. Characters not available on your word processor (Greek letters, mathematical symbols, etc.) should not be left open, but indicated by a unique code (e.g., gralpha, <alpha>, @, etc., for the Greek letter α). Such codes should be used consistently throughout the entire text; a list of codes used should accompany the electronic manuscript. Do not allow your word processor to introduce word breaks and do not use a justified layout. Please adhere strictly to the general instructions below on style, arrangement and, in particular, the reference style of the *Journal*.

Manuscripts should be typewritten on one side of the paper only, double-spaced with wide margins. All pages should be numbered consecutively. Titles and subtitles should be short. References, tables and legends for figures should be typed on separate pages. The legends and titles on tables and figures must be sufficiently descriptive such that they are understandable without reference to the text. The dimensions of figure axes and the body of tables must be clearly labeled in English.

4. **A short note** on the author's current position, affiliation, and other relevant biographical information, including publications, should also be provided.

5. **The first page** of the manuscript should contain the following information: (i) the title; (ii) the name(s) and institutional affiliation(s) of the author(s); (iii) an abstract of not more than 100 words; (iv) at least one classification code according to the Classification System used by the *Journal of Economic Literature*, in addition, up to five key words should be supplied. A footnote on the same sheet should give the name and present address of the author to whom proofs and reprint order form should be addressed.

6. **Acknowledgements** and information on grants received can be given before the References or in a first footnote, which should not be included in the consecutive numbering of footnotes.

7. **Important formulae** (displayed) should be numbered consecutively throughout the manuscript as (1), (2), etc., on the right-hand side of the page. Where the derivation of formulae has been abbreviated, it is of great help to referees if the full derivation can be presented on a separate sheet (not to be published).

8. **Footnotes** should be kept to a minimum and be numbered consecutively throughout the text with superscripts Arabic numerals.

9. **The References** should include only the most relevant papers. In the text, references to publications should appear as follows: "Smith (1969) reported that..." or "This problem has been a subject in literature before [e.g., Smith (1969, p. 102)]". The author should make sure that there is a strict "one-to-one correspondence" between the names (years) in the text and those on the list. At the end of the manuscript (after any appendices), the complete references should be listed as:

For monographs
Tobin, James, 1971, Essays in economics, vol. 1, Macroeconomics (North-Holland, Amsterdam).
For contributions to collective works
Glejser, Herbert, 1970, Predictive World models, In: Colette Duprez and Bienne Sadi Kirschen, eds., Megistos, A world income and trade model for 1975 North-Holland, Amsterdam, 3-16.
For periodicals
Goldfeld, Stephen M. and Richard E. Quandt, 1973, A Markov model for switching regressions, Journal of Econometrics, 1, 3-15.

10. **Illustrations** should be provided in triplicate (1 original drawn in black ink on white paper plus 2 photocopies). Care should be taken that lettering and symbols are of a comparable size. The drawings should not be inserted in the text and should be marked on the back with figure numbers, title of paper, and name of author. All graphs and diagrams should be referred to as figures and should be numbered consecutively in the text in Arabic numerals. Graph paper should be ruled in blue and any grid lines to be shown should be inked black. Illustrations of insufficient quality, which have to be redrawn by the publisher, will be charged to the author. Further information is available on the website: http://authors.elsevier.com or http://elsevier/homepage/sae/econworld/econbase/jebo/frame.htm.

11. All unessential tables should be eliminated from the manuscript. Tables should be numbered consecutively in the text in Arabic numerals and typed on separate sheets.

Important Notes for Authors

On Referencing

- On first citation, use the date but not on subsequent citations to the same piece unless there are two by the same author(s) in the same year.
- Avoid gratuitous referencing. Cite only the directly relevant references, explaining, of course, how your own work is related. When there are many possible references, the seminal or classic one and perhaps one or two of the most recent important examples should be included.
- Do not cite references for self-evident observations or generally known facts, e.g., the formation of weather is turbulent (Lorenz 1962, 1963).
- Try to phrase referencing where possible like this: "Lorenz (1963) showed that certain salient features of weather formations, e.g., turbulence, could be represented mathematically." Not this: "Weather turbulence can be modeled mathematically (Lorenz 1963)."

Prose Style

Strive for a clear, economical or "crisp" style. Avoid repetition. Abstracts should be cogent summaries not exceeding 100 words. They should contain details. Introductions should briefly describe the purpose, motivation, and approach of the paper and explain its relation directly to the relevant literature. Get straight to the point. If a substantial discussion of the literature and issues involved is justified, it should be in a separate section. Also, please minimize the repeated use of acronyms.

Mathematical Style

Define variables and equations as you go along. Don't provide a long list of equations followed by a long list of variable definitions, although it is okay to define the parameters of a single equation after it has been presented. When only a little calculus or algebra (such as the marginal conditions for a maximum or minimum) is required, don't go through all the obvious elementary steps. In more advanced proofs try to find an intuitive argument to help the reader through the formalities.

On Gender Non-Specific Usage

The English language uses the masculine for gender non-specific settings. Some authors are now substituting the feminine for the masculine in places where the person is not gender specific. While this is perhaps "politically correct," it is in fact the substitution for an arguably offensive linguistic convention of another equally arbitrary linguistic convention which is arguably just as offensive. This is not progress in improving equality of opportunity among the sexes. If you wish to change the age old convention of gender, then please do so by using "he or she," "the agent," "the person," "Humanity" for "Man," etc. This is awkward, of course, but not silly or discriminatory to anyone. Out of respect for custom and for the great writers, female and male who have shaped the language, the masculine will still be accepted as the gender non-specific convention until specific gender non-specific words are coined. An invention of your own would be considered.

Proofs

If your corrected proofs are not received within 2 weeks, proofing will be done by the publisher or the paper will be rescheduled for a later date.

682

Any manuscript, which does not conform to the above instructions, may be returned for the necessary revision before publication. Page proofs will be sent to the authors. Corrections other than printer's errors may be charged to the author. 25 reprints of each paper are supplied free; additional reprints are available at cost if they are ordered when the proof is returned.

All questions arising after acceptance of the manuscript, especially those relating to proofs, should be directed to Elsevier Science Ireland Ltd., Elsevier House, Brookvale Plaza, East Park, Shannon, Co. Clare, Ireland. Tel. +35 3 61-709-677. Fax +35 3 61-709-114.

Journal of Economic Development

ADDRESS FOR SUBMISSION:

Kookshin Ahn, Editor
Journal of Economic Development
Chung-Ang University
Department of Economics
Heukseok-Dong, Dongjak-Ku
Seoul,
Korea
Phone: 82 2 820 5497
Fax: 82 2 812 9718
E-Mail: ksahn@cau.ac.kr
Web: http://jed.econ.cau.ac.kr
Address May Change:

PUBLICATION GUIDELINES:

Manuscript Length: 16-20
Copies Required: Three
Computer Submission: Yes
Format: MS Word
Fees to Review: 0.00 US$

Manuscript Style:
    See Manuscript Guidelines

CIRCULATION DATA:

Reader: Academics
Frequency of Issue: 2 Times/Year
Copies per Issue: 500-1,000
Sponsor/Publisher: Economic Research
    Institute of Chung-Ang University
Subscribe Price: 26.00 US$ Individual
    46.00 US$ Institution

REVIEW INFORMATION:

Type of Review: Blind Review
No. of External Reviewers: 2
No. of In House Reviewers: 1
Acceptance Rate: 21-30%
Time to Review: 2 - 3 Months
Reviewers Comments: Yes
Invited Articles: 0%
Fees to Publish: 0.00 US$

MANUSCRIPT TOPICS:
Economic Development; Economic Growth; International Trade & Finance

MANUSCRIPT GUIDELINES/COMMENTS:

Journal of Economic Development, JED, is published biannually (June and December) by the Economic Research Institute of Chung-Ang University.

The purpose of *JED* is to support and encourage research in economic development, economic growth, international trade and finance, and share the economic analysis of the experience of economic development from all the countries of the world. Both theoretical and empirical manuscripts are equally welcomed.

JED welcomes unsolicited manuscripts, which will be considered for publication by the Editorial Board. The manuscript should be sent to the Editor.

Preparation and Submission of Manuscripts

1. Authors are strongly advised to consult one or more recent issues of the *Journal of Economic Development* before submitting manuscripts for publication.

2. Manuscripts should be written in English.

3. Unsolicited contribution should be accompanied by a statement that they have not already been published, and that if accepted for publication in the *JED* they will not be submitted for publication elsewhere without the agreement of the editor.

4. Articles are accepted for publication on the understanding that they are subject to editorial revision and that the right of publication in any form or language is reserved by the *JED*.

5. Send a clean original (ribbon) copy and two photocopies along with a diskette with the file in Micro-Soft Word format. The preferred maximum length of manuscripts is 25 typed pages.

6. The entire manuscripts including quotations and notes should be typed with double spaced, and are preferred not more than 25 pages in length.

7. An abstract of not more than 100 words should be included in all manuscripts submitted. Both JEL classification and key words should be provided.

8. All notes, except those included in tables and diagrams, should be numbered consecutively throughout the article. Tables and diagrams should be numbered consecutively. Tables and diagram should bear a descriptive title.

9. References should contain the following information as a minimum:
   a) For books, author's name and initials (in that order), title of book (*underlined*), place of publication, publisher, date of publication (in parentheses) and page (p.) or pages (pp.) cited;
   b) For articles, author's name and initials, title of article in inverted commas (quotes), date of the issues, title of periodical (*underlined*), place of publication, and page (p.) or pages (pp.) cited. The titles of articles, books and periodicals should always be given in the original language.

10. Authors are reminded that they must observe the usual rules and practices regarding the reproduction of copyright material in their articles.

For rights of reproduction or translation of articles application should be made to the Editor.

Request to reproduce materials published in the *JED* should be addressed to:
   The Editor
   Journal of Economic Development
   The Economic Research Institute
   Chung-Ang University
   Seoul, 156-756, Korea.

Journal of Economic Education

ADDRESS FOR SUBMISSION:

William Becker, Editor
Journal of Economic Education
Indiana University
Department of Economics
Wylie Hall, 105
Bloomington, IN 47405
USA
Phone: 812-855-3577
Fax: 812-855-3736
E-Mail: becker@indiana.edu
Web:
Address May Change:

PUBLICATION GUIDELINES:

Manuscript Length: 16-20
Copies Required: Five
Computer Submission: No
Format: N/A
Fees to Review: 0.00 US$

Manuscript Style:
    Chicago Manual of Style

CIRCULATION DATA:

Reader: Academics
Frequency of Issue: Quarterly
Copies per Issue: 1,001 - 2,000
Sponsor/Publisher: Nat'l Council on Econ
    Educ, Amer Econ Assn Committee on
    Econ Educ/Heldref Publications
Subscribe Price: 41.00 US$ Individual
    82.00 US$ Institution

REVIEW INFORMATION:

Type of Review: Blind Review
No. of External Reviewers: 2
No. of In House Reviewers: 2
Acceptance Rate: 21-30%
Time to Review: 4 - 6 Months
Reviewers Comments: Yes
Invited Articles: 6-10%
Fees to Publish: 0.00 US$

MANUSCRIPT TOPICS:
Accounting Information Systems; Econometrics; Economic Education; Economic History;
Public Policy Economics

MANUSCRIPT GUIDELINES/COMMENTS:

Manuscripts for the *Journal of Economic Education* should fall within one of the following
categories:

- **Research in Economic Education**. Original theoretical and empirical studies dealing
  with the analysis and evaluation of teaching methods, learning attitudes and interests,
  materials, or processes.
- **Economic Content**. Substantive issues, new ideas, and research findings in economics
  that may influence or can be used in the teaching of economics.
- **Economic Instruction**. Innovations in pedagogy, hardware, materials, and methods for
  treating traditional and newer subject matter. Issues involving the way economics is taught
  are emphasized.

- **Professional Information**. Reports on the status of the profession (the labor market for economists, status of women and minorities, and developments in the economics major); reviews of books and materials; announcements of conferences and professional development and research grant opportunities; and related topics of interest to the profession.

Send five copies of all manuscripts, including a 125-word abstract, to the Editor. Receipt of manuscripts will be acknowledged, and authors will be notified of editorial decisions.

Text

Manuscripts submitted for publication typically will be evaluated by two or more reviewers. Pertinent comments will be brought to the author's attention, but manuscripts will not be returned or stored.

Submissions should be clear and concise. Authors should keep in mind that our readers are economists and educators with diverse preparation in economics, statistics, and educational theory.

- State the problem or subject to be discussed, indicating its nature and significance
- Mention previous research concisely. The author's own methodology, assumptions, statistics, and validity of measures should be clearly indicated.
- Include a precise statement of the findings and conclusions. Conflicting views, if any, should be mentioned.
- Do not repeat in the text information contained in the tables; merely refer to the table in order to prove or interpret a statement.
- Use figures only if they present something that cannot be conveyed easily by the written word. Legends should be short. Those that are longer than two lines should be rewritten as part of the text.
- Give a brief summary interpretation of the article at the end. (For shorter articles, this may not be necessary.)
- Be consistent in the usage of capitals, italicized words and letters, hyphenated words, and quotation marks.
- Check all references, quotations, and formulas carefully. Make sure that thee article faithfully represents what you want to say. Look at it with the eye of an "outsider" and see if it still makes sense. In most disciplines, it is extremely easy to make "jumps" in reasoning that cannot be followed by the interested layman. Also bear in mind the diversity of the readers' preparation in economics, statistics, and educational theory, as well as their varied backgrounds. Your audience is composed of economists, professors of education, social studies supervisors, and twelfth grade teachers.

Manuscript Requirements

All Copy. Text, explanatory notes, and references should be typed double-spaced on 8½" x 11" white paper.

Title Page. To retain anonymity in the review process, show the author's name only on this title page. Also include the author's complete mailing address, telephone and fax numbers, and a short statement noting professional title and institutional affiliation.

Tables and Figures. Submit on separate pages and supply short titles for each. Repeat in the text only information from the tables that interprets a statement. Use figures only if they present concepts that cannot be conveyed easily in words. Upon acceptance of a manuscript for publication, the author will be asked to submit camera-ready artwork. Printing specifications will be supplied at that time.

Mathematical Symbols and Equations. Present clearly. Distinguish numbers from letters (one and the letter l; zero from the letter o). Identify all vectors and Greek letters; align sub and superscripts.

Notes and References. Follow Style B of *Manual Of Style*, 13th ed., University of Chicago Press 1982. Number notes sequentially and list at the end of the text. For text citations, use the author/date style (Smith 1980). Include a page number for quotations. List full citations, alphabetically by author, in the references and include year of publication, title, location, and publisher or volume, issue, and page numbers. See examples:

Johnson, J. 1972. Econometric methods. ed. St. Louis, MO: McGraw-Hill.

Samuelson, P.A. 1954. The pure theory of public expenditures and taxation. In Public economics, ed. J. Margolis and H. Guitton. New York: St. Martin's.

Soper, J.C., and W.B. Walstad. 1983. On measuring economic attitudes. Journal of Economic Education 14 (Fall): 4-17.

Artwork Requirements

Printing specifications for camera-ready figures for the *Journal Of Economic Education.*

1. Figures should be no larger than 7¼" (44 picas) high and 4¼" (25 picas) wide.
2. Figures should be vertical if possible.
3. Figures should be done in black and white.
4. All lines and curves should be labeled (as in example below.
5. Each figure should have a short title, which will be typeset at the journal for consistency.
6. Please indicate any screened areas but do not screen.
7. If lines or curves are of different weight, please make that obvious with thicker lines, dotted lines, etc.
8. If you reproduce a figure used in another publication, be sure to obtain permission to publish from the holder of the copyright.

Journal of Economic Growth

ADDRESS FOR SUBMISSION:

Oded Galor, Editor
Journal of Economic Growth
c/o Linda Singer
Kluwer Academic Publishers
Journal Editorial Office
101 Philip Drive
Norwell, MA 02061
USA
Phone: 781-871-6600
Fax: 781-878-0449
E-Mail: Linda.Singer@wkap.com
Web: www.kluweronline.com
Address May Change:

CIRCULATION DATA:

Reader: Academics
Frequency of Issue: Quarterly
Copies per Issue: Less than 1,000
Sponsor/Publisher: Kluwer Academic
 Publishers
Subscribe Price: 71.00 US$ Individual
 483.00 US$ Institution
 75.00 Euro Indv, 482 Euro Institution

PUBLICATION GUIDELINES:

Manuscript Length: Any
Copies Required: Four
Computer Submission: Yes Disk, Email,
 Web
Format: See Manuscript Guidelines
Fees to Review: 50.00 US$

Manuscript Style:
 See Manuscript Guidelines

REVIEW INFORMATION:

Type of Review: Editorial Review
No. of External Reviewers: 2
No. of In House Reviewers: 1
Acceptance Rate: 11-20%
Time to Review: 2 - 3 Months
Reviewers Comments: Yes
Invited Articles: 6-10%
Fees to Publish: 50.00 US$

MANUSCRIPT TOPICS:
Economic Development; International Economics & Trade; Macro Economics

MANUSCRIPT GUIDELINES/COMMENTS:

Four copies of submitted manuscripts accompanied by a US$50 submission fee should be forwarded to the Editor, c/o Linda Singer, address above.

Manuscript Preparation of Accepted Manuscripts
Final versions of accepted manuscripts (including notes, references, tables, and legends) should be typed double-spaced on 8½ x 11" (22 x 29cm) white paper with 1" (2.5cm) margins on all sides. Sections should appear in the following order: title page, abstract, text, notes, references, tables, figure legends, and figures.

- **Title Page**. The title page should include the article title, authors' names and permanent affiliations, and the name, current address, e-mail address and telephone number of the person to whom page proofs and reprints should be sent.

- **Abstract**. The following page should include an abstract of not more than 100 words and a list of two to six keywords. Also include JEL classification number.

- **Text**. The text of the article should begin on a new page. Each heading should be designated by Arabic numerals (1, 2, etc.) and subsection headings should be numbered 1.1, 1.2, etc.

- **Figures, tables** and **displayed equations** should be numbered consecutively throughout the text (1, 2, etc.). Equation numbers should appear flush right in parentheses.

- **Notes**. Acknowledgments and related information should appear in a note designated by an asterisk after the last author's name, and subsequent notes should be numbered consecutively and designated by superscripts (1, 2, etc.) in the text. All notes should be typed double-spaced beginning on a separate page following the text.

- **References** in the text should follow the author-date format (e.g. Brown (1986), Jones (1978a, 1978b), Smith and Johnson (1983). References should be typed double-spaced beginning on a separate page following the notes, according to the following samples (journal and book titles may be underlined rather than italicized). References with up to three authors should include the names of each author; references with four or more authors should cite the first author and add "et al."

Sample References
Becker, G., M. DeGroot, and J. Marschak. (1964). "Measuring Utility by a Single-Response Sequential Method," Behavioral Science 9, 226-232.

Schoemaker, P. (1980). Experiments on Decisions Under Risk: The Expected Utility Hypothesis. Boston: Kluwer-Nijhoff Publishing.

Smith, V.K. (1986). "A Conceptual Overview of the Foundations of Benefit-Cost Analysis." In Judith Bentkover, Vincent Covello, and Jeryl Mumpower (eds), Benefits Assessment: The State of the Art. Dordrecht: D. Reidel Publishing Co.

- **Tables** should be titled and typed double-spaced, each on a separate sheet, following the references. Notes to tables should be designated by superscript letters (a, b, etc.) within each table and typed double-spaced on the same page as the table. Use descriptive labels rather than computer acronyms, and explain all abbreviations. When tables are typed on oversized paper, please submit both the original and a reduced copy.

- **Figures** for accepted manuscripts should be submitted in camera-ready form, i.e. clear glossy prints or drawn in India ink on drafting paper or high quality white paper. Lettering in figures should be large enough to be legible after half-size reproduction. Authors should submit one 5 x 7" (13 x 18cm) original and two photocopies of each figure, with authors' names, manuscript title, and figure number on the back of each original and copy (use gummed labels if necessary to avoid damaging originals). Figures should be enclosed in a separate envelope backed by cardboard and without staples or paper clips. Figure legends should be typed double-spaced on a separate sheet following the tables.

Electronic Delivery of Accepted Manuscripts (Optional)

Please send only the electronic version (of ACCEPTED papers) via one of the methods listed below. Note, in the event of minor discrepancies between the electronic version and hard copy, the electronic file will be used as the final version.

Via Electronic Mail

1. Please e-mail electronic version to KAPfiles@wkap.com

2. Recommended formats for sending files via e-mail:
   - Binary files—uuencode or binhex
   - Compressing files—compress, pkzip, or gzip
   - Collecting files—tar

3. The e-mail message should include the author's last name, the name of the journal to which the paper has been accepted, and the type of file (e.g., LaTeX or ASCII).

Via Anonymous FTP

- ftp: ftp.wkap.com
- cd: /incoming/production

Send e-mail to KAPfiles@wkap.com to inform Kluwer electronic version is at this FTP site.

Via Disk

Label a 3.5" floppy disk with the operating system and word processing program along with the authors' names, manuscript title, and name of journal to which the paper has been accepted. Mail disk to Kluwer Academic Publishers, Desktop Department, 101 Philip Drive, Assinippi Park, Norwell, MA 02061 U.S.A.

Any questions about the above procedures please send e-mail to dthelp@wkap.com.

Page Proofs and Reprints

Corrected page proofs must be returned within three days of receipt. Authors will receive 50 free reprints, and may order additional copies when returning the corrected proofs.

Journal of Economic History (The)

ADDRESS FOR SUBMISSION:

Jeremy Atack, Editor
Journal of Economic History (The)
Vanderbilt University
Department of Economics
Station B Box 351819
Nashville, TN 37235
USA
Phone:
Fax:
E-Mail: jeremy.atack@vanderbilt.edu
Web: http://jstor.org
Address May Change:

PUBLICATION GUIDELINES:

Manuscript Length: 35 Page/15,000 Words
Copies Required: Three
Computer Submission: Yes Contact Editor
Format: MS Word, WordPerfect
Fees to Review: 25.00 US$ Non-Members

Manuscript Style:
    See Manuscript Guidelines

CIRCULATION DATA:

Reader: Academics
Frequency of Issue: Quarterly
Copies per Issue: 3,001 - 4,000
Sponsor/Publisher: Economic History Assn.
    /Cambridge University Press
Subscribe Price: 0.00 US$ in EHA Mem
    159.00 US$ Institution - Print+Online
    138.00 US$ Inst. Online or Print Only

REVIEW INFORMATION:

Type of Review: Blind Review
No. of External Reviewers: 2-3
No. of In House Reviewers: 0
Acceptance Rate: 11-20%
Time to Review: 3-4 Months
Reviewers Comments: Yes
Invited Articles: 0-5%
Fees to Publish: 0.00 US$

MANUSCRIPT TOPICS:
Economic History

MANUSCRIPT GUIDELINES/COMMENTS:

Aims and Scope
The *Journal of Economic History* is devoted to the interdisciplinary study of history and economics, and is of interest not only to economic historians but to social and demographic historians as well as economists in general. The journal has broad coverage, in terms of both method and geographic scope. Topics examined include money and banking, trade, manufacturing, technology, transportation, industrial organisation, labour, agriculture, servitude, demography, education, economic growth, and the role of government and regulation. In addition, an extensive review section keeps readers informed about the latest books in economic history and related fields.

Instructions for Contributors
Articles on economic history and related aspects of history or economics will be considered for publication by the Editors on the understanding that the articles have not previously been

published and are not under consideration elsewhere. Papers should indicate the wider significance of detailed original research findings as well as the logic and limitations of specialized techniques of analysis. Comments and shorter notes are also welcome. The Journal does not accept unsolicited book reviews, nor can it honor requests to review particular works. Contributions should be kept within 35 double-spaced pages, inclusive of footnotes, references, figures, and tables—approximately 15,000 words. Three printed copies of each manuscript should be submitted, or a computer file in Word or WordPerfect format may be substituted if compatible with the editors' systems. Prospective contributors may obtain a copy of the Style Sheet for the *Journal* from the Editorial Office. A submission fee, payable to the Economic History Association, of $25.00 or a year's membership (fee schedule below) is required from nonmembers of the Association.

Editorial Office Addresses
For submissions dealing with English-speaking North America: Jeremy Atack, Editor; *Journal of Economic History*; Department of Economics; Station B Box 351819; Vanderbilt Univ, Nashville, TN 37235; jeremy.atack@vanderbilt.edu.

For submissions dealing with all other regions: The Editors; *Journal of Economic History*; Department of Economics; Social Science Centre; University of Western Ontario; London, Ontario N6A 5C2, Canada; charley@uwo.ca.

For style sheets and general inquiries please contact: Susan Isaac, Production Editor, *Journal of Economic History*, Department of Economics, Florida State University, Tallahassee, FL 32306-2180; (850) 644-9130; sisaac@mailer.fsu.edu.

Journal of Economic Integration

ADDRESS FOR SUBMISSION:

Myung-gun Choo
Journal of Economic Integration
Sejong University
Sejong Institution
Center for International Economics
Kunja-Gong
Kwangjin-Ku, Seoul, 143-747
South Korea
Phone: +82-2-34-08-3151
Fax: +82-2-34-08-3338
E-Mail: hhlee@sejong.ac.kr
Web: www.sejong.ac.kr/~cie
Address May Change:

PUBLICATION GUIDELINES:

Manuscript Length: 26-30
Copies Required: Three
Computer Submission: Yes - Disk
Format:
Fees to Review: 0.00 US$

Manuscript Style:
    Chicago Manual of Style

CIRCULATION DATA:

Reader: Academics, Policy Makers
Frequency of Issue: Quarterly
Copies per Issue: 1,001 - 2,000
Sponsor/Publisher: Sejong University
Subscribe Price: 60.00 US$ Individual
    120.00 US$ Institution

REVIEW INFORMATION:

Type of Review: Blind Review
No. of External Reviewers: 3
No. of In House Reviewers: 0
Acceptance Rate: 21-30%
Time to Review: 4 - 6 Months
Reviewers Comments: Yes
Invited Articles: 31-50%
Fees to Publish: 0.00 US$

MANUSCRIPT TOPICS:
International Economic Integration; International Economics & Trade

MANUSCRIPT GUIDELINES/COMMENTS:

All issues and methodology on the economic integration are welcome, only if the paper has clear policy implications on the subject.

1. **Submission**. Manuscripts must be original, unpublished, and must not be considered elsewhere for publication. Four copies of the typescript with a floppy diskette (if available) should be submitted to the editor.

2. **Manuscripts** should be written in English, typed in double spacing, with 3cm margins, on one side of standard paper. The preferred length of manuscripts is maximum 30 typed pages.

3. **The Title Page** should contain the full title, the affiliation and full address of all authors, an abstract of less than 100 words. The name, full postal address, telephone and fax numbers, e-

mail address of the author who will be responsible for correspondence and proofs should be clearly indicated. This page should also contain *Journal of Economic Literature* classification numbers and key words.

4. **Variables and equations** should be written in italics.

5. **Figures and tables** should be on separate sheet, have descriptive titles, and consecutive numbers.

6. **References**—use the Harvard System. When quoted in the text the format is Lee (2000), or Brown and James, 1992), or Paul et al. (1997a). References are listed alphabetically after the text. The author should make sure that there is a strict "one-to-one correspondence" between the names (years) in the text and those on that list. Examples are:

Obstfeld, M. (1996) Models of Currency Crises with Self-fulfilling Features, *European Economic Review*, 40, 1037-48
Grossman, G., Helpman, E. (1995) Technology and Trade, in *Handbook of International Economics* (Ed.) Grossman, G., Rogoff, K., North-Holland, Amsterdam, pp. 1279-1338

For unpublished lectures or symposia, include title of the paper, name of the sponsoring society in full, and date. Journal and book titles must be underlined.

7. **Acknowledgements** can be after the conclusion section.

8. **Copyright**. Upon acceptance of an article by the *Journal*, authors will be asked to transfer copyright of the article to the publisher. The copyright covers the exclusive rights to reproduce and distribute the article, including reprints, photographic reproductions, microfilm or any other reproductions of similar nature, and translations.

Journal of Economic Issues

ADDRESS FOR SUBMISSION:

Glen Atkinson, Editor
Journal of Economic Issues
University of Nevada
Department of Economics
MS 030
Reno, NV 89557-0207
USA
Phone: 775-784-6678
Fax: 775-784-4728
E-Mail: atkinson@unr.nevada.edu
Web: www.orgs.bucknell.edu/afee/jei
Address May Change:

PUBLICATION GUIDELINES:

Manuscript Length: 16-30
Copies Required: Four
Computer Submission: Yes Disk, Email
Format: MS Word, WordPerfect, RTF
Fees to Review: 0.00 US$

Manuscript Style:
 Chicago Manual of Style, Merriam-
 Webster's Collegiate Dictionary

CIRCULATION DATA:

Reader: Academics
Frequency of Issue: Quarterly
Copies per Issue: 1,001 - 2,000
Sponsor/Publisher: Association for
 Evolutionary Economics
Subscribe Price: 45.00 US$
 55.00 US$ Library

REVIEW INFORMATION:

Type of Review: Blind Review
No. of External Reviewers: 2
No. of In House Reviewers: 0
Acceptance Rate: 21-30%
Time to Review: 1 - 2 Months
Reviewers Comments: Yes
Invited Articles: 11-20%
Fees to Publish: 0.00 US$

MANUSCRIPT TOPICS:
Economic History; Evolutionary Economics; Institutional Economics; International
Economics & Trade

MANUSCRIPT GUIDELINES/COMMENTS:

Submission
Send inquiries or manuscripts to Glen Atkinson, *Journal of Economic Issues,* Department of
Economics, Mail Stop 30, University of Nevada, Reno, USA, 89557. Manuscripts can be
attached to e-mail messages sent to atkinson@ unr.nevada.edu.

Please provide address, telephone number, e-mail address (if available), rank, and institutional
affiliation of author(s). Where necessary, designate the author to whom response and inquiries
should be directed. Please notify the editor of any change in address that may occur during the
time it will take to bring an accepted paper to publication. Note any special feature or
circumstance concerning the paper, such as its presentation at a meeting or conference.

We will assume that papers submitted to this journal are not under consideration elsewhere. Authors of accepted papers must agree to transfer copyright to the *JEI*.

The preferred method of submission is electronic, either as an e-mail attachment, on three-and-a-half-inch diskette, or on CD. Electronic submissions must be PC-compatible. Microsoft Word, WordPerfect, ASCII, and Rich Text Format files are acceptable. Tables and figures should be in separate files. They might be scanned, so submit hard copies of them even when you are submitting everything electronically.

If not submitting your manuscript electronically, send four hard copies. Number all pages and double-space all text, including block quotations, endnotes, references, and table headings. Your copyedited manuscript will be returned to you. After you have made the revisions, you will need to submit the revised manuscript in electronic format as described in the previous paragraph.

Style
The *JEI* follows the current editions of *The Chicago Manual of Style* and *Merriam-Webster's Collegiate Dictionary*.

The introductory section does not need a heading. Subsequent sections should be given subtitles; do not use a numbering system for headings.

The *JEI* no longer uses brackets for author/date citations; use parentheses instead. Be sure that all references cited in the text are listed in the references and that all works listed in the references are cited in the text. Do not use *op cit* or *ibid*.

If possible, put note numbers at the ends of sentences, after the punctuation. Do not use your word processor's footnote or endnote feature to code your notes. Instead, insert a number where you want the note and use your font feature to make it superscript. Avoid putting more than one note in a sentence. Instead, use one note number and collect all the notes as individual paragraphs under the same number. Place all the notes between the article and the references.

A first name or two initials must be supplied when each individual is first mentioned in the text or notes.

Mathematical Material, Tables, and Figures
If you use mathematical material, include a sheet clearly identifying all mathematical symbols you have used in the paper. Indicate in a marginal note the general area in the text where such material is to be incorporated. Type mathematical equations on separate lines and number them consecutively at the right margin, with Arabic numerals in parentheses. Use Greek letters only when necessary.

When creating tables and figures, keep in mind that the *JEI* page size is six inches by nine inches with a text area of four and three-quarters inches by seven inches. The minimum font size is eight points. In other words, a table in eight-point type that fills a standard sheet of paper is far too large for our format. Tables and figures with broadside (landscape) orientation and two-page tables may be used if necessary.

Tables and figures should be in separate electronic files. They might be scanned, so submit hard copies of them even when you are submitting everything electronically.

Questions
Questions about the production process of the *JEI* are welcome. Please contact the production editor, Laurel Busch, at lbusch@unr.edu (preferred) or (775) 784-4792.

A *JEI* manuscript preparation checklist and a list of commonly misused words are available upon request.

Journal of Economic Literature

ADDRESS FOR SUBMISSION:

John McMillan, Editor
Journal of Economic Literature
Stanford University
Graduate School of Business
Stanford, CA 94305-5015
USA
Phone: 650-724-4549
Fax: 650-725-0468
E-Mail: mcmillan_john@gsb.stanford.edu
Web: www.aeaweb.org
Address May Change:

PUBLICATION GUIDELINES:

Manuscript Length: 20+
Copies Required: Two Print or 1 Electronic
Computer Submission: Yes
Format: Any
Fees to Review: 0.00 US$

Manuscript Style:
    See Manuscript Guidelines

CIRCULATION DATA:

Reader: , Economists
Frequency of Issue: Quarterly
Copies per Issue: 25,000
Sponsor/Publisher: American Economic
    Association
Subscribe Price: 0.00 US$ Member

REVIEW INFORMATION:

Type of Review: Blind Review
No. of External Reviewers: 2-3
No. of In House Reviewers: 1
Acceptance Rate: 0-5%
Time to Review: 2 - 3 Months
Reviewers Comments: Yes
Invited Articles: 50% +
Fees to Publish: 0.00 US$

MANUSCRIPT TOPICS:
Accounting Information Systems; Econometrics; Economic History; International Economics
& Trade; International Finance; Public Policy Economics

MANUSCRIPT GUIDELINES/COMMENTS:

Editorship will change in early 2004—see Web site of the American Economic Association
    (www.aeaweb.org)

Editorial Policy
The editorial policy of the *Journal of Economic Literature* is explained by John McMillan,
Editor of *JEL*, in the Editor's Note on this page.

The *Journal of Economic Literature* has switched from using print to using electronic media
to disseminate bibliographic information. See the Editor's Note (March 2000) for further
information.

Editor's Note

The *Journal*'s purpose is to help economists keep up with the ever-increasing volume of economics research. This goal is effected by publishing survey articles and essays, book reviews, and an extensive bibliographic guide to the contents of current economics periodicals.

Survey Articles and Essays

Articles are usually commissioned by the editor, though unsolicited articles are sometimes published. Those interested in writing an article for the journal are requested to begin with an outline of about four pages, describing the contents of the proposed article, stating why the topic is deserving of our readers' attention, and listing the main references to be covered. Send the outline to the editor (see Correspondence).

The outline is sent to referees who are experts in the field, and if they see a promising journal article, the author is then invited to write it. The full article also is refereed. Most of the articles that have appeared in the journal have gone through several rounds of revision before being ready for publication; the *Journal* is not an outlet for authors seeking to get into print quickly.

Writing for the *Journal of Economic Literature*

The journals survey articles and essays seek to certify those lines of research that are significant and durable. The *Journal* aims to give the core areas of economics thorough attention, while being open to an eclectic range of topics that stretch the boundaries of economics. A successful *Journal* article has three features accessible exposition, selective coverage of the relevant literature, and synthesis.

Nontechnical exposition does not entail trivialization. Technicalities are needed in economics research. We do not really understand a new idea, nor know whether it is correct, until it has been rigorously modeled. We cannot do empirical work properly without painstaking attention to the econometrics. But after the modeling has been completed or the regressions run, the essential findings should be expressible in plain English. To quote the biologist Stephen J. Gould, "We must all pledge ourselves to recovering accessible science as an honorable intellectual tradition. The rules are simple: no compromises with conceptual richness; no bypassing of ambiguity or ignorance; removal of jargon, of course, but no dumbing down of ideas."[1] If it is an important idea, it can be put into everyday words.

Prospective journal authors might study D. N. McCloskey's useful guide, *The Writing of Economics*,[2] and heed George Orwell's warnings about poor writing habits in "Politics and the English Language."[3]

Literature coverage, the second ingredient, means addressing work that is both significant and pertinent. A *Journal* article should not only explain what is known about the subject, it should also highlight those questions that are unresolved and that deserve to be the focus of future research. It should be detailed enough that the reader can infer what research methods were used in the surveyed work.

Thoroughness, however, does not preclude discrimination. The reader should be told what work is most important and most convincing. A mere catalogue of who said what, exhaustively summarizing every article ever published in the area, is uninformative. It is better to risk offending people who have written in the field by not mentioning them than to bore the reader. When a field is marked by controversy and disagreement, the author should indicate the sources and substance of the disagreement. It is acceptable, even desirable, that the author's point of view shows through, provided opposing points of view are explained fully and fairly.

The crucial ingredient of a successful journal article, and perhaps the hardest to achieve, is synthesis. An effective synthesis is informative not only to economists outside the field but also to specialists. Ideas complement each other: they are worth more when combined than when separate. Synthesis gives a distinctive, and perhaps heretofore missing, shape to a subject. Synthesis often produces a clear statement of the important unanswered questions. Synthesizing scattered research adds as much value, and requires as much imagination and creativity, as doing the original research.

The need for the *Journal* as a record of the state of economics knowledge is heightened by the technological advances in electronic publishing. As Hal Varian put it, "In the future everything will be published, in the sense of being readily available, but the need for filtering will be even greater than it is now. Thus, more filtering will be done after the material is published." The *Journal*'s survey articles and essays do this filtering.

Much time can be saved by writing from the start in the *Journal*'s style, as described in the Style Guide; note especially the style for references.

Book Reviews
New books in economics are first annotated by the *Journal*'s Pittsburgh editorial office, and then some of these (currently about 160 per year, less than one-tenth of those received from publishers) are selected for review. Please send books for review to the Pittsburgh office.

Books that are well-researched and make original contributions to economics will tend to be those selected for review. Textbooks will not be reviewed. Second or revised editions will not be reviewed unless the revisions of the original edition are substantial. Collections of previously published articles will not be reviewed unless some value is added by bringing the articles together. Edited volumes such as festschrifts and conference volumes will be reviewed only if they are in some way distinctive; an edited volume is more likely to be reviewed if it is covering a single, coherent theme rather than mixing papers on a wide assortment of topics.

Book reviews are commissioned by the associate editor from reviewers who are knowledgeable in the field. Most reviews are short (up to 900 words). A review should be written so as to inform a wide readership of professional economists, explaining what the book is about and enabling a prospective reader to decide whether to read the book.

As a matter of policy, the *Journal* does not publish unsolicited reviews, nor does it accept offers to review specific books. The journal does welcome general expressions of interest from American Economic Association members who would like to review books.

Bibliographic Information
The Journal lists the contents of current periodicals. A complete list of articles published in economics along with some abstracts (currently from about 600 journals) is available electronically on EconLit.

EconLit can be accessed online through libraries that subscribe to the DIALOG, OCLC, OVID, and SilverPlatter services. Many libraries provide web access to *EconLit*. Individual American Economic Association members may subscribe to a low-priced shortened version of *EconLit*, covering the last 15-16 years.

[1]Stephen J. Gould, *Bully for Brontosaurus: Reflections in Natural History*, New York, Norton, 1991, p. 12.
[2]D.N. McCloskey, *The Writing of Economics*, New York, Macmillan, 1987.
[3]George Orwell, "Politics and the English Language," in Inside the Whale and Other Essays, London, Penguin, 1962; also in *The Collected Essays, Journalism and Letters of George Orwell*, Vol IV, New York, Harcourt, Brace, Jovanovich, 1968.
[4]Hal R. Varian, "The AEA's Electronic Publishing Plans: A Progress Report," *Journal of Economic Perspectives* 11, 3, Summer 1997, 95-104, p. 101.

Style Information for Articles
Manuscripts submitted to *JEL* for publication fall into one of three categories: those under initial consideration; those being revised but not yet formally accepted; and those accepted for publication. Please follow the appropriate guidelines listed here.

Manuscripts submitted for initial consideration. Submit three hard copies, double spaced and cleanly printed, with 1.25-inch margins on all sides.

Revised manuscripts submitted for reevaluation. Submit three hard copies, double spaced and cleanly printed, with 1.25-inch margins on all sides.

Accepted manuscripts submitted for publication. Manuscripts should be submitted in two formats: hard copy and computer file on diskette.

Hard Copy. Two copies, double spaced and cleanly printed, with 1.25-inch margins on all sides.

Disk Copy. The electronic version must exactly match the hard copy. Please use standard word processing software to prepare the text, tell us which software you have used, and supply a 3.5-inch disk. We prefer Microsoft Word, but can convert from most formats.

Manuscript Specifics
Abstract. For our CD-ROM and on-line bibliographic information, we require an abstract of no more than 100 words. This should be a separate file on your diskette and a separate page in your manuscript.

Title Page. Include the title of the article, author(s) name(s), and affiliation (s). Acknowledgements should also be on this page and should be the first footnote of the article.

Authors are expected to reveal the source of any financial or research support received in connection with the preparation of their article.

Tables and Figures. Number figures and tables consecutively (Table 1, Table 2, etc.). Do not number them according to the section in which they appear. Please do not insert figures and tables in the text. Instead, in the space immediately after the paragraph in which the figure or table is first referenced, insert a text tag as follows:

[Table 1 here]

Tables cannot be set broadside. Please format them to be set vertically on the journal page.

For the diskette version, please place figures and tables in files separate from the text file. For the hard copy, place the tables, then the figures in consecutive order at the end of the manuscript.

Art Work for Figures. When your article has been accepted, please submit camera-ready copies of your figures both with and without labels (numbers, letters, etc.). Figure legends should appear on a separate piece of paper. All copies should be laser printed on good bond paper. Do not submit photocopies.

Reference Citations. Include the first name of each author when first mentioned, either in text or in footnotes. Each subsequent reference to an author should include only the last name, unless two or more authors have the same last name.

Citations should take the place of footnotes whenever possible. Work them into the text smoothly. For material in quotation marks, include page number references. Try to avoid using e.g, cf, and "see also."

Allan Gibbard (1973) and Mark Satterthwaite (1975) independently asked the question of what happens when the agents studied by Kenneth Arrow in Social Choice and Individual Values (1963) decided ...others refocused attention on resource allocation (Charles Kindleberger 1964a,b; John Cornwall 1977).

Footnotes. Number footnotes in order, corresponding to numbers in the text, and place them at the bottom of the page (rather than as endnotes). Footnotes are not necessary for works cited; use citations instead as shown above.

Reference List. Verify references carefully; they must correspond to the citations in text. List alphabetically by author's last name and then by year. In references lists, only the first author's name is inverted. Please list all authors; avoid using et al. in lieu of authors' names. Include authors' first names unless the first names are not published. See the following examples.

Chapter in an Edited Volume
Alpert, Marc and Howard Raiffa. 1982. "A Progress Report on the Training of Probability Assessors, in Judgment Under Uncertainty: *Heuristics and Biases*. Daniel Kahneman, Paul Slovic, and Amos Tversky, eds. Cambridge: Cambridge U. Press, pp. 7-32.

Article in a Journal
Alston, Richard M.; J.R. Kearl, and Michael B. Vaughan. 1992. "Is There a Consensus Among Economists in the 1990's?" Amer. Econ. Rev. (Papers and Proceedings), 82:2, pp. 158-77.

Book
Atkinson, Anthony and Joseph Stiglitz. 1980. *Lectures in Public Economics*. New York: McGraw Hill.

For coauthored publications, only the first author's name is inverted: last name, first name. Subsequent authors' names are written normally: first name last name.

The year of publication or presentation appears directly after the author(s)' name(s); this applies to all references, whatever their form or forum.

All publication titles are capitalized: books, papers, articles, journals, etc.

Book titles are capitalized in standard fashion and italicized.

Paper/article titles are capitalized and put in quotation marks.

Journal titles are italicized and abbreviated.

Journal volume/issue numbers are written in Roman typeface: 22 :1. Note the colon. (Small caps, parentheses, italic, and bold typeface are not used.)

Journal of Economic Methodology

ADDRESS FOR SUBMISSION:

Matthias Klaes, Managing Editor
Journal of Economic Methodology
University of Stirling
Department of Economics
Stirling, FK9 4LA
UK
Phone: +44 (0)17 86-46-7480
Fax: +44 (0)17 86-46-7469
E-Mail: jem@mklaes.net
Web: www.econmethodology.org
Address May Change:

PUBLICATION GUIDELINES:

Manuscript Length: 26-30
Copies Required: Four
Computer Submission: Yes
Format: MS Word
Fees to Review: 0.00 US$

Manuscript Style:
   Uniform System of Citation (Harvard
   Blue Book)

CIRCULATION DATA:

Reader: Academics
Frequency of Issue: Quarterly
Copies per Issue: Less than 1,000
Sponsor/Publisher: International Network
   for Economic Method/Routledge, Taylor
   & Francis Group
Subscribe Price: 352.00 US$ Institution
   35.00 US$ INEM Membership

REVIEW INFORMATION:

Type of Review: Editorial Review
No. of External Reviewers: 2
No. of In House Reviewers: 2+
Acceptance Rate: 25%
Time to Review: 3 - 6 Months
Reviewers Comments: Yes
Invited Articles: 10%
Fees to Publish: 0.00 US$

MANUSCRIPT TOPICS:
Economic History; Economic Methodology

MANUSCRIPT GUIDELINES/COMMENTS:

Aims and Scope
The *Journal of Economic Methodology*, a leading journal in its field, addresses issues related to:
- The relationship between methodological work and economic practice
- Analysis of the methodological implications of new developments in economics
- The particular nature of economics and the types of methods that can be endorsed within it
- The relevance of ideas from outside economics (including feminism and postmodernism) for economic methodology
- The methodological writings and practice of earlier economists
- The sociology of economics
- The rhetoric of economics
- Peer-reviewed articles form the core of the *Journal*.

It also features mini-symposia on controversial issues. The Book Review section offers substantial reviews of key titles, and a Notes and Information section will enable the subscriber to stay up to date fully informed of international events and developments in the field.

Submission of Manuscripts

Authors should submit four copies of their paper, plus a floppy disk, to Managing Editor. Book reviews should be submitted to Jack Vromen, Department of Philosophy, Erasmus University, Rotterdam, PO Box 1738, 3000 DR Rotterdam, The Netherlands; E-mail vromen@fwb.eur.nl.

It will be assumed that the authors will keep a copy of their paper.

Submission should be in English typed in double spacing (including all notes and references) on one side only of the paper, preferably of A4 size. British or American spelling is acceptable provided usage is consistent.

Submission of a paper to the *Journal* will be taken to imply that it presents original, unpublished work not under consideration for publication elsewhere. By submitting a manuscript, the authors agree that the exclusive rights to reproduce and distribute the article have been given to the Publishers, including reprints, photographic reproductions, microfilm, or any other reproductions of a similar nature, and translations.

Permission to quote from or to reproduce copyright material in their article must be obtained by the authors before submission and acknowledgements given in a section at the end of the paper before the Notes or, in the case of illustrations, in the captions.

An abstract of the paper, of no more than 150 words, should accompany the article. Also please supply six key words suitable for on-line searching purposes.

Articles should not normally exceed 8,000 words in length. If your word-processor is capable of doing a word count, please use it to print this at the end of the text, together with the date of the manuscript.

Notes should be kept to a minimum and placed at the end of the article before the references; footnotes should be avoided.

A brief biographical note about each author should be supplied on a separate sheet. Details should also be given of authors' full postal and e-mail addresses as well as telephone and fax numbers.

If possible, authors are requested to send an electronic version of their article on disk, providing details of the make and model of the computer and the name and version number of the word-processing software used, including whether it is the Mac or PC version. It is important that authors ensure that their typescript is an exact printout of what is on the disk.

706

Illustrations
Tables and figures should not be inserted within the pages of the manuscript but included o separate sheets placed at the end of the article. The desired position for each table and figure should be indicated in the margin of the text.

Tables should be prepared with the minimum use of horizontal rules (usually three are sufficient) and avoiding vertical rules.

It is important to provide clear copy of figures (not photocopies or faxes), which can be reproduced by the printer and do not require redrawing. Photographs should be high-contrast black and white glossy prints.

All captions for figures and plates (including sources and acknowledgements) should be listed on a separate sheet.

References
The Harvard references system, preferred in this journal, uses the name of the author, the date of publication and following quoted material, and the page references, as a key to the full bibliographic details set out in the list of references; e.g. 'human decisions affecting the future...cannot depend on strict mathematical expectations since the basis for making such calculations does not exist' (Keynes 1936: 162-3).

Several authors have noted this trend (Smith 1970; Jones and Cook 1968; Dobbs et al. 1973). [N.B. et al. to be used when there are three or more authors].

The date of publication cited must be the date of the source referred to. When using a republished book, a translation or a modern version of an older edition; however, the date of the original publication may also be given. Where there are two or more works by one author in the same year, these should be distinguished by using 1980a, 1980b, etc.

The reference list should include every work cited in the text. Please ensure that dates, spelling and title used in the text are consistent with those listed in the References.

The content and form of the reference list should conform to the examples below. Please note that page numbers are required for articles; both place of publication and publisher are required for books cited; and, where relevant, translator and date of first publication should ' included. Do not use *et al.* in the reference list—spell out each author's full name or surn and initials.

Book/Multiple Authors
Key, John, Mayer, Colin and Thompson, David (1986) *Privatization and Regulation, (* Clarendon Press.

Article in Edited Volume
Kreile, Michael (1992) 'The political economy of the new Germany', in Paul B. Str: *The New Germany and the New Europe*, Washington DC: Brookings Institution, pp.

Article in Journal
Streeck, W. and Schmitter, P.C. (1991) 'From corporatism to transnational organised interests in the single European market', *Politics and Society*. 19: 133-6/

Edited Text
Smith, Adam (1976) [1776] An Inquiry into the Nature and Causes of the Wealth of Nations, ed. R.H. Campbell, A.S. Skinner and W.B. Todd, Oxford: Oxford University Press.
Translated Text
Jaspers, K. (1983) General Human Resource Management, 7th edn, trans. J. Hoenig and M. Hamilton, Manchester: Manchester University Press.
Article in Newspaper
Barber, L. (1993) 'The towering bureaucracy', *Financial Times*, 21 June.
Unpublished
Zito, A. (1994) 'Epistemic communities in European policy-making', Ph.D. dissertation, Department of Political Science, University of Pittsburgh.

Notes on Style
It would be helpful if contributors were to bear in mind the following points of style when preparing their papers for the *Journal of Economic Methodology*, particularly if they are submitting their articles on disk.

Justification of Text
If you are using a computer or word processor, use unjustified mode. Leave the right margin ragged, and avoid word divisions and hyphens at the ends of lines. Only insert hard returns at the end of paragraphs or headings.

Punctuation
Use a single (not a double) space after a full point, and after commas, colons, semicolons, etc. Do not put a space in front of a question mark, or in front of any other closing quotation mark.

Spelling
Please be consistent in your use of British or American spelling. Use -ize, in preference to -ise, as verbal ending (e.g., realize, specialize, recognize, etc.). Note, however, several words correctly end in -ise (e.g., advertise, enfranchise, exercise, etc.); note also analyse (British spelling), analyze (American).

Initial Capitalization
Please keep capitalization to a minimum. When possible, use lower case for government, church, state, party, volume, etc.; north, south, etc. are only capitalized if used as part of a recognized place name, e.g., Western Australia, South Africa; use lower case for general terms, e.g., eastern France, south-west of Paris.

Full Points
Use full points after abbreviations (p.m., e.g., i.e., etc.) and contractions where the end of the word is cut (p., ed., ch.). Omit the full points in acronyms (HMSO, USA, BBC, NATO, plc), after contractions that end in the last letter of the word (Dr, Mr, St, edn, Ltd) and after metric units (cm, m, km, kg). Note especially ed. eds; vol. vols; no. nos; ch. chs; etc.

Italics
Indicate italics by underlining, in preference to the italic font, and use for titles of books, journals, newspapers, plays, films, long poems, paintings and ships. Extensive use of italic for emphasis should be avoided.

Quotations
Use single quotation marks for quoted material within the text; double quotation marks should only be used for quotes within quotes. Do not use leader dots at the beginning or end of a quotation unless the sense absolutely demands. For ellipsis within a quotation use three leader dots for a mid-sentence break, four if the break is followed by a new sentence. Quotations of over forty words should be extracted and indented and no quotation marks used.

Numerals
In general spell out numbers under 100; but use numerals for measurements (e.g., 12 km) and ages (e.g., 10 years old). Insert a comma for both thousands and tens of thousands (e.g., 1,000 and 20,000). Always use the minimum number of figures in page numbers, dates, etc.; e.g., 22-4, 105-6, 1968-9; but use 112-13, 1914-18, etc. for 'teen numbers. Use the percentage sign only in figures and tables; spell out 'per cent' in the text using a numeral for the number (e.g., 84 per cent).

Dates
Set out as follows: 8 July 1990 (no comma), on 8 July, or on the 8th; 1990s (not spelt out, no apostrophe); nineteenth century (not 19th century) and insert hyphen when used adjectivally (e.g., nineteenth-century art).

En Rules
Since there is no en rule on a standard keyboard, use a double hyphen for en rules; use these to link number spans (e.g., 24--8); to connect two items linked in a political context (e.g., 'Labour--Liberal alliance', 'Rome--Berlin axis') and to link the names of joint authors (e.g., Temple--Hardcastle project).

Proofs
Authors are expected to correct proofs quickly and any alteration to the original text is strongly discouraged. Authors should correct typesetters' errors in red; minimal alterations of their own should be in black.

Offprints
Twenty-five offprints and a copy of the *Journal* will be supplied free of charge to main contributors; offprints must be shared in the case of joint authorship. See Web site for more details.

Journal of Economic Perspectives

ADDRESS FOR SUBMISSION:

Timothy Taylor, Managing Editor
Journal of Economic Perspectives
Macalester College
1600 Grand Avenue
St. Paul, MN 55105
USA
Phone: 651-696-6822
Fax: 651-696-6825
E-Mail: jep@macalester.edu
Web: www.aeaweb.org
Address May Change:

PUBLICATION GUIDELINES:

Manuscript Length: No Reply
Copies Required: Four
Computer Submission: Yes Email, Disk
Format: MS Word, WordPerfect
Fees to Review: 0.00 US$

Manuscript Style:
    Chicago Manual of Style, Webster's 9th
    New Collegiate Dictionary

CIRCULATION DATA:

Reader: Academics, Business Persons
Frequency of Issue: Quarterly
Copies per Issue: More than 25,000
Sponsor/Publisher: American Economic
    Association
Subscribe Price:
    See Web Site

REVIEW INFORMATION:

Type of Review: No Reply
No. of External Reviewers: 0
No. of In House Reviewers: 3
Acceptance Rate: No Reply
Time to Review: No Reply
Reviewers Comments: No Reply
Invited Articles: 50% +
Fees to Publish: 0.00 US$

MANUSCRIPT TOPICS:

Econometrics; Economic History; International Economics & Trade; International Finance;
Public Policy Economics

MANUSCRIPT GUIDELINES/COMMENTS:

Editorial Policy

Policy on Data Availability. It is the policy of the *Journal of Economic Perspectives* to publish papers only if the data used in the analysis are clearly and precisely documented and are readily available to any researcher for purposes of replication. Details of the computations sufficient to permit replication must be provided. The Editor should be notified at the time of submission if the data used in a paper are proprietary, or if, for some other reason, the above requirements cannot be met.

Policy on Disclosure. Authors of articles appearing the *JEP* are expected to disclose any potential conflicts of interest that may arise from their consulting activities, financial interests, or other non-academic activities.

Submission Policy. Articles appearing in the *Journal* are normally solicited by the editors and associate editors. Proposals for topics and authors should be directed to the *Journal* editorial office. See Submission Guidelines for complete submission guidelines for authors.

SUBMISSION GUIDELINES
Philosophy and Style

The *Journal of Economic Perspectives* attempts to fill part of the gap between refereed economics research journals and the popular press, while falling considerably closer to the former than the latter. These notes should help authors to understand the aims and procedures of the *Journal*. There is considerably more here than the typical admonitions to watch your spelling and punctuation, so please take a couple of minutes to read through.

Many articles in economics journals are addressed to the author's peers in a subspecialty; thus, they can use tools and terminology of that specialty and presume that readers know the context and general direction of the inquiry. By contrast, this *Journal* is aimed at all economists, including those not conversant with recent work in the subspecialty of the author, including those who apply their economics in teaching undergraduates or work outside academia, and including those with rusty technical tools. The goal is to have articles that can be read by 90 percent or more of the AEA membership, as opposed to articles that can be figured out given enough time and energy. Articles should be as complex as they need to be, but not more so. Moreover, the necessary complexity should be explained in terms appropriate to an audience that can be presumed to have a specialized knowledge of economics generally, but not of the author's methods or previous work.

The focus of articles in the *Journal of Economic Perspectives* should be on understanding the central economic ideas of a dispute, what is fundamentally at issue, why a particular question is important, what the latest advances are and what questions remain to be examined. In every case, articles should argue for the author's point of view, explain how recent theoretical or empirical work has affected that view, and lay out the points of departure for other views. The focus is not to instruct in a textbook or classroom sense, although we hope and intend that many of the articles will be useful supplements for instructors. The focus is not to survey thoroughly the relevant literature in a field (the *Journal of Economic Literature* does that), although articles may often serve as an entry to further reading.

We hope that most articles will offer a kind of intellectual arbitrage that will be useful for every economist. For some, it will be a look into the insights and issues in a specialty or discipline in which they do not specialize. For specialists, the articles will lead to thoughts about the questions underlying their research, which directions have been most productive, and what the key questions are. Since most of us are sometimes specialist, sometimes non-specialist, sometimes teacher, sometimes student, good articles will speak to each of us in different ways.

These goals have some stylistic implications. Articles should begin with a few paragraphs introducing the topic and what the paper will say about it, paragraphs that will serve as both lead-in and mini-abstract. Major sections of the paper should also begin with a short explanation.

The *Journal of Economic Perspectives* is intended to be scholarly without relying too heavily on mathematical notation or mathematical insights. Think twice (and perhaps three times) before offering a mathematical derivation of an economic relationship. Deriving the formula may occasionally be appropriate, but it's even more appropriate to explain why that formula makes sense, and to tie it to economic intuition. Relying on intuition about constrained optimization or linear algebra is no substitute for that explanation. In general, the explanation should precede the formula. When symbols are used in a formula, the explanation should rely on the words rather than the symbols.

Don't get us wrong. Mathematics provides a concise and powerful way to make many arguments. But it is also a shorthand that some read better than others, and a shorthand that should be made plausible in non-mathematical terms in every article. Starting off a section by saying "Consider a model in which . . ." or "To illustrate this, see equation 3 . . ." will tend to put the equation cart before the explanation horse. Mathematical explanations are available from a variety of other sources, ranging from textbooks to other published articles; this *Journal* is one of the few places that readers can rely on finding a more verbal style of exposition.

Minimize the number and obtrusiveness of notes and appendixes. This *Journal* is scholarly, but it is not a law review. Consider whether explanatory footnotes should be part of the text; if not, is the thought necessary for the article? Footnotes that serve only as acknowledgement can be incorporated into the text by giving the author's name and year of publication. Anyone who is interested can look up the reference in the listing at the end of the article. If your article includes a (brief!) guide to further reading, it may deserve a place in the text, or it may appear in an explanatory footnote. As a general guideline, try to limit the number of footnotes to an average of one on every other page.

The official rulebooks here in the office will be the *Chicago Manual of Style* and *Webster's Ninth New Collegiate Dictionary*. See our sample of journal reference style for more information.

Procedure and Format

When submitting the first draft of an article to the *Journal*, four copies should be sent to the editorial office: *Journal of Economic Perspectives*, Macalester College, 1600 Grand Ave., St. Paul, Minnesota 55105. In addition, we also need an e-version of the paper, written in WordPerfect or Word. This can be sent either on a diskette or as an e-mail attachment to jep@macalester.edu. Don't forget to keep a backup file.

Please submit papers double-spaced, printing only on one side of the paper. Number the pages, so we don't assume that a missing page is just a jump in syntax. Also number tables and charts, and put them on separate pages. Footnotes and references should be double-spaced at the end of the article. If you have no diagrams, graphs, or tables in your article, consider the possibility of adding one. If you have eight or ten exhibits already attached to your article, consider the possibility that you have gotten carried away with your graphics software.

The article will be read by the editor and co-editors, by the managing editor Timothy Taylor, and in some cases by the appropriate member of the editorial board. Some of the comments will focus on the economic analysis of the argument; the managing editor's comments will be aimed not at changing the argument, but at keeping the style as accessible and convincing as possible, while maintaining the necessary complexity and precision. For many articles, the comments are lengthy and in-depth. Generally, one set of comments and revisions by the author will be adequate, but in some cases the editors will request an additional secondary round of revisions.

Getting the paper in electronic form helps to speed our editing and production process, and will allow the managing editor to make the many small style changes that make a paper more readable. Of course, you will have a chance to check through those changes when the comments are returned to you, but our presumption is that style changes of this sort are often necessary and important to carrying out the functions of the *Journal*.

After you have revised the draft and dealt with comments to your satisfaction, it should be returned to the *Journal* offices at the University of Minnesota. Again, please send an e-version of the revision, along with two paper copies. The article will then be sent to the typesetter, and you will have a chance to check and correct the galleys (but please, not to rewrite them extensively) before they are printed.

Thanks for your interest in the *Journal of Economic Perspectives*. We trust that your contribution will be amply repaid by the opportunity to read the contributions of others, by the chance to clarify and extend your own thoughts, and by our sincere thanks.

Sample of *Journal* Reference Style

Here's a short list of general rules to follow when creating your citation list. This is not an exhaustive list, but we've tried to include as many scenarios as possible.

Please try to verify that all the references in the citation list correspond to citations in the text.

List the references alphabetically by last name; if you use several references by the same author, then sort the references by date in ascending order. If a particular author has two or more publications in the same year, please differentiate between them with the letters a, b, c, and so on.

In a list of two or more authors, please invert the first author's name only. If the reference has more than three authors, please list the primary author's name, followed by "et al." When possible, we prefer that you use full names for authors, rather than using initials for first names.

The publication year should appear right after the author's name.

All publication titles should be capitalized.

Book and journal titles should be written in italics; everything else in the reference should be regular Roman text.

Titles of articles should be listed in parentheses.

When indicating the volume and number of a journal, please use a colon between the two, like this: 12:1. Please do not use italics, bold, parentheses, or any other identifiers.

Here are some examples.
To reference a book
Atkinson, Alan and Joseph Stiglitz. 1980. *Lectures in Public Economics*. New York: McGraw Hill.

To reference a journal article
Elinor Ostrom. 2000. "Collective Action and the Evolution of Social Norms." *Journal of Economic Perspectives*. Summer, 14:3, pp. 137-158.

To reference a chapter in an edited volume
Alpert, Marc and Howard Raiffa. 1982. "A Progress Report on the Training of Probability Assesors," in *Judgment Under Uncertainty: Heuristics and Biases*. Daniel Kahneman, Paul Slovic and Amos Tversky, eds. Cambridge: Cambridge University Press, pp. 7-32.

Journal of Economic Psychology

ADDRESS FOR SUBMISSION:

Simon Kemp/Peter E. Earl, Editors
Journal of Economic Psychology
University of Canterbury
Department of Psychology
Private Bag 4800
Christchurch 1,
New Zealand
Phone: +64 3 364 2968
Fax: +64 3 364 2181
E-Mail: joep@psyc.canterbury.ac.nz
Web: www.elsevier.com
Address May Change:

PUBLICATION GUIDELINES:

Manuscript Length: 16-20
Copies Required: Four
Computer Submission: Yes - Email is faster
Format: MS Word 95, RTF
Fees to Review: 0.00 US$

Manuscript Style:
American Psychological Association

CIRCULATION DATA:

Reader: Academics, Economists, Policy
    Makers, Practioners
Frequency of Issue: 6 Times/Year
Copies per Issue: Less than 1,000
Sponsor/Publisher: Elsevier Science
    Publishing Co.
Subscribe Price: 181.00 US$ Individual
    514.00 US$ Institution
    161.00 Euro Indv, 460 Euro Institution

REVIEW INFORMATION:

Type of Review: Editorial Review
No. of External Reviewers: 2
No. of In House Reviewers: 0
Acceptance Rate: 50%
Time to Review: 4 - 6 Months
Reviewers Comments: Yes
Invited Articles: 6-10%
Fees to Publish: 0.00 US$

MANUSCRIPT TOPICS:
Cost Accounting; Economic Psychology; Marketing Research; Marketing Theory &
Application; Non-Profit Organizations

MANUSCRIPT GUIDELINES/COMMENTS:

Editors
Peter E. Earl, Senior Lecturer of Economics, Department of Economics, University of
Queensland, St. Lucia, Brisbane, Queensland 4072, Australia p.earl@economics.uq.edu.au

Simon Kemp, University of Canterbury, Dept Psychology, Private Bag 4800, Christchurch 1,
New Zealand S.Kemp@psyc.canterbury.ac.nz

Description
The *Journal* aims to present research that will improve understanding of behavioral, especially
socio-psychological, aspects of economic phenomena and processes. The *Journal* seeks to be
a channel for the increased interest in using behavioral science methods for the study of
economic behavior, and so to contribute to better solutions of societal problems, by

stimulating new approaches and new theorizing about economic affairs. Economic psychology as a discipline studies the psychological mechanisms that underlie consumption and other economic behavior. It deals with preferences, choices, decisions, and factors influencing these, as well as the consequences of decisions and choices with respect to the satisfaction of needs. This includes the impact of external economic phenomena upon human behavior and well-being. Studies in economic psychology may relate to different levels of aggregation, from the household and the individual consumer to the macro level of whole nations. Economic behavior in connection with inflation, unemployment, taxation, economic development, as well as consumer information and economic behavior in the market place are thus the major fields of interest.

The *Journal of Economic Psychology* contains: (a) reports of empirical research on economic behavior; (b) assessments of the state of the art in various subfields of economic psychology; (c) articles providing a theoretical perspective or a frame of reference for the study of economic behavior; (d) articles explaining the implications of theoretical developments for practical applications; (e) book reviews; (f) announcements of meetings, conferences and seminars.

Special issues of the *Journal* may be devoted to themes of particular interest. The *Journal* will encourage exchange of information between researchers and practitioners by being a forum for discussion and debate of issues in both theoretical and applied research.

The *Journal* is published under the auspices of the *International Association for Research in Economic Psychology* http://www.ex.ac.uk/IAREP/.

The aim of the Association is to promote interdisciplinary work relating to economic behavior.

Guide for Authors

Submissions will be received either via email or as typed manuscripts. Processing is likely be faster if they are electronically submitted.

Electronic manuscripts. Please send to joep@psyc.canterbury.ac.nz as an attachment. Submissions in MS-word 95 or in Rich Text Format are preferred. The paper may be returned if for some reason it or some part of it is unreadable for either the editors or the reviewers. On final acceptance of the paper we will also require a disk version and a matching double-spaced typed copy.

Typed manuscripts. Please send four copies to The Editors, *Journal of Economic Psychology*, Department of Psychology, University of Canterbury, Christchurch, New Zealand.

Papers should not normally exceed 25 pages of double spaced text (minimum 12 point Times New Roman font). Authors submitting longer articles may expect to be asked to shorten them before thay are put into the refereeing process. All pages should be numbered consecutively. The cover page should contain: (i) the title of the article, (ii) author(s), (iii) complete affiliation(s), and (iv) e-mail address, fax and telephone number of the corresponding author.

An **Abstract** should be provided conforming to the "Outline for Preparation of Abstracts" in Psychological Abstracts (PA), to be printed at the beginning of the paper. French articles should also be accompanied by an Abstract in English. Following the Abstract, one to five **Keywords** (from the American Psychological Association's (APA) "Thesaurus of Psychological Index Terms") and at least one **PsycINFO Classification code** (from the APA's "PsycINFO Classification Categories and Codes") and JEL Classification code (from the *Journal of Economic Literature*) should be added.

Titles and subtitles should be numbered. If the paper is an experimental one, it should be divided, for each experiment, into appropriate headings like: Method, Results, Discussion/Conclusions.

References. In the text of the manuscript, reference to a publication should be made by the name of its author, followed by the year of its publication between parentheses, thus: Katona (1964) found that ..., or .. as studied previously (Katona, 1964). The complete references must be given on a separate list, arranged alphabetically with respect to the first author's name. In the case of a publication brought out jointly by three or more authors, it should be quoted in the text as Smith et al. (1990); in the list, however, all names must be given in full. If an author or a particular group of authors have brought out several publications in one year, the corresponding references should be distinguished in the text as (1990a, 1990b) and in the list as 1990a, 1990b. Examples (please note that journal titles should not be abbreviated):
For Book
Lewis, A., Webley, P., & Furnham, A. (1995). *The new economic mind*. Hemel Hempstead, U.K.: Harvester Wheatsheaf.
For Contributed Volume
Tversky, A. (1996). Rational theory and constructive choice. In K. J. Arrow et al., *The rational foundations of economic behaviour* (pp. 185-197). Basingstoke, U.K.: Macmillan.
For Journal Article
Kemp, S. (1998). Rating the values of government and market supplied goods. *Journal of Economic Psychology, 19* (4), 447-461.

Figures should be large-size originals (each on a separate sheet), drawn in India ink and carefully lettered, or should be produced using professional quality graphics software and a laser - or equivalent printer. They should have an Arabic number and a caption. In the text, figures must be referred to as: see Fig. 1; or Figs. 2 and 3, etc. Their approximate location in the text should be indicated as follows:

<u>Insert Fig. 1 about here</u>

Tables must be typed on separate sheets and should have a short title and an Arabic number. The reference to tables in the main text and the indication of their approximate location is the same as for figures.

Formulae in the text and mathematical symbols. Avoid superposition of symbols (fractions or complicated exponents) which would necessitate a greater space between the lines; when superposition cannot be avoided place the expression on a separate line. Decimal numbers should have a zero before the decimal point, thus: 0.05.

Footnotes. The use of footnotes should be minimized. Footnotes to the text should be numbered consecutively throughout the contribution with superscript Arabic numerals.

Authors are requested to follow the 'Guidelines for Nonsexist Use of Language' as stated in Section 2.12 of the *APA Publication Manual*, 5th ed.

Any manuscripts not conforming to the above specifications or not written in impeccable English or French may be returned for necessary revision before publication.

Proofs. One proof will be sent to the corresponding author. Corrected proofs should be returned within 2 days to the publisher.

Authors' benefits. (1) 25 reprints per contribution free of charge. (2) 30% discount on all Elsevier Science books.

Journal of Economic Studies

ADDRESS FOR SUBMISSION:

Frank H. Stephen, Managing Editor
Journal of Economic Studies
University of Strathclyde
Department of Economics
Strathclyde
Glasgow, G4 0LN
UK
Phone: 0 1415 484326
Fax: 0 1415 525589
E-Mail: f.stephen@strath.ac.uk
Web: www.emeraldinsight.com
Address May Change:

PUBLICATION GUIDELINES:

Manuscript Length: 30+
Copies Required: Three
Computer Submission: No
Format: N/A
Fees to Review: 0.00 US$

Manuscript Style:
    Uniform System of Citation (Harvard
    Blue Book)

CIRCULATION DATA:

Reader: Academics
Frequency of Issue: 6 Times/Year
Copies per Issue: No Reply
Sponsor/Publisher: Emerald Group
    Publishing Ltd.
Subscribe Price: 8945.00 US$
    11332.00 AUS$
    9089.00 Euro /5,681 Pounds +VAT

REVIEW INFORMATION:

Type of Review: Editorial Review
No. of External Reviewers: 2
No. of In House Reviewers: 0
Acceptance Rate: 6-10%
Time to Review: 4 - 6 Months
Reviewers Comments: Yes
Invited Articles: 0-5%
Fees to Publish: 0.00 US$

MANUSCRIPT TOPICS:

Accounting Information Systems; Econometrics; Economic Development; Economic History;
Fiscal Policy; Industrial Organization; International Economics & Trade; International
Finance; Macro Economics; Micro Economics; Monetary Policy; Regional Economics

MANUSCRIPT GUIDELINES/COMMENTS:

About the Journal

The *Journal of Economic Studies* is dedicated to enhancing the link between academic theory
and its application at both micro and macro levels. The editorial team encourages all authors
to present their material in such a way that the implications for economists are fully explored.
Thus, the research community benefits by linking academic activity to end-user concerns.
This journal can extend your understanding of key issues and build a framework for future
research and policy formulation. By highlighting new perspectives on major economic trends,
the *Journal of Economic Studies* helps to find solutions to the problems facing many
economies around the world today.

NOTES FOR CONTRIBUTORS
Copyright
Articles submitted to the journal should be original contributions and should not be under consideration for any other publication at the same time. Authors submitting articles for publication warrant that the work is not an infringement of any existing copyright and will indemnify the publisher against any breach of such warranty. For ease of dissemination and to ensure proper policing of use, papers and contributions become the legal copyright of the publisher unless otherwise agreed. Submissions should be sent to the Editor.

Editorial Objectives
To provide economists with research findings and commentary on international developments in economics. It is our intention to maintain a sound balance between economic theory and application at both the micro and the macro levels. Articles on economic issues between individual nations, emerging and evolving trading blocs will be particularly welcomed. Contributors are encouraged to spell out the practical implications of their work for economists in government and industry.

Reviewing Process
Each paper is reviewed by the editor and, if it is judged suitable for this publication, it is then sent to two referees for double blind peer review. Based on their recommendations, the editor then decides whether the paper should be accepted as is, revised or rejected.

Emerald Literati Editing Service
The Literati Club can recommend the services of a number of freelance copy editors, all themselves experienced authors, to contributors who wish to improve the standard of English in their paper before submission. This is particularly useful for those whose first language is not English. http://www.emeraldinsight.com/literaticlub/editingservice.htm

Manuscript Requirements
Three copies of the manuscript should be submitted in double line spacing with wide margins. All authors should be shown and author's details must be printed on a separate sheet and the author should not be identified anywhere else in the article.

As a guide, articles should be between 3,000 and 6,000 words in length. A title of not more than eight words should be provided. A brief **autobiographical note** should be supplied including full name, affiliation, e-mail address and full international contact details. Authors must supply an **abstract** of 100-150 words. Up to six **keywords** should be included which encapsulate the principal subjects covered by the article.

Where there is a **methodology**, it should be clearly described under a separate heading. **Headings** must be short, clearly defined and not numbered.

Notes and **endnotes** should be used only if absolutely necessary. They should, however, always be used for citing Web sites. They should be identified in the text by consecutive numbers enclosed in square brackets and listed at the end of the article. Please then provide full Web site addresses in the end list.

Figures, charts and **diagrams** should be kept to a minimum. They should be provided both electronically and as good quality originals. They must be black and white with minimum shading and numbered consecutively using Arabic numerals.

Artwork should be either copied or pasted from the origination software into a blank Microsoft Word document, or saved and imported into a blank Microsoft Word document. Artwork created in MS PowerPoint is also acceptable. Artwork may be submitted in the following standard image formats: .eps—PostScript, .pdf—Adobe Acrobat portable document, .ai—Adobe Acrobat portable document, .wmf—Windows Metafile. If it is not possible to supply graphics in the formats listed above, authors should ensure that figures supplied as .tif, .gif, .jpeg, .bmp, .pcx, .pic, .pct are supplied as files of at least 300 dpi and at least 10cm wide.

In the text the position of a figure should be shown by typing on a separate line the words "take in Figure 2". Authors should supply succinct captions.

For photographic images good quality original **photographs** should be submitted. If submitted electronically they should be saved as tif files of at least 300dpi and at least 10cm wide. Their position in the text should be shown by typing on a separate line the words "take in Plate 2".

Tables should be kept to a minimum. They must be numbered consecutively with roman numerals and a brief title. In the text, the position of the table should be shown by typing on a separate line the words "take in Table IV".

Photos and **illustrations** must be supplied as good quality black and white original half tones with captions. Their position should be shown in the text by typing on a separate line the words "take in Plate 2".

References to other publications should be complete and in Harvard style. They should contain full bibliographical details and journal titles should not be abbreviated. For multiple citations in the same year use a, b, c immediately following the year of publication. References should be shown within the text by giving the author's last name followed by a comma and year of publication all in round brackets, e.g. (Fox, 1994). At the end of the article should be a reference list in alphabetical order as follows:

a) *For Books*
Surname, initials and year of publication, title, publisher, place of publication, e.g. Casson, M. (1979), Alternatives to the Multinational Enterprise, Macmillan, London.

b) *For Chapter in Edited Book*
Surname, initials and year, "title", editor's surname, initials, title, publisher, place, pages, e.g. Bessley, M. and Wilson, P. (1984), "Public policy and small firms in Britain", in Levicki, C. (Ed.), Small Business Theory and Policy, Croom Helm, London, pp. 111-26. Please note that the chapter title must be underlined.

c) *For Articles*

Surname, initials, year "title", journal, volume, number, pages, e.g. Fox, S. (1994) "Empowerment as a catalyst for change: an example from the food industry", Supply Chain Management, Vol 2 No 3, pp. 29-33

If there is more than one author list surnames followed by initials. All authors should be shown.

Electronic sources should include the URL of the electronic site at which they may be found, as follows:

Neuman, B.C. (1995), "Security, payment, and privacy for network commerce", IEEE Journal on Selected Areas in Communications, Vol. 13 No.8, October, pp. 1523-31. Available (IEEE SEPTEMBER) http://www.research.att.com/jsac/

Final Submission of the Article

Once accepted for publication, the final version of the manuscript must be provided, accompanied by a 3.5" disk of the same version labelled with: disk format; author name(s); title of article; journal title; file name.

Each article must be accompanied by a completed and signed Journal Article Record Form available from the Editor or on http://www.emeraldinsight.com/literaticlub Authors should note that proofs are not supplied prior to publication.

The manuscript will be considered to be the definitive version of the article. The author must ensure that it is complete, grammatically correct and without spelling or typographical errors.

In preparing the disk, please use one of the following preferred formats: Word, WordPerfect, Rich Text Format or TeX/LaTeX.

Technical assistance is available from Emerald's Literati Club http://www.emeraldinsight.com/literaticlub or by contacting Mike Massey at Emerald mmassey@emeraldinsight.com.

Summary of Submission Requirements
- Good quality hard copy manuscript
- A labelled disk
- A brief professional biography of each author
- An abstract and keywords
- Figures, photos and graphics electronically and as good quality originals
- Harvard style references where appropriate
- A completed Journal Article Record form

Journal of Economic Surveys

ADDRESS FOR SUBMISSION:

Stuart T. Sayer, Editor
Journal of Economic Surveys
University of Edinburgh, UK
William Robertson Building
Department of Economics
George Square
Edinburgh, EH8 9JY
Scotland
Phone: +44 (0) 131-650-8356
Fax: +44 (0) 131-650-4514
E-Mail: s.t.sayer@ed.ac.uk
Web: www.blackwellpublishing.com
Address May Change:

PUBLICATION GUIDELINES:

Manuscript Length: 20-30
Copies Required: Four
Computer Submission: Yes + Hard Copy
Format: MS Word
Fees to Review: 0.00 US$

Manuscript Style:
    See Manuscript Guidelines

CIRCULATION DATA:

Reader: Academics
Frequency of Issue: 5 Times/Year
Copies per Issue: Less than 1,000
Sponsor/Publisher: Blackwell Publishing
Subscribe Price: 86.00 US$ Indv P+PO
    640.00 US$ Inst Print+Premium Online
    80.00 Euro Indv, 337 Pounds Inst

REVIEW INFORMATION:

Type of Review: Blind Review
No. of External Reviewers: 2
No. of In House Reviewers: 1
Acceptance Rate: 11-20%
Time to Review: 2 - 3 Months
Reviewers Comments: No
Invited Articles: 6-10%
Fees to Publish: 0.00 US$

MANUSCRIPT TOPICS:

Econometrics; Economic Development; Economic History; Financial Institutions & Markets; Fiscal Policy; Industrial Organization; International Economics & Trade; International Finance; Macro Economics; Micro Economics; Monetary Policy; Public Policy Economics; Regional Economics

MANUSCRIPT GUIDELINES/COMMENTS:

Additional Editors
Donald A. R. George, University of Edinburgh, UK
Tel 44 (0)131 650-3849, Fax 44 (0)131 650-4514, Email: d.george@ed.ac.uk

Leslie T. Oxley, University of Canterbury, Christchurch, New Zealand
Tel 64 3 364-2134, Fax 64 3 364-2635, Email: les.oxley@canterbury.ac.nz

Colin J. Roberts, University of Edinburgh, UK
Tel 44 (0)131 650-8356, Fax 44 (0)131 650-4514, Email: c.Roberts@ed.ac.uk

Web. http://www.blackwellpublishing.com/journal.asp?ref=0950-0804

As economics becomes increasingly specialized, communication amongst economists becomes even more important. The *Journal of Economic Surveys* seeks to improve the communication of new ideas. It provides a means by which economists can keep abreast of recent developments beyond their immediate specialization. Areas covered include: economics, econometrics, economic history and business economics.

Key Features

- The ideal way for economists to keep abreast of developments across the broad spectrum of economics
- Up to date surveys of economics, econometrics, economic history and business economics
- Comprehensive review articles on books, software and conferences
- Synthesizes and appraises the literature rather than simply summarizing it
- Helps to reverse the present dangerous trend towards the balkanization of economics by providing a means of cross-fertilization of ideas
- Publishes articles that are submitted and refereed rather than commissioned—they provide ideal teaching material for graduates and undergraduates
- An annual special issue covering a particular theme, published jointly as a Blackwell book

Notes for Contributors

Survey articles should:

- Be accessible to the non-specialist reader (i.e. a 'representative' professional economist)
- Provide a creative synthesis of existing research as distinct from a simple catalogue of recent articles.
- Place the topic in perspective in the introductory section, to help motivate the non-specialist reader.

It can be helpful to:

- Set up an encompassing model and treat contributions to the literature as special cases
- Use summary tables to highlight the key differentiating characteristics of different contributions.
- Excessive repetition of material available in textbook form should be avoided. The aim is to survey recent research that has yet to be assimilated in standard texts.

Manuscript Preparation

1. Surveys should normally be 20-30 *Journal* pages in length (10,000-15,000 words), depending on the breadth of the topic. The normal language of the publication will be English.

2. Manuscripts should be typed, double-spaced on A4 paper, with ample left- and right-hand margins. Four copies should be submitted. All pages should be numbered consecutively. A cover page should contain only the title, author's name and affiliation, and the address to which proofs should be sent. This information should not appear elsewhere in the manuscript as the normal practice will be to referee 'double-blind'.

724

3. An abstract should be included. This should not exceed 200 words.

4. To facilitate the production of an annual subject index, please provide a list of key words (not more than six) under which the paper can be indexed.

5. Specialist terms should be explained so as to be understandable by non-specialist, professional economists.

6. Footnotes should be avoided. In particular, references to the literature should be included in the text (see point 8 below). Essential notes should be numbered in the text and grouped together at the end of the article.

7. Acknowledgements should be separated from the notes and should not be numbered. They should appear, under the heading 'Acknowledgements' at the end of the article, under the heading 'Notes'.

8. References to the literature in the main text or notes should use the form: Stiglitz (1997); Stiglitz (1997a). If a reference occurs within parentheses, the author and date should be separated by a comma, for example: (see Stiglitz, 1997; Stiglitz, 1992). Quotations should cite the source page of the quote, for example: (Stiglitz, 1997, p.376).

9. References should be set out in alphabetical order of the author's name in a list at the end of the article. They should be given in a standard form, as in the following examples.

Dasgupta, Partha and Stiglitz, Joseph (1980a) Industrial structure and the nature of innovative activity. *Economic Journal* 90, 266-93
_____ (1980b) Uncertainty, industrial structure, and the speed of R. & D. *Bell Journal of Economics* 2, 1-28
Turnovsky, Stephen J. (1995) Methods of Macroeconomic Dynamics. Cambridge, MA: MIT Press
Stein, J.L. (1976) Inside the monetarist black box. In J.L. Stein (ed.), Monetarism (pp. 183-232). Amsterdam: North-Holland

10. Sections should be numbered consecutively, using Arabic numerals (i.e. 1, 2, 3 etc.). Subsections may be double-numbered (e.g., 1.1, 1.2, etc.) or treble-numbered (e.g., 1.1.1, 1.1.2, etc.) where appropriate.

11. Short quotations (less than c. 60 words) should run on in the text. Longer quotations should be indented, with a line space above and below.

12. Tables and figures should be numbered consecutively (e.g., Table 1, Table 2; Figure 1; Figure 2). References in the text should be by number (e.g., 'See Table 1') rather than ' in the following table'. Figures should be on a separate page from the main text, and where possible, camera-ready copy should be provided by the author.

Special Notes for Mathematical Papers

It is important to distinguish symbols that may be confused, and in particular to distinguish carefully between (a) capitals and small letters, (b) ordinary and bold-faced letters, (c) certain Greek letters and similar Roman letters, (d) subscripts, superscripts and 'ordinary' symbols, and (e) numbers 0 and 1 and letters O and I. Boldfaced symbols should be underlined with a wiggly line in pencil. Mathematical variables should be underlined to prevent ambiguity and indicate that they are to be set in italics. However, certain standard abbreviations are set in roman font, not italic font, e.g., log, lim, exp (but not e), max, min, sup, var, cov, sin, cos.

- Small font setting is technically difficult, expensive and sometimes impossible. To reduce the use of small fonts:
- Avoid elaborate notations involving multiple suffices.
- Use the expression 'exp' for the exponential function when the argument is longer than a single compact group of symbols, e.g., exp $(a+ bt +ct^2)$ but e ^{t}.
- *Arrangement of formulae*—See *Journal* for further information

Manuscript Submission

1. Four hard copies of the manuscript should be submitted, together with a copy on floppy disk in Microsoft Word 6.0 format if possible.

2. Submission of a paper is held to imply that its content represents original and unpublished work, that it has not been submitted for publication elsewhere, and that full copyright clearance has been obtained for any material quoted in it. If the author has submitted related work elsewhere or does so while the paper is under consideration, then the Editors should be informed.

3. A typescript that is well prepared in accordance with the above guidelines will greatly assist the ease and speed of publication.

4. The principal author of a paper accepted for publication will receive a page proof for correction. This stage must not be used as an opportunity to revise the paper, because alterations are extremely costly. Extensive changes will be charged to the author and will probably result in the article being delayed to a later issue. Speedy return of corrected proofs is important.

5. There is neither a submission charge, nor page fee, nor is payment made to authors, but the principle author will receive 10 copies of the *Journal* free of charge. Additional copies may be ordered when returning corrected proofs.

Submissions should normally be addressed to Stuart Sayer, Editor (see Address for Submission), or if more convenient, to Les Oxley, Co-Editor. Papers submitted, providing they appear to be broadly in line with the aims of the *Journal*, undergo a standard refereeing process. The Editor's decision is based on the referees' reports, together with the consideration of the aims of the *Journal* and the balance of the *Journal*'s contents. We endeavor to reach a decision as quickly as possible.

Journal of Economic Theory

ADDRESS FOR SUBMISSION:

Karl Shell, Jess Benhabib, Co-Editors
Journal of Economic Theory
Cornell University
402 Uris Hall
Ithaca, NY 14853-7601
USA
Phone: 607-255-4878
Fax: 607-255-8838
E-Mail: jetoffice@cornell.edu
Web: www.academicpress.com/jet
Address May Change:

PUBLICATION GUIDELINES:

Manuscript Length: 20-30 Articles,1-10N
Copies Required: Three
Computer Submission: No
Format: N/A
Fees to Review: 0.00 US$

Manuscript Style:
    Chicago Manual of Style

CIRCULATION DATA:

Reader: Academics
Frequency of Issue: Monthly
Copies per Issue: No Reply
Sponsor/Publisher: Elsevier Science
    Publishing Co.
Subscribe Price: 95.00 US$ Individual
    2372.00 US$ Institution
    113.00 Euro Indv, 2,878 Euro Inst

REVIEW INFORMATION:

Type of Review: Editorial Review
No. of External Reviewers: 2
No. of In House Reviewers: No Reply
Acceptance Rate: No Reply
Time to Review: 2 - 3 Months
Reviewers Comments: Yes
Invited Articles: No Reply
Fees to Publish: 0.00 US$

MANUSCRIPT TOPICS:

Economic Development; Industrial Organization; International Economics & Trade;
International Finance; Macro Economics; Micro Economics; Monetary Policy; Portfolio &
Security Analysis; Public Policy Economics; Regional Economics

MANUSCRIPT GUIDELINES/COMMENTS:

Editors
Jess Benhabib   www.econ.nyu.edu/user/benhabib
Karl Shell   www.karlshell.com

Length of Manuscript: 1-10 for notes; 20-30 for articles

The *Journal of Economic Theory* publishes original articles on economic theory. JET also
publishes articles on mathematical and computational techniques. Manuscripts must be written
in English and may initially be submitted in pdf, dvi, or ps format. These files may be sent on
floppy disks to the address below or by email to jetoffice@nyu.edu. Hard-copy manuscripts
may also be submitted, in triplicate, including three sets of good-quality figures, to: Journal of

Economic Theory, New York University, Room 440, 6 Washington Square North, New York, NY 10003, USA.

Manuscripts are accepted for review with the understanding that the same work has not been and will not be nor is presently submitted elsewhere. While under editorial review, *it is the responsibility of the authors to keep the Editor informed about submissions, publication plans, and publication of related research (or abstracts thereof) in other outlets--including letters, journals, journals in other disciplines, collections of articles, and published dissertations.*

It is understood that submission of the paper for publication has been approved by all of the authors and by the institution where the work was carried out; further, that any person cited as a source of personal communications has approved such citation. Written authorization may be required at the Editor's discretion. Articles and any other materials published in the *Journal of Economic Theory* represent the opinions of the author(s) and should not be construed to reflect the opinion of the Editorial Board or the Publisher.

Authors submitting a manuscript do so on the understanding that if it is accepted for publication, copyright in the article, including the right to reproduce the article in all forms and media, shall be assigned exclusively to the Publisher. The Copyright Transfer Agreement, which may be found on www.academicpress.com should be signed by the appropriate person(s) and should accompany the original submission of a manuscript to this journal. The transfer of copyright does not take effect until the manuscript is accepted for publication.

Manuscripts should be prepared according to the following style rules (deviation from these rules causes publication delays).

Form of Manuscript. Submit manuscripts in triplicate and double-spaced on one side of 8.5 x 11 inch white paper. Number each page. *Page 1* should contain the article title, author names and complete affiliations (including email addresses), a running title of less than 35 characters, and the name, mailing address, telephone number, fax number and e-mail address of the corresponding author. At the bottom of page 1 place any footnotes to the title (indicated by superscript *, †, ‡). *Page 2* should contain an abstract of no more than 100 words. This abstract will appear at the beginning of the article in the journal. *Key words* should be listed immediately after the abstract.

List of Symbols. Attach to the manuscript a complete typewritten list of symbols, identified typographically, not mathematically. This list will not appear in print but is essential in order to avoid costly author's corrections in proof. [If equations are handwritten in the text then the list of symbols should also be handwritten.] Distinguish between "oh," "zero"; "el," "one"; "kappa," "kay"; upper- and lowercase "kay"; etc. Indicate also when special type is required (German, Greek, vector, scalar, script, etc.); all other letters will be set in *italic*.

Tables. Number tables consecutively with Roman numerals. Extensive tables will be reproduce photographically and so should be typed carefully and in the **exact** format desired. Authors will be charged for any new photo reproductions necessitated by changes in proof. Use superscript lowercase italic letters (a, b, c) for tables footnotes, which should be typed

728

immediately below the table. Type tables at least double-spaced, including titles and footnotes. Do not underline table titles.

Equations should be typewritten and with the number placed in parentheses at the right margin. Reference to equations should use the form "Eq. (3)" or simply (3). Superscripts and subscripts should be typed or handwritten clearly above and below the line, respectively. Use the exponent $^{1/2}$ wherever possible.

"Style". In general, authors should be guided by *A Manual for Authors* ($3.00) published in 1962 (an revised in 1980) by the American Mathematical Society, P.O. Box 6248, Providence, R. I. 02904, but

References should be styled and punctuated according to the following examples:

1. R.E. Lucas, Jr., Expectations and the neutrality of money, *J. Econ. Theory* 4 (1972), 103-124. [Do not underline titles of articles or books.]

2. D. Duffie, "Security Markets: Stochastic Models," Academic Press, San Diego, 1989. [For books, include name of publisher, city, state (if city is not well known), and year.] J.D. Peck, "Essays in Intertemporal Economic Theory," Ph.D. thesis, University of Pennsylvania, Philadelphia, May 1985.

3. J.D. Peck, "Essays in Intertemporal Economic Theory," Ph.D. thesis, University of Pennsylvania, Philadelphis, May 1985.

4. J. Benhabib and A. Rustichini, A vintage capital model of investment and growth: Theory and evidence, *in* "General Equilibrium, Growth, and Trade II: The Legacy of Lionel McKenzie" (R. Becker, M. Boldrin, R.W. Jones, and W. Thompson, Eds.), pp. 248-301, Academic Press, San Diego, 1993.

For unpublished lectures or symposia, include title of the paper, name of the sponsoring society in full, and date. For journal names, follow the *Journal of Economic Literature* abbreviations. Cite references in the text by an Arabic number between square brackets, as [1], [1, 2], [1, Theorem 1.5], etc. Type references double-spaced throughout.

Footnotes in text should be avoided if at all possible. If they must be used, identify by superscript numbers and type together on a separate page, double-spaced.

Figures. All illustrations are to be considered as figures. Number each graph or drawing in sequence with Arabic numerals. Supply a descriptive legend for each figure. Type legends double- or triple-spaced consecutively on a separate sheet. **Figures must be submitted in a form suitable for reproduction**. Plan figures to fit the proportion of the printed page. The final size of letters after reduction to fit the printed page should be between 8 and 10 points. Identify each figure in a margin with the name of the journal, author's name, and figure number; avoid marking the backs of figures.

Proofs. Proofs will be sent to the author, with a reprint order form. Authors will be charged for alterations in excess of 10% of the cost of composition.

Reprints. Fifty reprints without covers will be provided free of charge. Additional reprints may be purchased; an order form will be included with proofs.

Electronic Transmission. Authors are requested to transmit the text and art of the manuscript in electronic form, via either computer disk or FTP, after all revisions have been incorporated and the manuscript has been accepted for publication. Hard-copy printouts of the manuscript and art that exactly match the electronic files must be supplied. The manuscript will be edited according to the style of the journal, and the author must read the proofs carefully.

Complete instructions for electronic submission can be found on the *Journal of Economic Theory* home page (http://www.academicpress.com/jet).

Journal of Economics

ADDRESS FOR SUBMISSION:

David R. Hakes, Co-Editor
Journal of Economics
University of Nothern Iowa
Department of Economics
Cedar Falls, IA 50614-0129
USA
Phone: 319-273-3597
Fax: 319-273-2922
E-Mail: hakes@uni.edu
Web: www.cba.uni.edu/economics/joe.htm
Address May Change:

PUBLICATION GUIDELINES:

Manuscript Length: 10-25
Copies Required: Three
Computer Submission: Yes
Format: IBM
Fees to Review: 50.00 US$ Non Members
    25.00 US$ MVEA Members

Manuscript Style:
    Chicago Manual of Style

CIRCULATION DATA:

Reader: Academics
Frequency of Issue: 2 Times/Year
Copies per Issue: Less than 1,000
Sponsor/Publisher: Missouri Valley
    Economics Association
Subscribe Price: 32.00 US$ Individual
    100.00 US$ Institution

REVIEW INFORMATION:

Type of Review: Blind Review
No. of External Reviewers: 2
No. of In House Reviewers: 0
Acceptance Rate: 21-30%
Time to Review: 2 - 3 Months
Reviewers Comments: Yes
Invited Articles: 0-5%
Fees to Publish: 0.00 US$

MANUSCRIPT TOPICS:

Econometrics; Economic Development; Economic History; Fiscal Policy; Government &
Non-Profit Accounting; Industrial Organization; International Economics & Trade;
International Finance; Macro Economics; Micro Economics; Monetary Policy; Portfolio &
Security Analysis; Public Policy Economics; Real Estate; Regional Economics

MANUSCRIPT GUIDELINES/COMMENTS:

Journal of Economics and Business

ADDRESS FOR SUBMISSION:

Kenneth J. Kopecky, Editor
Journal of Economics and Business
Temple University
School of Business and Management
Speakman Hall
Philadelphia, PA 19122
USA
Phone: 215-204-8101
Fax: 215-204-2431
E-Mail: jeconbus@sbm.temple.edu
Web: www.sbm.temple.edu/jeb
Address May Change:

PUBLICATION GUIDELINES:

Manuscript Length: 30
Copies Required: Four
Computer Submission: Yes
Format: N/A
Fees to Review: 45.00 US$

Manuscript Style:
    See Manuscript Guidelines

CIRCULATION DATA:

Reader: Academics
Frequency of Issue: 6 Times/Year
Copies per Issue: 1,001 - 2,000
Sponsor/Publisher: Elsevier Science
    Publishing Co.
Subscribe Price: 86.00 US$ Individual
    510.00 US$ Institution
    82.00 Euro Indiv, 457 Euro Institution

REVIEW INFORMATION:

Type of Review: Blind Review
No. of External Reviewers: 2
No. of In House Reviewers: 0
Acceptance Rate: 21-30%
Time to Review: No Reply
Reviewers Comments: Yes
Invited Articles: 0-5%
Fees to Publish: 0.00 US$

MANUSCRIPT TOPICS:

Corporate Finance; Financial Institutions & Markets; Financial Services; Industrial Organization; International Finance; Monetary Policy; Portfolio & Security Analysis

MANUSCRIPT GUIDELINES/COMMENTS:

Description

The *Journal of Economics and Business* is published six times a year and focuses on theoretical and applied research in economics and finance in areas such as corporate finance, monetary and fiscal theory and policy, financial institutions and markets, and industrial organization.

Guide for Authors

All manuscripts should be submitted to the Editor. Manuscripts are submitted with the understanding that they are original, unpublished works and are not being submitted elsewhere.

Manuscript. Submit the four photocopies of the manuscript, typed double-spaced on 8½ x 11-inch bond paper. On the title page include names and addresses of authors, academic or professional affiliations, and the complete address of the author to whom proofs and reprint requests should be sent. Also, provide a running title of less than 45 characters and spaces, which will appear on alternate pages in the *Journal*. Include an Abstract and list Key Words that best code the contents of the article for indexing purposes. The text proper begins on the following page and ends with a citation of acknowledgments, whenever appropriate. References, tabular material, figure captions, and footnotes follow. Tables and figures are numbered in order of their appearance with Arabic numerals and each should have a brief descriptive title. Footnotes to the text are numbered consecutively with superior Arabic numerals.

Mathematical Notation. Use typewritten letters, numbers, and symbols whenever possible. Identify boldface, script letters, etc., at their first occurrence. Distinguish between one and the letter "l" and between zero and the letter "O" whenever confusion might result.

References. Citation in the text is by name(s) of author(s), followed by year of publication in parentheses. For references authored by more than two contributors use first authored by more than two contributors use first author's name and et al. For multiple citations in the same year use a, b, c after year of publication. The reference list should be typed alphabetically according to the following style:

Journal
Agapos, A.M., and Dunlap, P.R. (Feb. 1970.) The theory of price determination in government-industry relationships. *Quarterly Journal of Economics* 84 (1): 85-99.
Book
Fisher, F.M. (1966.) *The Identification Problem in Econometrics*. New York: McGraw-Hill.
Edited Book
Weiss, L.W. (1974.) The concentration profits relationship and antitrust. In *Industrial Concentration: The New Learning* (H.J. Goldschmidt, H.M. Mann, and J.F. Weston, eds.). Boston: Little Brown, pp. 184-233.

Illustrations. Unmounted, glossy, black and white photographs or India ink drawings on white paper should accompany the final version of the manuscript. Photocopies are suitable for the other copies of the manuscript. To facilitate identification and processing, on the back of each figure write the number, first author's name, and indicate which side is the top. Captions appear on a separate page.

Proofs and Reprints. The corresponding author will receive proofs, which should be corrected and returned within ten days of receipt or the article will be published without author's corrections. The author is responsible for proofreading the manuscript; the publisher is not responsible for any error not marked by the author on proof. Corrections on proof are limited to printer's errors; no substantial author changes are allowed at this stage. Reprints may be ordered prior to publication; consult the price list accompanying proofs.

Copyright. Upon acceptance of an article by the *Journal*, the author(s) will be asked to transfer copyright of the article to the publisher, Temple University of the Commonwealth

System of Higher Education, School of Business Administration. This transfer will insure the widest possible dissemination of information under the U.S. Copyright law.

Submission Fee. Please submit a $30 check payable to Temple University, *Journal of Economics and Business*. If the manuscript is not formally accepted for review, the fee will be returned.

Journal of Economics and Economic Education Researcl

ADDRESS FOR SUBMISSION:

Current Editor's Name/Check Web Site
Journal of Economics and Economic
    Education Research
Digital Submission Through Web Site
Address Other Questions to:
 Jim or JoAnn Carland at #s below
USA
Phone: 828-293-9151
Fax: 828-293-9407
E-Mail: info@alliedacademies.org
Web: www.alliedacademies.org
Address May Change:

PUBLICATION GUIDELINES:

Manuscript Length: 26-30
Copies Required: Submit Through Website
Computer Submission: Yes
Format: MS Word, WordPerfect
Fees to Review: 0.00 US$

Manuscript Style:
    American Psychological Association

CIRCULATION DATA:

Reader: Academics
Frequency of Issue: 2 Times/Year
Copies per Issue: Less than 1,000
Sponsor/Publisher: Allied Academies, Inc.
Subscribe Price: 75.00 US$ Individual
    150.00 US$ Foreign

REVIEW INFORMATION:

Type of Review: Blind Review
No. of External Reviewers: 2
No. of In House Reviewers: 2
Acceptance Rate: 21-30%
Time to Review: 3-4 Months
Reviewers Comments: Yes
Invited Articles: 0-5%
Fees to Publish: 75.00 US$ Membership

MANUSCRIPT TOPICS:
Economic Development; Economic Education; Macro Economics; Micro Economics; Public
Policy Economics

MANUSCRIPT GUIDELINES/COMMENTS:

The *Journal* publishes theoretical or empirical research concerning any of the Manuscript
Topics.

Comments. All authors of published manuscripts must be members of the appropriate
academy affiliate of Allied Academies. The current membership fee is $75.00 U.S.

Editorial Policy Guidelines
The primary criterion upon which manuscripts are judged is whether the research advances the
discipline. Key points include currency, interest and relevancy.

In order for a theoretical manuscript to advance the discipline, it must address the literature to
support conclusions or models which extend knowledge and understanding. Consequently,

referees pay particular attention to completeness of literature review and appropriateness of conclusions drawn from that review.

In order for an empirical manuscript to advance the discipline, it must employ appropriate and effective sampling and statistical analysis techniques, and must be grounded by a thorough literature review. Consequently, referees pay particular attention to the research methodology and to the conclusions drawn from statistical analyses and their consistency with the literature.

Journal of Economics and Finance

ADDRESS FOR SUBMISSION:

Richard Robinson/James Payne, Editors
Journal of Economics and Finance
Eastern Kentucky University
MBA Office
316 Combs Academic Building
Richmond, KY 40475
USA
Phone: 859-622-1775
Fax: 859-622-1413
E-Mail: rich.robinson@eku.edu
Web: www.jeandf.org
Address May Change:

PUBLICATION GUIDELINES:

Manuscript Length: 5-30
Copies Required: Two Paper+Electronic
Computer Submission: Yes Through Web
  Site
Format: WP
Fees to Review: 25.00 US$ Members
  50.00 US$ Non-Members

Manuscript Style:
  , See Web Site

CIRCULATION DATA:

Reader: Academics
Frequency of Issue: 3 Times/Year
Copies per Issue: Less than 1,000
Sponsor/Publisher: Academy of Economics
  and Finance
Subscribe Price: 25.00 US$ Individual
  50.00 US$ Library
  75.00 US$ Foreign Library

REVIEW INFORMATION:

Type of Review: Blind Review
No. of External Reviewers: 2+
No. of In House Reviewers: 0
Acceptance Rate: 15-20%
Time to Review: 2 Months
Reviewers Comments: Yes
Invited Articles: 0%
Fees to Publish: 0.00 US$

MANUSCRIPT TOPICS:

Behavioral Economics; Corporate Finance; Econometrics; Economic Development; Economic History; Financial Institutions & Markets; Financial Services; Fiscal Policy; Industrial Organization; International Economics & Trade; International Finance; Macro Economics; Micro Economics; Monetary Policy; Portfolio & Security Analysis; Public Policy Economics; Regional Economics

MANUSCRIPT GUIDELINES/COMMENTS:

James Payne, Economics Editor, james.payne@eku.edu; Tel 859-622-1771

The *Journal of Economics and Finance* (*JEF*) is a general interest academic journal covering both economics and finance. *JEF* invites theoretical, empirical, and methodological contributions. The principal criteria for acceptance are (a) the paper's overall quality, (b) its contribution to the fields of economics or finance, and (c) its potential usefulness to the general interest reader. The manuscript, or parts of it, must not have been previously published or submitted elsewhere while under review by *JEF*. See guidelines from www.jeandf.org.

Journal of Economics and Finance Education

ADDRESS FOR SUBMISSION:

Luther D. Lawson, Editor
Journal of Economics and Finance
  Education
University of North Carolina
  at Wilmington
Dept. of Economics & Finance Education
Electronic Submission Only
Wilmington, NC 28403
USA
Phone: 910-962-3524
Fax: 910-962-7464
E-Mail: jefeedit@unc.edu
Web: jeandfe.org
Address May Change: 12/31/2008

PUBLICATION GUIDELINES:

Manuscript Length: 21-25
Copies Required: One (if desired)
Computer Submission: Yes - Email
Format: MS Word
Fees to Review: 47.00 US$
    21.00 US$

Manuscript Style:
    Chicago Manual of Style

CIRCULATION DATA:

Reader: Academics
Frequency of Issue: 2 Times/Year
Copies per Issue: Electronic Journal
Sponsor/Publisher: Academy of Economics
    & Finance
Subscribe Price: 0.00 US$

REVIEW INFORMATION:

Type of Review: Blind Review
No. of External Reviewers: 2
No. of In House Reviewers: 0
Acceptance Rate: 11-20%
Time to Review: 1 - 2 Months
Reviewers Comments: Yes
Invited Articles: 0-5%
Fees to Publish: 0.00 US$

MANUSCRIPT TOPICS:

Econometrics; Economic Education; Financial Education

MANUSCRIPT GUIDELINES/COMMENTS:

Submission Fees

JEFE requires a submission fee of US$21 from members of the *Academy of Economics and Finance* and US$47 from non-members. The non-member submission fee of US$47 includes a one-year membership to the *Academy of Economics and Finance* and a one-year subscription to the *Journal of Economics and Finance*.

Payment has to be made by check, in US$ drawn on a U.S. bank. Make your check payable to the *Journal of Economics and Finance Education*. The check must be received within 10 days from the date of the electronic submission before manuscript consideration. Mail to the Editor.

How to Submit Electronically

As this is an electronic journal, all submissions must be submitted by email to: jefeedit@uncw.edu. The following guidelines must be adhered to.

Your e-mail message must contain:
a) The name of the lead or primary author
b) The title of your paper
c) A statement indicating that you are not submitting simultaneously to another journal
d) A statement that your paper has not been published in whole or part in a journal or book with an ISSN or ISBN number, respectively, and
e) A check in the amount of the submission fee.

The e-mail should include your manuscript in the following two separate Microsoft Word attachments, with DOC extensions:
a) The abstract, including author information
b) The manuscript itself (see: How to prepare your manuscript for initial review), including author information. Author information will be removed for manuscript review

Remember, the two attachments to your e-mail need to be in Microsoft Word format, with DOC extensions, with all links and graphics intact for simple editorial conversion to PDF format.

If you have questions on how to submit electronically, please contact the editorial office at jefeedit@uncw.edu.

How to Prepare Your Manuscript for Initial Review
1. Cover Page
The cover page contains the paper title, the author(s), their affiliation, and a maximum of five key words. The cover page also provides complete correspondence information: (a) postal addresses, (b) telephone and fax numbers, and, in particular, (c) e-mail addresses.

2. The Body of Your Paper
Page One
The first page of the manuscript for review contains the title of the paper and the *abstract* but no author information; no other information is to be included on the first page. Please note that the abstract must not exceed 100 words!

Page Two
The second page of the manuscript for review is the beginning of the text and includes the title of the paper but no author information. The body of the text is to be double spaced. All pages except the abstract page are numbered consecutively at the bottom of the page. The references are inserted after the main body of the paper. They are followed by appendices, tables (one per page), and figures (one per page). All material has to be part of the paper. Separate files for figures, tables, or other material are not acceptable.

Notes that are designed to help the reviewer in his/her evaluation of the paper should be placed at the very end of the paper. These notes should be labeled NOTES TO REVIEWERS.

They will not be published. In the case of papers containing complicated mathematics, these notes may detail the mathematical derivations. For empirical papers, the notes may consist of the key command files that are used to manipulate the data and to generate the results.

Please note that if your paper is accepted for publication, you will be asked to revise the above format (see <u>How to Revise Your Paper That Has Positive Peer-Reviewed Remarks</u>).

3. General Considerations in Preparing the Manuscript

Avoid typographical errors; missing pages; inconsistent footnotes, headings, or references; and other similar blunders. They communicate to the reader that the paper was prepared hastily. Remember that the time of referees is valuable. They do not want to be bothered with papers that are half finished. They want to read the final draft, not the first one. Therefore, the editorial office will not start the refereeing process for papers that give the impression of being slapped together with little care. Authors of such papers will be notified and given the opportunity to resubmit or to withdraw.

Most referees determine whether they like a paper or not during the first fifteen minutes of reading it. Often, they spend this time concentrating on the introduction and the conclusion sections as well as the list of references. If these sections of your paper are weak and if your paper gives the impression of being put together sloppily, most referees will conclude that this is indicative of your whole paper. In most cases, they will lose interest at this point and recommend rejection without wasting their time going over the main body of your paper. This means that you will need to spend a very considerable amount of time perfecting your introduction, conclusion, and reference sections. You should also make sure that your paper has a professional look. A typewriter font, a large number of tables, tables with missing horizontal lines, missing page numbers, and the like, do not give the paper a professional look. Without a professional look, your paper has hardly any chance of getting published.

The editorial office will remove the cover page before papers are sent on to the referees. This is done to allow for double-blind refereeing. Authors are urged to avoid anything that undercuts the idea of double-blind refereeing. The main body must not contain anything that may reveal the identity of the author(s). This includes, inter alia, the citation of one's own working papers or forthcoming books or articles and an unreasonable number of self-citations. References to working papers and forthcoming publications can be added once an article has been accepted for publication but not before. Papers that do not strictly adhere to the spirit of these standards are not sent out to the referees. The editorial office will give the author(s) the chance to resubmit or to withdraw.

Omit all information on how many times the paper has been revised, when and where it was presented, and who provided comments, encouragement, and so forth.

Keep the paper as concise as possible by sticking to the main point. There are few referees who will want to report on an article that contains more than 20 pages of text. Manuscripts in excess of 25 pages are not acceptable!!

Think carefully about the number of tables and figures you need. Often, tables can be combined and cut in size. Include figures only when they are essential.

Use footnotes rather than endnotes to make the paper easier to read.

Finally, it is highly recommended that anyone new or relatively new to the publication process read what Professor Choi of Iowa State University has to say on getting articles published. His comments and suggestions are based on many years of experience both as an author and as editor of the *Review of International Economics*: How to Publish in Top Journals. Another good source of information on how to get published is provided by Professor Starbuck of New York University's Stern School of Business.

When and How to Contact the Editorial Office

If you are waiting for the referees' comments
If you have not heard from the editorial office for two months after the submission of your paper has been acknowledged, you should send an e-mail message to inquire about the status of your paper. Please do not send letters or call.

If you have received a rejection
Please refrain from calling the editorial office of *JEFE* immediately after you have received a rejection letter. Think carefully about why your paper was rejected. Is your point not made clearly enough? Is your presentation inadequate? Does your paper give the overall impression of being slapped together without much care? Are there serious logical or other flaws in your paper? Is its contribution to the literature marginal at best? Does your paper contain unsubstantiated opinion? Only if you find that there is absolutely no good reason for the paper's rejection should you consider sending an e-mail to the editorial office. Again, please do not call. Write down your comments in detail. This will help to clarify your thinking.

No action will be taken by the editorial office unless you follow these rules. Also, you cannot expect any action if your paper was rejected because more than one referee has misread your intentions, methodology, or results. Remember that it is up to you, not the editors, to convince the referees that your paper is worthy of publication.

How to Revise Your Paper that has Positive Peer-Reviewed Remarks
1. The time limit for resubmission is *45 days* from the date of *JEFE*'s notice to you.

2. Please advise the editorial office within a week or two whether you will revise and resubmit or whether you will try a different journal instead. In deciding whether you should resubmit or whether you should try a different journal, it may be helpful to look at a list of journals in economics and finance, (which may or may not accept economic and finance education articles, such as Economics Journal on the Web and WebEc, or at a list of finance, management, and marketing journals, available from biz/ed.

3. If you have an important question concerning your revision, you may e-mail the editorial office. All questions need to be in a form such that they can be answered with yes or no. Do not try to make referees explain their decisions or engage in any type of ongoing dialogue.

4. If you decide to revise, please give the paper sufficient attention. Most likely, this will be your last chance to get accepted by *JEFE*.

5. When you resubmit, please indicate that this is a revision to previous peer reviewed remarks and include a detailed description of what the referees asked you to change and how you responded to their requests. Remember, the attached revision of your e-mail must be in Microsoft Word format, with DOC extensions, with all links and graphics intact for simple editorial conversion to PDF format.

Journal Style for Accepted Manuscripts

Initial submissions must follow the *JEFE* style and submitted in the following format. Authors who do not strictly adhere to these standards will be asked to resubmit. This may delay the publication of the article.

Organize the sections of your paper as follows: (a) abstract, (b) main body, (c) references, and (d) appendices. Author information and acknowledgments are provided as a footnote to the author's name. Use footnotes rather than endnotes. Insert tables where they belong in the text and attach figures at the end or in separate files.

1. Set the *title* of the article in Times Roman 20-point bold italic, left justified. Below the title, write the names of the authors (first name, last name) in 12 point bold italic, left justified.

2. The text of the *abstract* must be in Times Roman 10-point, centered, and fully justified. Use two and a quarter inch left and right margins. Center, capitalize, and bold the heading of the abstract. Do not exceed 100 words for the abstract.

3. For the *main text*, use Times Roman 10-point, **single spacing,** with all text fully justified. Leave only **one space** between sentences, not two! Set left and write margins to 1¼-inch, top and bottom margins to 1-inch. Indent new paragraphs 0.2 inches from the left margin.

Subheadings need to be set up as follows: (a) first-level, centered, bold, 12-point, first letter of main words capitalized, not numbered; (b) second-level, centered, bold, italic, 11-point, first letter of main words capitalized, not numbered; and (c) third-level, flush left, bold, italic, 10-point, first letter of main words capitalized. Double-space before all subheadings and after first- and second-level subheadings.

All references to books, articles, monographs, etc., should be identified at the appropriate point in the text by last name of author and year of publication, e.g., (Author 1994). Add page numbers when ideas are used or words are quoted, e.g., (Author 1997, pp. 123- 124). When an author's name is used as part of the text, set only the date in parentheses, with page number if necessary, e.g., Author (1997) and Author (1997, pp. 123-124). If more than one work by the same author is cited for the same year, use a, b, etc., behind the year, e.g., Dixon (1990a).

Include a comma before the last item in a series, e.g., travel by car, rail, and bus. All variable names that appear in the text need to be italicized to separate them from the text.

4. Other font settings
- Information on authors should be set at 8-point
- Notes at the bottom of tables should be set at 8-point
- Footnotes should be set at 8-point

5. All page headers will be identified as:

JOURNAL OF ECONOMICS AND FINANCE EDUCATION (by volume, number and edition, followed by the page number). The header font is to be set at 10-point. The first page of the paper will not be assigned a number; whereas, the succeeding pages will be ascending in order. The editor will provide your page numbers. (See previous articles at jeandfe.org for further clarity)

6. Indent each footnote by 0.2 inches from the left margin. Use single spacing and leave one blank line between the footnotes. Do not start a new page. Keep the text in all footnotes to a minimum. Bullets, indents, elaborate equations or formulas, and long explanations are not acceptable in footnotes.

7. List all items cited by author in alphabetical order in a separate section entitled *References*. Do not use indents, and do not number the references. Refer to the *Chicago Manual of Style, 14th edition* for the style to be used. When possible, the reference section uses full author names. Names of first authors are represented as Last, First Middle Initial, and subsequent author names as First Middle Initial Last with an "and" preceding the last author. The references are sorted by Author + Year + Title and make use of a letter after year to distinguish citations of the same author in the same year, e.g., 1978a, 1978b. Journal articles, books, and book sections are referenced as follows:

Journal Articles. Engle, Robert F., David M. Lilien, and Russell P. Robins. 1987. "Estimating Time Varying Risk Premia in the Term Structure: The ARCH-M Model." *Econometrica* 55: 391-407.

Books. Fama, Eugene F. 1976. *Foundations of Finance*. New York: Basic Books.

Book Sections. Geweke, John. 1977. "The Dynamic Factor Analysis of Economic Time-Series Models." In *Latent Variables in Socioeconomic Models*, edited by Dennis J. Aigner and Arthur S. Goldberg. Amsterdam: North-Holland.

8. Center, capitalize, and bold the heading of the *appendix* or appendices. Do not start a new page.

9. *All tables are to be placed in the body of the text where they are discussed. Do not place tables at the end of the manuscript. Tables* need to be in the style used, inter alia, by the *American Economic Review/Journal of Economic Perspectives*. There are no vertical lines anywhere in the table. Minimize the number of tables. Make every effort to combine tables. This can often be done by presenting regression results in columnar form (one column for each regression equation). It is highly recommended to insert a table with variable definitions and data sources, and possibly basic statistics, as Table 1. The same variable names should be

used throughout, including in the tables. Please use variable names that make some sense and only capitalize the first character of your variable names.

Make sure your table columns are aligned by the decimal points of the estimated coefficients or key variables. Use a table editor or tabs. Do not use simple spaces. To report regression results, do not use very large or very small numbers and E-format (e.g., -0.1E-08). Please rescale your variables and run your regressions again to generate coefficients of a similar size!! The scaling of your variables can be conveniently reported in Table 1—Definitions of Variables (see above). Keep the number of digits to the right of the decimal point to a minimum (no more than three) and the same for all coefficients—again, rescale your variables to make this possible. Use the same number of digits to the right of the decimal point for all coefficients. Use the same internal consistency for all values, etc. T-values must not have more than two digits to the right of the decimal point. Use probability values whenever possible (again no more than three digits to the right of the decimal point). This avoids the need for stars in addition to t-values!! If you use stars to indicate significance, use one star for 5 or 10 percent and two stars for 1 percent, not the other way around! The coefficient of multiple determinations should be reported with three digits to the right of the decimal point. Each regression equation needs to have a sufficient number of statistical adequacy tests reported to make the results believable (autocorrelation, heteroskedasticity, reset for functional form, chow, cusum, etc.). Use probability values (p-values) to report statistical significance on these tests. Do not use the same explanatory symbol next to each number in column or row, such as %; rather put the explanation into the column heading or the row label. You may divide your table into sections, but do not separate sections with a horizontal line; use a heading in italic to indicate a new section within a table.

Explanatory notes appear at the bottom of the table, below a horizontal line, and not at the top of the table!! The word *Notes* precedes the table notes and has to be set in italic. Do not start each note on a new line, but write all notes consecutively on the same line, separating them by semicolon or colon. Do not repeat variable definitions in notes and do not repeat equations in notes. Refer to the text or other tables if there is a need. Notations, such as [Table I about here], have to be inserted in the body of the text to indicate the approximate location of tables.

Until the *Journal* develops a history of publications, potential authors may wish to review the *Journal of Economics and Finance* for style and format.

10. Concerning *figures,* headings and notes need to be in the same style as those for tables. Do not use shading for your figures. Use line charts whenever possible, not bar charts. Make sure that different lines can be identified when they are printed in black and white. Use different line styles (e.g., solid, broken, thick, thin) for different series, but do not use line markers.

11. The rule for manuscripts accepted for publication must be submitted in MS Word format.

12. You need to send a filled-out and signed *Copyright Transfer Form.* The Copyright Transfer Form is available from the main page of *JEFE*'s **Web site**: http://www.jeandfe.org/copyright/pdf. Please fill out the form from within your Acrobat PDF Reader. You can use the Reader to type the paper's title and your name in the appropriate spaces. Then print out the form, sign it, date it, and send it along with the hard copy of your

paper and your diskette. All authors need to sign the *same* form. CGI list form posted web forms

13. Before a *Journal* issue is printed, all authors receive *galley proofs*. The proof will be sent via e-mail in Adobe Acrobat PDF format. Please make sure your e-mail address is functioning and check your e-mail for incoming mail. Please read the article very carefully! This is your last chance to make corrections. All corrections need to be back at the editorial office within two weeks. If you are out of town or out of the country, please make sure you leave an e-mail address. Please edit the galley proof and return by email. This will be the last you will see it until it is posted on the Web.

Journal of Economics Business and Finance

ADDRESS FOR SUBMISSION:

Ali Bilge, Editor
Journal of Economics Business and Finance
Cemal Nadir Sok.23/5 06680
Cankaya/Ankara,
Turkey
Phone: +90 312-441-5219
Fax: +90 312-441-5113
E-Mail: isletme-finans@kolaymail.com
Web: www.isletme-finans.com
Address May Change:

PUBLICATION GUIDELINES:

Manuscript Length: 21-25
Copies Required: Two
Computer Submission: Yes Disk, Email
Format: MS Word-English or Turkish
Fees to Review: 50.00 US$

Manuscript Style:

CIRCULATION DATA:

Reader: Academics, Business Persons,
   Government & Media, Students
Frequency of Issue: Monthly
Copies per Issue: 1,001 - 2,000
Sponsor/Publisher: No Reply
Subscribe Price: 50.00 US$

REVIEW INFORMATION:

Type of Review: Blind Review
No. of External Reviewers: 2
No. of In House Reviewers: 2
Acceptance Rate: 55%
Time to Review: No Reply
Reviewers Comments: Yes
Invited Articles: 0-5%
Fees to Publish: 50.00 US$

MANUSCRIPT TOPICS:

Accounting Information Systems; Auditing; Corporate Finance; Cost Accounting;
Econometrics; Economic Development; Economic History; Financial Institutions & Markets;
Financial Services; Fiscal Policy; Government & Non-Profit Accounting; Industrial
Organization; Insurance; International Economics & Trade; International Finance; Macro
Economics; Micro Economics; Monetary Policy; Portfolio & Security Analysis; Public Policy
Economics; Regional Economics

MANUSCRIPT GUIDELINES/COMMENTS:

Terms and Conditions of Publishing

1. The papers must not be published in anywhere else before.

2. The typing format is 2 line blank between each line and a total of 5-15 pages. The
document should be delivered or mailed to our headquarter together with a WinWord
computer output in a 3 1/4 diskette. For the deliveries via internet, our e-mail address is
info:isletme-finans@kolaymail.com.

3. Footnotes should have relatively smaller fonts and be *italic*, and take place on the page they are mentioned.

4. The name and abstract of the paper in English should be included.

5. Tables, graphs, illustrations should take place on the page or the following page they are mentioned.

6. References should take place at the end of the paper.

7. A brief CV, address, phone and telefax numbers, as well as a summary about the previous writings of the author should be included.

8. The papers are to be published following the examination and the approval of the referees.

9. The papers can be mailed to the following e-mail address: isletme-finans@kolaymail.com.

10. The papers are not available to be returned with no exception whether they are published or not.

11. The translations may also be published if they are appropriate to the general publishing principles of the periodical. If this is the case, CV, institution and title of the translator, as well as the origin of the translation should be included.

The opinions expressed in the published papers reflect solely the ones of authors own and do not bound the periodical. The papers are published in Turkish in general. However, the ones in English may also be published if found appropriate by the advising board of the periodical.

Journal of Educators Online

ADDRESS FOR SUBMISSION:

Matthew A. Elbeck, Editor
Journal of Educators Online
500 University Drive
Dothan, AL 36303
USA
Phone: 334-983-6556 ext. 356
Fax: 334-983-6322
E-Mail: melbeck@troyst.edu
Web: www.thejeo.com
Address May Change:

PUBLICATION GUIDELINES:

Manuscript Length: 16-20
Copies Required:
Computer Submission: Yes Disk, Email
Format: MS Word, Excel
Fees to Review: 0.00 US$

Manuscript Style:
    American Psychological Association

CIRCULATION DATA:

Reader: Academics
Frequency of Issue: 2 Times/Year
Copies per Issue:
Sponsor/Publisher: Troy State University
    Dothan
Subscribe Price: 0.00 US$

REVIEW INFORMATION:

Type of Review: Blind Review
No. of External Reviewers: 2
No. of In House Reviewers: 0
Acceptance Rate:
Time to Review: 1 - 2 Months
Reviewers Comments: Yes
Invited Articles: 0-5%
Fees to Publish: 0.00 US$

MANUSCRIPT TOPICS:

Accounting Theory & Practice; Economic Development; Economic History; International Economics & Trade; International Finance

MANUSCRIPT GUIDELINES/COMMENTS:

We accept articles related to teaching or to researching online or in cyber-enhanced classes anywhere in the world; or articles discussing how traditional knowledge and/or conventional cognitive processing is enhanced, destroyed, or transformed by the medium of cyberspace.

Journal of Emerging Markets

ADDRESS FOR SUBMISSION:

Maximo Eng, Francis Lees, Co-Editors
Journal of Emerging Markets
St. John's University
Center for Global Education
8000 Utopia Parkway
Jamaica, NY 11439
USA
Phone: 718-990-7305
Fax: 718-990-1868
E-Mail: leesf@stjohns.edu
Web:
Address May Change:

PUBLICATION GUIDELINES:

Manuscript Length: 12-16
Copies Required: Three
Computer Submission: Yes After
    Acceptance
Format: MS Word
Fees to Review: 40.00 US$

Manuscript Style:
    Chicago Manual of Style

CIRCULATION DATA:

Reader: Academics, Business Persons
Frequency of Issue: 3 Times/Year
Copies per Issue: Less than 1,000
Sponsor/Publisher: Emerging Market
    Traders Assn., St. Johns U., Chase
    Manhattan, Merrill Lynch
Subscribe Price: 60.00 US$ Individual
    110.00 US$ Institution
    90.00 US$ Academic Library

REVIEW INFORMATION:

Type of Review: Blind Review
No. of External Reviewers: 1
No. of In House Reviewers: 1
Acceptance Rate: 38%
Time to Review: 2 - 3 Months
Reviewers Comments: Yes
Invited Articles: 0-5%
Fees to Publish: 0.00 US$

MANUSCRIPT TOPICS:
Economic Development; Financial Institutions & Markets; Financial Services; International Finance

MANUSCRIPT GUIDELINES/COMMENTS:

Submit two copies of the manuscript with the submission fee ($40) to Editor. Manuscripts must be in English and should conform to the following guidelines.

Electronic Publishing
Upon completion of the review process, and after acceptance, *JEM* requires authors make final corrections to the manuscript. The length of the manuscript should not exceed 14 pages, single-spaced (including references, charts, and tables). Longer manuscripts may be published, with a cost overrun charge of $15 per page. The final manuscript version must be submitted in both printed (hard copy) and diskette, using a 3.5 diskette. Please check diskettes to be sure they are virus-free. Pack diskettes securely when sending them to *JEM*.

1. All manuscripts should be completed in Microsoft Word 6.0. Inquires concerning alternative formats should be directed to 718-990-1951.

2. Manuscripts should follow *The Chicago Manual of Style*.

3. Please double-space all text, including the abstract, quotations, and references.

4. On title page include title, author's name, affiliation, address for correspondence, and a telephone number.

5. An abstract of no more than 100 words should follow the title page. The one paragraph abstract should be preceded by the title, but not the author's name.

6. Primary headings should be centered using Roman numerals. Subsection headings should begin at the left margin.

7. Tables should stand independently of text. Column headings should be clear, descriptive and easily understood. Use tabs (not spaces) to separate columns in tables.

8. Number tables with Arabic numbers, and figures with Roman numerals.

9. Present each figure or table on a separate page, and indicate in the text where each table and figure is to appear. Figures may be submitted originally in rough form. However, if the article is accepted for publication, the author must supply camera-ready copy.

10. References should be cited in the text by placing the publication date in parentheses, such as 'Adler (1987) reports that...' or 'Several analyses (e.g., Prochnow (1991), Richardson (1988)...)'.

11. Please list references alphabetically at the end of the manuscript using format shown below. When citing more than one publication that appears in the same year by one author, add a, b, c, etc., to the publication date.

Clark, J., 1986, Options arid Futures (Macmillan, London).

Frank, B., 1991, The use of registered bonds, Journal of Managerial Finance 11, 164-186.

Martin, S., 1990, Germany's stock market system, In E.S. Chandler and L. Pratt, eds. Recent Developments in European Sock Markers (Atlantic Press, New York).

Journal of Empirical Finance

ADDRESS FOR SUBMISSION:

Franz C. Palm, Editor
Journal of Empirical Finance
Maastricht University
P.O. Box 616
6200 MD
Maastricht,
The Netherlands
Phone:
Fax: 31 43 3 88 4874
E-Mail: f.palm@ke.unimaas.nl
Web: www.elsevier.com
Address May Change:

PUBLICATION GUIDELINES:

Manuscript Length: N/A
Copies Required: Three
Computer Submission: No
Format: N/A
Fees to Review: 75.00 US$
          50.00 US$ Current Subscriber

Manuscript Style:
     See Manuscript Guidelines

CIRCULATION DATA:

Reader: Academics
Frequency of Issue: Quarterly
Copies per Issue: Less than 1,000
Sponsor/Publisher: Elsevier Science
   Publishing Co.
Subscribe Price: 50.00 US$ Individual
   355.00 US$ Institution
   44.92 Euro Indv., 317.19 Euro Inst.

REVIEW INFORMATION:

Type of Review: Blind Review
No. of External Reviewers: 2
No. of In House Reviewers: 0
Acceptance Rate: 11-20%
Time to Review: 4 - 6 Months
Reviewers Comments: Yes
Invited Articles: 6-10%
Fees to Publish: 0.00 US$

MANUSCRIPT TOPICS:

Econometrics; Financial Institutions & Markets; Financial Services; International Finance;
Portfolio & Security Analysis

MANUSCRIPT GUIDELINES/COMMENTS:

Description

The Journal of Empirical Finance provides an international forum for empirical researchers in
the intersection of the fields of econometrics and finance. The *Journal* welcomes high quality
articles in empirical finance. Empirical finance encompasses the testing of well-established or
new theories using financial data, the measurement of variables relevant in financial decision-
making, the econometric analysis of financial market data or the development of new
econometric methodology with finance applications. Submissions in any field of finance,
corporate, international, asset pricing, market microstructure, etc. are welcome.

Possible topics include but are not limited to:
• Modelling and forecasting asset returns
• Modelling, measuring and forecasting volatility and risk premia

- The capital asset pricing model, multifactor models
- Term structure of interest rate models
- Empirical pricing models for options and other derivatives
- Empirical studies in corporate finance
- Exchange rate determination and other empirical studies in international finance
- Microstructure of security markets
- Modelling emerging markets
- Evaluating the performance of portfolio management
- Modelling high frequency data, transactions data, non-synchronous trading
- Risk management and hedging
- Empirical credit risk modelling

Editorial Policy

The main features of the *Journal of Empirical Finance* are the following:

High Quality Contributions and Double-Blind Refereeing Process. This implies that articles accepted for publication in the *Journal* will be in accord with high methodological standards involving the sophisticated use of economic reasoning, use of appropriate statistical techniques, and thorough analyses of data. Each paper will be reviewed by one associate editor and as a rule by (at least) two referees.

Significant Results. The *Journal* favors articles with empirical results that have important implications for the understanding of financial markets and institutions, asset pricing, forecasting and other financial decision problems.

Intellectual Integrity. Originality and high standards of reporting results, data, and description of computer programs will be strictly enforced. The information obtained by the author(s) must be sufficient for interested readers to be able to reproduce the results.

Guide for Authors

1. Papers must be in English.

2. Papers for publication should be sent in quadruplicate to: Professor Franz C. Palm accompanied by a submission fee of US$50.00 for authors who currently subscribe to this *Journal* and US$75.00 for non-subscribers. The submission fee of US$75.00 includes a one-year subscription to the *Journal of Empirical Finance*. Cheques should be made payable to Elsevier Science Publishers. There are no page charges. Submission of a paper will be held to imply that it contains original unpublished work and is not being submitted for publication elsewhere. The Editor does not accept responsibility for damage or loss of papers submitted. Upon acceptance of an article, author(s) will be asked to transfer copyright of the article to the publisher. This transfer will ensure the widest possible dissemination of information.

3. **Submission of accepted papers** as electronic manuscripts, i.e., on disk with accompanying manuscript, is encouraged. Electronic manuscripts have the advantage that there is no need for rekeying of text, thereby avoiding the possibility of introducing errors and resulting in reliable and fast delivery of proofs. The preferred storage medium is a 3.5-inch disk in MS-DOS

format, although other systems are welcome, e.g., Macintosh (in this case, save your file in the usual manner; do not use the option 'save in MS-DOS format'). Do not submit your original paper as electronic manuscript but hold on to disk until asked for this by the Editor (in case your paper is accepted without revisions). Do submit the accepted version of your paper as electronic manuscript. Make absolutely sure that the file on the disk and the printout are identical. Please use a new and correctly formatted disk and label this with your name; also specify the software and hardware used as well as the title of the file to be processed. Do not convert the file to plain ASCII. Ensure that the letter 'l' and digit '1', and also the letter 'O' and digit '0' are used properly, and format your article (tabs, indents, etc.) consistently. Characters not available on your word processor (Greek letters mathematical symbols, etc.) should not be left open, but be indicated by a unique code (e.g., gralpha, alpha, etc., for the Greek letter α). Such codes should be used consistently throughout the entire text; a list of codes used should accompany the electronic manuscript. Do not allow your word processor to introduce word breaks and do not use a justified layout. Please adhere strictly to the general instructions below on style, arrangement and, in particular, the reference style of the *Journal*.

4. **Manuscripts** should be double-spaced, with wide margins, and printed on one side of the paper only. All pages should be numbered consequently. Titles and subtitles should be short. References, tables, and legends for the figures should be printed on separate pages.

5. The **first page** of the manuscript should contain the following information: (i) the title; (ii) the name(s) and institutional affiliation(s) of the author(s); (iii) an abstract of not more than 100 words. A footnote on the same sheet should give the name, address, and telephone and fax numbers of the corresponding author [as well as an e-mail address].

6. The **first page** of the manuscript should also contain at least one classification code according to the Classification System for Journal Articles as used by the *Journal of Economic Literature*; in addition, up to five key words should be supplied.

7. **Acknowledgements** and information on grants received can be given in a first footnote, which should not be included in the consecutive numbering of footnotes.

8. **Footnotes** should be kept to a minimum and numbered consecutively throughout the text with superscript Arabic numerals. Footnotes should be double-spaced and not include displayed formulae or tables.

9. **Displayed formulae** should be numbered consecutively throughout the manuscript as (1), (2), etc., against the right-hand margin of the page. In cases where the derivation of formulae has been abbreviated, it is of great help to the referees if the full derivation can be presented on a separate sheet (not to be published).

10. **References** to publications should be as follows: 'Smith (1992) reported that...' or 'This problem has been studied previously (e.g., Smith et al., 1969)'. The author should make sure that there is a strict one-to-one correspondence between the names and years in the text and those on the list. The list of references should appear at the end of the main text (after any appendices, but before tables and legends for figures). It should be double spaced and listed in alphabetical order by author's name. References should appear as follows:

For monographs
Hawawini, G. and I. Swary, 1990, Mergers and acquisitions in the U.S. banking industry: Evidence from the capital markets (North-Holland, Amsterdam).

For contributions to collective works
Brunner, K. and A.H. Meltzer, 1990, Money supply, in: B.M. Friedman and F.H. Hahn, Handbook of monetary economics, Vol. 1 (North-Holland, Amsterdam) 357-396.

For periodicals
Griffiths, W. and G. Judge, 1992, Testing and estimating location vectors when the error covariance matrix is unknown, Journal of Econometrics 54, 121-138.
Note that journal titles should not be abbreviated.

11. **Illustrations** will be reproduced photographically from originals supplied by the author; they will not be redrawn by the publisher. Please provide all illustrations in quadruplicate (one high-contrast original and three photocopies). Care should be taken that lettering and symbols are of a comparable size. The illustrations should not be inserted in the text, and should be marked on the back with figure number, title of paper, and author's name. All graphs and diagrams should be referred to as figures, and should be numbered consecutively in the text in Arabic numerals. Illustration for papers submitted as electronic manuscripts should be in traditional form.

12. **Tables** should be numbered consecutively in the text in Arabic numerals and printed on separate sheets.

Any manuscript, which does not conform to the above instructions, may be returned for the necessary revision before publication. Proofs should be corrected carefully; the responsibility for detecting errors lies with the author. Corrections should be restricted to instances in which the proof is at variance with the manuscript. Extensive alterations will be charged. Fifty reprints of each paper are supplied free of charge to the corresponding author; additional reprints are available at cost if they are ordered when the proof is returned.

Journal of Entrepreneurship Education

ADDRESS FOR SUBMISSION:

Current Editor/Check Web Site
Journal of Entrepreneurship Education
Digital Submission Through Web Site
Address other questions to:
 Jim or JoAnn Carland at #s below
USA
Phone: 828-293-9151
Fax: 828-293-9407
E-Mail: info@alliedacademies.org
Web: www.alliedacademies.org
Address May Change:

PUBLICATION GUIDELINES:

Manuscript Length: 16-20
Copies Required: Submit Through Web
Computer Submission: Yes
Format: MS Word, WordPerfect
Fees to Review: 0.00 US$

Manuscript Style:
    American Psychological Association

CIRCULATION DATA:

Reader: Academics
Frequency of Issue: Yearly
Copies per Issue: 1,001 - 2,000
Sponsor/Publisher: Allied Academies, Inc.
Subscribe Price: 75.00 US$
    150.00 US$ Foreign

REVIEW INFORMATION:

Type of Review: Blind Review
No. of External Reviewers: 3
No. of In House Reviewers: 2
Acceptance Rate: 21-30%
Time to Review: 3-4 Months
Reviewers Comments: Yes
Invited Articles: 0-5%
Fees to Publish: US$

MANUSCRIPT TOPICS:
Economic Development; Entrepreneurship Education

MANUSCRIPT GUIDELINES/COMMENTS:

Theoretical or empirical research concerning entrepreneurship education, or educational research which describes or illustrates effective teaching of entrepreneurship or entrepreneurship principles or examines pedagogies appropriate to entrepreneurship education.

Comments. All authors of published manuscripts must be members of the appropriate academy affiliate of Allied Academies. The current membership fee is $75.00 US.

Editorial Policy Guidelines. The primary criterion upon which manuscripts are judged is whether the research advances the art and science of teaching entrepreneurship. Key points include currency, relevancy and usefulness to entrepreneurship educators.

In order for a theoretical manuscript to advance the discipline, it must address the literature to support conclusions or models which extend knowledge and understanding. Consequently, referees pay particular attention to completeness of literature review and appropriateness of conclusions drawn from that review.

In order for an empirical manuscript to advance the discipline, it must employ appropriate and effective sampling and statistical analysis techniques, and must be grounded by a thorough literature review. Consequently, referees pay particular attention to the research methodology and to the conclusions drawn from statistical analyses and their consistency with the literature.

Journal of Environmental Economics and Management

ADDRESS FOR SUBMISSION:

Joseph A. Herriges, Managing Editor
Journal of Environmental Economics and
    Management
Iowa State University
Department of Economics
260 Heady Hall
Ames, IA 50011-1070
USA
Phone:
Fax: 515-294-0221
E-Mail: jeem@iastate.edu
Web: www.elsevier.com
Address May Change:

PUBLICATION GUIDELINES:

Manuscript Length: 25 Avg
Copies Required: Four
Computer Submission: Yes - Email
Format: PDF
Fees to Review: 40.00 US$ Member
    80.00 US$ Non-Member

Manuscript Style:
    See Manuscript Guidelines

CIRCULATION DATA:

Reader: Academics
Frequency of Issue: Bi-Monthly
Copies per Issue: 1,001 - 2,000
Sponsor/Publisher: Elsevier Science
    Publishing Co.
Subscribe Price: 95.00 US$ Individual
    857.00 US$ Institution
    120.00 Euro Indv, 1,091 Euro Inst

REVIEW INFORMATION:

Type of Review: Blind Review
No. of External Reviewers: 2
No. of In House Reviewers: No Reply
Acceptance Rate: 16-18%
Time to Review: 2 - 3 Months
Reviewers Comments: Yes
Invited Articles: 0-5%
Fees to Publish: 0.00 US$

MANUSCRIPT TOPICS:
Econometrics; Environmental Economics; Micro Economics; Natural Resource Economics;
Public Policy Economics

MANUSCRIPT GUIDELINES/COMMENTS:

The Journal of Environmental Economics and Management publishes theoretical and
empirical papers devoted to specific natural resources and environmental issues. For
consideration, papers should (1) contain a substantial element embodying the linkage between
economic systems and environmental and natural resources systems or (2) be of substantial
importance in understanding the management and/or social control of the economy in its
relations with the natural environment. Although the general orientation of the journal is
toward economics, interdisciplinary papers by researchers in other fields of interest to
resource and environmental economists will be welcomed. The journal is intended to be of
interest not only to research economists but also to the scientific community concerned with
resource and environmental management research.

JEEM **Policy Concerning Replication**. For any paper published in this *Journal*, all data used must be clearly documented. Computational methods must be explained in sufficient detail to permit replication, and data used in analyses must be made available to any researcher for purposes of replication. The Editor must be notified at the time that a paper is submitted to the *Journal*, if these conditions cannot be met.

Submission of Manuscripts. All manuscripts should be submitted to: Joseph A. Herriges, *Journal of Environmental Economics and Management*, Department of Economics, Iowa State University, Ames, Iowa 50011-1070. Manuscripts may be submitted in one of two ways. First, four copies of the manuscript, including four sets of good-quality figures, can be submitted through the regular postal or an express service to the above address. Second, authors can send a PDF version of their manuscript by e-mail to JEEM@iastate.edu. When creating the PDF file, be sure that all fonts are embedded into the PDF file. A single hard copy of the paper, along with a cover letter and submission fee, should be sent at the same time to the above address through the regular postal or an express service. Manuscripts submitted electronically will be processed as soon as they are received.

The Association has established a submission fee of $80.00 for non-AERE members and $40.00 for AERE members. Checks should be in U.S. dollars drawn on U.S. banks only (no Eurocheques, please), should be made payable to Iowa State University, and must accompany the original submission of the manuscript. For international wire transfers, please send the submission fee to Bankers Trust Company, Des Moines, Iowa, U.S.A. The Payee is "Iowa State University." The ABA Routing number is 073000642 with the Iowa State University Account Number 057150. Please add the reference *JEEM*. Payment can also be made by VISA or MasterCard, in which case the credit card number, expiration date, and cardholder's name should be provided in a letter accompanying the submitted paper.

Manuscripts submitted to *JEEM* must be written in English and double-spaced throughout. Margins must be at least one inch on all sides and fonts should be no smaller than 11-point. The title and abstract page, described below, must be included. Papers not meeting these minimal formatting guidelines will be returned to the authors without review. *JEEM* will not normally consider for publication manuscripts exceeding forty pages (everything included).

Original papers only will be considered. Manuscripts are accepted for review with the understanding that the same work has not been and will not be nor is presently submitted elsewhere, and that its submission for publication has been approved by all of the authors and by the institution where the work was carried out; further, that any person cited as a source of personal communications has approved such citation. Written authorization may be required at the Editor's discretion. Articles and any other material published in the *Journal of Environmental Economics and Management* represent the opinions of the author(s) and should not be construed to reflect the opinions of the Editor(s) and the Publisher.

Authors submitting a manuscript do so on the understanding that if the manuscript is accepted for publication, copyright in the article, including the right to reproduce the article in all forms and media, shall be assigned exclusively to the Publisher. The Copyright Transfer Agreement, which may be copied from the journal home page listed here, should be signed by the appropriate person and should accompany the original submission of a manuscript to this journal. The transfer of copyright does not take place until the manuscript is accepted for publication.

Authors are responsible for obtaining permissions to reprint previously published figures, tables, and other material. Letters of permission should accompany the final submission.

Electronic Transmission of Accepted Manuscripts. Authors are requested to transmit the text and art of the manuscript in electronic form, via computer disk, e-mail, or FTP, after all revisions have been incorporated and the manuscript has been accepted for publication. Submission as an e-mail attachment is acceptable provided that all files are included in a single archive the size of which does not exceed 2 megabytes (jeem@elsevier.com). Manuscripts prepared using TeX or LaTeX are welcome; however, LaTeX(2e) is strongly preferred. Note that the use of other specialized versions of TeX or extensive use of custom macros may necessitate conventional typesetting from the hard-copy manuscript. Hard-copy printouts of the manuscript and art must also be supplied. The manuscript will be edited according to the style of the journal, and authors must read the proofs carefully. Complete instructions for electronic transmission can be found on the journal home page (http://www.elsevier.com/locate/jeem).

Preparation of Manuscript. Manuscripts should be double-spaced throughout on one side of 8.5 x 11-inch or A4 while paper. Pages should be numbered consecutively and organized as follows:

The **Title Page** (p. 1) should contain the article title, authors' name and complete affiliations, footnotes to the title, a running title of less than 50 characters, and the address for manuscript correspondence (including e-mail address and telephone and fax numbers).

The **Abstract Page** (p. 2) must contain the article title and a single paragraph abstract summarizing the main findings of the paper in less than 150 words. After the abstract a list of up to 10 key words that will be useful for indexing or searching should be included.

References should be cited in the text by Arabic numerals in brackets, e.g., [1], [2], etc. For abbreviations of journal titles, consult "Abbreviations of Names of Serials" reviewed in Mathematical Reviews (Mathematical Reviews Annual Index, American Mathematical Society, 1990). Only articles that have been published or are in press should be included in the references. Unpublished results or personal communications should be cited as such in the text.

1. J.K. Stranlund and K.K. Dhanda, Endogenous monitoring and enforcement of a transferable emissions permit system, J. Environ. Econom. Management 38, 267-282 (1999).
2. A. Ulph, Harmonization and optimal environmental policy in a federal system with asymmetric information, J. Environ. Econom, Management, doi:10.1066/jeem.1999.1098.
3. G. Peterson and T. Mueller, Regional impact of federal tax and spending policies, in "Alternatives to Confrontation" (E. Arnold, Ed.), Heath, Lexington, MA (1980).

Figures should be in a finished form suitable for publication. Number figures consecutively with Arabic numeral, and indicate the top and the authors on the back of each figure. Lettering on drawings should be professional quality or generated by high-resolution computer graphics and must be large enough to withstand appropriate reduction for publication.

Color Figures. Illustrations in color can be accepted only if the authors defray the cost.

Tables should be numbered consecutively with Roman numerals in order of appearance in the text. Type each table double-spaced on a separate page with a short descriptive title typed directly above and with essential footnotes below. Authors should submit complex tables as camera-ready copy.

Proofs will be sent to the corresponding author. To avoid delay in publication, only necessary changes should be made, and proofs should be returned promptly. Authors will be charged for alterations that exceed 10% of the total cost of composition.

Reprints. Twenty-five (25) reprints will be provided free of charge. Additional reprints may be ordered.

Journal of Finance

ADDRESS FOR SUBMISSION:

Robert F. Stambaugh, Editor
Journal of Finance
Wharton School
Dept. of Finance
Electronic Submissions Only
http://services.bepress.com/jof/
Phone: 215-898-5734
Fax:
E-Mail:
Web: www.afajof.org/jofihome.shtml
Address May Change:

PUBLICATION GUIDELINES:

Manuscript Length: Any
Copies Required: Electronic Submission
Computer Submission: Yes - Required
Format: Word, Adobe Acrobat, RTF
Fees to Review: 70.00 US$ AFA Member
   140.00 US$ Non-Member AFA

Manuscript Style:
   See Manuscript Guidelines

CIRCULATION DATA:

Reader: Academics
Frequency of Issue: Bi-Monthly
Copies per Issue: 5,001 - 10,000
Sponsor/Publisher: American Finance
   Association (AFA)/Blackwell Publishing
Subscribe Price:
   See Web Site

REVIEW INFORMATION:

Type of Review: Blind Review
No. of External Reviewers: 1
No. of In House Reviewers: 1
Acceptance Rate: 6-7%
Time to Review: 1 - 2 Months
Reviewers Comments: Yes
Invited Articles: 0-5%
Fees to Publish: 0.00 US$

MANUSCRIPT TOPICS:
Econometrics; International Finance; Portfolio & Security Analysis

MANUSCRIPT GUIDELINES/COMMENTS:

The *Journal of Finance* is the world's leading journal in financial economics, published by The American Finance Association (AFA).

The *Journal of Finance* publishes leading research across all the major fields of financial research. It is the most widely cited academic journal in finance and one of the most widely cited journals in economics as well. Each issue of the *Journal* reaches over 8,000 academics, finance professionals, libraries, government and financial institutions around the world. Published six times a year, the *Journal* is the official publication of The American Finance Association, the premier academic organization devoted to the study and promotion of knowledge about financial economics. Membership in the AFA includes a subscription to the *Journal of Finance*.

Electronic Submission Information

All papers must be submitted electronically. To enter the submission site, go to http://services.bepress.com/jof/.

Acceptable formats for electronic submission include Adobe Acrobat, Microsoft Word, and RTF. In preparing Acrobat files, make sure that all fonts are embedded, and it is recommended that the document be created using Distiller.

Fees for submission are US$70.00 for AFA members and US$140.00 for nonmembers. Submission fees will be paid via credit card (Visa, MasterCard or American Express) as part of the submission procedure.

The following style instructions should be followed in manuscripts submitted for publication in the *Journal of Finance*.

1. All submitted manuscripts must be original work that is not under submission at another journal or under consideration for publication in another form, such as a monograph or chapter of a book. Authors of submitted papers are obligated not to submit their paper for publication elsewhere until an editorial decision is rendered on their submission. Further, authors of accepted papers are prohibited from publishing the results in other publications that appear before the paper is published in the *Journal* unless they receive approval for doing so from the managing editor.

2. Manuscripts must be clearly typed with double spacing throughout. The pitch must not exceed 12 characters per inch, and the character height must be at least 10 points. All text should be double-spaced.

3. The cover page shall contain the title of the manuscript, and an abstract of not more than 100 words. *The title page should not include the names of the authors, their affiliations, or any other identifying information. That information must be input separately as part of the on-line submission.*

4. *An abstract, of no more than 100 words, must be entered or pasted into a separate text box as part of the on-line submission.*

5. The **introductory** section must have no heading or number. Subsequent headings should be given Roman numerals. Subsection headings should be lettered A, B, C, etc.

6. The article should end with a non-technical **summary statement** of the main conclusions. Lengthy mathematical proofs and very extensive detailed tables should be placed in an appendix or omitted entirely. The author should make every effort to explain the meaning of mathematical proofs.

7. **Footnotes**. An initial acknowledgement footnote should not be included. Acknowledgements must be entered or pasted into a separate text box as part of the on-line submission. Footnotes in the text must be numbered consecutively and typed on a separate

page, double-spaced, following the reference section. Footnotes to tables must also be double-spaced and typed on the bottom of the page with the table.

8. **Tables**. Tables must be numbered with Roman numerals. Please check that your text contains a reference to each table. Indicate in the text approximately where each table should be placed. Type each table on a separate page at the end of the paper. Tables must be self-contained, in the sense that the reader must be able to understand them without going back to the text of the paper. Each table must have a title followed by a descriptive legend. Authors must check tables to be sure that the title, column headings, captions, etc., are clear and to the point.

9. **Figures** must be numbered with Arabic numerals. All figure captions must be typed in double space on a separate sheet following the footnotes. A figure's title should be part of the caption. Figures must be self-contained. Each figure must have a title followed by a descriptive legend. *Final figures for accepted papers must be submitted in native electronic form and uploaded as separate files on the submission site.*

10. **Equations**. All but very short mathematical expressions should be displayed on a separate line and centered. Equations must be numbered consecutively on the right margin, using Arabic numerals in parentheses. Use Greek letters only when necessary. Do not use a dot over a variable to denote time derivative; only D operator notations are acceptable.

11. **References** must be typed on a separate page, double-spaced, at the end of the paper. References to publications in the text should appear as follows: "Jensen and Meckling (1976) report that..." or "(Jenson and Meckling (1976))." At the end of the manuscript (before tables and figures), the complete list of references should be as follows:

For Monographs
Fama, Eugene F., and Merton H. Miller, 1972. The Theory of Finance (Dryden Press, Hinsdale, Ill.).

For Contributions to Collective Works
Grossman, Sanford J., and Oliver D. Hart, 1982, Corporate financial structure and managerial incentives, in John J. McCall, ed.: The Economics of Information and Uncertainty (University of Chicago Press, Chicago, Ill.).

For Periodicals
Jensen, Michael C., and William H. Meckling, 1976, Theory of the firm: Managerial behavior, agency costs and ownership structure, Journal of Financial Economics 3, 305-360

Journal of Finance Case Research

ADDRESS FOR SUBMISSION:

Robert Stretcher, Managing Editor
Journal of Finance Case Research
Department of General
  Business and Finance
Box 2062 SHSU
Huntsville, TX 77341
USA
Phone: 936-294-3308
Fax: 936-294-3074
E-Mail: editor@jfcr.org
Web: www.jfcr.org
Address May Change:

PUBLICATION GUIDELINES:

Manuscript Length: Up to 80
Copies Required: One Electronic
Computer Submission: Yes
Format: MS Word, WordPerfect
Fees to Review:
    See Guidelines

Manuscript Style:
    American Psychological Association,
    except use italics instead of underline

CIRCULATION DATA:

Reader: Academics
Frequency of Issue: 2 Times/Year
Copies per Issue: Less than 1,000
Sponsor/Publisher: Institute of Finance
  Case Research
Subscribe Price: 0.00 US$ IFCR Member
  70.00 US$ Library

REVIEW INFORMATION:

Type of Review: Blind Review
No. of External Reviewers: 2
No. of In House Reviewers: 1
Acceptance Rate: 20-25%
Time to Review: 4 - 5 Months
Reviewers Comments: Yes
Invited Articles: 0-5%
Fees to Publish: 47.00 US$

MANUSCRIPT TOPICS:

Cases in Finance; International Finance; Micro Economics; Monetary Policy; Portfolio &
Security Analysis

MANUSCRIPT GUIDELINES/COMMENTS:

Submission of Manuscripts. Electronic, via email. Fees and submissions details at
www.jfcr.org

Types of Manuscripts. Decision cases or discussion cases in finance topic areas

Style Sheets and Editorial Guidelines are available by direct request or at www.jfcr.org.

Journal of Financial and Economic Practice

ADDRESS FOR SUBMISSION:

Allen L. Webster, Editor
Journal of Financial and Economic Practice
Bradley University
Foster College of Business
Dept of Finance & Quantitative Methods
Peoria, IL 61625
USA
Phone: 309-677-2312
Fax: 309-677-3374
E-Mail: alw@bradley.edu
Web: www.bradley.edu/fcba/fin/jfep
Address May Change:

PUBLICATION GUIDELINES:

Manuscript Length: 16-20
Copies Required: Four
Computer Submission: Yes Disk, Email
Format: MS Word
Fees to Review: 30.00 US$

Manuscript Style:
    Chicago Manual of Style

CIRCULATION DATA:

Reader: Academics, Business Persons
Frequency of Issue: 2 Times/Year
Copies per Issue: Less than 1,000
Sponsor/Publisher: Department of Finance
    and Quantitative Methods, Foster College
    of Business
Subscribe Price: 30.00 US$ Individual

REVIEW INFORMATION:

Type of Review: Blind Review
No. of External Reviewers: 3
No. of In House Reviewers: 1
Acceptance Rate: 11-20%
Time to Review: 2 - 3 Months
Reviewers Comments: Yes
Invited Articles: 0-5%
Fees to Publish: 0.00 US$

MANUSCRIPT TOPICS:

Econometrics; Economic Development; Economic History; Financial Services; Fiscal Policy; Insurance; International Economics & Trade; International Finance; Macro Economics; Micro Economics; Monetary Policy; Portfolio & Security Analysis; Real Estate

MANUSCRIPT GUIDELINES/COMMENTS:

Editors. Dr. Allen L. Webster and Dr. Philip Horvath, Foster College of Business, Bradley University

A journal dedicated to challenge conventional theory, energize empirical research and enlighten practice in finance, economics, and financial economics.

The *Journal of Financial and Economic Practice* is a peer-reviewed, refereed journal designed to serve as an outlet for quality research that combines academic rigor with the practical applications of financial and economic principles. The *Journal* is published by the Department of Finance and Quantitative Methods, Foster College of Business Administration, Bradley University. Manuscripts pertaining to all popular aspect of economics and finance are solicited for review. Articles of interest to both academicians and practitioners will be considered.

Articles previously published or currently under review with another journal are not acceptable.

Although the *Journal* will seriously consider empirical studies designed to test hypotheses and examine economic and financial models, we are not seeking papers that simply contain another regression model. Instead, the *Journal* is interested in introspective and insightful discourse and discussion that scrutinizes and evaluates economic and financial issues of a topical and timely nature. An intuitive, innovative and perceptive assessment of pressing economic and financial concerns is of particular interest. Emphasis is placed on the manner in which the relevant economic and financial concepts presented in the paper can be applied in a business setting.

Please submit four (4) copies of your manuscript to the addresses of the editors shown below. A submission fee of $30.00, which also entitles the author(s) to a one-year subscription to the *Journal*, must accompany the submission. Checks should be made payable to The *Journal of Financial and Economic Practice* (*JFEP*). Articles may also be submitted electronically in a Microsoft Word file to jfep@bradley.edu or to alw@bradley.edu.

The manuscript must be single-spaced with one inch margins accompanied by a cover letter containing the 1) title of the manuscript, 2) author name, title, affiliation, mailing address, and e-mail if available. The first page of the manuscript should begin with the title in 12-point Times New Roman font followed by an abstract in 10-point font, italicized, and not to exceed 200 words indented one tab space on both sides. The rest of the paper should also be in 10-point font.

Tables, etc. All tables, charts, graphs and other insertions should appear at the end of the manuscript just prior to the REFERENCES page(s). They should be centered horizontally on the page, numbered and contain an appropriate heading such as Table 4—Productivity Estimates of Japanese Firms and American Firms (notice the method of capitalization used).

Headings. Section headings should be left justified in **bold** and all capitalized such as **MAIN HEADING** while subheadings should be left justified in **bold** with only first letter of each word capitalized such as **Subheading.**

Equations. Equations should be centered on the page on which they are first referenced and identified with Arabic numbers that are right justified.

References. Citations within the text should be identified in parentheses such as, "Earlier research (Smith) has shown that..." If cited authors(s) have more than one paper listed on the REFERENCES page a date must be used to distinguish citations such as (Smith, 2002). Latin letters are to be used if the same author(s) have two or more papers cited in the same year (Smith, 2002A). This distinction must also appear in the REFERENCES page. If the author's name is used in the text of the paper only the date should be enclosed in parentheses, such as "In his earlier research, Smith (2002) showed that..."

Footnotes. Footnotes should be kept to a minimum. All footnotes should be numbered consecutively and placed at the end of the manuscript just before the REFERENCES page(s).

Pages should not be numbered.

The reference page(s) should appear at the end of the document with the word REFERENCES centered at the top. The reference entries should follow the *Chicago Manual of Style*.

Below is an example of what the first page should look like.

Title Centered Here In Twelve-Point Font

Author Name; Title; Affiliation; e-mail (in 10-point font)

Abstract here in italics and indented one tab stop on both right and left ends (10-point font)

Begin main body here in 10-point font.

Journal of Financial and Quantitative Analysis

ADDRESS FOR SUBMISSION:

Paul Malatestra, Managing Editor
Journal of Financial and Quantitative
   Analysis
University of Washington
School of Business Administration
115 Lewis Hall
Box 353200
Seattle, WA 98195-3200
USA
Phone: 206-543-4598
Fax: 206-616-1894
E-Mail: jfqa@u.washington.edu
Web: http://depts.washington.edu/jfqa/
Address May Change:

PUBLICATION GUIDELINES:

Manuscript Length: No Limit
Copies Required: Two
Computer Submission: Yes
Format: PDF, MS Word
Fees to Review: 200.00 US$ Subscribers
   255.00 US$ Non-Subscribers

Manuscript Style:
   See Manuscript Guidelines

CIRCULATION DATA:

Reader: Academics, Business Persons,
   Practitioners
Frequency of Issue: Quarterly
Copies per Issue: 3,001 - 4,000
Sponsor/Publisher: University of
   Washington
Subscribe Price: 60.00 US$ Individual
   130.00 US$ Library, Firm
   25.00 US$ Student

REVIEW INFORMATION:

Type of Review: Blind Review
No. of External Reviewers: 1
No. of In House Reviewers: No Reply
Acceptance Rate: 10-12%
Time to Review: 2 - 3 Months
Reviewers Comments: Yes
Invited Articles: No Reply
Fees to Publish: 0.00 US$

MANUSCRIPT TOPICS:
Cost Accounting; International Economics & Trade

MANUSCRIPT GUIDELINES/COMMENTS:

The *Journal of Financial and Quantitative Analysis* (*JFQA*) is published quarterly in March, June, September, and December by the School of Business Administration at the University of Washington in Seattle, Washington, USA.

Submission of Articles
The *JFQA* publishes theoretical and empirical research in financial economics. Topics include corporate finance, investments, capital and security markets, and quantitative methods of particular relevance to financial researchers.

The *JFQA* gives prompt attention to all submitted manuscripts. Consistent with this policy, honoraria are paid to referees who provide timely reviews.

Send manuscripts via email in PDF or Word (or alternately hard copy manuscripts may be sent in duplicate), with a cover letter and $200 submission fee for subscribers ($255 for non-subscribers) to:

Managing Editors
Journal of Financial and Quantitative Analysis
University of Washington, School of Business Administration
115 Lewis, Box 353200, Seattle, WA 98195-3200 USA
or jfqa@u.washington.edu.

Payment. Checks must be payable to the *JFQA* in U.S. dollars for deposit in a U.S. bank. VISA, MasterCard, and American Express are also accepted.

Style Requirements
Send manuscripts via e-mail in PDF or mail hard copy manuscripts in duplicate on 8.5" x 11" paper. The cover page must show title, author name(s) and affiliation(s), e-mail address(es), and work phone number(s). The first page of text should begin with the title only. A one-paragraph abstract of no more than 100 words must be included. Manuscripts must be double-spaced on one side of the page. All sections of the paper, beginning with the introduction and ending with a conclusion or summary, must be numbered with Roman numerals. Subsection headings must be lettered A, B, C, etc.

The manuscript should explain its relation to other research in the field, especially recently published material. References cited in the text should be noted by the last name(s) of the author(s) followed by the publication year enclosed in parentheses without punctuation: Smith (1988). When a particular page, section, or equation is referred to, the reference also should be placed within parentheses: (Smith and Jones (1988), p. 222), (Green (1988a), eq. 3).

Lengthy mathematical proofs and extensive tables should be placed in an appendix or omitted from the manuscript entirely. In the latter case, the author may indicate in a footnote that proofs or tables are available on request. The author should make every effort to explain the meaning of mathematical proofs.

The author should check the manuscript for clarity, grammar, spelling, and punctuation to minimize editorial changes and the necessity of extensive corrections at the proof stage. All abbreviations must be defined.

Equations
All but very short mathematical expressions should be displayed on a separate line and centered. Important displayed equations must be identified by consecutive Arabic numerals in parentheses on the left. Expressions should be aligned and subscripts and superscripts clearly marked to avoid confusion.

Tables
Each table must be titled and numbered consecutively with Arabic numerals. Please check the text to make sure there is a reference to each table. General footnotes should be marked as a, b, c, etc., for specific footnotes. Asterisks * or ** indicate significance at the 5% and 1%

levels, respectively. The author should check tables to be sure that totals are correct and that the title, column headings, and footnotes clearly explain the content of the table. If tables are on separate pages at the end of the article, indicate approximate placement within the text.

Figures

Figures must be titled and numbered consecutively with Arabic numerals. Captions should present sufficient information to describe the purpose of the figure. Figures for accepted manuscripts must be of professional quality and ready for reproduction.

Footnotes

Footnotes must be double-spaced. Footnotes must not be used for the purpose of citation. Footnotes with extensive content should be avoided.

References

All works cited in the text must be alphabetically arranged in a double-spaced list at the end of the manuscript. Examples:

Brown, S., and J. Warner. "Using Daily Stock Returns: The Case of Event Studies." *Journal of Financial Economics,* 14 (1985), 1-31.

Ross, S.A. "Return, Risk and Arbitrage." In *Risk and Return in Finance,* Vol. I, I. Friend and J. L. Bicksler, eds. Cambridge, MA: Ballinger (1977).

Journal of Financial Crime

ADDRESS FOR SUBMISSION:

Daryn Moody, Editor
Journal of Financial Crime
Henry Stewart Publications
Museum House
25 Museum Street
London, WC1A 1JT
UK
Phone: 44 (0)20.7323.2916
Fax: 44 (0)20.7323.2918
E-Mail: daryn@hspublications.co.uk
Web: www.henrystewart.co.uk
Address May Change:

PUBLICATION GUIDELINES:

Manuscript Length: 10-30
Copies Required: Three
Computer Submission: Yes
Format: MS Word
Fees to Review: 0.00 US$

Manuscript Style:
, Vancouver

CIRCULATION DATA:

Reader: Academics, Business Persons
Frequency of Issue: Quarterly
Copies per Issue: 1,001 - 2,000
Sponsor/Publisher: Henry Stewart
  Publications
Subscribe Price: 130.00 US$ Individual
  400.00 US$ Institution
  85.00 Pounds Indv, 270 Pounds Inst

REVIEW INFORMATION:

Type of Review: Blind Review
No. of External Reviewers: 2
No. of In House Reviewers: 1
Acceptance Rate: 21-30%
Time to Review: 1 - 2 Months
Reviewers Comments: Yes
Invited Articles: 6-10%
Fees to Publish: 0.00 US$

MANUSCRIPT TOPICS:
Accounting Theory & Practice; Auditing; Criminology; Economic Crime; Financial
Institutions & Markets; Financial Services; Fiscal Policy; International Economics & Trade;
International Finance; Tax Accounting

MANUSCRIPT GUIDELINES/COMMENTS:

1. Papers should be between 2,000 and 6,000 words in length. They should be typewritten,
double-spaced, on A4 or US letter-sized paper. A copy should also be submitted on disk with
a note of the hardware and software used.

2. All papers should be accompanied by a short abstract, outlining the aims and subject matter.

3. All papers should be accompanied by a short (about 80 words) description of the author(s)
and, if appropriate, the organization of which he or she is a member.

4. Papers should be supported by actual or hypothetical examples, wherever possible and appropriate. Authors should not seek to use the *Journal* as a vehicle for marketing any specific product or service.

5. Authors should avoid the use of language or slang, which is not in keeping with the academic and professional style of the *Journal*.

6. Titles of organizations, etc., should be written out first in full, followed by the organization's initials in brackets, and thereafter, only their initials should be used.

7. Papers should be supported by references. These should be set out in accordance with the Vancouver style—that is, they should be referred to by number in the text and set out in full in numerical order at the end of the text.

8. Photographs and illustrations supporting papers should be submitted where appropriate. Photographs should be good quality positives, printed from the original negatives and in black and white only. Figures and other line illustrations should be submitted in good quality originals and a copy of the data should also be included.

9. Authors are asked to ensure the references to named people and/or organizations are accurate and without libelous implications.

10. All contributions sent to the publisher, whether they are invited or not, will be sent to the Editor and also submitted to two members of the Editorial Board for double-blind peer review. Any such contribution must bear the author's full name and address, even if this is not for publication. Contributions, whether published pseudonymously or not, are accepted on the strict understanding that the author is responsible for the accuracy of all opinion, technical comment, factual report, data figures, illustrations, and photographs. Publication does not necessarily imply that these are the opinions of the editors, Editorial Board or the publisher, nor does the Board accept any liability for the accuracy of such comment, report, and other technical and factual information. The publisher will, however, strive to ensure that all opinions, comments, reports, data, figures, illustrations, and photographs are accurate, insofar as it is within its abilities to do so. The publisher reserves the right to edit, abridge or omit material submitted for publication.

11. The author bears the responsibility for checking whether material submitted is subject to copyright or ownership rights, e.g., photographs, illustrations, trade literature, and data. Where use is so restricted, the publisher must be informed with the submission of the material.

12. No contribution will be accepted which has been published elsewhere, unless it is expressly invited or agreed by the editors and the publisher. Papers and contributions published become the copyright of the publisher, unless otherwise stated.

13. All reasonable efforts are made to ensure accurate reproduction of text, photographs, and illustrations. The publisher does not accept responsibility for mistakes, be they editorial or typographical, nor for consequences resulting from them.

Journal of Financial Economics

ADDRESS FOR SUBMISSION:

G. William Schwert, Managing Editor
Journal of Financial Economics
University of Rochester
William E. Simon Graduate School
  of Business
Rochester, NY 14627
USA
Phone: 585-275-2470
Fax: 585-461-5475
E-Mail: jfe@jfe.rochester.edu
Web: jfe.rochester.edu
Address May Change:

PUBLICATION GUIDELINES:

Manuscript Length: 20-50
Copies Required: Four
Computer Submission: Optional
Format: N/A
Fees to Review: 400.00 US$ Subscribers
    450.00 US$ Non-Subscribers

Manuscript Style:
    See Manuscript Guidelines

CIRCULATION DATA:

Reader: Academics
Frequency of Issue: Monthly
Copies per Issue: 2,000-2,500
Sponsor/Publisher: University of Rochester
  /Elsevier Publishing
Subscribe Price: 95.00 US$ Individual
    1339.00 US$ Institution
    91.00 Euro Indv., 1,681 Euro Inst.

REVIEW INFORMATION:

Type of Review: Blind Review
No. of External Reviewers: 1-2
No. of In House Reviewers: 0
Acceptance Rate: 11-20%
Time to Review: 2 - 3 Months
Reviewers Comments: Yes
Invited Articles: 0-5%
Fees to Publish: 0.00 US$

MANUSCRIPT TOPICS:

Corporate Finance; Financial Institutions & Markets; Financial Services; International Finance; Portfolio & Security Analysis

MANUSCRIPT GUIDELINES/COMMENTS:

Description

The Journal of Financial Economics began a new section containing applied papers and case studies in 1989. This section provides a high-quality professional outlet for scholarly studies of actual cases, events or practice. Such phenomena provide a rich source of data that illustrate or challenge accepted theory and lead to new insights about the world. These studies currently have few professional outlets, and with this section *The Journal of Financial Economics* takes a leading role in encouraging such work. Applications and case study papers are often different in form, scope and content and can be more conjectural. The papers deal with issues that are often less quantifiable, more descriptive and normative than usual. Papers that raise a new question or pose an old one in an innovative way and papers that test theories in specialized ways or document interesting phenomena which are likely to stimulate new research are emphasized.

Guide for Authors
1. Papers must be in English.

2. Papers for publication should be sent in quadruplicate to:
    Professor G. William Schwert
    Managing Editor
    William E. Simon Graduate School of Business Administration
    University of Rochester
    Rochester, NY 14627, USA
    E-mail: Schwert@schwert.ssb.rochester.edu

Submission fee: Unsolicited manuscripts must be accompanied by a submission fee of $400 for authors who are current *Journal of Financial Economics* subscribers and $450 for non-subscribers. This submission fee will be refunded for all accepted manuscripts. To encourage quicker response, referees are paid an honorarium out of the submission fee. There are no page charges.

Payment may be made by Visa or MasterCard. The cardholder's name, credit card number, and expiration date must be included with the submission. Alternatively, the submission fee can be paid by check made payable to the *Journal of Financial Economics*, but it must be drawn on a U.S. Bank and in U.S. currency.

Submission of a paper will be held to imply that it contains original unpublished work and is not being submitted for publication elsewhere. The Editor does not accept responsibility for damage or loss of papers submitted. Upon acceptance of an article, author(s) will be asked to transfer copyright of the article to the publisher. This transfer will ensure the widest possible dissemination of information.

3. Submission of accepted papers as electronic manuscripts, i.e., on disk with accompanying manuscript, is encouraged. Electronic manuscripts have the advantage that there is no need for rekeying of text, thereby avoiding the possibility of introducing errors and resulting in reliable and fast delivery of proofs. The preferred storage medium is a 5.25 or 3.5 inch disk in MS-DOS format, although other systems are welcome, e.g., Macintosh (in this case, save your file in the usual manner; do not use the option 'save in MS-DOS format'). Do not submit your original paper as electronic manuscript but hold on to disk until asked for this by the Editor (in case your paper is accepted without revisions). Do submit the accepted version of your paper as electronic manuscript. Make absolutely sure that the file on the disk and the printout are identical. Please use a new and correctly formatted disk and label this with your name; also specify the software and hardware used as well as the title of the file to be processed. Do not convert the file to plain ASCII. Ensure that the letter 'l' and digit '1', and also the letter 'O' and digit '0' are used properly, and format your article (tabs, indents, etc.) consistently. Characters not available on your word processor (Greek letters mathematical symbols, etc.) should not be left open but indicated by a unique code (e.g. gralpha, alpha, etc., for the Greek letter α). Such codes should be used consistently throughout the entire text; a list of codes used should accompany the electronic manuscript. Do not allow your word processor to

introduce word breaks and do not use a justified layout. Please adhere strictly to the general instructions below on style, arrangement and, in particular, the reference style of the *Journal*.

4. Manuscripts should be double spaced, with wide margins, and printed on one side of the paper only. All pages should be numbered consequently. Titles and subtitles should be short. References, tables, and legends for the figures should be printed on separate pages.

5. The first page of the manuscript should contain the following information: (i) the title; (ii) the name(s) and institutional affiliation(s) of the author(s); (iii) an abstract of not more than 100 words. A footnote on the same sheet should give the name, address, and telephone and fax numbers of the corresponding author [as well as an e-mail address].

6. The first page of the manuscript should also contain at least one classification code according to the Classification System for Journal Articles as used by the *Journal of Economic Literature*; in addition, up to five key words should be supplied.

7. Acknowledgements and information on grants received can be given in a first footnote, which should not be included in the consecutive numbering of footnotes.

8. Footnotes should be kept to a minimum and numbered consecutively throughout the text with superscript Arabic numerals.

9. Displayed formulae should be numbered consecutively throughout the manuscript as (1), (2), etc. against the right-hand margin of the page. In cases where the derivation of formulae has been abbreviated, it is of great help to the referees if the full derivation can be presented on a separate sheet (not to be published).

10. References to publications should be as follows: 'Smith (1992) reported that...' or 'This problem has been studied previously (e.g., Smith et al., 1969)'. The author should make sure that there is a strict one-to-one correspondence between the names and years in the text and those on the list. The list of references should appear at the end of the main text (after any appendices, but before tables and legends for figures). It should be double spaced and listed in alphabetical order by author's name. References should appear as follows:

For monographs
Hawawini, G. and I. Swary, 1990, Mergers and acquisitions in the U.S. banking industry: Evidence from the capital markets (North-Holland, Amsterdam).

For contributions to collective works
Brunner, K., Meltzer, A., 1990. Money supply. in: B.M. Friedman and F.H. Hahn, eds., Handbook of monetary economics, Vol. 1 (North- Holland, Amsterdam) 357-396.

For periodicals
Griffiths, W. and G. Judge, 1992, Testing and estimating location vectors when the error covariance matrix is unknown, Journal of Econometrics 54, 121-138.

Note that journal titles should not be abbreviated.

11. Illustrations will be reproduced photographically from originals supplied by the author; they will not be redrawn by the publisher. Please provide all illustrations in quadruplicate (one high-contrast original and three photocopies). Care should be taken that lettering and symbols are of a comparable size. The illustrations should not be inserted in the text, and should be marked on the back with figure number, title of paper, and author's name. All graphs and diagrams should be referred to as figures, and should be numbered consecutively in the text in Arabic numerals. Illustration for papers submitted as electronic manuscripts should be in traditional form.

12 Tables should be numbered consecutively in the text in Arabic numerals and printed on separate sheets.

Any manuscript which does not conform to the above instructions may be returned for the necessary revision before publication.

Page proofs will be sent to the corresponding author. Proofs should be corrected carefully; the responsibility for detecting errors lies with the author. Corrections should be restricted to instances in which the proof is at variance with the manuscript. No deviations from the version accepted by the Editors are permissible without the prior and explicit approval by the Editors; these alterations will be charged. Fifty reprints of each paper are supplied free of charge to the corresponding author; additional reprints are available at cost if they are ordered when the proof is returned.

Journal of Financial Education

ADDRESS FOR SUBMISSION:

Jean L. Heck, Editor
Journal of Financial Education
Villanova University
Department of Finance
Villanova, PA 19085
USA
Phone: 610-519-4325
Fax: 610-519-6881
E-Mail: jean.heck@villanoval.edu
Web: www.fea.villanova.edu
Address May Change:

PUBLICATION GUIDELINES:

Manuscript Length: Any
Copies Required: Three
Computer Submission: Yes Email
Format: See Web Site
Fees to Review: 30.00 US$

Manuscript Style:
    See Manuscript Guidelines

CIRCULATION DATA:

Reader: Academics
Frequency of Issue: Quarterly
Copies per Issue: Less than 1,000
Sponsor/Publisher: Financial Education
    Association
Subscribe Price: 40.00 US$ Individual
    80.00 US$ Institution
    10.00 US$ Xtra International (Air)

REVIEW INFORMATION:

Type of Review: Blind Review
No. of External Reviewers: 2
No. of In House Reviewers: 0
Acceptance Rate: 25-30%
Time to Review: 3 Months
Reviewers Comments: Yes
Invited Articles: 0%
Fees to Publish: 0.00 US$

MANUSCRIPT TOPICS:
Corporate Finance; Financial Institutions & Markets; Insurance; International Finance;
Portfolio & Security Analysis; Real Estate

MANUSCRIPT GUIDELINES/COMMENTS:

Topics
All finance subject areas regarding educational research, teaching/pedagogy, cases, literature
reviews and special topics of interest to finance educators.

1. Statement of Editorial Policy
The *Journal of Financial Education* is to bring to the finance discipline important educational
research results, innovative classroom approaches and tools to enhance teaching. The journal
seeks submissions for the following journal sections:
a.   Educational Research - statistical testing of questions on the educational process
b.   Pedagogical Tools - interesting and unique ways concepts can be covered in class or
      otherwise enhance student learning
c.   Financial Cases - learning by applying finance principles in real world-like situations
d.   Review Articles - papers bringing readers up to date on a narrowly defined topical area

e.   Book and Software Reviews - brief looks into book and computer resources relevant to the classroom and research

2. Manuscript Submissions

Three copies of the manuscript should be sent to the Editor.

Submitted manuscripts should conform to the following style specifications.

Authors of accepted manuscripts will receive specific instructions on preparing manuscript for final publication.

3. Author Information

First page of the manuscript is the cover page and should include:

a.   paper title
b.   author(s) names
c.   institutional affiliations
d.   address, phone and fax of contact person

Second page of manuscript is the abstract page and should include:

a.   paper title
b.   paper abstract not to exceed 150 words

Third page of manuscript begins paper and begins with paper title.

4. Headings

Three levels of headings are allowed. The first level of heading is left justified with all letters capitalized. The second level of heading is left justified with the first letter of each word capitalized. The third level of heading is left justified and italicized.

The first section of paper is titled "INTRODUCTION."

5. Manuscript Text

All text of paper should be double-spaced with paragraphs indented.

6. Endnotes/Footnotes

No footnotes! Keep endnotes to a minimum, numbered consecutively throughout the text with superscripted Arabic numerals. Endnotes should appear at the end of the paper, but before **References** section.

7. Equations

Number all equations consecutively and place the number in parentheses at the right margin.

8. Tables and Figures

Tables and figures should be on a separate pages at end of paper following REFERENCES section. Note approximate position of tables and figures in body of paper with "PUT TABLE NO.1 HERE" between double lines. Table and figure headings should be at top of tables/figures, left justified and appear like as "TABLE 1: Title of Table." Camera ready copy of figures must be provided by author for accepted manuscripts.

9. References

References should be at end of the paper in alphabetical order by author's last name. Text citations should refer to author and year in brackets as [Smith, 1979].

10. Professional Presentation

Manuscript should be written in the third person. Check the manuscript for clarity, grammar, spelling and punctuation.

12. Requirements For Accepted Manuscripts

Manuscripts accepted for publication must be provided on a 3.5" disk using either WordPerfect, Microsoft Word or ASCII formats. Specific instructions provided upon acceptance.

Journal of Financial Intermediation

ADDRESS FOR SUBMISSION:

Anjan Thakor, Editor
Journal of Financial Intermediation
Washington University
Olin School of Business
Campus Box 1133
One Brookings Drive
St. Louis, MO 63130-4899
USA
Phone: 314-935-5614
Fax: 314-935-6392
E-Mail: jfi@olin.wustl.edu
Web: www.olin.wustl.edu/jfi/
Address May Change:

PUBLICATION GUIDELINES:

Manuscript Length: 21-30
Copies Required: Disk
Computer Submission: Yes
Format: PDF
Fees to Review: 75.00 US$ Subscribers
125.00 US$ Non-Subscribers

Manuscript Style:
See Manuscript Guidelines

CIRCULATION DATA:

Reader: Academics
Frequency of Issue: Quarterly
Copies per Issue: 1,001 - 2,000
Sponsor/Publisher: Academic Press, Inc.,
Elsevier Science Publishing Co.
Subscribe Price: 65.00 US$ Individual
330.00 US$ Institution
65.00 Euro Indv, 424 Euro Institution

REVIEW INFORMATION:

Type of Review: Blind Review
No. of External Reviewers: 2
No. of In House Reviewers: 0
Acceptance Rate: 6-10%
Time to Review: 1 - 2 Months
Reviewers Comments: Yes
Invited Articles: 0-5%
Fees to Publish: 0.00 US$

MANUSCRIPT TOPICS:

Banking & Finance; Corporate Finance; Insurance; International Economics & Trade; International Finance; Stock Market

MANUSCRIPT GUIDELINES/COMMENTS:

The *Journal of Financial Intermediation* stresses the use of contemporary analytical and empirical tools to collect and stimulate research in the design of financial contracts and institutions. Interest in this field is related to the development of information economics and options pricing.

Research areas include
- Theory of financial intermediation, especially the evolution and role of financial institutions
- Informational bases for the design of financial contracts
- The role of insurance firms in influencing allocations and the efficiency of market equilibrium

- Choices among financing sources
- The role of investment bankers in the development of new financial contracts and methods of raising capital
- Lending and funding behavior of depository financial institutions under informational asymmetry and uncertainty
- Economics of financial engineering
- Interactions between real and financial decisions
- Public regulation of financial markets and institutions in the context of market globalization

Submission of manuscripts. Submit manuscripts in quadruplicate (original and three copies), including four sets of illustrations, to: Professor Anjan V. Thakor e-mail: jfi@umich.edu. There is submission fee of $75.00 for subscribers to the *Journal* and $125.00 for nonsubscribers. Revisions will not require additional fees. Checks should be made payable to *Journal of Financial Intermediation* and must accompany the original submission of the manuscript.

Original papers only will be considered. Manuscripts are accepted for review with the understanding that the same work has not been published, that it is not under consideration for publication elsewhere, and that its submission for publication has been approved by all of the authors and by the institution where the work was carried out. It is further understood that any person cited as a source of personal communications has approved such citation; written authorization may be required at the Editors' discretion. Articles and any other material published in *Journal of Financial Intermediation* represent the opinions of the authors and should not be construed to reflect the opinions of the Editors or the Publisher. For inquiries on pending manuscripts please contact the editorial office at (734) 647-6433 or jfi@umich.edu.

Authors submitting a manuscript do so on the understanding that if it is accepted for publication, copyright in the article, including the right to reproduce the article in all forms and media, shall be assigned exclusively to the Publisher. The Copyright Transfer Agreement, which may be copied from the pages following the Information for Authors or found on the *Journal* home page listed here, should be signed by the appropriate person(s) and should accompany the original submission of a manuscript to this *Journal*. The transfer of copyright does not take effect until the manuscript is accepted for publication.

Form of manuscript. Submit manuscripts in quadruplicate and double-spaced on one side of 8.5 x 11-inch white paper. Number all pages consecutively. *Page 1* should contain the article title, author(s) name(s), and complete affiliation(s) (name of institution, city, state, and zip code). At the bottom of page 1 place any footnotes to the title (indicated by superscript *, †, ‡). *Page 2* should contain a proposed running head (abbreviated form of the title) of less than 40 characters including letters and spaces, the name and mailing address of the author to whom proofs should be sent, and an abstract of no more than 100 words. The Abstract will appear at the beginning of the article in the *Journal*; use the abstract format and classification numbers which are required by the *Journal of Economic Literature*. *Key words* should be listed immediately after the abstract.

List of symbols. *Page 3* should be a complete typewritten list of symbols used, identified typographically, not mathematically. This list will not appear in print but is *essential* in order to avoid costly corrections in proof. If equations in text are handwritten, the symbols list should be handwritten as well. Distinguish between "oh," "zero,"; "ell," "one,"; "kappa," "kay,"; "vee," "nu"; upper- and lowercase "kay"; etc. Also indicate when special type is required (e.g., German, Greek, boldface, script); all other letters in formulas will be set *italic*.

Tables. Number tables consecutively with Roman numerals in order of appearance in the text. Type each table double-spaced on a separate page. Extensive tables may be reproduced photographically and so should be typed carefully and in the *exact* format desired. Authors will be charged for any new photo reproductions necessitated by changes in proof. A short descriptive caption should be typed directly above each table, and any necessary footnotes (indicated by superscript lowercase italic letters) should be typed double-spaced directly below the table.

Figures. All illustrations are to be considered as figures. Cite figures consecutively in the text with Arabic numerals. Type legends double-spaced consecutively on a separate sheet. **Figures must be submitted in a form suitable for reproduction.** Plan all figures to fit the proportions of the printed page (4.5 x 7.4 in.). Lettering on the original figure should be of professional quality or generated by *high-resolution* computer graphics and should be large enough (10-12 points) to take a reduction of 50 to 60%. *Differences in type size within a single figure should be no more than approximately 15%.* Drawings should be made with black India ink on tracing linen, smooth-surface white paper, or Bristol board. Alternatively, *high-quality* computer graphics may be acceptable. *Symbols used to identify points within a graph should be large enough that they will be easily distinguishable after reduction.* Plot graphs on blue coordinate or white paper no larger than 8.5 x 11 in. Grid lines that are to reproduce must be shown in black. Identify each figure in a margin with the name of the journal, author's name, and figure number; avoid marking the backs of figures.

Submit halftones in duplicate, no larger than 6.5 x 4.5 in. Illustrations in color can be accepted only if the authors defray the cost.

Equations. All equations should be typewritten and the numbers for displayed equations should be placed in parentheses at the right margin. References to equations should use the form "Eq. (3)" or simply "(3)." Superscripts and subscripts should be typed or handwritten clearly above and below the line, respectively. Use the exponent $1/2$ wherever possible.

"Style." In general, authors should be guided by *A Manual for Authors* published in 1962 (and revised in 1980) by the American Mathematical Society, P.O. Box 6248, Providence, RI 02904.

References. Cite references in the text by the author's surname and date of publication. The text citations can be given in the form "As Cummins (1988) showed ..."or "As already shown (Cummins, 1988; Shah and Thakor, 1987)...."Where there are more than two authors, use the first author's surname followed by *et al.*: "In Laffont *et al.* (1987) it was ...."List references in alphabetical order. *Type the references double-spaced throughout.* Style and punctuate references according to the following examples.

CUMMINS, J. D. (1988). Risk-based premiums for insurance guaranty funds, *J. Finance* 43, 823-839.

KAMIEN, M., AND SCHWARTZ, N. (1981). "Dynamic Optimization," North Holland, New York.

LAFFONT, J.-J., MASKIN, E., AND ROCHET, J.-C. (1987). Optimal nonlinear pricing with two dimensional characteristics, *in* "Information, Incentives, and Economic Mechanisms" (T. Groves, R. Radner, and S. Reiter, Eds.), pp. 256-266. Univ. of Minnesota Press, Minneapolis.

SHAH, S., AND THAKOR, A. V. (1987). Optimal capital structure and project financing, *J. Econ. Theory* 42, 209-243.

For unpublished lectures or symposia, include the title of the paper, name of the sponsoring society in full, and date. For journal names, follow the *Journal of Economic Literature* abbreviations.

Footnotes. In text, footnotes should be avoided if at all possible. If they must be used, identify them by superscript Arabic numerals in order of their appearance and type them together on a separate page, double-spaced.

Proofs. Proofs will be sent to the author, with a reprint order form. Authors will be charged for alterations in excess of 10% of the cost of original composition.

Reprints. Fifty reprints (without covers) of each article will be provided free of charge. Authors may purchase additional reprints; an order form will be included with the proofs.

Electronic transmission. Authors are requested to transmit the text and art of the manuscript in electronic form, via either computer disk or FTP, after all revisions have been incorporated and the manuscript has been accepted for publication. Hard-copy printouts of the manuscript and art that exactly match the electronic files must be supplied. The manuscript will be edited according to the style of the *Journal*, and the proofs must be read carefully by the author.

Journal of Financial Management and Analysis

ADDRESS FOR SUBMISSION:

M. R. K. Swamy, Managing Editor
Journal of Financial Management and
   Analysis
Om Sai Ram Centre for
  Financial Management Research
15 Prakash Co-operative Housing Society
Relief Road
Santacruz (West), Mumbai, 400054
India
Phone: 91 22 2660 7715
Fax:
E-Mail: jfmaosr@lycos.com
Web:
Address May Change:

PUBLICATION GUIDELINES:

Manuscript Length: 11-15
Copies Required: Three
Computer Submission: No
Format:
Fees to Review: 30.00 US$

Manuscript Style:
  See Manuscript Guidelines

CIRCULATION DATA:

Reader: Academics, Policy Makers
Frequency of Issue: 2 Times/Year
Copies per Issue: 1,001 - 2,000
Sponsor/Publisher: Om Sai Ram Centre for
  Financial Management Research
Subscribe Price: 120.00 US$

REVIEW INFORMATION:

Type of Review: Blind Review
No. of External Reviewers: 2
No. of In House Reviewers: 3+
Acceptance Rate: 21-30%
Time to Review: 4 - 6 Months
Reviewers Comments: Yes
Invited Articles: 0-5%
Fees to Publish: 0.00 US$

MANUSCRIPT TOPICS:
Corporate Finance; Economic Development; Financial Institutions & Markets; Fiscal Policy;
International Economics & Trade; International Finance; Portfolio & Security Analysis

MANUSCRIPT GUIDELINES/COMMENTS:

Aim
JFMA, a refereed journal, is a unique and a new brand all-purpose reference offering
techniques and new concepts backed up by case studies and provides an excellent bridge
between financial management theory and practice in line with demands of to-day's techno-
economic corporate, cooperative business and public sector business environments. The
Journal, a useful decision kit for finance practitioners, policy makers and scholars from
throughout the world; is published half-yearly (January-June and July-December) every year
by the Om Sai Ram Centre for Financial Management Research, Mumbai, India and the
endeavor is to maintain the highest international quality standards.

784

Submission Guidelines
Submit three typed copies of manuscript with submission fee of US$ 30 or in equivalent Euro along with floppy disk. Check should be payable to Journal of Financial Management and Analysis.

Include an abstract of 300 words along with Journal of Economic Literature (JEL) classification and key words about the manuscript. JEL classification can be found at:
   http://www.aeaweb.org/journal/elclasjn.html

Tables and Figures should have brief descriptive titles and be numbered consecutively. Each table and figure must appear on separate sheets and placed at the end of the article. Indicate the approximate locations of tables and figures in the text with caption such as: "INSERT TABLE 1 OR FIGURE 1 HERE".

All references should appear on the last page under title "REFERENCES".

To minimize editorial changes check the manuscript for figures, quotes, data, etc. from original sources of reference to ensure cent per cent accuracy.

Manuscripts should be sent to: Managing Editor, Journal of Financial Management and Analysis, Om Sai Ram Centre for Financial Management Research, 15 Prakash Co-operative Housing Society, Relief Road, Santacruz (West), Mumbai, 400054, India.

Journal of Financial Markets

ADDRESS FOR SUBMISSION:

Matthew Spiegel, Co-Editor
Journal of Financial Markets
Yale University
School of Management
P.O. Box 208200
New Haven, CT 06520-8200
USA
Phone: 203-432-6017
Fax: 203-432-8931
E-Mail: matthew.spiegel@yale.edu
Web: som.yale.edu/jfm
Address May Change:

PUBLICATION GUIDELINES:

Manuscript Length: 26-30
Copies Required: Four
Computer Submission: No
Format: N/A
Fees to Review: 170.00 US$ Subscriber
    190.00 US$ Non-Subscriber

Manuscript Style:
  , Elsevier Web Site

CIRCULATION DATA:

Reader: Academics
Frequency of Issue: Quarterly
Copies per Issue: Less than 1,000
Sponsor/Publisher: Elsevier Science
    Publishing Co.
Subscribe Price: 50.00 US$ Individual
    301.00 US$ Institution
    48.00 Pounds Indv, 269 Pounds Inst

REVIEW INFORMATION:

Type of Review: Blind Review
No. of External Reviewers: 1
No. of In House Reviewers: 0
Acceptance Rate: 11-20%
Time to Review: 2 - 3 Months
Reviewers Comments: Yes
Invited Articles: 6-10%
Fees to Publish: 0.00 US$

MANUSCRIPT TOPICS:
Financial Institutions & Markets; Portfolio & Security Analysis

MANUSCRIPT GUIDELINES/COMMENTS:

Editors
Professor Bruce Lehmann, University of California, San Diego, blehmann@ucsd.edu
Professor Matthew Spiegel, Yale School of Management, matthew.spiegel@yale.edu,
    http://som.yale.edu/~spiegel
Professor Avanidhar Subrahmanyam, University of California, Los Angeles, subra@anderson
    .ucla.edu, http://www.agsm.ucla.edu/finance/subrabio.htm

Guide for Authors
1. Papers must be in English.

2. Papers for publication should be sent in quadruplicate to Professor Matthew Spiegel.

Manuscripts will be processed by the editor who, in the opinion of the three Co-Editors, is the most familiar with the topic of the paper. A new simplified submission fee structure is now in place. All submissions are now US$170 for both subscribers and non-subscribers. See the submissions page online for details.

Manuscripts will be processed by that editor who, in the opinion of the three Co-Editors, is the most familiar with the topic of the paper. The submission is accompanied by a submission fee of US$ 170.00. Payments can be by cheque; or by credit card having printed and completed the manuscript transmittal form online. The payment should be sent to the Editorial Office together with the submitted article. The above fee reflects the *Journal*'s transactions costs.

If a decision on a manuscript is not rendered within 100 days the *Journal* will refund the submission fee. If one or more authors are current Ph.D. students, the *Journal* guarantees a response in 45 days. In order to fall under the expedited policy for Ph.D. students the cover letter should state which author or authors are students, and include the institution from which they are seeking a degree.

There are no page charges. Submission of a paper will be held to imply that it contains original unpublished work and is not being submitted for publication elsewhere. The Editors do not accept responsibility for damage or loss of papers submitted. Upon acceptance of an article, author(s) will be asked to transfer copyright of the article to the publisher. This transfer will ensure the widest possible dissemination of information. A portion of the submission fees will be used to compensate referees who turn in prompt and helpful reports.

3. Submission of accepted papers as electronic manuscripts, i.e., on disk with accompanying manuscript, is encouraged. Electronic manuscripts have the advantage that there is no need for rekeying of text, thereby avoiding the possibility of introducing errors and resulting in reliable and fast delivery of proofs. The preferred storage medium is a 5.25-inch or 3.5-inch disk in MS-DOS format, although other systems are welcome, e.g., Macintosh (in this case, save your file in the usual manner; do not use the option "save in MS-DOS format"). Do not submit your original paper as electronic manuscript but hold on to the disk until asked for this by the Editors (in case your paper is accepted without revisions). Do submit the accepted version of your paper as electronic manuscript. Make absolutely sure that the file on the disk and the printout are identical. Please use a new and correctly formatted disk and label this with your name; also specify the software and hardware used as well as the title of the file to be processed. Do not convert the file to plain ASCII. Ensure that the letter 'I' and digit '1' and the letter 'O' and digit '0' are used properly, and format your article (tabs, indents, etc.) consistently. Characters not available on your word processor (Greek letters, mathematical symbols, etc.) should not be left open, but indicated by a unique code (e.g., gralpha, alpha, etc., for the Greek letter α). Such codes should be used consistently throughout the entire text; a list of codes used should accompany the electronic manuscript. Do not allow your word processor to introduce word breaks and do not use a justified layout. Please adhere strictly to the general instructions below on style, arrangement and, in particular, the reference style of the *Journal*.

4. Manuscripts should be double-spaced, with wide margins, and printed on one side of the paper only. All pages should be numbered consecutively. Titles and subtitles should be short. References, tables, and legends for the figures should be printed on separate pages.

5. The first page of the manuscript should contain the following information:
i)   The title
ii) The name(s) and institutional affiliation(s) of the author(s)
iii) An abstract of not more than 100 words—A footnote on the same sheet should give the name, address, telephone and fax numbers, and e-mail address of the corresponding author.

6. The first page of the manuscript should also contain at least one classification code according to the Classification System for Journal Articles as used by the *Journal of Economic Literature*; in addition, up to five key words should be supplied.

7. Acknowledgements and information on grants received can be given in a first footnote, which should not be included in the consecutive numbering of footnotes.

8. Footnotes should be kept to a minimum and numbered consecutively throughout the text with superscript Arabic numerals. They should be double-spaced and not include displayed formulae or tables.

9. Displayed formulae should be numbered consecutively throughout the manuscript as (1), (2), etc., against the right-hand margin of the page. In cases where the derivation of formulae has been abbreviated, it is of great help to the referees if the full derivation can be presented on a separate sheet (not to be published).

10. References to publications should be as follows: 'Smith (1992) reported that...' or 'This problem has been studied previously (e.g., Smith et al., 1969)'. The author should make sure that there is a strict one-to-one correspondence between the names and years in the text and those on the list. The list of references should appear at the end of the main text (after any appendices, but before tables and legends for figures). It should be double-spaced and listed in alphabetical order by author's name. References should appear as follows:
For monographs
Hawawini, G. and I. Swary, 1990, Mergers and acquisitions in the U.S. banking industry: Evidence from the capital markets (North-Holland, Amsterdam).
For contributions to collective works
Brunner, K. and A.H. Meltzer, 1990, Money supply, in: B.M. Friedman and F.H. Hahn, eds., Handbook of monetary economics, Vol. 1 (North-Holland, Amsterdam) 357-396.
For periodicals
Griffiths, W. and G. Judge, 1992, Testing and estimating location vectors when the error covariance matrix is unknown, Journal of Econometrics 54, 121-138.

11. Illustrations will be reproduced photographically from originals supplied by the author; they will not be redrawn by the publisher. Please provide all illustrations in quadruplicate (one high-contrast original and three photocopies). Care should be taken that lettering and symbols are of a comparable size. The illustrations should not be inserted in the text, and should be

marked on the back with figure number, title of paper, and author's name. All graphs and diagrams should be referred to as figures, and should be numbered consecutively in the text in Arabic numerals. Illustration for papers submitted as electronic manuscripts should be in traditional form.

12. Tables should be numbered consecutively in the text in Arabic numerals and printed on separate sheets. Any manuscript, which does not conform to the above instructions, may be returned for the necessary revision before publication.

13. Page proofs will be sent to the corresponding author. Proofs should be corrected carefully; the responsibility for detecting errors lies with the author. Corrections should be restricted to instances in which the proof is at variance with the manuscript. Extensive alterations will be charged. Fifty reprints of each paper are supplied free of charge to the corresponding author; additional reprints are available at cost if they are ordered when the proof is returned.

Journal of Financial Planning

ADDRESS FOR SUBMISSION:

Mary Corbin, Editorial Svcs Coordinator
Journal of Financial Planning
Financial Planning Association
3801 E. Florida Avenue, Suite 708
Denver, CO 80210
USA
Phone: 303-759-4900 x7143
Fax: 303-759-0749
E-Mail: mary.corbin@fpanet.org
Web: www.journalfp.net
Address May Change:

PUBLICATION GUIDELINES:

Manuscript Length: 3,000-5,000 Words
Copies Required: Four
Computer Submission: Yes
Format: Word Processing Format
Fees to Review: 0.00 US$

Manuscript Style:
    Chicago Manual of Style

CIRCULATION DATA:

Reader: Business Persons
Frequency of Issue: Monthly
Copies per Issue: More Than 50,000
Sponsor/Publisher: Financial Planning
    Association
Subscribe Price: 90.00 US$

REVIEW INFORMATION:

Type of Review: Blind Review
No. of External Reviewers: 4
No. of In House Reviewers: 3+
Acceptance Rate: 21-30%
Time to Review: 2 - 3 Months
Reviewers Comments: Yes
Invited Articles: 6-10%
Fees to Publish: 0.00 US$

MANUSCRIPT TOPICS:

Behavioral Economics; Corporate Finance; Financial Services; Insurance; International
Economics & Trade; International Finance; Real Estate

MANUSCRIPT GUIDELINES/COMMENTS:

The *Journal of Financial Planning* is a professional publication that aims to inform its readers
of innovative, timely, and constructive concepts, theories, applications, and current trends in
financial planning. The *Journal* welcomes original articles on any aspect of financial
planning. To submit an article for possible publication, please follow these guidelines:

Financial planners, financial services professionals, and academicians should submit articles
or article ideas to Mary Corbin, Editorial Services Coordinator, *Journal of Financial
Planning*, 3801 E. Florida Avenue, Suite 708, Denver, CO 80210. The receipt of all
manuscripts will be acknowledged.

The editor will initially screen manuscripts for appropriateness and quality, and may suggest
revisions. Articles with merit will then be sent out for peer review by members of the

Journal's Editorial Review Board. The initial screening and peer-review process takes six to eight weeks.

As an author, strive to provide the reader with timely, practical material that apply to, or will in some way directly benefit, the financial planner in his or her work. State early in the article the purpose of the article, the material it will cover, and why that material is important and useful to the reader. Be clear, concise, and organized. Avoid passive voice when possible, and use active, declarative English. Examples that illustrate key points are encouraged.

While academic research in financial planning is welcome, please keep in mind that this is a **professional** journal and that the research should have a direct and demonstrable application or benefit for financial planners. Assume the reader has a fundamental but not esoteric knowledge.

Material should be objective and avoid, when possible, mentioning or promoting specific financial products or services.

Footnotes are welcome but should not be excessive. Please list footnotes or references as they appear in the text, and place them at the end of the article.

Tables, drawings, graphs, charts, or other visual support material are welcome. Place them on separate pages and indicate their approximate placement within the text.

Manuscripts should run, ideally, 10-20 typewritten pages, and should not exceed 25 pages, including supporting material. Type manuscripts on one side of 8½-inch white paper, numbered consecutively, beginning with the first page.

As the author, your name, address, and phone number should be included on the cover page. For blind review purposes, the second page should consist of the title and a 50-100 word abstract, but NOT your name. Biographical information should be on a separate page.

If the article is accepted for publication, you will be asked to provide five true/false and multiple-choice questions and answers based on the article (to be used as part of the *Journal*'s continuing education exam). In addition, include the article on a 3½-inch disk in a word processing format or attach it to an email.

Potential *Journal* authors who wish to discuss prospective articles or who need additional information on subject matter, approach, guidelines, and so on, should contact Mary Corbin at 303-759-4900 x7143.

Journal of Financial Regulation and Compliance

ADDRESS FOR SUBMISSION:

Daryn Moody, Publishing Editor
Journal of Financial Regulation and
    Compliance
Henry Stewart Publications
Museum House
25 Museum Street
London, WC1A 1JT
UK
Phone: +44 (0)20 7323-2916
Fax: +44 (0)20 7323-2918
E-Mail: daryn@hspublications.co.uk
Web: www.henrystewart.co.uk
Address May Change:

PUBLICATION GUIDELINES:

Manuscript Length: 11-30
Copies Required: Three
Computer Submission: Yes
Format: MS Word
Fees to Review: 0.00 US$

Manuscript Style:
    , Vancouver

CIRCULATION DATA:

Reader: Academics, Business Persons
Frequency of Issue: Quarterly
Copies per Issue: 1,001 - 2,000
Sponsor/Publisher: Henry Stewart
    Publications
Subscribe Price: 465.00 US$ N America
    305.00 Pounds Europe
    320.00 Pounds ROW

REVIEW INFORMATION:

Type of Review: Blind Review
No. of External Reviewers: 2
No. of In House Reviewers: 1
Acceptance Rate: 30-40%
Time to Review: 1 Month or Less
Reviewers Comments: Yes
Invited Articles: 20%
Fees to Publish: 0.00 US$

MANUSCRIPT TOPICS:

Accounting Theory & Practice; Auditing; Financial Institutions & Markets; Financial
Regulation & Law; Financial Services; Fiscal Policy; International Economics & Trade;
International Finance

MANUSCRIPT GUIDELINES/COMMENTS:

Journal of Financial Regulation and Compliance consistently publishes authoritative,
intelligent articles and research of direct relevance both to banking supervisors and the
regulated institutions, addressing:
- *what* is happening...
- *why* it's happening...
- *where* it's happening...
- to *whom* it's happening...
- and *how* it impacts the work of compliance professionals.

In addition to articles and case studies on latest thinking and techniques in regulation and compliance, the *Journal* features comment from Joanna Gray on important regulatory rule updates and significant case law developments. It also publishes regulatory bodies' discussion papers, and book reviews of relevance to compliance personnel.

Notes for Contributors

1. Contributions should be between 2,000 and 5,000 words in length. All submissions should be typewritten and double spaced.

2. The *Journal*'s Editors and Editorial Board particularly welcome submissions which present case study material, new approaches, techniques, empirical research or conceptual papers.

3. All articles should be accompanied by a short abstract outlining the paper's aims and subject matter.

4. All articles should be accompanied by up to six keywords.

5. Articles should be accompanied by a short (about 80 words) description of the author(s) and, if appropriate, the organization of which he or she is a member.

6. Authors should not seek to use the *Journal* as a vehicle for marketing any specific product or service.

7. Authors should avoid the use of language or slang which is not in keeping with the professional and academic style of the *Journal*.

8. Titles of organizations etc should be written out first in full and thereafter in initials.

9. Papers should be supported by references. References should be set out in accordance with the Vancouver style—that is, they should be numbered consecutively in the text and the set out in full in a corresponding numbered list at the end of the text in the following form: [for journal articles] Author (year) 'Title of article', Journal name, Vol., No., pp,; [for books] Author (year) 'Title of chapter' in 'Editor' (ed), 'Book title', Publisher, place of publication.

10. Photographs and illustrations supporting articles should be submitted where appropriate. Photographs should be good quality positives, printed from the original negatives and preferably in black and white only. Figures and other line illustrations should be submitted in good quality originals and a copy of the data should also be included.

11. Authors must ensure that references to named people and/or organizations are accurate, not racist or sexist and without libellous implications.

12. All contributions sent to the Publisher, whether invited or not, will be submitted to the *Journal*'s Editors and Editorial Board. Any such contribution must bear the author's full name and address, even if this is not for publication. Contributions, whether published pseudonymously or not, are accepted on the strict understanding that the author is responsible for the accuracy of all opinion, technical comment, factual report, data, figures, illustrations

and photographs. Publication does not necessarily imply that these are the opinions of the Editorial Board, Editors or the Publisher, nor does the Board, Editors or Publisher accept any liability for the accuracy of such comment, report and other technical and factual information. The Publisher will, however, strive to ensure that all opinion, comments, reports, data, figures, illustrations and photographs are accurate, insofar as it is within its abilities to do so. The Publisher reserves the right to edit, abridge or omit material submitted for publication.

13. All Articles submitted for publication will be subject to a double-blind refereeing procedure.

14. The author bears the responsibility for checking whether material submitted is subject to copyright or ownership rights, eg photographs, illustrations, trade literature and data. Where use is so restricted, the Publisher must be informed with the submission of the material.

15. No contribution will be accepted which has been published elsewhere, unless it is expressly invited or agreed by the Publisher. Articles and contributions published become the copyright of the Publisher, unless otherwise agreed.

16. All reasonable efforts are made to ensure accurate reproduction of text, photographs and illustrations. The Publisher does not accept responsibility for mistakes, be they editorial or typographical, nor for consequences resulting from them.

17. Submissions should be sent to Henry Stewart Publications, Museum House, 25 Museum Street, London WC1A 1JT, submissions@hspublications.co.uk. **Please clearly state for which journal you are contributing.**

Journal of Financial Research

ADDRESS FOR SUBMISSION:

William T. Moore, Editor
Journal of Financial Research
Univesity of South Carolina
Moore School of Business
Columbia, SC 29208
USA
Phone: 803-777-1512
Fax: 803-777-6876
E-Mail: moore-ted@sc.edu
Web: www.blackwellpublishing.com/
Address May Change:

PUBLICATION GUIDELINES:

Manuscript Length: 16-25
Copies Required: Three
Computer Submission: No
Format: N/A
Fees to Review: 85.00 US$ Non-Member
          50.00 US$ Member of SFA or SWFA

Manuscript Style:
   Chicago Manual of Style

CIRCULATION DATA:

Reader: Academics
Frequency of Issue: Quarterly
Copies per Issue: 1,001 - 2,000
Sponsor/Publisher: Southern Financial
   Assn. & Southwestern Assn/Blackwell
   Publishing
Subscribe Price: 230.00 US$ Inst-Print
   266.00 US$ Inst-Premium Online+Print
   See Web Site For Others

REVIEW INFORMATION:

Type of Review: Blind Review
No. of External Reviewers: 1
No. of In House Reviewers: 0
Acceptance Rate: 11-15%
Time to Review: 2 - 3 Months
Reviewers Comments: Yes
Invited Articles: 0-5%
Fees to Publish: 0.00 US$

MANUSCRIPT TOPICS:
Capital Markets; Corporate Finance; Financial Institutions & Markets; International Finance;
Investments

MANUSCRIPT GUIDELINES/COMMENTS:

Aims and Scope
The *Journal of Financial Research* is a quarterly academic journal devoted to publication of
original scholarly research in investment and portfolio management, capital markets and
institutions, and corporate finance, corporate governance, and capital investment. The *JFR,* as
it is popularly known, has been in continuous publication since 1978 and is sponsored by the
Southern Finance Association (SFA) and the Southwestern Finance Association (SWFA).

Manuscript Style Guide
Submit three copies of the manuscript with the appropriate submission fee ($50 for members
of the Southern Finance Association or Southwestern Finance Association; $85 for
nonmembers, which includes a one-year's subscription to the Journal of Financial Research)
to the Editor. Checks for submission fees must be drawn on U.S. banks. Please include your e-
mail address along with other contact information.

Manuscripts should conform to the following guidelines:

1. In general, manuscripts should follow *The Chicago Manual of Style*.

2. Please edit manuscripts carefully, writing in the active voice. Avoid expressions such as "This paper tests." Do not use italics to indicate emphasis.

3. Eliminate excess verbiage and avoid redundancies. In the introduction do not describe the contents of the subsequent sections.

4. On the title page, include the title, author's name, author's affiliation, JEL classification code, and personal footnote, if desired. Double-space all text, including abstract, footnotes, and references. Print on one side of page only.

5. Include a single-paragraph abstract of no more than 100 words after the title page.

6. Use footnotes instead of endnotes. Keep number and length of footnotes to a minimum.

7. Center primary headings, using Roman numerals. Begin subsection headings at the left margin.

8. Tables should be able to stand alone. Make column headings descriptive and easily understood. Define all variables and abbreviations.

9. Number tables and equations with Arabic numbers, and number figures with Roman numerals. Enclose equation numbers in parentheses and place them in the right margin.

10. Present each table or figure on a separate page. Figures accepted for publication must be camera ready and may not exceed 5 inches in width and 7 inches in length.

11. Cite references in the text by placing the publication date in parentheses, for example:

Cornell (1986) finds...

Or

Several studies (e.g., Bierwag 1987; Cox 1990) report...

12. List source references alphabetically at the end of the manuscript using the format shown below. Do not list any reference not cited in the text. When citing several publications that appear in the same year by one author, add a, b, c, etc. to the publication date.

Cornell, B., 1986, Inflation measurement, inflation risk, and the pricing of Treasury bills, Journal of Financial Research 9, 193-202.

Cox, J. and M. Rubinstein, 1983, Option Markets (Prentice Hall, Englewood Cliffs, NJ).

Ho, T.S.Y., 1985, The value of a sinking fund provision under interest-rate risk, in E.I. Altman and M.G. Subrahmanyan, eds.: Recent Advances in Corporate Finance (Irwin, Homewood, IL), 45-75.

Journal of Financial Service Professionals

ADDRESS FOR SUBMISSION:

Kenn B. Tacchino, Editor
Journal of Financial Service Professionals
Widener University
One University Place
Chester, PA 19013-5792
USA
Phone: 610-499-1180
Fax: 610-499-4615
E-Mail: kenn.b.tacchino@widener.edu
Web: www.financialpro.org
Address May Change:

PUBLICATION GUIDELINES:

Manuscript Length: 11-20
Copies Required: One
Computer Submission: Yes Email (pref),
   Disk
Format: MS Word, WordPerfect, Excel
Fees to Review: 0.00 US$

Manuscript Style:
   Chicago Manual of Style

CIRCULATION DATA:

Reader: Academics, Business Persons
Frequency of Issue: Bi-Monthly
Copies per Issue: More than 25,000
Sponsor/Publisher: Society of Financial
   Service Professionals
Subscribe Price: 86.00 US$ Individual
   95.00 US$ Institution
   15.00 US$ Add For Foreign

REVIEW INFORMATION:

Type of Review: Blind Review
No. of External Reviewers: 3
No. of In House Reviewers: 1
Acceptance Rate: 45%
Time to Review: 1 - 2 Months
Reviewers Comments: Yes
Invited Articles: 6-10%
Fees to Publish: 0.00 US$

MANUSCRIPT TOPICS:

Corporate Finance; Estate Planning; Financial Institutions & Markets; Financial Services;
Insurance; Monetary Policy; Pensions; Portfolio & Security Analysis; Retirement Planning;
Tax Accounting; Tax Planning

MANUSCRIPT GUIDELINES/COMMENTS:

Publisher's Office
Mary Anne Mennite, Director, Publications
Kathleen Assenmacher,
Assistant Managing Editor
Society of Financial Service Professionals
270 S. Bryn Mawr Avenue
Bryn Mawr, PA 19010-2195
Tel 610-526-2525
Fax 610-526-2587
Email journal@financialpro.org

Editor's Office
Kenn B. Tacchino, JD, LLM, Editor
Suzanne W. Rettew, Associate Editor
Journal of Financial Service Professionals
Widener University
One University Place
Chester, PA 19013-5792
Tel 610-499-1180
Fax 610-499-4615
Email kenn.b.tacchino@widener.edu
    suzanne.w.rettew@widener.edu

The *Journal of Financial Service Professionals* (formerly the *Journal of the American Society of CLU & ChFC)* is one of the oldest and most prestigious journals in the financial planning field. From its roots in insurance, pensions, and estate planning, the *Journal* has evolved into a vehicle for groundbreaking applied research in all areas of financial planning, including retirement planning, investments, tax, health care, economics, ethics, information management, and other topics of concern to the holistic financial planner.

The *Journal* reaches almost 30,000 subscribers including practitioners, academics, and policymakers in the financial services industry. It is a blind peer-reviewed journal with a competitive nature for publishing insightful articles of the highest level that enhance the ability of financial planners to serve their client base.

On the following pages are guidelines for submitting manuscripts to the *Journal of Financial Service Professionals*.

A. Editorial Policies
1. Topical Content
In keeping with the Society's mission to promote professionalism among its members, the *Journal* will consider for publication an original professional manuscript on any aspect of financial services, as long as it evidences research, has its facts properly authenticated and objectively presented, and is well-written and thought-provoking.

2. Multiple Submissions
In submitting an article to the *Journal*, authors agree that they have not submitted, and will not submit, the same (or a substantially similar) article to any other publication. In exchange, the *Journal* agrees to process articles promptly and accept or reject manuscripts in a timely manner. Upon learning of a multiple submission, the Journal will cease further consideration of the manuscript.

3. Copyright
The copyright to an accepted/published article will be held by the Society of Financial Service Professionals in all cases. Authors will be required to complete and return a Copyright transfer Form. *No article will be accepted until this completed form has been received.* The Journal reserves the right to reprint all articles and publish them either alone or in collected and composite works, in printed, electronic, or such other formats as the Society deems appropriate.

If any material in an article is based on a study or research data, please note that the Copyright Transfer Form does not preclude in any way the author's use of the data from this study in future articles, nor does the Society assume ownership of the data—just the submission based on it.

Authors should be aware that permission to republish to republish their articles in any other publication, or to reprint them in any form, can be granted only by the office of the Managing editor of the *Journal*. For all information on reprints, contact Kathleen Assenmacher, Assistant Managing Editor, at the Publisher's Office address above.

4. Publication Commitment

Because of space limitations, the *Journal*, which is published bimonthly in the months of January, March, May, July, September, and November, cannot commit in advance to publish an accepted article in a particular issue. Articles are processed in the order in which they are received. However, special consideration may be extended to articles that are of current or timely importance, or that may become dated (such as articles regarding tax-related matters). After the review process has been completed and all changes have been made to the Editor's satisfaction, a tentative publication date will be communicated to the author.

5. Company/Product Names

The *Journal* will NOT publish articles, which name specific companies or the brand names of products, policies, computer software or hardware, if the information presented appears to be solely an attempt to market the product or company.

B. Submission Procedures
1. Manuscript Submission

Authors should submit the following through e-mail.

a. **Manuscript**. Attached Word or WordPerfect document of the article, set double-spaced in 12-point type with numbered pages. (Please note. we now prefer e-mail submissions as opposed to regular mail submissions.)

b. **Biographical Sketch**. One or two paragraphs about each author, limited to 50 words which should include designations, past education, company and job title (with responsibilities), other published works, industry awards or recognition, and e-mail addressor phone number for readers to contact them. The bio(s) should be typed at the end of the article.

c. **Abstract**. An abstract, between 50 and 100 words, that is a synopsis of the article, giving a preview of its contents and explaining why the topic is important to the reader. The abstract should precede the body of the article.

d. **Contact Information**. Complete address, phone, fax and e-mail address of each author.

These materials should be e-mailed to both the following addresses:
suzanne.w.rettew@widener.edu   kenn.b.tacchino@widener.edu

IMPORTANT NOTE. Articles cannot be processed until the biographical sketch and abstract have been received. If there are two or more authors of an article, the person who sends the manuscript to the *Journal* will be deemed the contact person for all correspondence regarding that article (corresponding author).

2. Review Process and Revisions

Each manuscript submitted is sent to reviewers who comment on various editorial and technical aspects of the article, including its suitability for inclusion in the *Journal*. This part of the review process takes approximately four (4) weeks. Reviewers' recommendations may be forwarded to the author for use in preparing revisions. After reviewing and incorporating these recommendations, the author is asked to e-mail a revised draft of the manuscript, using the tracking tool on his or her computer to show where the changes were made. In lieu of clicking on the tracking feature, the author may simply type a note outlining where he or she made changes. Please note that the author's failure to submit revisions deemed necessary for technical accuracy or the manuscript's tone may result in the rejection of the manuscript for publication.

At the Editor's discretion, the revised manuscript may be sent back to the original reviewers to determine if the requested changes were successfully incorporated.

IMPORTANT. All manuscripts should be spell-checked by the computer *before* final submission. Whenever there is a discrepancy between the copy on the final revised version and any previous copies, the Editor will assume that the document labeled "final," or dated the most recent, is the correct version. It is, therefore, imperative to send the most recent manuscript and to make sure it is as accurate as possible.

Authors may use Word or WordPerfect, on either a Macintosh or IBM PC compatible computer, to prepare their documents. Figures and tables may be prepared in Excel.

3. Final Proofreading
Before publication of an article, the corresponding author will receive page proofs of his or her article to ensure that the manuscript has been typeset properly and to minimize the chance of errors. Cost considerations will not permit significant revisions to be made at this stage of the process. The *Journal* reserves the right to make changes deemed necessary by the editorial staff up until the *Journal's* press time and following the author's final review.

4. Copies of Published Article
Please call the Bryn Mawr office at 610-526-2525 for details about receiving copies of published articles.

5. Author Award Program
Eligible articles published in each volume (six issues within the same calendar year) are automatically submitted to the Kenneth Black, Jr., *Journal* Author Award competition. Honoraria of US$1,500, US$1,000, and US$500 are awarded to the authors of the winning entries for first, second, and third place, respectively. Members of the staffs of the Society of Financial Service Professionals and The American College are not eligible.

C. Format and Writing Style
1. Writing Style
Manuscripts should be written in the third-person style. Articles using first- and second-person pronouns (i.e., I, me, my, we, us, our, ours, you, your, yours, etc.) will be returned to the author for rewriting in the third person. To ensure anonymous review, authors should not identify themselves directly or indirectly in their manuscripts.

2. Inclusive Language
Every effort should be made to use inclusive language, avoiding the sexist use of "he," "she," "salesman," or other such terms unless the content clearly demands it. The *Journal's* style is either to use the plural pronoun forms (they, them, their, etc.), to include both sexes ("he or she," "him or her," etc.), or to use a neuter term ("salesperson," "persons," etc.)

3. Tax-Oriented Articles

All tax-oriented articles should, where possible, provide easy-to-understand statements of the IRC sections to which they refer by number. Authors should assume that readers are *not* sufficiently familiar with the Code reference and that the mention of a Code section does not constitute an adequate reference.

4. Quantitatively Oriented Articles

All quantitatively oriented articles should, where possible, provide simply understood English statements explaining the use of notations and the interpretation of quantitative results. The results should be presented in terms of their *practical* significance. Only quantitative results that the text of the article discusses should be presented in the body of the article, with other relevant quantitative material reserved for an appendix to the article.

- Keep your discussion of the research methodology you used concise (or put it in an appendix at the end of the article). Focus on the new knowledge you are creating, not how you created it.
- Show the relevance of your mathematical analysis with practical examples, charts, and tables that enable the result to be the focus, rather than the equation that was used to arrive at the result.
- Focus on the information the reader needs, not the information that authors sometimes feel obligated to give.
- Point out the application of your insight in a financial services practice by adding examples that account for an understanding of the reader's practice or adding a section to the paper titled "How This Applies to Your Practice."

5. Length and Page Setup

Feature articles should be a minimum of 8 *double-spaced* pages, in 12-point type, up to a maximum of approximately 25 pages (2,000 to 8,000 words). Manuscripts should be set on 8½ x 11-inch size, *with a page number assigned to each page.* Margins should be at traditional settings (top and bottom margins at 1 inch and side margins at 1¼ inches).

6. Article Titles

Article titles should be a scholarly reflection of the subject matter of the article. Authors should avoid language that appears boastful, overreaching, or nonobjective in nature (i.e., not "revolutionize" or "the greatest"). Titles should be *no longer than 12 words.* The *Journal* reserves the right to change an article's title without the express permission of the author. Because the manuscripts are sent out for blind reviews, the author's name must *not* appear on any page of the body of the text. Instead, submit a *title page* with the article's title and the author's name, designations, address, phone, fax, and e-mail address preceding the first page of the article. Repeat the title on the first page of the article.

7. Charts, Graphs, and Tables

All charts, graphs, and tables should be inserted at their appropriate places within the body of the manuscript. If such items cannot be produced by the author within the document, the author should insert a reference to each table at the point where it should eventually appear (i.e., [Insert Table 1 here.]), then include each insert as a separate file. The art department will recreate the charts, graphs, and tables, if necessary, based on what the author submits. In instances of line, scatter line, and bar charts, include the data file that was used to create the original chart in order for the art department to recreate it accurately for publication. If submitting a computer file created from graphics or spreadsheet software, the author should include the name and version of the software.

8. Endnotes

When appropriate for credit to a source, clarity, or completeness, articles should contain: (1) endnotes that provide simplified explanations of, or rigorous technical support for, a complex concept used in the article (as, for example, with regression analysis); (2) endnotes that provide references to bibliographical materials that either support a statement, represent the source of a quotation, or should be read if further information is desired.

All endnotes should be numbered consecutively and double-spaced. They should also appear at the END of the article, beginning on a new page but continuing the page numbers of the body of the article. Do not cite parenthetically in the text.

The *Journal* uses the *Chicago Manual of Style, 14th ed.*, as a standard for documentation of books and periodicals.

Endnotes with legal citations may conform to the style prescribed by *A Uniform System of Citation,* 17th ed. *("The Bluebook")*, published by the Harvard Law Review Association, or may follow a simplified system shown here.

Sample Citations for Cases

Smith v. Comm'r 99-2 USTC ¶ 50,826	Smith v. Comm'r 209 US 337
Smith v. Comm'r 24 S. Ct. 771	Smith v. Comm'r 150 F. 2d. 837
Smith v. Comm'r 243 F. Supp. 894	Smith v. Comm'r 32 TC 1222
Smith v. Comm'r 2 TCM 622	Smith v. Comm'r TC Memo 1997-171
Smith v. Comm'r 45 B.T.A. 671	

Source	Sample Citation
Internal Revenue Code	IRC Sec. 401(a)(4)
Treasury Decision	TD 8346
IRS Final Regulation	Final Reg. Sec. 1.1031(k)(1)
IRS Proposed Regulation	Prop. Reg. Sec. 1.125-1
Temporary Regulation	Temp. Reg. Sec. 1.72-16(a)
Revenue Ruling	Rev. Rul. 58-430
Revenue Procedures	Rev. Proc. 92-65
Private Letter Ruling	PLR 9407007
IRS Announcement	IRS Announcement 96-24
IRS Notice	Notice 88-97
IRS News Release	IR 86-172
IRS Publications	IRS Publ. No. 334
General Council Memorandum	GCM 36921
Technical Advice Memorandum	TAM 8504005
United States Code	42 U.S.C. Sec. 1983
Public Law	PL 96-104

Alternatives: Cumulative Bulletin cites may be given. For example, 1986-1 CB 544.

9. Headings

Authors should subdivide their material to show the logical sequencing of the article. In typing manuscripts, insert main headings and subheadings at appropriate places throughout the article.

D. Publication Time Factor
1. Review Processing Time

Every effort is made to respond to authors within four to six weeks after their article has been sent to *Journal* reviewers. However, depending on the complexity, length, subject matter, etc., the review processing time period may occasionally take longer.

2. Publication Date

The Editor, who tentatively plans two or three issues in advance of publication, decides on the publication date of each article. Authors can be assured that their articles will be published as soon as possible after the review process has been completed, depending on available editorial space in each issue and the timeliness of the articles in question.

If at any time following the acceptance of an article for publication, the author(s), editors, or publishers find the information to be out of date (i.e., due to tax law changes, new developments in products or coverage's, etc.), every attempt will be made to give the author(s) the opportunity to update the article. However, it is the prerogative of the editors/publishers to cancel publication of the article despite any previous agreement to publish it.

Journal of Financial Services Marketing

ADDRESS FOR SUBMISSION:

Kerry Barner, Editor
Journal of Financial Services Marketing
Henry Stewart Publications
Museum House
25 Museum Street
London, WC1A 1JT
UK
Phone: 44 (0) 207-323-2916
Fax: 44 (0) 207-323-2918
E-Mail: kerry@hspublications.co.uk
Web: www.henrystewart.com
Address May Change:

PUBLICATION GUIDELINES:

Manuscript Length: 2,500-5,000 Words
Copies Required: Three
Computer Submission: Yes
Format: MS Word, WordPerfect
Fees to Review: 0.00 US$

Manuscript Style:
, Vancouver

CIRCULATION DATA:

Reader: , 65% Business, 35% Academic
Frequency of Issue: Quarterly
Copies per Issue: 1,001 - 2,000
Sponsor/Publisher: Henry Stewart
    Publications
Subscribe Price: 495.00 US$ USA
      330.00 Pounds Europe
      345.00 Pounds ROW

REVIEW INFORMATION:

Type of Review: Blind Review
No. of External Reviewers: 3
No. of In House Reviewers: 2
Acceptance Rate: 50%
Time to Review: 1 - 2 Months
Reviewers Comments: Yes
Invited Articles: 31-50%
Fees to Publish: 0.00 US$

MANUSCRIPT TOPICS:
Financial Services

MANUSCRIPT GUIDELINES/COMMENTS:

1. Contributions should be between 2,000 and 5,000 words in length. All submissions should be typewritten and double spaced.

2. The *Journal*'s Editors and Editorial Board particularly welcome submissions which present case study material, new approaches, techniques, empirical research or conceptual papers.

3. All articles should be accompanied by a short abstract outlining the paper's aims and subject matter.

4. All articles should be accompanied by up to six keywords.

5. Articles should be accompanied by a short (about 80 words) description of the author(s) and, if appropriate, the organization of which he or she is a member.

6. Authors should not seek to use the *Journal* as a vehicle for marketing any specific product or service.

7. Authors should avoid the use of language or slang which is not in keeping with the professional and academic style of the *Journal*.

8. Titles of organizations etc should be written out first in full and thereafter in initials.

9. Papers should be supported by references. These should be set out in accordance with the Vancouver style—that is, they should be referred to by number in the text and set out in full at the end of the text. Any repeated references should use the same number as the original reference [for journal articles] Author (year) 'Title of article', Journal name, Vol., No., pp,; [for books] Author (year) 'Title of chapter' in 'Editor' (ed), 'Book title', Publisher, place of publication.

10. Photographs and illustrations supporting articles should be submitted where appropriate. Photographs should be good quality positives, printed from the original negatives and preferably in black and white only. Figures and other line illustrations should be submitted in good quality originals and a copy of the data should also be included.

11. Authors must ensure that references to named people and/or organizations are accurate, not racist or sexist and without libellous implications.

12. All contributions sent to the Publisher, whether invited or not, will be submitted to the *Journal*'s Editors and Editorial Board. Any such contribution must bear the author's full name and address, even if this is not for publication. Contributions, whether published pseudonymously or not, are accepted on the strict understanding that the author is responsible for the accuracy of all opinion, technical comment, factual report, data, figures, illustrations and photographs. Publication does not necessarily imply that these are the opinions of the Editorial Board, Editors or the Publisher, nor does the Board, Editors or Publisher accept any liability for the accuracy of such comment, report and other technical and factual information. The Publisher will, however, strive to ensure that all opinion, comments, reports, data, figures, illustrations and photographs are accurate, insofar as it is within its abilities to do so. The Publisher reserves the right to edit, abridge or omit material submitted for publication.

13. All Articles submitted for publication will be subject to a double-blind refereeing procedure.

14. The author bears the responsibility for checking whether material submitted is subject to copyright or ownership rights, eg photographs, illustrations, trade literature and data. Where use is so restricted, the Publisher must be informed with the submission of the material.

15. No contribution will be accepted which has been published elsewhere, unless it is expressly invited or agreed by the Publisher. Articles and contributions published become the copyright of the Publisher, unless otherwise agreed.

16. All reasonable efforts are made to ensure accurate reproduction of text, photographs and illustrations. The Publisher does not accept responsibility for mistakes, be they editorial or typographical, nor for consequences resulting from them.

17. Submissions should be sent to Henry Stewart Publications, Museum House, 25 Museum Street, London WC1A 1JT, email: submissions@hspublications.co.uk. **Please clearly state for which journal you are contributing.**

Journal of Financial Services Research

ADDRESS FOR SUBMISSION:

Haluk Unal, Managing Editor
Journal of Financial Services Research
University of Maryland
R. H. Smith School of Business
Van Munching Hall 4429
College Park, MD 20742
USA
Phone: 301-405-0498
Fax: 301-405-2389
E-Mail: jfsr@rhsmith.umd.edu
Web: www.kluweronline.com
Address May Change:

PUBLICATION GUIDELINES:

Manuscript Length: 11-15
Copies Required: Three
Computer Submission: Yes
Format: See Guidelines
Fees to Review: 60.00 US$

Manuscript Style:
, The Elements of Style

CIRCULATION DATA:

Reader: Academics
Frequency of Issue: 6 Times/Year
Copies per Issue: Less than 1,000
Sponsor/Publisher: Kluwer Academic
   Publishers
Subscribe Price: 248.00 US$ Individual
   615.00 US$ Institution

REVIEW INFORMATION:

Type of Review: Blind Review
No. of External Reviewers: 2
No. of In House Reviewers: 0 1-2
Acceptance Rate: 11-20%
Time to Review: 2 - 3 Months
Reviewers Comments: Yes
Invited Articles: 0-5%
Fees to Publish: 0.00 US$

MANUSCRIPT TOPICS:

Financial Institutions & Markets; Financial Services; Insurance; International Finance;
Investment Banking; Monetary Policy; Real Estate; Securities & Investments

MANUSCRIPT GUIDELINES/COMMENTS:

Aims & Scope

The *Journal of Financial Services Research* publishes original research dealing with private
and public policy questions arising from the evolution of the financial services sector. The
journal emphasizes, but is not limited to, the microanalysis of financial services providers,
financial services regulation, financial innovation, the management of financial institutions,
and related topics.

The *Journal of Financial Services Research* is required reading for all those involved in the
provision, development, regulation and study of financial services on an international,
national, and local level, whether in private practice, or industrial, state, or academic
employment.

The papers published in the journal fall mostly in the areas of financial services, insurance, banking, finance, real estate, securities and investments, and investment banking.

The financial revolution is sweeping the world. Its effects are not yet completely apparent and are, in many cases, unpredictable and contrary to what many had expected. The *Journal of Financial Services Research* is the most cost-effective means for keeping abreast of developments.

Submissions Policy
There is no fixed limit on the length of articles, although concise presentation is encouraged. All articles will be reviewed. The journal welcomes comments dealing with material that has previously appeared in the journal. The journal will also publish longer articles of opinion or speculation and review articles on selected topics; these will normally be by invitation, but interested persons are invited to contact the editors. Manuscripts submitted to the journal must not be under simultaneous consideration by any other journal and should not have been published elsewhere in a substantially similar form. No part of a paper that has been published in the *Journal of Financial Services Research* may be reproduced elsewhere without the written permission of the publisher. A reviewing fee of US$60 will be imposed on all submissions. This fee will be employed to provide an incentive for reviewers to return their manuscript reviews in a timely manner.

Submission Fee. US$60 (foreign checks accepted if drawn against U.S. bank). Please make checks payable to Journal of Financial Services Research.

Manuscript Preparation (Articles)
Manuscripts must be submitted in English in triplicate (one original and two copies) and typed double-spaced on 22cm x 29cm (8½ x 11in) white bond paper. This applies to all parts of the manuscript, including references, legends, etc. Liberal margins (2.5cm/1in) should be left at the top and bottom, and at the sides. The manuscript should be submitted in the following order: title page, summary, text, notes, references, tables, figure legends, and figures. Authors should retain a copy for reference as accepted manuscripts will not be returned. Abbreviations should be kept to a minimum and must be explained when they first appear; after the first use, an abbreviation may be used.

Title Page. The title page of each manuscript should include: (i) article title; (ii) authors names (including first and middle names and degrees); (iii) name and address of the institution(s) from which the work originated, plus information about grants (including city and state of all foundations, funds and institutions): and (iv) name, address, and telephone number of person(s) to whom proofs and reprint requests should be addressed. This page will be removed before the manuscript is sent to a referee. The first page of the text should show the title but NOT the author's name.

Summary Page. The page following the title page should include a brief abstract of 125 words describing the article.

Text. The text of the article should begin on a new page. The introduction should have no heading or number; subsequent headings should be designated by Arabic numbers. Sub-headings should be numbered 1.1, 1.2, etc., according to the main head that it appears under.

Note—There should be no references to the author(s) on any text, figure, and table pages or reference sheet.

Figures. Figures must be submitted in camera-ready form, with lettering large enough to be legible in the event of half-size reduction. Submit one 13cm x 18cm (5in x 7in) and two photocopies of each figure. On the back of each figure, give authors name, the figure number, and indicate the top with an arrow. Do not write directly on the back of the figure; rather, write on a gummed label and affix it to the back of the figure. Do not use paper clips or staples. Figure numbers should be Arabic corresponding with the order in which the figures are presented in the text. Identify all abbreviations appearing on the figure in alphabetical order at the end of each legend. Figures are limited to the number necessary for clarity. You must submit written permission from the author(s) and publisher to use any figure that has already been published.

Tables. Tables should be typed double-spaced, each on a separate sheet, with title in bold above. Following the title, there should be a descriptive legend. This legend enables the reader to follow the information presented in the table without the need to read the text. All variables, acronyms, and sources of information should be given in the legend. Tables and table numbers should be in Arabic, corresponding with the order in which the tables are presented in the text. You must obtain permission to use all tables that have already been published. Please be certain that the text contains a reference to each table. Significance levels for statistical tests are shown at the bottom of the table as *, **, and ***, representing 10%, 5%, and 1% respectively.

References. References in the text should appear as a name, date citation (Borch, 1984) within parentheses. The references section should be double-spaced on a separate page at the end of the text, following the sample formats given below. All authors' names must be provided for up to three individuals; when there are four or more authors, list the first three and add et al. It is the responsibility of the author(s) to verify all references.

Sample References

Aspinwall, Richard. "Shifting Institutional Frontiers in Financial Markets in the United States." In: D.E. Fair, ed., *Shifting Frontiers in Financial Markets*. Dordrecht: Martinus Nijhoff Publishing. 1986, pp. 223-239.

Bergendahl, G. "DEA and Benchmarks for Nordic Banks." Working Paper, Gothenburg University, Gothenburg, Sweden (December 1995).

Borch, Karl. "Equilibrium Premiums in an Insurance Market", *Journal of Risk and Insurance* 51 (September 1984), 468-476.

Schoemaker, Paul J.H. *Experiments on Decisions Under Risk: The Expected Utility Hypothesis*. Boston: Kluwer-Nijhoff Publishing. 1980, pp. 13-16.

Comments and Replies. Comments and replies should follow the same general rule for articles, except that a separate title page and summary are not required. A table or figure may be included. If references are needed, they should follow the standard format. The full names and addresses of the writers should follow the text.

Style. The following book is an extremely valuable general, nonscientific style manual: Strunk, W. Jr., and White, E.B., *The Elements of Style*. New York: Macmillan, 1972.

Proofs and Offprints. Page proofs must be returned within three days of receipt; late return may cause delays in publication of an article. Please check text, tables, legends, and references carefully. To expedite publication, page proof, rather than galleys, will be sent. Alterations other than the correction of printing errors will be charged to the author(s). Authors will receive fifty offprints free of charge. Order information for additional offprints will accompany author's proofs.

Journal of Fixed Income (The)

ADDRESS FOR SUBMISSION:

Bobbie S. Griffin, Editorial Assistant
Journal of Fixed Income (The)
Smith Breeden Associates
100 Europa Drive, Suite 200
Chapel Hill, NC 27517
USA
Phone: 919-967-7221
Fax: 919-967-1820
E-Mail: bgriffin@smithbreeden.com
Web: http://www.iijfi.com/
Address May Change:

PUBLICATION GUIDELINES:

Manuscript Length: 16-20
Copies Required: Three
Computer Submission: Yes
Format: MS Word
Fees to Review: 0.00 US$

Manuscript Style:
　　See Manuscript Guidelines

CIRCULATION DATA:

Reader: Business Persons
Frequency of Issue: Quarterly
Copies per Issue: 2,001 - 3,000
Sponsor/Publisher: Institutional Investor,
　　Inc.
Subscribe Price: 360.00 US$ Institution
　　180.00 US$ Academics

REVIEW INFORMATION:

Type of Review: Editorial Review
No. of External Reviewers: 2
No. of In House Reviewers: 0
Acceptance Rate: No Reply
Time to Review: 2 - 3 Months
Reviewers Comments: No
Invited Articles: 50% +
Fees to Publish: 0.00 US$

MANUSCRIPT TOPICS:
Financial Institutions & Markets; Financial Services; Fixed Income Portfolio Management;
International Finance; Portfolio & Security Analysis

MANUSCRIPT GUIDELINES/COMMENTS:

The *Journal of Fixed Income* provides technical, sophisticated research in bonds: mortgage-backed securities, high-yield bonds, futures and options, municipal and global bonds, corporate and asset-backed securities. Industry experts offer penetrating analysis on fixed income structuring, asset allocation, performance measurement, risk management and more.

Submission of Manuscripts
Please refer to the following guidelines when submitting a manuscript for publication. We may return any paper to the author for revisions that does not follow these instructions. The editors reserve the right to make changes for clarity and consistency.

1. Submit three copies of the manuscript double-spaced with wide margins and pages numbered. The front page should include the authors' full names, titles, addresses, zip codes, and phone/fax numbers. If the paper is accepted for publication, the authors must supply a

diskette copy of the paper. Please note the type of word processing software used and securely attach the article title, author's name, and address to the diskette.

2. Supply an abstract that describes the paper succinctly for the editor and referees.

3. References, endnotes, tables, and figures should appear on separate pages at the end of the text.

4. Limit references to works cited in the text and list them alphabetically. Citations in the text should appear as "Smith [1990] suggests that..." Use page numbers for quotes.

5. Minimize the number of endnotes. Use periods instead of comas between authors' names and titles of references. Use superscript Arabic numbers in the text and on the endnote page.

6. Number and title all exhibits, with one to a page. Write out the column heads and legends; they should be understandable without reference to the text. Submit graphs in camera-ready form and as large as possible because they will be shrunk for the text.

Note. We cannot draw graphs for you.

7. Center each equation on a separate line, numbered consecutively with Arabic numbers, in parentheses, in the right margin. Identify Greek letters in the margin for the typesetter. Please make clear markings when inserting Greek letters or equations into the text.

8. *The Journal of Fixed Income*'s copyright agreement form must be signed prior to publication.

Send two copies to the Editor. Send one copy to Noelle Schultz, Editorial Production Director, The Journal of Fixed Income, Institutional Investor, Inc., 488 Madison Avenue, New York, NY 10022.

Inquiries regarding the status of papers under review should be directed to Bobbie Griffin, Editorial Assistant.

The Journal of Fixed Income is published by Institutional Investor, Inc., 488 Madison Avenue, New York, NY 10022. Tel: 212-224-3545 Fax: 212-224-3527.

Journal of Forecasting

ADDRESS FOR SUBMISSION:

Derek W. Bunn, Editor-in-Chief
Journal of Forecasting
London Business School
Sussex Place
Regent's Park
London, NW1 4SA
UK
Phone:
Fax: +44 (0) 20 7724-7875
E-Mail: dbunn@london.edu
Web: www3.interscience.wiley.com
Address May Change:

PUBLICATION GUIDELINES:

Manuscript Length: 16-20
Copies Required: Three
Computer Submission: Yes - Final
     Submission
Format: Prefer Word, WordPerfect, TeX
Fees to Review: 0.00 US$

Manuscript Style:
     See Manuscript Guidelines

CIRCULATION DATA:

Reader: Academics, Practitioners
Frequency of Issue: 8 Times/Year
Copies per Issue: 1,001 - 2,000
Sponsor/Publisher: Wiley InterScience
Subscribe Price: 325.00 US$ Individual
     1115.00 US$ Institution
     210.00 Pounds UK - Individual

REVIEW INFORMATION:

Type of Review: Editorial Review
No. of External Reviewers: 2
No. of In House Reviewers: 1
Acceptance Rate: 35%
Time to Review: 4 - 6 Months
Reviewers Comments: Yes
Invited Articles: 0-5%
Fees to Publish: 0.00 US$

MANUSCRIPT TOPICS:
Applied Econometrics; Econometrics

MANUSCRIPT GUIDELINES/COMMENTS:

Aims and Scope
The *Journal of Forecasting* is an international journal that publishes refereed papers on forecasting. It is multidisciplinary, welcoming papers dealing with any aspect of forecasting: theoretical, practical, computational and methodological. A broad interpretation of the topic is taken with approaches from various subject areas, such as statistics, economics, psychology, systems engineering and social sciences, all encouraged. Furthermore, the *Journal* welcomes a wide diversity of applications in such fields as business, government, technology and the environment. Of particular interest are papers dealing with modelling issues and the relationship of forecasting systems to decision-making processes. New concepts of modelling are especially encouraged as well as practical details of actual applications of particular models. Apart from research reports and review articles, other materials of interest that will be published include book reviews, software reviews, descriptions of data sources and notices of general interest.

814

Readership
Academics and practitioners in management science, decision analysis and operations research, Business forecasters, Economists, Statisticians, Operations Researchers.

INSTRUCTIONS TO AUTHORS
Initial Manuscript Submission. Submit four copies of the manuscript (including copies of tables and illustrations) to the Editor-in-Chief or to any of the Departmental Editors.

Authors must also supply:
- An electronic copy of the final version (see section below)
- A Copyright Transfer Agreement (available online) with original signature(s)—without this we are unable to accept the submission
- Permission Grants—If the manuscript contains extracts, including illustrations, from other copyright works (including material from on-line or intranet sources), it is the author's responsibility to obtain written permission from the owners of the publishing rights to reproduce such extracts using the Wiley Permission Request Form. Permission grants should be submitted with the manuscript.

Submitted manuscripts should not have been previously published and should not be submitted for publication elsewhere while they are under consideration by Wiley. Submitted material will not be returned to the author unless specifically requested.

Electronic Submission. The electronic copy of the final, revised manuscript must be sent to the Editor together with the paper copy. Disks should be PC or Mac formatted; write on the disk the software package used, the name of the author and the name of the journal. We are able to use most word processing packages, but prefer Word or WordPerfect and TeX or one of its derivatives.

Illustrations must be submitted in electronic format where possible. Save each figure as a separate file, in TIFF or EPS format preferably, and include the source file. Write on the disk the software package used to create them; we favour dedicated illustration packages over tools such as Excel or PowerPoint.

Manuscript Style. The language of the *Journal* is English. All submissions including book reviews must have a title, be printed on one side of the paper, be double-line spaced and have a margin of 3cm all round. Illustrations and tables must be printed on separate sheets, and not be incorporated into the text.

- The title page must list the full title, short title of up to 70 characters and names and affiliations of all authors. Give the full address, including email, telephone and fax, of the author who is to check the proofs.
- Include the name(s) of any sponsor(s) of the research contained in the paper, along with grant number(s).
- Supply an abstract of up to 150 words for all articles [except book reviews]. An abstract is a concise summary of the whole paper, not just the conclusions, and is understandable

without reference to the rest of the paper. It should contain no citation to other published work.

- Include up to five keywords that describe your paper for indexing purposes.
- Include also a brief biography of up to 50 words for each author.

Reference Style. References should be quoted in the text as name and year within brackets and listed at the end of the paper alphabetically. Where reference is made to more than one work by the same author published in the same year, identify each citation in the text as follows: (Collins, 1998a), (Collins, 1998b). Where three or more authors are listed in the reference list, please cite in the text as (Collins *et al.*, 1998).

All references must be complete and accurate. Online citations should include date of access. If necessary, cite unpublished or personal work in the text but do not include it in the reference list. References should be listed in the following style:

Caporaletti LE, Dorsey RE, Johnson JD, Powell WA. 1994. A decision support system for in-sample simultaneous equation systems forecasting using artificial neural systems. *Decision Support Systems* **11**: 481-495.

Judge GG, Hill RC, Griffiths WE, Lütkepohl H, Lee TC. 1988. *Introduction to the Theory and Practice of Econometrics,* 2nd edn. John Wiley: New York.

Moody J, Saffell M, Liao Y, Wu L. 1998. Reinforcement learning for trading systems and portfolios: Immediate vs future rewards. In *Decision Technologies for Financial Engineering*, Refenes AN, Burgess N, Moody J (eds); Kluwer: Amsterdam.

Journal of Forecasting homepage. 2000. http://www.interscience.wiley.com/jpages/0277-6693 [1 June 2000]

Illustrations. Supply each illustration on a separate sheet, with the lead author's name and the figure number, with the top of the figure indicated, on the reverse. Supply original **photographs**; photocopies or previously printed material will not be used. Line artwork must be high-quality laser output (not photocopies). Grey shading is not acceptable; lettering must be of a reasonable size that would still be clearly legible upon reduction, and consistent within each figure and set of figures. Supply artwork at the intended size for printing. The artwork must be sized to a maximum text width of 13cm.

The cost of printing **colour** illustrations in the *Journal* will be charged to the author. There is a charge for printing colour illustrations of approximately £700 per page. If colour illustrations are supplied electronically in either **TIFF** or **EPS** format, they **may** be used in the PDF of the article at no cost to the author, even if this illustration was printed in black and white in the *Journal*. The PDF will appear on the *Wiley InterScience* site.

Copyright. To enable the publisher to disseminate the author's work to the fullest extent, the author must sign a Copyright Transfer Agreement, transferring copyright in the article from the author to the publisher, and submit the original signed agreement with the article presented for publication. A copy of the agreement to be used (which may be photocopied) can be found in *Journal of Forecasting*. Copies may also be obtained from the *Journal* editor or publisher, or may be printed from the Web site.

Further Information. Proofs will be sent to the author for checking. This stage is to be used only to correct errors that may have been introduced during the production process. Prompt return of the corrected proofs, preferably within two days of receipt, will minimise the risk of the paper being held over to a later issue. 25 complimentary offprints will be provided to the author who checked the proofs, unless otherwise indicated. Further offprints and copies of the *Journal* may be ordered. There is no page charge to authors.

Journal of Forensic Economics

ADDRESS FOR SUBMISSION:

John O. Ward, Managing Editor
Journal of Forensic Economics
National Association of
  Forensic Economics
Box 30067
Kansas City, MO 64112-0067
USA
Phone: 816-235-2833
Fax: 816-235-5263
E-Mail: umkcnafe@umkc.edu
Web: www.nafe.net
Address May Change:

PUBLICATION GUIDELINES:

Manuscript Length: 16-20
Copies Required: Four
Computer Submission: No
Format: N/A
Fees to Review: 50.00 US$
  25.00 US$ Members

Manuscript Style:
  See Manuscript Guidelines

CIRCULATION DATA:

Reader: Academics
Frequency of Issue: 3 Times/Year
Copies per Issue: 1,200
Sponsor/Publisher: National Association of
  Forensic Economics
Subscribe Price: 110.00 US$

REVIEW INFORMATION:

Type of Review: Blind Review
No. of External Reviewers: 3
No. of In House Reviewers: 0
Acceptance Rate: 21-30%
Time to Review: 2 - 3 Months
Reviewers Comments: Yes
Invited Articles: 0-5%
Fees to Publish: 0.00 US$

MANUSCRIPT TOPICS:

Econometrics; Industrial Organization; Law & Economics; Micro Economics; Portfolio & Security Analysis; Public Policy Economics; Regional Economics

MANUSCRIPT GUIDELINES/COMMENTS:

Submission Guidelines for Consideration of Publication

1. **Submission Fee**. In order to cover the expense of distribution of manuscripts through the review process, the *Journal of Forensic Economics* requires a fee for each manuscript title sent for consideration of publication. The fee is $25.00 for members of the National Association of Forensic Economics and $50.00 for non-members. (Canadian and foreign payments must be in the form of a draft or check drawn on a United States bank payable in United States dollars.) Submission fees are not required for requested revisions.

2. **Format**. Four paper copies of the manuscript must be submitted. Manuscripts should be arranged on separate sheets in the following order and format:
- Title Page—Title, author(s), complete mailing address and telephone numbers of author(s), and date written

818

- Abstract—150 words or less; not required for Comments, Replies, etc.
- Text—Double-spacing of all material; 1-inch margins at the top, bottom, and left and right sides; justification on left margin only
- Appendix—Same format as text
- References—Should be bibliographic form and should not be used as footnotes
- Figures & Tables—Each figure and table should be on a separate sheet and numbered consecutively; text should be double-spaced

Mail submissions to the Managing Editor. Call or fax if you have questions.

Book Review Submission Guidelines
There is no submission fee for Book Reviews but they should be sent in the form listed below direct to the Book Review Editor Dr. Robert Thornton, Economics Department, Rauch Business Center, 621 Taylor Street, Lehigh University, Bethlehem, PA 18015-3144

1. Clearly but briefly indicate the contents and purpose of the volume.
2. Relate the volume to the important literature in the field, and evaluate its contribution to the existing literature.
3. Reviews should be between 600-800 words in length, with the upper limit reserved for collective volumes.
4. Format should be that used in the *Journal of Economic Literature*. For example, the beginning of the review should contain information about the volume like the following:

A Hedonics Primer for Economists and Attorneys
Compiled and edited by John O. Ward
Tucson: Lawyers and Judges Publishing Company, 1992, 306 pages
ISBN 0-88450-087-X $54.00

Following the review, the author's name and affiliation are then given.

5. Avoid the following in the review:
- Lists of typographical errors
- Footnotes
- Digressions unrelated to the volume

6. Please submit two paper copies of the review to the Book Review Editor.

Questions? Phone (610) 758-3460 — FAX: (610) 758-4677

Journal of Futures Markets

ADDRESS FOR SUBMISSION:

Robert I. Webb, Editor
Journal of Futures Markets
1595 Old Oaks Drive
Charlottesville, VA 22901
USA
Phone: 434-295-4550
Fax: 434-295-4550
E-Mail: rwebb@adelphia.net
Web: www.wiley.com
Address May Change:

PUBLICATION GUIDELINES:

Manuscript Length: Any
Copies Required: Three
Computer Submission: Yes - Disk
Format: See Web Site
Fees to Review: 0.00 US$

Manuscript Style:
See Manuscript Guidelines

CIRCULATION DATA:

Reader: Academics, Business Researchers
Frequency of Issue: Monthly
Copies per Issue: Less than 1,000
Sponsor/Publisher: Wiley InterScience
Subscribe Price: 1555.00 US$ USA
1675.00 US$ Canada, Mexico
1777.00 US$

REVIEW INFORMATION:

Type of Review: Blind Review
No. of External Reviewers: 1-2
No. of In House Reviewers: 1
Acceptance Rate: 20%
Time to Review: 2 - 3 Months
Reviewers Comments: Yes
Invited Articles: 0-5%
Fees to Publish: 0.00 US$

MANUSCRIPT TOPICS:

Derivative Securities & Markets; Derivative Securities & Markets; Derivative Securities & Markets; Derivative Securities & Markets; Financial Institutions & Markets

MANUSCRIPT GUIDELINES/COMMENTS:

Web. http://www3.interscience.wiley.com/cgi-bin/jhome/34434

Description of Journal Content

The *Journal of Futures Markets* is an academic finance journal specializing in articles on futures and other derivative securities and markets. It publishes timely, innovative articles written by leading finance academics and professionals. Coverage ranges from the highly practical to theoretical topics that include futures, derivatives, risk management and control, financial engineering, new financial instruments, hedging strategies, analysis of trading systems, legal, accounting, and regulatory issues, and portfolio optimization, among others.

It is intended that articles should present research results and focus on the discussion of ideas. Most readers are more interested in the implications and meaning of research results than in mathematical notation per se. To be sure, some articles deal solely with techniques, and it is necessary in many articles to include a description of the research technique used so that the reader can judge for himself its appropriateness. At times, also, some mathematical notation may be the best way of making a point. Generally, however, it is preferred that mathematical details be kept to a minimum or relegated to an appendix.

Information for Contributors

Send manuscripts for submission and other editorial correspondence to the Editor.

All other correspondence should be addressed to the publisher, Professional, Reference, & Trade Group, John Wiley & Sons, Inc., 111 River Street, Hoboken, NJ 07030.

Submission of a manuscript to this journal implies that the material has not been copyrighted or published, that it is not being submitted for publication elsewhere, and that, if the material is sponsored, it has been released for publication.

No article can be published unless accompanied by a **signed publication agreement**, which serves as a transfer of copyright from author to publisher. A publication agreement may be obtained from the editor or the publisher. A copy of the publication agreement appears in most issues of the journal. Only **original papers** will be accepted and copyright of published papers will be vested in the publisher. It is the author's responsibility to obtain written permission to reproduce material that has appeared in another publication. If the article is a "work made for hire," the agreement must be signed by the employer.

Notes (brief communications) will be considered for publication as well as letters of a discursive nature (e.g., commenting on recent articles).

Submit three copies of manuscript (including all tables and artwork) typed on one side only on standard 8½ x 11-inch paper. All copy must be typed double-spaced with 1-inch margins. All ambiguous characters and symbols must be clearly marked in the margins.

Divide the manuscript into subsections for clarity. Wherever possible, detailed mathematical analysis should be placed in an Appendix.

Figures should be professionally prepared and submitted in a form suitable for reproduction (camera-ready copy). Computer-generated graphs are acceptable only if they have been printed with a good quality laser printer.

Complete descriptive captions for all figures should be supplied on a separate sheet. All figures must be cited in text and assigned **Arabic numbers**.

Complete captions for all tabular material must be supplied. All columns in tabular material should have explanatory headings. Each table should be typed on a separate sheet. All tables must be cited in text and assigned **Roman numbers**.

Expository footnotes should be cited in text with a superscript Arabic number and **typed double-spaced on a separate sheet** that is inserted at the end of the manuscript. When typeset, the footnotes will appear at the bottom of the page on which they are cited.

Literature citations in the text should indicate the author and the year of publication (e.g., "Smith (1978) built on certain earlier work (Jones, 1969, pp. 38–99) which was inaccurate..."). All literature citations should appear alphabetically under the heading "Bibliography" at the end of the text. Sample entries for a book and a journal article follow:

Powers, M.J., & Castelino, M.G. (1991). Inside the financial markets (3rd ed.). New York: Wiley.

Ma, C.K., Rao, R.P., & Sears, R.S. (1992). Limit moves and price resolution: A reply. *The Journal of Futures Markets*, 12, 361–363.

A complete mailing address and telephone number (and fax number, if available) for the author(s) must be supplied. In case of multiple authors, indicate which author is to handle the correspondence and review the proofs. Supply the **professional title and affiliation** of each author.

Supply an abstract that succinctly and accurately describes the paper so that appropriate referees can be matched to the topic. Abstracts should not exceed 100 words.

The introduction should include a statement of the problem being addressed, why it is important, and to whom it is important. How is the study related to other work? Is it an extension? Major or minor? Is it a correction or difference of interpretation?

The conclusion should tell the reader clearly what the paper finds or demonstrates. It should coincide with the objectives set forth in the introduction. It should describe the implications of the results for researchers, traders, policy makers, etc.

Do not use personal pronouns (I, we, our, etc.).

Use present tense throughout (introduction, main body, conclusion). Past tense should be reserved for description of past research.

Use simple, straightforward, declarative sentences. Compound sentences are all right if they are clear in their meaning. Hint: Avoid starting a sentence with a phrase.

A final version of your accepted manuscript should be submitted on diskette as well as hard copy, using the guidelines in the Diskette Submission Instructions, usually included in most issues of the journal.

Journal of Human Resources

ADDRESS FOR SUBMISSION:

Jan Levine Thal, Managing Editor
Journal of Human Resources
University of Wisconsin
Social Science Building
c/o James R. Walker, Editor
1180 Observatory Drive
Madison, WI 53706
USA
Phone: 608-262-4867
Fax: 608-262-6290
E-Mail: thal@ssc.wisc.edu
Web: www.ssc.wisc.edu/jhr/
Address May Change:

PUBLICATION GUIDELINES:

Manuscript Length: 20+
Copies Required: Five
Computer Submission: Yes - Required
Format: See Guidelines
Fees to Review: 0.00 US$

Manuscript Style:
    Chicago Manual of Style

CIRCULATION DATA:

Reader: Academics, Government Officials,
    Practitioners
Frequency of Issue: Quarterly
Copies per Issue: 2,001 - 3,000
Sponsor/Publisher: University of Wisconsin
Subscribe Price: 62.00 US$ Individual
    180.00 US$ Institution/Library

REVIEW INFORMATION:

Type of Review: Blind Review
No. of External Reviewers: 1-3
No. of In House Reviewers: 1-2
Acceptance Rate: 11-20%
Time to Review: 2 - 6 Months
Reviewers Comments: Yes
Invited Articles: 0-5%
Fees to Publish:
    See Guidelines

MANUSCRIPT TOPICS:
Demography; Econometrics; Health Economics; Public Policy Economics

MANUSCRIPT GUIDELINES/COMMENTS:

The *Journal of Human Resources* (*JHR*) publishes academic papers that use the best available empirical methods. It is not a personnel publication.

The *JHR* has no submission fee.

Send your paper as two separate MS Word or .PDF files, via email, to the *JHR*'s managing editor, Jan Levine Thal, thal@ssc.wisc.edu. Please put all the identifying information in your covering email or in a file that includes any cover letter, title page, or other accompanying information. The manuscript must be sent in a separate file containing no identifying information about the authors, because it may be forwarded to reviewers. Check the manuscript properties under "file" to make sure the identifying information has been deleted.

Authors who submit electronically must also send five hard copies of the paper and follow all of the required formatting directions below.

Required
Failure to comply with any of these guidelines may result in the JHR *returning manuscripts to authors for formatting.*
- **Five** copies of each manuscript
- Single-sided pages
- Double-spaced lines throughout all text and endnotes
- One-inch or wider margins
- All text and endnotes in 12-point type or larger
- Include an abstract of **no more than 100 words**
- Author name(s), address(es), institutional affiliation(s), and any acknowledgements should appear **only on the title page** of the manuscript

Do not send submissions directly to the Editor or Co-Editors. Failing to send submissions to the Madison office will only delay consideration.

Fee to Publish. Authors must provide own camera-ready figures that follow JGR specifications exactly.

Journal of Industrial Economics

ADDRESS FOR SUBMISSION:

General Editor
Journal of Industrial Economics
New York University
Stern School of Business
Department of Economics
44 West 4th Street
New York, NY 10012-1126
USA
Phone: 510-643-1048
Fax: 510-643-1048
E-Mail: jindec@stern.nyu.edu
Web: www.essex.ac.uk/jindec/
Address May Change:

PUBLICATION GUIDELINES:

Manuscript Length: No Reply
Copies Required: Three
Computer Submission: Yes Online
  Preferred
Format: See Web Site
Fees to Review: 0.00 US$

Manuscript Style:
  See Manuscript Guidelines

CIRCULATION DATA:

Reader: Academics
Frequency of Issue: Quarterly
Copies per Issue: 1,001 - 2,000
Sponsor/Publisher: Blackwell Publishing
Subscribe Price: 62.00 US$ Individual
  184.00 US$ Institution
  25.00 US$ Student

REVIEW INFORMATION:

Type of Review: Editorial Review
No. of External Reviewers: 2
No. of In House Reviewers: 1
Acceptance Rate: 11-20%
Time to Review: 2 - 3 Months
Reviewers Comments: Yes
Invited Articles: 0-5%
Fees to Publish: 0.00 US$

MANUSCRIPT TOPICS:
Capital Budgeting; Industrial Organization; Public Policy Economics

MANUSCRIPT GUIDELINES/COMMENTS:

General Editor
Pierre Régibeau, University of Essex, UK

Editors
Yeon-Koo Che, University of Wisconsin at Madison, USA
Kenneth Hendricks, University of Texas at Austin, USA
Frank Verboven, Catholic University of Leuven, Netherlands

Editorial Assistants
Amanda Broomell, New York University, USA
Jan Stevenson, University of Essex, UK

Aims and Scope
First published in 1952 the *Journal* has a very wide international circulation and is recognised as a leading journal in the field. It was founded to promote and publish the analysis of modern industry, particularly the behaviour of firms and the functioning of markets. Contributions are welcomed in all areas of industrial economics including: organization of industry, applied oligopoly theory, product differentiation and technical change, theory of the firm and internal organization, regulation, monopoly, merger and technology policy. Necessarily, these subjects will often draw on adjacent areas such as international economics, labour economics and law.

The *Journal* has a tradition of publishing a blend of theory and evidence. Theoretical papers are welcomed and should be presented so as to highlight their implications for policy and/ or empirical analysis. Likewise, empirical papers should have a sound theoretical base; and where novel econometric techniques are applied these should be clearly explained. Case studies should be motivated by, and inform, economic theory and should avoid pure description. The *Journal* editors are ready to publish shorter notes which report significant new data or empirical results or are short comments on subjects which have featured in previous issues of the *Journal*.

Author Guidelines
The *Journal* has a tradition of publishing a blend of theory and evidence. Theoretical discussion is welcomed. It should include sufficient explanation to convey the robustness and potential empirical relevance of the material to the general reader who wants to decide whether to follow the analysis. Empirical analysis, and especially econometric analysis, should include an explanation of the data sources used, of the methods applied and of the theoretical or conceptual of the study. The *Journal* has a particular tradition of case studies of firms and industries, which the Editors actively wish to continue. Contributors of case studies of firms, markets, or related organisations should illustrate the behaviour that can be explained by recognized economic principles, as well as the puzzles that arise when those principles do not seem to govern behaviour.

The Editors are ready to publish shorter notes, which report significant new data or empirical results, or are short comments on subjects which have featured in previous issues of the *Journal*. Books are not reviewed, but substantial review articles will be considered for publication.

Authors should send three copies (preferably printed double-sided) of a manuscript to the appropriate editorial office. If a paper is accepted, the author will be asked to prepare it in accordance with the *Journal* style guide (available on the JIE editorial Web site). There is no submission fee.

Typescripts from North America should be sent to the General Editor, address above. Typescripts from *all* other countries should be sent to the Editors, Journal of Industrial Economics, Dept of Economics, Univ of Essex, Wivenhoe Park, Colchester, CO4 3SQ, UK.

Turnaround time from manuscript receipt to decision historically has averaged about twelve weeks.

Journal of Industrial, Business and Economic Research

ADDRESS FOR SUBMISSION:

Emmanuel Emenyonu, Editor
Journal of Industrial, Business and
    Economic Research
Southern Connecticut State University
School of Business
Department of Accounting
501 Cresscent Street
New Haven, CT 06515
USA
Phone: 203-392-6148
Fax: 203-392-5863
E-Mail: emenyonu1@aol.com
Web:
Address May Change:

PUBLICATION GUIDELINES:

Manuscript Length: 16-20
Copies Required: Four
Computer Submission: Yes Disk
Format: MS Word 97 or 2000
Fees to Review: 30.00 US$

Manuscript Style:
    Chicago Manual of Style

CIRCULATION DATA:

Reader: Academics, Business Persons
Frequency of Issue: 2 Times/Year
Copies per Issue: 1,001 - 2,000
Sponsor/Publisher: Markowitz Center for
    Research & Department of Economics,
    University of Port Harcourt
Subscribe Price: 50.00 US$ Individual
    90.00 US$ Institution

REVIEW INFORMATION:

Type of Review: Blind Review
No. of External Reviewers: 2
No. of In House Reviewers: 1
Acceptance Rate: 11-20%
Time to Review: 4 - 6 Months
Reviewers Comments: Yes
Invited Articles: 0-5%
Fees to Publish: 0.00 US$

MANUSCRIPT TOPICS:
Accounting; Accounting Information Systems; Accounting Theory & Practice; Auditing;
Behavioral Accounting; Behavioral Economics; Cost Accounting; Econometrics; Economic
Development; Economic History; Economics; Finance; Financial Services; Fiscal Policy;
Government & Non-Profit Accounting; Industrial & Public Policy; Industrial Organization;
Insurance; International Economics & Trade; International Finance; Macro Economics;
Management & Entrepreneurial; Marketing & Transportation; Micro Economics; Monetary
Policy; Portfolio & Security Analysis; Public Policy Economics; Regional Economics; Tax
Accounting

MANUSCRIPT GUIDELINES/COMMENTS:

Authors should adopt the *Chicago Manual of Style* in preparing their manuscripts for
submission to *JIBER*.

The *JIBER* is a publication of Markowitz Center for Research and Development (MCRD) in association with the Department of Economics, University of Port Harcourt. It is the primary objective of *JIBER* to disseminate research findings by top scholars, researchers and professionals from around the world. *JIBER* is oriented towards bringing the industrial world, the professionals and the academia together in bid to stimulate meaningful exchange of ideas. *JIBER* is targeted to a wide spectrum of readers covering industrialists, business practitioners, academics, and research students.

The Editorial board of the *Journal of Industrial, Business and Economic Research* (*JIBER*) calls for well-researched papers from Researchers on the themes and sub-themes highlighted below.

Papers submitted must show evidence of contribution to existing knowledge and originality. The *Journal* insists on originality and would by no means be liable for works that are not the original contributions of the authors. While reasonable effort would be made to ensure that no such copied works are published, the Board assumes no liability for the unauthorized use of other people's work.

Manuscripts should be submitted in triplicates and should not be more than 20 pages (8½" x 11"), typed double-spaced with 1" margins—tables and references included.

The first page should contain the title of paper, the names and affiliations of authors and contact address of one of the authors at the footnote. The second page should contain the title of the paper and the Abstract of not more than 200 words. The third page should start with the title of the paper and the introduction with the rest of the article continuing.

The authors-and-date style of citation should be used; for example, (Agiobenebo, 2001). Footnotes should be avoided except if absolutely necessary.

References should be arranged in alphabetical order at the end of the article. All tables and figures should be positioned wherever they should appear.

Addresses for Submissions
Submission fee of US$30.00 is payable to Emmanuel N. Emenyonu, International Editor, *JIBER* for those in US, Canada, and Mexico (address above).

Submission fee of US$30.00 is payable to Chinedu B. Ezirim, Managing Editor, *JIBER*, for those in other parts of the world, including Nigeria. Send to Journal of Industrial, Business, and Economic Research, Markowitz Center for Research and Development, University of Port Harcourt, P. O. Box 97, Port Harcourt, Nigeria. Email: markowitzcg@yahoo.com or cberzirim@yahoo.com.

Journal of Insurance Issues

ADDRESS FOR SUBMISSION:

James M. Carson, Editor
Journal of Insurance Issues
Florida State University
College of Business
RMI, RE, & BL Department
Tallahassee, FL 32306-1110
USA
Phone: 850-644-5858
Fax: 850-644-5842
E-Mail: jcarson@cob.fsu.edu
Web: www.wria.org
Address May Change:

PUBLICATION GUIDELINES:

Manuscript Length: 14-30
Copies Required: Four
Computer Submission: Yes
Format: MS Word (preferred), PDF
Fees to Review: 35.00 US$ Non-Member

Manuscript Style:
    See Manuscript Guidelines

CIRCULATION DATA:

Reader: Academics
Frequency of Issue: 2 Times/Year
Copies per Issue: Less than 1,000
Sponsor/Publisher: Western Risk &
    Insurance Association
Subscribe Price: 30.00 US$
    35.00 US$ Overseas

REVIEW INFORMATION:

Type of Review: Blind Review
No. of External Reviewers: 3
No. of In House Reviewers: 1
Acceptance Rate: 0-50%
Time to Review: 3-6 Months
Reviewers Comments: Yes
Invited Articles: 0-5%
Fees to Publish: 0.00 US$

MANUSCRIPT TOPICS:

Corporate Finance; Financial Institutions & Markets; Financial Services; Insurance; Portfolio
& Security Analysis

MANUSCRIPT GUIDELINES/COMMENTS:

The *Journal of Insurance Issues* deals with current issues, problems or practices, which
inform the reader about changes in the insurance industry and risk management applications.
Also publishable would be articles that make new contributions to the existing body of
knowledge in this field.

Manuscripts may be submitted within the following guidelines:

1. Authors should submit manuscripts (as attachments to email) directly to the Editor. MS
Word is the preferred format.

2. The first page should include the title of the manuscript, author contact information
(including email addresses), and author biographies (not to exceed 50 words for each author).

3. The second page of the manuscript should include the title, abstract, and three key words; e.g., cycles, reinsurance, and regulation. No author information should appear on this page.

4. The *Journal* requires a US$35 submission fee (check payable to WRIA); this fee is waived for WRIA members. To become a WRIA member, see Web—www.wira.org.

5. Endnotes should be placed on a separate page and placed at the end of the manuscript. Endnotes should be placed in numerical order (not alphabetically) in the text as well as on the endnote page.

6. The reference style of the *Journal* is an alphabetical, unnumbered list at the end of the manuscript. For example:
Barnea, A., R.A. Haugen, and L.W. Senbet (1985) *Agency Problems and Financial Contracting.* Englewood Cliffs, NJ: Prentice-Hall.

Keleher, R.E. (1982) "Evidence Relating to Supply-Side Tax Policy," *Supply-Side Economics: A Critical Appraisal,* R.H. Fink, editor. Frederick, MD: University Publications.

Miller, M. (1977) "Debt and Taxes," *Journal of Finance,* 32, May, pp. 261-278.

In the text, a reference should show an author's last name followed by the year of publication in parentheses. For example: (Posey, 1998; Louberge et al., 1999).

For direct quotes, a page number is added to the reference. For example: Hoyt (1989, p. 23).

7. Each manuscript should end with a non-technical summary of the main conclusions of the paper.

8. Papers should be formatted in the style of *JII* articles. See, for example, Colquitt and Dumm (1999).

9. Once a manuscript is accepted for publication, authors will be asked to submit three copies of the final paper and an electronic file (email preferred) in MS Word or WordPerfect. All tables, graphs, charts, formulae, and equations should be placed in the body of the manuscript.

Journal of Insurance Regulation

ADDRESS FOR SUBMISSION:

Mike Barth, Editor
Journal of Insurance Regulation
Georgia Southern University
Department of Finance and
  Quantitative Methods
Statesboro, GA 30460-8151
USA
Phone: 912-681-0259
Fax: 912-871-1835
E-Mail: mbarth@georgiasouthern.edu
Web: www.naic.org/insprod/jir/
Address May Change:

PUBLICATION GUIDELINES:

Manuscript Length: 6-25
Copies Required: One
Computer Submission: Yes Email
Format: MS Word, WordPerfect
Fees to Review: 0.00 US$

Manuscript Style:
    See Manuscript Guidelines, Simplified
    Law Review

CIRCULATION DATA:

Reader: Academics, Business Persons
Frequency of Issue: Quarterly
Copies per Issue: 1,001 - 2,000
Sponsor/Publisher: National Association of
  Insurance Commissioners
Subscribe Price: 70.00 US$ Domestic
  85.00 US$ Outside USA

REVIEW INFORMATION:

Type of Review: Blind Review
No. of External Reviewers: 2
No. of In House Reviewers: 1
Acceptance Rate: 21-30%
Time to Review: 1 - 2 Months
Reviewers Comments: Yes
Invited Articles: 21-30%
Fees to Publish: 0.00 US$

MANUSCRIPT TOPICS:
Insurance; Insurance Regulatory Issues; International Topics in Insurance Regulation; Public Policy

MANUSCRIPT GUIDELINES/COMMENTS:

Purpose
The *Journal of Insurance Regulation* is sponsored by the National Association of Insurance Commissioners. The objectives of the National Association of Insurance Commissioners in sponsoring the *Journal of Insurance Regulation* are:

1.   To provide a forum for opinion and discussion on major insurance regulatory issues,
2.   To provide wide distribution of rigorous, high quality research regarding insurance regulatory issues,
3.   To make state insurance departments more aware of insurance regulatory research efforts,
4.   To increase the rigor, quality, and quantity of the research efforts on insurance regulatory issues, and

5. To be an important force for the overall improvement of insurance regulation.

To meet these objectives, the National Association of Insurance Commissioners will provide an open forum for the discussion of a broad spectrum of ideas. However, the ideas expressed in the *Journal* are not endorsed by the National Association of Insurance Commissioners, the editorial staff, or the *Journal*'s Board.

Editorial Policy

The *Journal of Insurance Regulation* is published quarterly by the National Association of Insurance Commissioners ("NAIC"). The purpose of the *Journal* is to provide a medium for the critical examination of issues pertinent to insurance regulation through the publication of rigorous, high quality research and by providing a forum for the exchange of opinion on such issues.

Subjects Considered for Publication. Consistent with its goal of providing a medium for expression of competent opinions and results of original research, the *Journal* will consider topics of current interest to its diverse readership that includes regulators, actuaries, economists, insurance personnel, lawyers, and academicians. Both theoretical and practical approaches to contemporary regulatory issues are appropriate for the *Journal*. The *Journal* does not support any specific position, welcoming all viewpoints as long as they are objectively presented, properly authenticated, and thought-provoking. Although sponsored by the NAIC, the *Journal* is editorially independent of the NAIC.

Character of Acceptable Manuscripts. A manuscript's acceptability for publication will be evaluated on the following criteria:

1. Significance of contribution to the literature of insurance regulation.
2. Style of writing that communicates the author's message clearly and concisely.
3. Thorough documentation of controversial material with adequate coverage of opposing positions.

Significance of contribution to the literature is not dependent upon the research methodology employed. Rather, emphasis is given to the quality of the research methods and interpretation of the findings. Reflective essays of superior quality demonstrating creative thought and analysis may satisfy the requirement of significant contribution. The importance of the topic to national or international insurance regulation substantially influences the significance of a manuscript's contribution to the literature.

Originality of Material. Generally, only original, unpublished material will be considered for publication with the exception of republication of a report or judicial opinion that is of widespread interest or material to which the readership is not likely to be exposed. Analysis, explanation, or critique of such reports, however, is preferred.

Multiple Submissions. It is understood that manuscripts submitted to the *Journal* or substantially similar manuscripts will not be concurrently submitted to any other publication. In exchange for this commitment, the *Journal* agrees to conduct the review process promptly, ideally within two months. The *Journal* will discontinue consideration of a manuscript when multiple submissions are identified.

Copyright. The copyright to an accepted/published article will be held by the National Association of Insurance Commissioners. The *Journal* reserves the right to reprint articles and publish them in composite works and may permit others to republish articles (with appropriate credit) at its discretion. Reasonable requests by authors for reprint permission are normally granted with the stipulation that proper credit to the *Journal* and the author must be included.

Publication Commitment. Due to space constraints, the *Journal* can make no advance commitment to publish an accepted manuscript in a particular issue. While articles are generally processed in the order in which they are received, special consideration occasionally is given to manuscripts whose expedient publication is of critical importance. Ordinarily a manuscript is published within two to six months after its acceptance.

Guidelines for Authors. The format of the *Journal* includes three general categories of material: articles, legal reviews, and commentary from readers. Frequently, articles representing divergent views on a subject are juxtaposed in a "point-counterpoint" format. The guidelines specified here apply to articles and legal reviews. Commentary from readers, by contrast, is subject only to space limitations and general standards of good taste.

Submission and Review Procedures

1. One copy of the manuscript should be submitted to the Editor, whose address appears at the end of these Guidelines. Electronic submission through email is strongly encouraged. Receipt of all manuscripts is acknowledged. Authors should indicate the word processing package and computer system used in preparing the manuscript.

2. The name of the author should appear on a separate sheet together with any professional designations, academic degrees, and company, university, or department affiliation. Acknowledgments and disclaimers should also appear on this sheet. The separate sheet is necessary so that the manuscript can be evaluated by one or more members of the Editorial Review Board without his or her having knowledge of the identity of the author. The background information is used when a manuscript is accepted for publication. It has no bearing on whether an article is accepted.

3. A short, one or two page executive summary should be included. The executive summary should be thorough enough to be read alone.

4. For accepted manuscripts, a valid street address with zip code must be submitted to the editor, along with a daytime phone number. Complimentary copies are provided through UPS or other private shipper and require a street address for delivery.

5. Completion of the review process is generally accomplished within eight weeks of the receipt of a manuscript. The complexity of the subject or difficulty in identifying a suitable reviewer, however, occasionally lengthens the required reviewing time.

6. The *Journal* uses a simplified law review form of citation for legal citations. Three examples are provided below.

- Carlton v.s. Mut. Ins. Co., 72 Ga. 3171 (1884).
- C.A. KULP & J.W. HALL, CASUALTY INSURANCE (4th ed. 1968).
- Cassidy, State Insurance Department Funding, 1970-1982, 5 J. INS. REG. 444 (1987).

7. Cited literature should be shown in a "References" section containing an alphabetical list of authors as shown below:

Klein, Robert W. and Michael M. Barth, 1995. "Solvency Monitoring in the Twenty-First Century," *Journal of Insurance Regulation*, 13:256-277.

Becker, Gary S., 1983. "A Theory of Competition Among Pressure Groups for Political Influence," *Quarterly Journal of Economics*, 48:371-399.

Binder, John J., 1985a. "Measuring the Effects of Regulation with Stock Price Data," *Rand Journal of Economics*, 16:167-183.

Binder, John J., 1985b. "On the Use of the Multivariate Regression Model in Event Studies," *Journal of Accounting Research*, 23:370-383.

Cummins, J. David, Richard D. Phillips, and Sharon Tennyson, 2001. "Regulation, Political Influence and the Price of Automobile Insurance," *Journal of Insurance Regulation*, 20:9-50.

Meier, Kenneth J., 1988. *The Political Economy of Regulation: The Case of Insurance*, Albany: SUNY Press.

Business Insurance, 2000. "Floods Highlight Climate Risk," Oct. 16: 70.

Challis, S., 2002. "Insurers Press for Climate-Change Controls," Feb. 20, *Reuters* (found at www.planetark.org/dailynewsstory.cfm/newsid/14618/story.htm, accessed March 31, 2002).

A more extensive listing of citation styles can be found on the *Journal* Web site under the link *Guidelines for Authors*.

8. Length should be governed by the complexity of the subject matter. In general, shorter manuscripts should be at least five pages but no longer than 10 pages. For longer articles, 20-30 pages of double-spaced manuscript, including relevant tables and charts, is preferable. Very long manuscripts will be divided and published in consecutive issues, if they cannot be appropriately shortened.

9. Authors are encouraged to use subdivisions to give continuity. Headings and subheadings should be appropriately marked throughout the manuscript.

SPECIAL CONSIDERATIONS

Tables, Graphs, Figures. Each table, graph, or figure should be on a separate page and identified. Its place of insertion should be indicated in the margin of the text. The legends, axis, row and column headings, and footnotes should be clear enough so that the exhibit is self-contained.

Mathematical Formula. To enable the typesetter to enter mathematical formula correctly, carets (^) should be placed over all subscripts, "vees" (v) under all superscripts, and a slash mark through each zero (0) with a colored pencil. Since determining to which pan of a formula a divisor applies is frequently difficult, parentheses should be used to clarify whenever possible. Care should be taken to differentiate lower case letters from numerals with which they may be confused (e.g., "i" and "1"). Longhand is encouraged to facilitate clarification of formulas.

Equations should be numbered consecutively, with the number in parenthesis and flush with the right margin. All definitions are listed flush with the Left margin (e.g., $x=q2r$). Authors are contacted prior to publication to confirm that the editor understands the author's intent.

Legal Reviews. In general the same writing and submission guides apply to Legal reviews as apply to regular articles. Legal reviews, however, are shorter, normally running a minimum of 500 words in Length to a maximum of 1,500 words.

1. Most legal reviews analyze a single case. In general these reviews should follow standard law review form. Since many of the cases do not yet appear in any type of reporter (official or otherwise), as much information as possible should be included so that the reader can locate the case. This information would include the docket number of the case and, if possible, some means by which the opinion can be found. if the opinion is obscure, a copy of the opinion should be included for the Legal Reviews Editors.

2. Sometimes a jurisdiction will decide a series of related cases that deserve extensive comment. In that case, the general guidelines for articles should be followed.

3. Frequently authors will spend an inordinate amount of space discussing procedural maneuvers or preliminary matters that are of slight interest to persons involved generally in insurance regulation. It is important, of course, to know that an opinion was issued merely on the basis of alleged facts or that a court held that a particular matter is not a proper subject for decision on a motion for summary judgment. But normally the details of legal maneuvering are not a subject of general interest.

Submission of Manuscripts
Send all manuscripts to the Editor.

Journal of International Business and Economics

ADDRESS FOR SUBMISSION:

Alan S. Khade, Editor
Journal of International Business and
    Economics
California State University, Stanislaus
College of Business Administration
983 Woodland Drive
Turlock, CA 95382-7281
USA
Phone: 209-667-3074
Fax: 209-667-3210
E-Mail: akhade@csustan.edu
Web: www.aibe.org
Address May Change: 10/10/2010

PUBLICATION GUIDELINES:

Manuscript Length: 10-20
Copies Required: Two
Computer Submission: Yes - Disk, Email
Format: MS Word
Fees to Review: 0.00 US$

Manuscript Style:
    Chicago Manual of Style

CIRCULATION DATA:

Reader: Academics, Business Persons
Frequency of Issue: 2 Times/Year
Copies per Issue: Less than 1,000
Sponsor/Publisher: AIBE
Subscribe Price: 50.00 US$ Individual

REVIEW INFORMATION:

Type of Review: Blind Review
No. of External Reviewers: 2
No. of In House Reviewers: 1
Acceptance Rate: 21-30%
Time to Review: 1 - 2 Months
Reviewers Comments: Yes
Invited Articles: 21-30%
Fees to Publish: 0.00 US$

MANUSCRIPT TOPICS:

Corporate Finance; Econometrics; Economic Development; Economics; Financial Institutions
& Markets; Financial Services; Fiscal Policy; Global Business; Industrial Organization;
Insurance; International Economics & Trade; International Finance; Macro Economics;
Monetary Policy; Portfolio & Security Analysis; Public Policy Economics; Regional
Economics

MANUSCRIPT GUIDELINES/COMMENTS:

Journal of International Business and Economics (*JIBE*) is a refereed research journal
published by the AIBE. *JIBE* will serve and provide a forum for the exchange of
research/teaching ideas among faculty and executives in Business and Economics.

The original, high-quality research papers and articles (not currently under review or
published in other publications) on all topics related to business and economics will be
considered for publication in *JIBE*.

836

Please follow these following Manuscript Guidelines for *Journal of International Business and Economics*. For more information, please visit our Web site.

I. **Copyright**. Articles, papers, abstracts or cases submitted for publication should be original contributions and should not be under consideration for any other publication at the same time. Authors submitting articles/papers/abstracts/cases for publication warrant that the work is not an infringement of any existing copyright, infringement of proprietary right, invasion of privacy, or libel and will indemnify, defend, and hold AIBE/IABE harmless from any damages, expenses, and costs against any breach of such warranty. For ease of dissemination and to ensure proper policing of use, papers/articles/abstracts/cases and contributions become the legal copyright of the AIBE/IABE unless otherwise agreed in writing.

II. **Typing**. Paper must be laser printed on 8.5" x 11" white sheets in *Arial 10-point font, single-spaced lines, justify style in MS Word*. All four margins must be 1" each.

III. **First Page**. Paper title, not exceeding two lines, must be **CAPITALIZED AND CENTERED IN BOLD LETTERS**. Author name and university/organizational affiliation of each author must be printed on one line each. Do NOT include titles such as, Dr., Professor, Ph.D., department, address, email address etc. Please print the word "**ABSTRACT**" in capitalized bold letters, left justified, and double-spaced from last author's name/affiliation. Abstract should be in italic. Please see the sample manuscript.

IV. **All Other Headings**. All other section headings starting with **INTRODUCTION** must be numbered, in capitalized bold letters, left justified, and double-spaced from last line above them.

V. **Tables, Figures, and Charts**. All tables, figures or charts must be inserted in the body of the manuscripts within the margins with headings/titles in centered **CAPITALIZED BOLD** letters.

VI. **References and Bibliography**. All references listed in this section must be cited in the article and vice-versa. The reference citations in the text must be inserted in parentheses within sentences with author name followed by a comma and year of publication. Please follow the following formats:

Journal Articles:	Khade, Alan S. and Metlen, Scott K., "An Application of Benchmarking in Dairy Industry", *International Journal of Benchmarking*, Vol. III (4), 1996, 17-27.
Books:	Harrison, Norma and Samson, D., Technology Management: Text and Cases, McGraw-Hill Publishing, New York, 2002.
Internet:	Hesterbrink, C., E-Business and ERP: Bringing two Paradigms together, October 1999; PricewaterhouseCoopers, www.pwc.com.

VII. **Author Profile(s)**. At the end of paper, include author profile(s), not exceeding <u>five</u> lines each author, including name, highest degree/university/year, current position/ university, and major achievements. For example:

Dr. Andrew J. Wagner earned his Ph.D. at Texas A and M University in 1997. Currently he is an associate professor of finance at California State University, Stanislaus, and Program Chair of the IABE.

VIII. **Manuscript**. Absolutely **no** footnotes allowed! Please do not forget to run spelling and grammar check for the completed paper. **Save the manuscript on a diskette** and label the diskette with title of your paper, your name, and email address.

IX. **Submission**
Submissions by Mail
Please mail the following items in a 9" x 12" envelope:
1. Two camera-ready laser-printed copies of the manuscript
2. Diskette containing your manuscript

Submissions by Email
Send your paper as an attachment to the email to: AKhade@csustan.edu.

Journal of International Business Research

ADDRESS FOR SUBMISSION:

Current Editor's Name/See Web Site
Journal of International Business Research
Digital Submission Through Web Site
Address Other Questions to:
  Jim or JoAnn Carland at #s below
USA
Phone: 828-293-9151
Fax: 828-293-9407
E-Mail: info@alliedacademies.org
Web: www.alliedacademies.org
Address May Change:

PUBLICATION GUIDELINES:

Manuscript Length: 25 Pages
Copies Required: Submit Through Web
Computer Submission: Yes
Format: MS Word, WordPerfect
Fees to Review: 0.00 US$

Manuscript Style:
    American Psychological Association

CIRCULATION DATA:

Reader: Academics
Frequency of Issue: Yearly
Copies per Issue: Less than 1,000
Sponsor/Publisher: Allied Academies, Inc.
Subscribe Price: 75.00 US$ Individual
    150.00 US$ Foreign

REVIEW INFORMATION:

Type of Review: Blind Review
No. of External Reviewers: 2
No. of In House Reviewers: 2
Acceptance Rate: 21-30%
Time to Review: 3-4 Months
Reviewers Comments: Yes
Invited Articles: 0-5%
Fees to Publish: 75.00 US$ Membership

MANUSCRIPT TOPICS:
International Economics & Trade; International Finance

MANUSCRIPT GUIDELINES/COMMENTS:

The journal publishes theoretical or empirical research concerning: any of the Manuscript Topics.

Comments. All authors of published manuscripts must be members of the appropriate academy affiliate of Allied Academies. The current membership fee is $75.00 U.S.

Editorial Policy Guidelines
The primary criterion upon which manuscripts are judged is whether the research advances the discipline. Key points include currency, interest and relevancy.

In order for a theoretical manuscript to advance the discipline, it must address the literature to support conclusions or models which extend knowledge and understanding. Consequently, referees pay particular attention to completeness of literature review and appropriateness of conclusions drawn from that review.

In order for an empirical manuscript to advance the discipline, it must employ appropriate and effective sampling and statistical analysis techniques, and must be grounded by a thorough literature review. Consequently, referees pay particular attention to the research methodology and to the conclusions drawn from statistical analyses and their consistency with the literature.

Journal of International Economics

ADDRESS FOR SUBMISSION:

Jonathan Eaton, Charles Engel, Co-Eds
Journal of International Economics
University of Wisconsin
Center for World Affairs & the Global
 Economy, c/o Dept of Economics
1180 Observatory Dr, Soc Sciences Bldg
Madison, WI 53706-1393
USA
Phone: 608-262-2081
Fax: 608-263-3876
E-Mail: jie@intl-institute.wisc.edu
Web: www.ssc.wisc.edu/~cengel/JIE.htm
Address May Change:

PUBLICATION GUIDELINES:

Manuscript Length: 30+
Copies Required: Four
Computer Submission: Yes
Format: PDF
Fees to Review: 95.00 US$ Hard Copy
     65.00 US$ Electronic Submission

Manuscript Style:
     See Manuscript Guidelines

CIRCULATION DATA:

Reader: Academics
Frequency of Issue: Bi-Monthly
Copies per Issue: 1,001 - 2,000
Sponsor/Publisher: Elsevier Science
    Publishing Co.
Subscribe Price: 125.00 US$ Individual
    1201.00 US$ Institution
    120.00 Pounds /1,075 Pounds Indv/Inst

REVIEW INFORMATION:

Type of Review: Editorial Review
No. of External Reviewers: 2
No. of In House Reviewers: 1
Acceptance Rate: 11-20%
Time to Review: 4 - 6 Months
Reviewers Comments: Yes
Invited Articles: 0-5%
Fees to Publish: 0.00 US$

MANUSCRIPT TOPICS:
International Economics & Trade; International Finance

MANUSCRIPT GUIDELINES/COMMENTS:

General Submission Information
1.   Papers must be in English.

2.   Papers may be submitted electronically or in hard copy. The fee for electronic submissions is US$65, and for hard-copy submissions US$95. The fee may be paid by any of the following: Checks in U.S. currency from American banks or banks with American branches; International Money Orders; Cash or Travelers Checks. Checks should be made payable to the Journal of International Economics. Under exceptional circumstances, the submission fee can be waived, upon application to the Editors. We are unable to accept credit card payments. The submission fee should be mailed to the editorial office (address above).

3. Electronic submissions should be in PDF format and e-mailed to JIE@intl-institute.wisc.edu. It is the author's responsibility to ensure that the PDF file is completely readable on any personal computer (not just the computer on which the paper was composed.) Unreadable files will not be accepted. Some suggestions for preparation of PDF files may be found at http://www.ssc.wisc.edu/~cengel/JIE.htm.

Hard-copy submissions should be sent in quadruplicate to the *JIE* Editorial office.

4. Submission of a paper will be held to imply that it contains original unpublished work and is not being submitted for publication elsewhere.

5. The Editors do not accept responsibility for damage or loss of papers submitted. Upon acceptance of an article, author(s) will be asked to transfer copyright of the article to the publisher. This transfer will ensure the widest possible dissemination of information.

Paper Format Requirements

1. Papers in excess of 35 pages will not ordinarily be considered for publication.

2. Manuscripts should be typewritten and double-spaced with wide margins. The size of type font used should be large enough to be easily read (not smaller than 10 point). All pages should be numbered consecutively.

3. Tables, references, and legends for figures should be typed on separate pages. Titles and subtitles should be short.

4. The first page of the manuscript should contain the following information:
- Title
- Name(s) and institutional affiliation(s) of the author(s)
- An abstract of not more than 100 words
- A footnote on the same sheet should give the name, address, telephone and FAX numbers, and E-mail address, if available, of the corresponding author (addresses for all authors are requested).
- Classification code: at least one classification code according to the Classification System for Journal Articles as used by the *Journal of Economic Literature*
- Five key words should be supplied.
- Acknowledgments and information on grants received can be given in a footnote on the first page of the manuscript or before the References.

5. Footnotes should be kept to a minimum and numbered consecutively throughout the text with superscript Arabic numerals. Footnotes should be double-spaced, and not include formulae.

6. Important formulae (displayed) should be numbered consecutively throughout the manuscript as (1), (2), etc. on the right-hand side of the page. Where the derivation of formulae has been abbreviated, it is of great help to referees if the full derivation can be presented on a separate sheet (not to be published).

7. Illustrations will be reproduced photographically from originals supplied by the author. Illustrations of insufficient quality, which have to be redrawn by the publisher, will be charged to the author. Please provide all illustrations in quadruplicate (one high-contrast original and three photocopies). Care should be taken that lettering and symbols are of a comparable size. The illustrations should not be inserted in the text, and should be marked on the back with figure number, title of paper, and author's name. All graphs and diagrams should be referred to as figures, and should be numbered consecutively in the text in Arabic numerals. Illustrations of papers submitted as electronic manuscripts should be in traditional (i.e. hard-copy) form.

For additional information on preparing artwork for publication, please see the Author Artwork Guidelines, available on the Elsevier website at:
    http://authors.Elsevier.com/ArtworkInstructions.html?dc=AI1

8. Tables. All unessential tables should be eliminated from the manuscript. Tables should be numbered consecutively in the text in Arabic numerals and typed on separate sheets.

References
1. References should include only the most relevant papers. In the text, references to publications should appear as follows:
"Smith (1992) reported that..." or "This problem has been studied previously (e.g. Smith et al. 1969).

2. The author should make sure that there is a strict "one-to-one correspondence" between the names and years in the text and those on the list.

3. The list of references should appear at the end of the main text (after any appendices, but before tables and legends for figures). It should be double-spaced and listed in alphabetical order by author's name. References should appear as follows:

For Monographs
Hawawini, G., Swary, I., 1990. Mergers and Acquisitions in the U.S. Banking Industry: Evidence from the Capital Markets. North-Holland, Amsterdam.

For Contributions to Collective Works
Brunner, K., Meltzer, A.H., 1990. Money supply, in: Friedman, B.M., Hahn, F.H. (Eds.), Handbook of Monetary Economics, Vol. 1. North-Holland, Amsterdam, pp. 357--396.

For Periodicals
Griffiths, W., Judge, G., 1992. Testing and estimating location vectors when the error covariance matrix is unknown. Journal of Econometrics 54, 121--138.

Note that journal titles should not be abbreviated.

Accepted Manuscripts

After notification that a paper has been accepted for publication, four copies of the final manuscript, along with a disk with electronic files (if available), should be sent to the *Journal*'s editorial office in Madison. Please also include the "Checklist for files on diskette".

General Information

Please adhere strictly to the general instructions above on format, arrangement and, in particular, the reference style of the *Journal*. Any manuscript which does not conform to the above instructions will be returned for the necessary revision before publication.

Page proofs will be sent directly from Elsevier to the corresponding author. Proofs should be corrected carefully; the responsibility for detecting errors lies with the author. Corrections should be restricted to instances in which the proof is at variance with the manuscript. Extensive alterations will be charged.

Fifty reprints of each paper are supplied free of charge to the corresponding author; additional reprints are available at cost if they are ordered when the proof is returned.

All questions arising after the manuscript has been sent from the *JIE* office at the University of Wisconsin to the Elsevier Editorial Office, especially those relating to proofs, should be directed to Elsevier Science Ireland Ltd., Elsevier House, Brookvale Plaza, East Park, Shannon, Co. Clare, Ireland.

Electronic Files on Disk

Submission of accepted papers as electronic manuscripts, i.e. on disk with four copies of the accompanying manuscript, is encouraged. Electronic manuscripts have the advantage that there is no need for re-keying of text, thereby avoiding the possibility of introducing errors and resulting in reliable and fast delivery of proofs. The preferred storage medium is a 5.25 or 3.5-inch disk in MS-DOS format, although other systems are welcome, e.g. Macintosh (in this case, save your file in the usual manner; do not use the option 'save in MS-DOS format').

When submitting the accepted version of your paper in electronic format:

- Make absolutely sure that the file on the disk and the printout are identical.
- Please use a new and correctly formatted disk and label this with the names of all the authors and the title of the paper; also, specify the software and hardware used as well as the title of the file to be processed.
- Do not convert the file to plain ASCII. Ensure that the letter 'I' and digit '1' and also the letter 'O' and digit '0' are used properly and format your article (tabs, indents, etc.) consistently. Characters unavailable on your word processor (Greek letters, mathematical symbols, etc.) should not be left open but indicated by a unique code (e.g., gralpha, @, etc. for the Greek letter α). Such codes should be used consistently throughout the entire text; a list of codes used should accompany the electronic manuscript.

Do not allow your word processor to introduce word breaks, and do not use a justified layout.

Journal of International Financial Management and Accounting

ADDRESS FOR SUBMISSION:

Deloris Lewis, Editorial Assistant
Journal of International Financial
   Management and Accounting
New York University
Stern School of Business
44 West Fourth Street
New York, NY 10012
USA
Phone: 212-998-4142
Fax: 212-995-4221
E-Mail: fchoie@stern.nyu.edu
Web: See Guidelines
Address May Change:

PUBLICATION GUIDELINES:

Manuscript Length: Under 30
Copies Required: Three
Computer Submission: Yes
Format: MS Word, WordPerfect
Fees to Review: 50.00 US$

Manuscript Style:
   See Manuscript Guidelines

CIRCULATION DATA:

Reader: Academics
Frequency of Issue: 3 Times/Year
Copies per Issue: Less than 1,000
Sponsor/Publisher: Blackwell Publishing
Subscribe Price: 130.00 US$ Indv - P+O
   549.00 US$ Inst - Premium P+O
   92.00 US$ IAAER Memb-Prem
   Prnt+Online

REVIEW INFORMATION:

Type of Review: Blind Review
No. of External Reviewers: 2
No. of In House Reviewers: 1
Acceptance Rate: 11-20%
Time to Review: 2 - 3 Months
Reviewers Comments: Yes
Invited Articles: 0-5%
Fees to Publish: 0.00 US$

MANUSCRIPT TOPICS:

Corporate Finance; Cost Accounting; Financial Institutions & Markets; Financial Services; International Finance

MANUSCRIPT GUIDELINES/COMMENTS:

Editors. Professor Frederick Choi and Professor Richard Levich, New York University, USA
   Fchoi@stern.nyu.edu — Tel 212-998-4010, Fax 212-995-4221
   Rlevich@stern.nyu.edu — Tel 212-998-0422, Fax 212-995-4220

Web. http://www.stern.nyu.edu/International/Journals/jifm.html

Aims and Scope

The *Journal of International Financial Management & Accounting* publishes original research dealing with international aspects of financial management and reporting, banking and financial services, auditing, and taxation. Both the theory and the successful practice of international financial management are increasingly dependent on an in-depth understanding of the impact of imperfections in the world product, factor and financial markets, as well as the impact of institutional, regulatory, and accounting differences across countries. Providing a forum for the interaction of ideas from both academics and practitioners, the *Journal of International Financial Management & Accounting* keeps you up-to-date with new developments and emerging trends.

Key Features

- Covers theory and practice—helps solve problems and maintain competitive edge
- Executive Perspectives section—top-level corporate executives, institutional leaders and policy-makers writing on contemporary research and policy issues
- Country Perspectives section—documents recent rule changes and/or institutional developments in a country or region and analyses the implications of these changes for corporate decision-making
- Cases section—presents well-reasoned analysis of important international financial management and accounting issues faced by firms, and demonstrates how these were resolved
- Main emphasis is on financial management of the firm, but also publishes research on related macro-economic issues

Form of the Manuscript

All manuscripts should be typed on one side of either international, standard A4 or 8½" x 11" paper, and should be double-spaced, except for indented quotations, endnotes, and references. Three copies should be submitted together with a check for $50.00, payable in US dollars, to JIFMA Corporation.

Manuscripts generally should not exceed 30 pages in length (including endnotes, references, supporting exhibits, and any appendices). Margins should be appropriate to facilitate editing and duplication. A cover page should give the title and author's name, affiliation, address, and phone number. Acknowledgements should also appear on this page.

Aside from the cover page, authors should not identify themselves directly or indirectly in their manuscripts.

An abstract, not to exceed 250 words, should also be provided. The abstract should summarize the manuscript's contents as well as its significance and potential usefulness for financial managers.

References

Citation in the text is by name(s) of author(s) followed by year of publication (and page numbers where relevant) in parentheses. For references authored by more than two contributors, use the first author's name and "et al. "For multiple citations in the same year, use a, b, c immediately following the year of publication. The source reference list should be typed in alphabetic order, and in accord with the following examples of style:

Doe, John, *A Manual of Style*, 3rd ed. (Oxford: Blackwell Publishers, 1999).

Lee, Terrence and Michael Fox, "Accounting for International Financial Innovations," in *Essays in International Corporate Finance*, A. Rusolo and S. Lachman, eds. (Oxford: Blackwell Publishers, 2001), pp. 279-300.

Smith, Roy, et al., "Research Issues in International Accounting and Finance," *Journal of International Financial Management and Accounting*" (Spring 2000), pp. 98-123.

Mathematical Notation

Mathematical notation should be used only when its rigor and precision are essential to comprehension, and authors should explain in narrative format the principal operations performed. Any equations used should be numbered sequentially in parentheses positioned flush with the right-hand margin. Whilst *JIFMA* does not wish to publish unnecessary mathematical statistical detail, or specimen questionnaires, supplementary information of these kinds may be of assistance to the editors and reviewers in assessing papers, and authors are invited to submit such supporting evidence as separate documents clearly marked as being for information rather than publication.

Illustrations

All graphs, charts, etc. submitted with papers must be referred to in the text, and be fully legible and clearly related to scales on the axes. If illustrations are numerous, a proportion may have to be deleted unless the author is able to supply artwork of camera-ready quality or to reimburse *JIFMA* for the cost of artwork.

Correction Procedure

The designated author will receive page-proofs, which should be corrected and returned within two weeks of their dispatch (or three weeks in the case of overseas contributors). The author is responsible for proofreading the manuscript—the editors/publishers are not responsible for any error not marked by the author on the proofs. Corrections to proofs are limited to rectifying errors; no substantial author's changes can be allowed at this stage unless agreement to pay full costs is communicated with the return of proofs. Similarly, copies in excess of the five free copies automatically supplied to the designated author (for sharing among any co-authors) must be ordered at the time of the return of proofs, in accord with the instructions and price list accompanying the proofs.

Comments

JIFMA welcomes non-trivial comments on papers published in previous issues. To avoid publishing comments based on misunderstandings, and to obtain replies that can be published simultaneously with the comments, draft comments should be sent directly to the original author(s) for reactions, prior to any formal submission to the editors for publication.

Manuscript submissions and business correspondence should be sent to Ms. Deloris Lewis.

Journal of International Financial Markets, Institutions & Money

ADDRESS FOR SUBMISSION:

Ike Mathur, Co-Editor
Journal of International Financial Markets,
    Institutions & Money
Southern Illinois University
College of Business & Administration
Carbondale, IL 62901-4626
USA
Phone: 618-453-1421
Fax: 618-453-5626
E-Mail: imathur@cba.siu.edu
Web: www.elsevier.nl/inca/publications
Address May Change:

PUBLICATION GUIDELINES:

Manuscript Length: 21-25
Copies Required: Three
Computer Submission: No
Format: N/A
Fees to Review: 30.00 US$ Subscriber
    50.00 US$ Non-Subscriber

Manuscript Style:
    , Journal of Finance Style

CIRCULATION DATA:

Reader: Academics
Frequency of Issue: Quarterly
Copies per Issue: Less than 1,000
Sponsor/Publisher: North-Holland /
    Elsevier Science Publishing Co.
Subscribe Price: 50.00 US$ Individual
    304.00 US$ Institution
    48.00 Euro Indv, 272 Euro Institution

REVIEW INFORMATION:

Type of Review: Blind Review
No. of External Reviewers: 1
No. of In House Reviewers: 1
Acceptance Rate: 11-20%
Time to Review: 2 - 3 Months
Reviewers Comments: Yes
Invited Articles: 6-10%
Fees to Publish: 0.00 US$

MANUSCRIPT TOPICS:
Financial Institutions & Markets; International Economics & Trade; International Finance;
Monetary Policy

MANUSCRIPT GUIDELINES/COMMENTS:

Web. http://www.elsevier.nl/inca/publications/store/6/0/0/1/1/3

Co-Editor. C. Neely, Federal Reserve Bank of St. Louis, St. Louis, Missouri, USA

Description
The purpose of the *Journal of International Financial Markets, Institutions & Money* is to publish rigorous, original articles dealing with the international aspects of financial markets, institutions and money. Theoretical/conceptual and empirical papers providing meaningful insights into the subject areas will be considered.

The following topic areas, although not exhaustive, are representative of the coverage in this *Journal*.

- International financial markets
- International securities markets
- Foreign exchange markets
- Eurocurrency markets
- International syndications
- Term structures of Eurocurrency rates
- Determination of exchange rates
- Information, speculation and parity
- Forward rates and swaps
- International payment mechanisms
- International commercial banking;
- International investment banking
- Central bank intervention
- International monetary systems
- Balance of payments

Guide for Authors

1. Papers must be in English

2. Papers for publication should be sent in triplicate to: Ike Mathur accompanied by a submission fee of US$30.00 for authors who currently subscribe to the *Journal* and US$50 for non-subscribers. The submission fee entitles the respective author(s) to a one year personal subscription to the *Journal of International Financial Markets, Institutions & Money*, with a maximum of 2 (two) subscriptions per submitted paper, upon indication. Cheques should be made payable to Elsevier Science. There are no page charges. Submission of a paper will be held to imply that it contains original unpublished work and is not being submitted for publication elsewhere. The Editor does not accept responsibility for damage or loss of papers submitted. Upon acceptance of an article, author(s) will be asked to transfer copyright of the article to the publisher. This transfer will ensure the widest possible dissemination of information.

3. Submission of accepted papers as electronic manuscripts, i.e., on disk with accompanying manuscript, is encouraged. Electronic manuscripts have the advantage that there is no need for rekeying of text, thereby avoiding the possibility of introducing errors and resulting in reliable and fast delivery of proofs. The preferred storage medium is a 5.25 or 3.5-inch disk in MS-DOS format, although other systems are welcome, e.g., Macintosh (in this case, save your file in the usual manner; do not use the option 'save in MS-DOS format"). Do not submit your original paper as electronic manuscript but hold on to disk until asked for this by the Editor (in case your paper is accepted without revisions). Do submit the accepted version of your paper as electronic manuscript. Make absolutely sure that the file on the disk and the printout are identical. Please use a new and correctly formatted disk and label this with your name; also specify the software and hardware used as well as the title of the file to be processed. Do not convert the file to plain ASCII. Ensure that the letter 'l' and digit '1', and also the letter 'O' and digit '0' are used properly, and format your article (tabs, indents, etc.) consistently. Characters not available on your word processor (Greek letters mathematical symbols, etc.) should not be left open but indicated by a unique code (e.g. gralpha, (alpha), @, etc., for the

Greek letter α). Such codes should be used consistently throughout the entire text; a list of codes used should accompany the electronic manuscript. Do not allow your word processor to introduce word breaks and do not use a justified layout. Please adhere strictly to the general instructions below on style, arrangement and, in particular, the reference style of the *Journal*.

4. **Manuscripts** should be double spaced, with wide margins, and printed on one side of the paper only. All pages should be numbered consequently. Titles and subtitles should be short. References, tables, and legends for the figures should be printed on separate pages.

5. **The first page of the manuscript** should contain the following information:

   i.   The title
   ii.   The name(s) and institutional affiliation(s) of the author(s)
   iii.   An abstract of not more than 100 words. A footnote on the same sheet should give the name, address, telephone and fax numbers and e-mail address of the corresponding author.

6. The first page of the manuscript should also contain at least one classification code according to the Classification System for Journal Articles as used by the *Journal of Economic Literature*; in addition, up to five key words should be supplied.

7. **Acknowledgements** and information on grants received can be given in a first footnote, which should not be included in the consecutive numbering of footnotes.

8. **Footnotes** should be kept to a minimum and numbered consecutively throughout the text with superscript Arabic numerals.

9. **Displayed formulae** should be numbered consecutively throughout the manuscript as (1), (2), etc. against the right-hand margin of the page. In cases where the derivation of formulae has been abbreviated, it is of great help to the referees if the full derivation can be presented on a separate sheet (not to be published).

10. **References** to publications should be as follows: 'Smith (1992) reported that...' or 'This problem has been studied previously (e.g., Smith et al., 1969)'. The author should make sure that there is a strict one-to-one correspondence between the names and years in the text and those on the list. The list of references should appear at the end of the main text (after any appendices, but before tables and legends for figures). It should be double spaced and listed in alphabetical order by author's name.

References should appear as follows:

For Monographs
Hawawini, G. and I. Swary, 1990, Mergers and acquisitions in the U.S. banking industry: Evidence from the capital markets (North-Holland, Amsterdam).

For Contributions to Collective Works
Brunner, K. and A.H. Meltzer, 1990, Money supply, in: B.M. Friedman and F.H. Hahn, eds., Handbook of monetary economics, Vol. 1 (North-Holland, Amsterdam) 357-396.

For Periodicals
Griffiths, W. and G. Judge, 1992, Testing and estimating location vectors when the error covariance matrix is unknown, Journal of Econometrics 54, 121-138. Note that journal titles should not be abbreviated.

11. **Illustrations** will be reproduced photographically from originals supplied by the author; they will not be redrawn by the publisher. Please provide all illustrations in quadruplicate (one high-contrast original and three photocopies). Care should be taken that lettering and symbols are of a comparable size. The illustrations should not be inserted in the text, and should be marked on the back with figure number, title of paper, and author's name. All graphs and diagrams should be referred to as figures, and should be numbered consecutively in the text in Arabic numerals. Illustration for papers submitted as electronic manuscripts should be in traditional form.

12. **Tables** should be numbered consecutively in the text in Arabic numerals and printed on separate sheets.

Any manuscript which does not conform to the above instructions may be returned for the necessary revision before publication.

13. **Page proofs** will be sent to the corresponding author. Proofs should be corrected carefully; the responsibility for detecting errors lies with the author. Corrections should be restricted to instances in which the proof is at variance with the manuscript. Extensive alterations will be charged. Fifty reprints of each paper are supplied free of charge to the corresponding author; additional reprints are available at cost if they are ordered when the proof is returned.

Journal of International Food & Agribusiness Marketing

ADDRESS FOR SUBMISSION:

Erdener Kaynak, Editor-in-Chief
Journal of International Food &
    Agribusiness Marketing
International Business Press Journals
Box 399
Middletown, PA 17057
USA
Phone: 717-566-3054
Fax: 717-566-8589
E-Mail: k9x@psu.edu
Web: www.haworthpress.com
Address May Change:

PUBLICATION GUIDELINES:

Manuscript Length: 21-25
Copies Required: Three
Computer Submission: Yes
Format: MS Word
Fees to Review: 0.00 US$

Manuscript Style:
    American Psychological Association

CIRCULATION DATA:

Reader: Academics
Frequency of Issue: Quarterly
Copies per Issue: Less than 1,000
Sponsor/Publisher: Haworth Press, Inc.
Subscribe Price: 75.00 US$ Individual
    150.00 US$ Institution
    250.00 US$ Agency / Library

REVIEW INFORMATION:

Type of Review: Blind Review
No. of External Reviewers: 2
No. of In House Reviewers: 1
Acceptance Rate: 21-30%
Time to Review: 2 - 3 Months
Reviewers Comments: Yes
Invited Articles: 6-10%
Fees to Publish: 0.00 US$

MANUSCRIPT TOPICS:

Economic Development; Financial Institutions & Markets; Food & Agribusiness Industry Marketing; Industrial Organization; International Economics & Trade; Macro Economics; Micro Economics; Regional Economics

MANUSCRIPT GUIDELINES/COMMENTS:

The *Journal of International Food & Agribusiness Marketing* is a timely journal that serves as a forum for the exchange and dissemination of food and agribusiness marketing knowledge and experiences on an international scale. Designed to study the characteristics and workings of food and agribusiness marketing systems around the world, the *Journal of International Food & Agribusiness Marketing* critically examines marketing issues in the total food business chain prevailing in different parts of the globe by using a systems and cross-cultural/national approach to explain the many facets of food marketing in a range of socioeconomic and political systems.

Scholars, practitioners, and public policymakers share up-to-date and insightful information-both descriptive and analytical-on international food and agribusiness marketing theory and practice. In particular, they place a special emphasis on the exporting and importing of food products between developed and developing countries. Methods for improving food and agribusiness marketing practices in developing countries and the transfer of food marketing technology from advanced countries are discussed.

It is an indispensable source of reference for all those involved in the planning and implementation of food and agribusiness marketing policy and practice, such as food business firms, government food departments, and agencies and institutions related to food marketing internationally. The journal will also be valuable to professionals in many other roles-executives from international food companies and agribusiness industries; policymakers from government; officials of international food agencies; administrators from public and cooperative sectors; financial institutions and monetary agencies; insurance company officials; transportation industry executives; and academicians, researchers, and consultants of food and agricultural marketing, economics, business administration, food science, nutrition, and home economics.

Instructions for Authors

1. **Original Articles Only**. Submission of a manuscript to this Journal represents a certification on the part of the author(s) that it is an original work, and that neither this manuscript nor a version of it has been published elsewhere nor is being considered for publication elsewhere.

2. **Manuscript Length**. Your manuscript may be approximately **5-25** typed pages, double-spaced (including references and abstract). Lengthier manuscripts may be considered, but only at the discretion of the Editor. Sometimes, lengthier manuscripts may be considered if they can be divided up into sections for publication in successive *Journal* issues.

3. **Manuscript Style**. References, citations, and general style of manuscripts for this *Journal* should follow the APA style (as outlined in the latest edition of the *Publication Manual of the American Psychological Association*). References should be double-spaced and placed in alphabetical order.

If an author wishes to submit a paper that has been already prepared in another style, he or she may do so. However, if the paper is accepted (with or without reviewer's alterations), the author is fully responsible for retyping the manuscript in the correct style as indicated above. Neither the Editor nor the Publisher is responsible for re-preparing manuscript copy to adhere to the *Journal*'s style.

4. **Manuscript Preparation**

Margins. Leave at least a 1" margin on all four sides.

Paper. Use clean white, 8½" x 11" bond paper.

Number of Copies. 4 (the original plus 3 photocopies)

Cover page. ***Important***—Staple a cover page to the manuscript, indicating only the article title (this is used for anonymous refereeing)

Second "Title Page". enclose a regular title page but do not staple it to the manuscript. Include the title again, plus:
- Full authorship
- An ABSTRACT of about 100 words. (Below the abstract provide 3-10 key words for index purposes.)
- An introductory footnote with authors' academic degrees, professional titles, affiliations, mailing addresses, and any desired acknowledgment of research support or other credit.

5. **Return Envelopes**. When you submit your four manuscript copies, also include:
- A 9" x 12" envelope, self-addressed and stamped (with sufficient postage to ensure return of your manuscript);
- A regular envelope, stamped and self-addressed. This is for the Editor to send you an "acknowledgement of receipt" letter.

6. **Spelling, Grammar, and Punctuation**. You are responsible for preparing manuscript copy which is clearly written in acceptable scholarly English, and which contains no errors of spelling, grammar, or punctuation. Neither the Editor nor the Publisher is responsible for correcting errors of spelling and grammar: the manuscript, after acceptance by the Editor, must be immediately ready for typesetting as it is finally submitted by the author(s).

Check your paper for the following common errors:
- Dangling modifiers
- Misplaced modifiers
- Unclear antecedents
- Incorrect or inconsistent abbreviations

Also, check the accuracy of all arithmetic calculations, statistics, numerical data, text citations, and references.

7. **Inconsistencies Must Be Avoided**. Be sure you are consistent in your use of abbreviations, terminology, and in citing references, from one part of your paper to another.

8. **Preparation of tables, figures, and illustrations**. Any material that is not textual is considered artwork. This includes tables, figures, diagrams, charts, graphs, illustrations, appendices, screen captures, and photos. Tables and figures (including legend, notes, and sources) should be no larger than 4½ x 6½". Type styles should be Helvetica (or Helvetica narrow if necessary) and no smaller than 8 point. We request that computer-generated figures be in black and white and/or shades of gray (preferably no color, for it does not reproduce well). Camera-ready art must contain no grammatical, typographical, or format errors and must reproduce sharply and clearly in the dimensions of the final printed page (4½ x 6½"). Photos and screen captures must be on disk as a TIF file, or other graphic file format such as JPEG or BMP. For rapid publication we must receive black-and-white glossy or matte positives (white background with black images and/or wording) in addition to files on disk. Tables should be created in the text document file using the software's Table feature.

9. **Submitting Art**. Both a printed hard copy and a disk copy of the art must be provided. We request that each piece of art be sent in its own file, on a disk separate from the disk containing the manuscript text file(s), and be clearly labeled. We reserve the right to (if necessary) request new art, alter art, or if all else has failed in achieving art that is presentable, delete art. If submitted art cannot be used, the Publisher reserves the right to redo the art and to change the author for a fee of $35.00 per hour for this service. The Haworth Press, Inc. is not responsible for errors incurred in the preparation of new artwork. Camera-ready artwork must be prepared on separate sheets of paper. Always use black ink and professional drawing instruments. On the back of these items, write your article title and the journal title lightly in soft-lead pencil (please do not write on the face of art). In the text file, skip extra lines and indicate where these figures are placed. Photos are considered part of the acceptable manuscript and remain with the Publisher for use in additional printings.

10. **Electronic Media**. Haworth's in-house typesetting unit is able to utilize your final manuscript material as prepared on most personal computers and word processors. This will minimize typographical errors and decrease overall production time. Please send the first draft and final draft copies of your manuscript to the journal Editor in print format for his/her final review and approval. After approval of your final manuscript, please submit the final approved version both on printed format ("hard copy") and floppy diskette. On the outside of the diskette package write:

i)   The brand name of your computer or word processor
ii) The word processing program and version that you used
iii) The title of your article
iv) The file name

Note. Disk and hard copy must agree. In case of discrepancies, it is The Haworth Press' policy to follow hard copy. Authors are advised that no revisions of the manuscript can be made after acceptance by the Editor for publication. The benefits of this procedure are many with speed and accuracy being the most obvious. We look forward to working with your electronic submission which will allow us to serve you more efficiently.

11. **Alterations Required by Referees and Reviewers**. Many times a paper is accepted by the Editor contingent upon changes that are mandated by anonymous specialist referees and members of the Editorial Board. If the Editor returns your manuscript for revisions, you are responsible for retyping any sections of the paper to incorporate these revisions (if applicable, revisions should also be put on disk).

12. **Typesetting**. You will not be receiving galley proofs of your article. Editorial revisions, if any, must therefore be made while your article is still in manuscript. The final version of the manuscript will be the version you see published. Typesetter's errors will be corrected by the production staff of The Haworth Press. Authors are expected to submit manuscripts, disks, and art that are free from error.

13. **Reprints**. The senior author will receive two copies of the journal issue and complimentary reprints of his or her article. The junior author will receive two copies of the journal issue. These are sent several weeks after the journal issue is published and in

circulation. An order form for the purchase of additional reprints will also be sent to all authors at this time. (Approximately 4–6 weeks is necessary for the preparation of reprints.) Please do not query the Journal's Editor about reprints. All such questions should be sent directly to The Haworth Press, Inc., Production Department, 37 West Broad Street, West Hazleton, PA 18202. To order additional reprints (minimum: 50 copies), please contact The Haworth Document Delivery Center, 10 Alice Street, Binghamton, NY 13904–1580; 1-800-429-6784 or Fax (607) 722–6362.

14. **Copyright**. Copyright ownership of your manuscript must be transferred officially to The Haworth Press, Inc. before we can begin the peer-review process. The Editor's letter acknowledging receipt of the manuscript will be accompanied by a form fully explaining this. All authors must sign the form and return the original to the Editor as soon as possible. Failure to return the copyright form in a timely fashion will result in a delay in review and subsequent publication.

Examples of Reference to Periodicals
1. Journal Article
One Author. Levitt, T. (1983). The Globalization of Markets, *Harvard Business Review*, (May-June), 61 (3), 92-102.

2. Journal Article: Multiple Authors
Kaynak, E. and Mitchell A.L. (1981). Analysis of Marketing Strategies Used in Diverse Cultures, *Journal of Advertising Research* (June), 21 (3), 25-32.

3. Magazine Article
Tinnin, D.B. (1981, November 16) The Heady Success of Holland's Heineken, *Fortune*, pp. 158-164

4. Newspaper Article
The opportunity of world brands, (1984, June 3). *The New York Times*, p. 6F.

5. Monograph
Franko, L.G. (1979). *A Survey of the Impact of Manufactured Exports From Industrializing Countries in Asia and Latin America*, Changing International Realities [Monograph] No. 6.

Examples of References to Books
1. Reference to an Entire Book
Kaynak, E. (1986) *Marketing and Economic Development*, New York: Praeger Publishers Inc.

2. Book with a Corporate Author
Committee For Economic Development (1981) *Transnational Corporation for Developing Countries*, New York: Author.

3. Edited Book
Kaynak, E. (ed.) (1985) *Global Perspectives in Marketing*, New York: Praeger Publishers Inc.

4. Book with No Author or Editor
Marketing Opportunities in Japan (1978). London: Dentsu Incorporated

5. Article or Chapter in an Edited Book
Bucklin, L.P. (1986). Improving Food Retailing in Less Developed Asian Countries. In E. Kaynak (Ed.) *World Food Marketing Systems* (pp. 73-81) London: Butterworth Scientific Publishers.

Proceedings of Meetings and Symposia
1. Published Proceedings, Published Contributions to a Symposium

Lee, K.H. (1981). From Production Orientation to Marketing Orientation-Hong Kong in the International Trade Setting. In D.B. Yeaman (Ed.) *Developing Global Corporate Strategies* (pp. 753-766). Conference held at the University of Navarra, Barcelona, Spain, 2 (December 17-19).

2. Unpublished Paper Presented at a Meeting

Yucelt, U. (1987). *Tourism Marketing Planning in Developing Economies.* Paper presented at the annual meeting of the Academy of Marketing Science, Bal Harbor, Florida.

Doctoral Dissertations
1. Unpublished Doctoral Dissertation

Czintoka, M.F. (1980). An Analysis of Export Development Strategies in Selected U.S. Industries. *Dissertations Abstract International* (University Microfilms No. 80-15, 865).

For reference to unpublished manuscripts, publications of limited circulation, reviews and interviews and non-print media please refer to the latest edition of Publication Manual of American Psychological Association.

MANUSCRIPT SUBMISSION FORM

This limited Copyright Transmittal Form, signed by all authors, *must* be included with any Journal article submission to the Editor.

Original signatures are preferred, but we will accept faxed and/or electronic signatures.

Name and EXACT Mailing Address of Contributor

Special Note. THIS ADDRESS WILL BE USED FOR MAILING REPRINTS. You *must* include exact street address, name of your department if at a university, and domestic or foreign ZIP CODE. The Haworth Press, Inc. cannot be responsible for lost reprints if you do not provide us with your exact mailing address.

In reference to your journal article/review
□ **If this box is checked...**
Thank you for your article submission! Please allow 10-15 weeks for the review process. Before sending out your article for review, however, the Publisher requires us to obtain your signature(s) confirming that you have read the official PUBLICATION AGREEMENT.

All co-authors must sign and return this limited copyright transfer form.

IT IS CONFIRMED that I/we have read the PUBLICATION AGREEMENT, and agree to and accept all conditions.

_____
Author's signature date

_____
Author's signature date

_____
Author's signature date

Please reply to:
( ) Journal Editor ( ) Guest Editor

□ **If this box is checked...**
Your article has been favorably reviewed. Our reviewers, however, require certain revisions which are indicated on the attached sheets. Please review and incorporate their suggestions, and return your manuscript/disk retyped within 14 days. A decision about publication will be made at that time. Thank you for your help and cooperation.

□ **If this box is checked...**
We are pleased to inform you that your article has been accepted for publication in the journal noted above; to be available in print and electronic versions. In addition to the standard journal editions, at the Editor's discretion, this issue may also be co-published in a hardcover and/or soft cover monographic co-edition.

Please note the following:
1. **Publication**. Your article is currently scheduled to appear in

    VOLUME: _____ ISSUE: _____

2. **Typesetting**. Your article will be sent to the Print Journal Production Department of The Haworth Press, Inc. They will typeset your article (from the required computer disk) exactly as submitted. In order to efficiently typeset the print version and to quickly produce a preliminary (before proofreading) electronic version, we require that all manuscripts be submitted conversion-ready. This means that the article on your computer disk must be clearly written with no errors of spelling, grammar, or punctuation. Also, inconsistencies must be avoided. Please refer to the Instructions for Authors for further submission requirements. Please note that you will not be receiving galley proofs. The production staff will proofread the galleys, for typesetting errors, against the final version of the manuscript as submitted.

(NOTE: Revisions to the galleys are not allowed.) **The disk *must* be the one from which the accompanying manuscript (finalized version) was printed out.**

3. Preparation of Tables, Figures, and Illustrations

Any material that is not textual is considered artwork. This includes tables, figures, diagrams, charts, graphs, illustrations, appendices, screen captures, and photos. Tables and figures (*including* legend, notes, and source) should be no larger than 4½ x 6½". Type style should be Helvetica (or Helvetica Narrow if necessary) and no smaller than 8 point. We request that computer-generated figures be in black and white and/or shades of gray (preferably no color, for it does not reproduce well). Camera-ready art must contain no grammatical, typographical, or format errors and must reproduce sharply and clearly in the dimensions of the final printed page (4½ x 6½"). Photos and screen captures must be on disk as a TIFF file, or other graphic file format such as JPEG or BMP. For rapid publication we must receive black-and-white glossy or matte positives (white background with black images and/or wording) in addition to files on disk. Tables should be created in the text document file using the software's *Table* feature.

4. Submitting Art.

Both a printed hard copy and a disk copy of the art must be provided. We request that each piece of art be sent in its own file, on a disk *separate* from the disk containing the manuscript text file(s), and be clearly labeled. We reserve the right to (if necessary) *request new art, alter art,* or if all else has failed in achieving art that is presentable, *delete art.* If submitted art cannot be used, the Publisher reserves the right to redo the art and to charge the author a fee of $35.00 per hour for this service. The Haworth Press, Inc. is not responsible for errors incurred in the preparation of new artwork. Camera-ready artwork must be prepared on separate sheets of paper. Always use black ink and professional drawing instruments. On the back of these items, write your article title and the journal title lightly in soft-lead pencil (please do not write on the face of art). In the text file, skip extra lines and indicate where these figures are to be placed. Photos are considered part of the acceptable manuscript and remain with the Publisher for use in additional printings.

5. Reprints.

Shortly after publication you will receive an order form for purchasing quantities of reprints. (About three weeks after publication, the senior author will receive two complimentary copies of the issue as well as complimentary reprints of the article. Junior author(s) will receive two complimentary copies of the issue.) Please note that preparation of reprints takes about eight weeks additional time after the actual issue is printed and in circulation.

□ If this box is checked...

We are sorry, but the reviewers for this journal did not agree that your article was appropriate for publication in this periodical. If the reviewers consented in having their comments forwarded to you, their critiques are attached. Your submission is appreciated, and we hope that you will contribute again in the future.

Journal of International Money and Finance

ADDRESS FOR SUBMISSION:

James R. Lothian, Editor
Journal of International Money and Finance
Fordham University at Lincoln Center
Graduate School of Business Admin
113 W. 60th Street, Room 616
New York, NY 10023
USA
Phone: 212-636-6147
Fax: 212-765-5573
E-Mail: jimf@fordham.edu
Web: www.elsevier.com
Address May Change:

PUBLICATION GUIDELINES:

Manuscript Length: 16-20
Copies Required: Two
Computer Submission: No
Format: N/A
Fees to Review: 75.00 US$ Subscribers
    125.00 US$ Non-Subscribers

Manuscript Style:
   , Journal of Economic Literature

CIRCULATION DATA:

Reader: Academics
Frequency of Issue: 8 Times/Year
Copies per Issue: No Reply
Sponsor/Publisher: Elsevier Science
    Publishing Co.
Subscribe Price: 95.00 US$ Individual
    997.00 US$ Institution
    85.00 Euro Indv, 890 Euro Instn

REVIEW INFORMATION:

Type of Review: Editorial Review
No. of External Reviewers: 2
No. of In House Reviewers: 0
Acceptance Rate: 11-20%
Time to Review: 2 - 3 Months
Reviewers Comments: Yes
Invited Articles: 0-5%
Fees to Publish: 0.00 US$

MANUSCRIPT TOPICS:
Accounting Information Systems; International Finance; Macro Economics; Monetary Policy

MANUSCRIPT GUIDELINES/COMMENTS:

Description
Since its launch in 1982, *Journal of International Money and Finance* has built up a solid reputation as a high quality scholarly journal devoted to theoretical and empirical research in the fields of international monetary economics, international finance, and the rapidly developing overlap area between the two. Researchers in these areas, and financial market professionals too, pay attention to the articles that the journal publishes.

Authors published in the journal are in the forefront of scholarly research on exchange rate behaviour, foreign exchange options, international capital markets, international monetary and fiscal policy, international transmission and related questions. With articles being submitted from economists and finance specialists in major research universities, smaller universities, central banks and private financial institutions worldwide, the journal achieves an extraordinary diversity, in both topic and approach, and provides a truly global perspective on international economic and financial questions.

Submission of Papers
Authors are requested to submit two hard copies of their manuscripts and figures and one electronic copy to the Editor.

Submission of a paper will be held to imply that it has not been published previously, that it is not under consideration for publication elsewhere, and that if accepted it will not be published elsewhere in the same form, in English or in any other language, without the written consent of the publisher.

Submission Fee
Personal subscribers should note that there is no longer a exemption but a reduced fee for submission. Authors who are not personal subscribers should include with articles submitted a non-refundable submission fee of US$125 and personal subscribers to the journal should include with articles a non-refundable submission fee to the journal of US$75. Payments should be in US funds by cheque payable to "James R. Lothian J.I.M.F. Account". Where required for exchange control, the submission fee will be billed on request.

Manuscript Preparation
Language. Papers must be in English.

General. Manuscripts must be typewritten, double-spaced with wide margins on one side of white paper. Good quality printouts with a font size of 12-pt or 10-pt are required. The corresponding author should be identified (include a Fax number and E-mail address). Full postal addresses must be given for all co-authors. Authors should consult a recent issue of the journal for style if possible. An electronic copy of the paper should accompany the **final** version. The Editors reserve the right to adjust style to certain standards of uniformity. Authors should retain a copy of their manuscript since we cannot accept responsibility for damage or loss of papers. Original manuscripts are discarded one month after publication unless the Publisher is asked to return original material after use.

Text. Follow this order when typing manuscripts: Title Page, Main Text, Acknowledgements, Appendix, References, Figures, Figure Captions and then Tables.

The **Title Page** should contain the following information: 1) Title; 2) Authors' Names; 3) Institutional Affiliations; 4) Abstract of not more than 100 words; 5) JEL code; at least one classification code according to the Classification System for Journal Articles as used by the *Journal of Economic Literature* is required; and 6) Keywords. On the title page the Corresponding Author should be identified with an asterisk and footnote.

The main-text sections, including the introduction, should be labelled with consecutive Arabic numbers. Subsections should be numbered in italic, *2.1*, *2.2* etc. Do not import the Figures or Tables into your text. All footnotes (except for table footnotes and the corresponding author footnote) should be identified with superscript Arabic numbers.

Units. Ensure that the letter "l" and the digit "1" and also the letter "O" and the digit "0" are used properly. Characters not available on your word processor (Greek letters, mathematical symbols, etc.,) should not be left open but indicated by a unique code (e.g. gralph, (alpha), @, etc., for the Greek letter α). Such codes should be used consistently throughout the text and a list of codes used should accompany the electronic manuscript.

Quotations. Quotations must correspond exactly with the original in wording, spelling, and punctuation. Page numbers must be given. Changes must be indicated: use brackets to identify insertions; use dots (...) to show omissions. Also indicate where emphasis has been added. Only quotations of over 50 words should be separated from the text; these should also be indented at beginning margin and double-spaced with page number to be shown in brackets.

Formulae. Displayed formulae should be numbered consecutively throughout the manuscript as (1), (2) etc., against the right-hand margin of the page. When used extensively, symbolic notations should be listed, summarised and briefly identified in a separate table. In cases where the derivation of formulae has been abbreviated, it is of great help to the referees if the full derivation can be presented on a separate sheet (not to be published).

References. All publications cited in the text should be presented in a list of references following the text of the manuscript. In the text refer to the author's name (without initials) and year of publication (e.g. "Since Peterson (1993) has shown that" or "This is in the agreement with results obtained later (Kramer, 1994)"). For three or more authors use the first author followed by "et al.", in the text.

The reference section should be double-spaced and begin on a new page. Items are to be listed alphabetically by authors' names and works by the same author in order of publication. The manuscript should be carefully checked to ensure that the spelling of authors' names and dates are exactly the same in the text as in the reference list.

References should be given in the following form:
For Monographs
Edwards, S., 1989. Real Exchange Rates, Devaluation, and Adjustment: Exchange Rate Policy in Developing Countries. MIT Press, Cambridge, MA.
For Contributions to Collective Works
Freebairn, J., 1990. Is the $A a commodity currency. In: Clements, K., Freebairn, J. (Eds.), Exchange Rates and Australian Commodity Exports. Centre for Policy Studies, Monash University, and Economic Research Centre, The University of Western Australia, Melbourne and Perth, pp. 6-30.
For Periodicals
Culver, S.E., Papell, D.H., 1999. Long-run purchasing power parity with short-run data: evidence with a null hypothesis of stationarity. Journal of International Money and Finance 18 (5), 751-768.

Figures. Charts and diagrams are all to be referred to as "Figure(s)" and should be numbered consecutively with numerals in the order to which they are referred. They should accompany the manuscript, but should not be included within the text. All illustrations should be clearly marked on the back with the figure number and the author's name. All figures are to have a caption. Captions should be supplied on a separate sheet. Legends, if any, should be typed on a covering sheet of paper.

Line Drawings. Good quality printouts on white paper produced in black ink are required. All lettering, graph lines and points on graphs should be sufficiently large and bold to permit reproduction when the diagram has been reduced to a size suitable for inclusion in the journal. Dye-line prints or photocopies are not suitable for reproduction. Do not use any type of shading on computer-generated illustrations.

Tables. Tables should be numbered consecutively and given a suitable caption and each table typed on a separate sheet. Footnotes to tables should be typed below the table and should be referred to by superscript lowercase letters. No vertical rules should be used. Tables should not duplicate results presented elsewhere in the manuscript, (e.g. in graphs).

Electronic Submission
Authors should submit an electronic copy of their paper with the final version of the manuscript. The electronic copy should match the hardcopy exactly. Always keep a backup copy of the electronic file for reference and safety. Full details of electronic submission and formats can be obtained from http://authors.elsevier.com.

Proofs
Proofs will be sent to the author (first named author if no corresponding author is identified of multi-authored papers) and should be returned within 48 hours of receipt. Corrections should be restricted to typesetting errors; any others may be charged to the author. Any queries should be answered in full. Please note that authors are urged to check their proofs carefully before return, since the inclusion of late corrections cannot be guaranteed.

Proofs are to be returned to the Log-in Department, Elsevier Science, Stover Court, Bampfylde Street, Exeter, Devon EX1 2AH, UK.

Offprints
Twenty-five offprints will be supplied free of charge. Additional offprints can be ordered at a specially reduced rate using the order form sent to the corresponding author after the manuscript has been accepted. Orders for reprints (produced after publication of an article) will incur a 50% surcharge.

Copyright
All authors must sign the "Transfer of Copyright" agreement before the article can be published. This transfer agreement enables Elsevier Science Ltd. to protect the copyrighted material for the authors, without the author relinquishing his/her proprietary rights. The copyright transfer covers the exclusive rights to reproduce and distribute the article, including reprints, photographic reproductions, microfilm or any other reproductions of a similar nature, and translations. It also includes the right to adapt the article for use in conjunction with computer systems and programs, including reproduction or publication in machine-readable form and incorporation in retrieval systems. Authors are responsible for obtaining from the copyright holder permission to reproduce any material for which copyright already exists.

Author Services
For queries relating to the general submission of manuscripts (including electronic text and artwork) and the status of accepted manuscripts, please contact the Author Services, Log-in Department, Elsevier Science, The Boulevard, Langford Lane, Kidlington, Oxford OX5 1GB, UK—Tel +44 (0) 1865 843900, Fax +44 (0) 1865 843905; authors@elsevier.co.uk

Authors can also keep a track on the progress of their accepted article, and set up e-mail alerts informing them of changes to their manuscript's status, by using the "Track a Paper" feature of Elsevier's Author Gateway.

Journal of International Trade and Economic Development

ADDRESS FOR SUBMISSION:

Pasquale M. Sgro, Co-Editor
Journal of International Trade and
    Economic Development
Deakin University
School of Economics
221 Burwood Highway
Burwood, Victoria, 3125
Australia
Phone: +61 (0)3 92-446-6034
Fax: +61 (0)3 92-446-6064
E-Mail: sgro@deakin.edu.au
Web: web.uvic.ca/~dgiles/jited
Address May Change:

PUBLICATION GUIDELINES:

Manuscript Length: 21-25
Copies Required: Three
Computer Submission: Yes
Format: MS Word
Fees to Review: 0.00 US$

Manuscript Style:
    Uniform System of Citation (Harvard
    Blue Book)

CIRCULATION DATA:

Reader: Academics
Frequency of Issue: Quarterly
Copies per Issue: Less than 1,000
Sponsor/Publisher: Routledge, Taylor &
    Francis
Subscribe Price: 89.00 US$ Individual
    579.00 US$ Institution
    57.00 Pounds Indv, 351 Pounds Inst

REVIEW INFORMATION:

Type of Review: Peer Review
No. of External Reviewers: 3
No. of In House Reviewers: 0
Acceptance Rate: 11-20%
Time to Review: 2 - 3 Months
Reviewers Comments: Yes
Invited Articles: 0-5%
Fees to Publish: 0.00 US$

MANUSCRIPT TOPICS:
Econometrics; Economic Development; International Economics & Trade; International
Finance; Macro Economics; Regional Economics

MANUSCRIPT GUIDELINES/COMMENTS:

Editors
Pasquale M. Sgro and Bharat R. Hazari, *Deakin University, Australia*
North American Editor David E.A. Giles, *University of Victoria, Canada*

Aims and Scope
JITED focuses on international economics, economic development and, more importantly, the
interface between trade and development. The links between trade and development
economics are critical at a time when both fluctuating commodity prices and trade
liberalization and agreements can radically affect the economies of developing countries.

JITED is designed to meet the needs of international and development economists, economic historians, applied economists, and policy makers. The international experts who make up the *Journal*'s Editorial Board encourage contributions from economists worldwide.

JITED covers:

- Theoretical and applied issues in international and development economics
- Econometric applications of trade and/or development models
- Models of structural change
- Trade and development issues of economies in Eastern Europe, Asia and the Pacific area
- Papers on specific topics
- Review articles on important branches of the literature

Instructions for Authors

Authors should submit three complete copies of their text, tables and figures, with any original illustrations, to Professor Pasquale M. Sgro, School of Economics, Deakin University, Burwood, Victoria 3125, Australia. It will be assumed that the authors keep a copy of their paper.

Submission of a paper to the *Journal* will be taken to imply that it presents original, unpublished work not under consideration for publication elsewhere. By submitting a manuscript, the authors agree that exclusive rights to reproduce and distribute the article have been given to the publishers, including reprints, photographic reproductions, microfilm, or any reproductions of a similar nature, and translations.

1. The submission should include a cover page showing the author's name, the department where the work was done, an address for correspondence, if different, telephone numbers, e-mail address and any acknowledgements.

2. Submissions should be in English, typed in double spacing with wide margins, one side only of the paper, preferably of A4 size. The title, but not the author's name should appear on the first page of the manuscript. Furthermore, to assist objectivity, the author should avoid any reference to him or herself, which would enable identification by referees. Articles should normally be as concise as possible and proceeded by an abstract of not more than 200 words and a list of up to 6 keywords for on-line searching purposes.

3. Tables and figures should not be inserted in the pages of the manuscript but should be on separate sheets. They should be numbered consecutively in Arabic numerals with a descriptive caption. The desired position in the text for each table and figure should be indicated in the margin of the manuscript. Permission to reproduce copyright material must be obtained by the authors before submission and any acknowledgements should be included in the typescript or captions as appropriate.

4. Use the Harvard System of referencing, which gives the name of the author and the date of publication as a key to the full bibliographical details that are set out in the list of references. When the author's name is mentioned in the text, the date is inserted in parentheses immediately after the name, as in 'Smith (1970)'. When a less direct reference is made to one

or more authors, both name and date are bracketed, with the references separated by a semi-colon, as in 'several authors have noted this trend (Smith, 1970; Cook, 1968; Dobbs, 1973)'. When the reference is to a work of dual or multiple authorship, use only surnames of the abbreviated form as in 'Smith and Dobbs (1978)' or 'Jones et al. (1976)'. If an author has two references published in the same year, add lower case letters after the date to distinguish them, as in 'Smith (1980a, 1980b)'. Always use the minimum number of figures in page numbers, dates, etc., e.g., 22-4, 105-6 (but 112-13 for 'teen numbers) and 1968-9.

5. Footnotes should be used only where necessary to avoid interrupting the continuity of the text. They should be numbered consecutively using superscript Arabic numerals. They should appear at the end of the main text, immediately before the list of references.

6. Submissions should include a reference list, in alphabetical order, at the end of the article. The content and format should conform to the following examples:

Book. Kennedy, W.P. (1987) Industrial Structure: Capital Markets and the Origins of British Economic Decline. Cambridge: Cambridge University Press.

Article in Journal. Chapman, S.D. (1985) 'British-based investment groups before 1914'. The Economic History Review 38, 230-51. (Note. please give journal title in full.)

Edited Text. Davenport-Hines, P.R.T. and Jones, G. (eds) (1989) British Business in Asia since 1860. Cambridge: Cambridge University Press.

Multiple Authors. Green, E. and Moss, M. (1982) A Business of National Importance, The Royal Mail Shipping Group 1902-b1937, London: Methuen.

Article in Edited Volume. Kitchen, J. (1974) Lawrence Dicksee, depreciation and the double-account system'. In Edey, H. and Yamey, B.S. (eds) Debits, Credits, Finance and Profits. London: Sweet & Maxwell, 109-30.

Unattributed. The Accountant (1939) 'Consolidation: the publication Stock Exchange moves'. 25 February 1939:246.

7. For any other matters of presentation not covered by the above notes, please refer to the usual custom and practice as indicated by the last few issues of the *Journal*.

8. On acceptance for publication, authors will be requested to provide a copy of their paper in exact accordance with the conventions listed in the preceding notes. If the final version of the paper is not submitted in accordance with these conventions then publication may be delayed by the need to return manuscripts to authors for necessary revisions. Authors should note that, following acceptance for publication, they will be required to provide not only a hard copy of the final version, but also a copy on a virus-free disk, preferably in MS Word 6 format, if possible. Authors will also be required to complete a Publishing Agreement form assigning copyright to the Publisher.

9. Twenty-five free offprints and one bound copy of the *Journal* will be supplied free of charge to main contributors; offprints must be shared in the case of joint ownership.

10. Page proofs will be sent for correction to a first-named author, unless otherwise requested. The difficulty and expense involved in making amendments at the page proof stage make it essential for authors to prepare their typescript carefully: any alteration to the original text is strongly discouraged Authors should correct printers' errors in red; minimal alterations of their own should be in black. Our aim is rapid publication. This will be helped if authors provide good copy, following the above instructions, and return their page proofs to the editor on the date requested.

Journal of Investing

ADDRESS FOR SUBMISSION:

Brian Bruce, Editor-in-Chief
Journal of Investing
Suite 267, PMB 310
1900 Preston Road #267
Plano, TX 75093
USA
Phone: 817-442-5404
Fax: 817-442-5406
E-Mail: journals@investmentresearch.org
Web: www.iijoi.com
Address May Change:

PUBLICATION GUIDELINES:

Manuscript Length: 16-20
Copies Required: Three
Computer Submission: Yes
Format: Word
Fees to Review: 0.00 US$

Manuscript Style:
    See Manuscript Guidelines

CIRCULATION DATA:

Reader: Business Persons
Frequency of Issue: Quarterly
Copies per Issue: 2,001 - 3,000
Sponsor/Publisher: Institutional Investor,
    Inc.
Subscribe Price: 350.00 US$
    175.00 US$ Academics

REVIEW INFORMATION:

Type of Review: Blind Review
No. of External Reviewers: 1
No. of In House Reviewers: 1
Acceptance Rate: 21-30%
Time to Review: 2 - 3 Months
Reviewers Comments: No
Invited Articles: 50% +
Fees to Publish: 0.00 US$

MANUSCRIPT TOPICS:

Asset Allocation; Consulting; Custody & Benefits; Global Investing; Marketing; Mutual Funds; Portfolio & Security Analysis; Real Estate; Risk Management; Technology; Trading Systems

MANUSCRIPT GUIDELINES/COMMENTS:

We invite investment professionals and scholars to contribute articles on the topics of asset allocation, global investing, risk management, real estate, technology, consulting, marketing, mutual finds, trading, custody, and benefits. *The Journal of Investing* is written in a style unique in the world of journals. In an attempt to help prospective authors understand that style, we have provided the following guidelines. The editors reserve the right to make changes for clarity and consistency.

1. Most journal articles follow the same format introduction, methodology and data, results, and finally conclusions. *The Journal of Investing,* however, is trying to create a new, more readable style. We therefore ask that you arrange articles in the following manner:
a.   What is the idea being conveyed by the article.
b.   How/why was this idea conceived.

c. What are the results of your investigation into the idea.
d. How can this idea be used by the investment community. This section should contain specific examples.

2. Some other suggestions of preferred writing style follow:
a. Keep in mind that writing is for the readers.
b. Write to express, not to impress.
c. Write the way you talk.
d. Keep it simple. Brevity and conciseness are valued.
e. Create interest. Colorful language and examples are encouraged.
f. Equations and formulas are discouraged, except in appendixes.

Authors should submit three hard copies of the manuscript (address below), along with a copy on diskette, in Microsoft Word if possible. Manuscripts should be no more than fifteen pages and should be double-spaced with wide margins and pages numbered. The front page should include the authors' full names, titles, addresses, zip codes, phone numbers, email addresses and type of software used.

4. References, endnotes, tables and figures should appear on separate pages at the end of the text.

5. Limit references to works cited in the text and list them alphabetically. Citations in the text should appear as "Smith [1990] suggests that..." Use page numbers for quotes.

6. Minimize the number of endnotes. Use periods instead of commas between authors' names and titles of references. Use superscript Arabic numbers in the text and on the endnote page.

7. Number and title all exhibits, with one to a page. Write out the column heads and legends; they should be understandable without reference to the text. Submit graphs in camera-ready form, we cannot draw graphs for you.

8. Center any equations on a separate line, numbered consecutively with Arabic numbers, in parenthesis in the right margin. Identify Greek letters in the margin for the typesetter. Please make clear markings, in a color other than black, when inserting Greek letters or equations into the text.

9. Include a brief article summary and short author biography for each author. The biographies should include details about education, prior affiliations, etc.

The Journal of Investing's permission form must be signed and returned to Institutional Investor in New York prior to publication.

Send three hard copies and a disk copy to:
   Mr. Brian Bruce, Editor-in-Chief, *The Journal of Investing*
   1900 Preston Road, #267, PMB 310, Plano, Texas 75093 USA
Or E-mail journals@InvestmentResearch.org

Journal of Investment Compliance (The)

ADDRESS FOR SUBMISSION:

Henry A. Davis, Managing Editor
Journal of Investment Compliance (The)
3133 Connecticut Avenue, NW #624
Washington, DC 20008-5147
USA
Phone: 202-328-7074
Fax: 202-483-0828
E-Mail: hdresearch@aobl.com
Web: www.iijic.com
Address May Change:

PUBLICATION GUIDELINES:

Manuscript Length: 16-25
Copies Required: Two
Computer Submission: Yes
Format: MS Word
Fees to Review: 0.00 US$

Manuscript Style:

CIRCULATION DATA:

Reader: Academics, Business Persons
Frequency of Issue: Quarterly
Copies per Issue: Less than 1,000
Sponsor/Publisher: Institutional Investor, Inc.
Subscribe Price: 500.00 US$

REVIEW INFORMATION:

Type of Review: Editorial Review
No. of External Reviewers: 2
No. of In House Reviewers: 0
Acceptance Rate: 11-20%
Time to Review: 2 - 3 Months
Reviewers Comments: Yes
Invited Articles: 11-20%
Fees to Publish: 0.00 US$

MANUSCRIPT TOPICS:
Accounting Theory & Practice; Financial Institutions & Markets; Financial Services

MANUSCRIPT GUIDELINES/COMMENTS:

Editor. James A. Tricarico, Jr.

Please follow the guidelines below when you prepare a manuscript for submission. The editors will edit and copyedit articles for clarity and consistency. *Please note that we reserve the right to return to an author any paper accepted for publication that is not prepared according to these instructions.*

1. **Article Submission**. Please submit 2 copies double-spaced sized on an 8.5"x11" page with 1.5"-2" margins and numbered pages. Include on the title page the authors' names and titles as they are to appear, including affiliation, mailing address, telephone and fax numbers, and e-mail address. Also submit an electronic file. Text should be formatted in 12-point type. If submitting a PDF file, please prepare with all fonts embedded and, if possible, include an accompanying Word file which would include the running text. We do not support articles submitted in WordPerfect. Please save any WordPerfect files as a text document and please provide separate eps files for any graphic elements. **All manuscripts are expected to be**

submitted in final form. We reserve the right to limit any changes following article formatting based upon content, not style.

2. **Abstract**. On the page after the title page, please provide a brief article summary or abstract suitable for the table of contents. Do not begin the paper with a heading such as "introduction." Do not number section or subsection headings.

3. Do not asterisk or footnote any authors' names listed as bylines. Footnoting should only begin in the body of the article.

4. **Exhibits**. Please put tables and graphs on separate individual pages at the end of the paper. Do not integrate them with the text; do not call them table 1 and figure 1. Please call any tabular or graphical material Exhibits, numbered in Arabic numbers consecutively in order of appearance in the text. We reserve the right to return to an author for reformatting any paper accepted for publication that does not conform to this style.

5. **Exhibit Presentation**. Please organize and present tables consistently throughout a paper, because we will print them the way they are presented to us. **Exhibits should be created as grayscale, as opposed to color, since the journal is printed in black and white. Please make sure that all categories in an exhibit can be distinguished from each other.** Align numbers correctly by decimal points; use the same number of decimal points for the same sorts of numbers; center headings, columns, and numbers correctly; use the exact same language in successive appearances; identify any bold-faced or italicized entries in exhibits; and provide any source notes necessary.

6. **Graphs**. Please submit graphs for accepted papers in electronic form. We cannot produce graphs for authors. Graphs will appear the way you submit them. Please be consistent as to fonts, capitalization, and abbreviations in graphs throughout the paper, and label all axes and lines in graphs clearly and absolutely consistently. When pasting graphs into Word, paste as an object, not as a picture, so we will be able to have access to original graph.

7. **Equations**. Please display called-out equations on separate lines, aligned on the exact same indents as the text paragraphs and with no punctuation following. Number equations consecutively throughout the paper in Arabic numbers at the right-hand margin. Clarify in handwriting any operations signs or Greek letters or any notation that may be unclear. Leave space around operations signs like plus and minus everywhere. We reserve the right to return for resubmission any accepted article that prepares equations in any other way. It would be preferable if manuscripts containing mathematical equations be submitted in Microsoft Word using either Equation Editor or MathType.

8. **Reference Citations**. In the text, please refer to authors and works as: Smith [2000]. Use brackets for the year, not parentheses. The same is true for references within parentheses, such as: "(see also Smith [2000])."

9. Reference Styles

Brokerage house internal publications	Askin, D.J., and S.D. Meyer. "Dollar Rolls: A Low-Cost Financing Technique." Mortgage-Backed Securities Research, Drexel Burnham Lambert, 1986.
Journal articles	Batlin, C.A. "Hedging Mortgage-Backed Securities with Treasury Bond Futures." *Journal of Futures Markets,* 7 (1987), pp. 675-693.
——. "Trading Mortgage-Backed Securities with Treasury Bond Futures." Journal of Futures Markets, 7 (1987), pp. 675-693.	Same author, alphabetized by title, two em-dashes instead of repeating name
Working papers	Boudoukh, J., M. Richardson, R. Stanton, and R.F. Whitelaw. "Pricing Mortgage-Backed Securities in a Multifactor Interest Rate Environment: A Multivariate Density Estimation Approach." Working Paper, New York University, 1995.
Sections of books	Breeden, D.T., and M.J. Giarla. "Hedging Interest Rate Risk with Futures, Swaps, and Options." In F. Fabozzi, ed., *The Handbook of Mortgage-Backed Securities.* Chicago: Probus Publishing, 1992, 3rd edition, pp. 847-960.
Books	Hull, J., ed. *Options, Futures and Other Derivative Securities.* Englewood Cliffs, NJ: Prentice-Hall, 1993, 2nd edition.

10. **Endnotes.** Please put in endnotes only material that is not essential to the understanding of an article. If it is essential, it belongs in the text. Do not place a footnote by the authors' names. Any biographical information can be indicated in a separate section and will not be footnoted. Authors' bio information appearing in the article will be limited to their titles, current affiliations, and locations. Do not include in endnotes full reference details; these belong in a separate references list; see below. We will delete non-essential endnotes in the interest of minimizing distraction and enhancing clarity. We also reserve the right to return to an author any article accepted for publication that includes endnotes with embedded reference detail and no separate references list in exchange for preparation of a paper with the appropriate endnotes and a separate references list.

11. **References lists.** Please list only those articles cited in a separate alphabetical references list at the end of the paper. Please follow absolutely the style you see in this journal. We reserve the right to return any accepted article for preparation of a references list according to this style.

12. **Electronic Files.** Word documents are preferred for the articles themselves. Excel can be used for the preparation of graphic elements, making sure that they are embedded in the Word document prior to submission. For those working with .tek or LaTeX files: ***PDF files of the articles must be submitted***, making sure to embed all fonts when the PDF file is prepared. Please also include a Word file which contains the text of the article.

13. **Copyright Agreement**: Institutional Investor Inc.'s copyright agreement form—giving us non-exclusive rights to publish the material in all media—must be signed prior to publication.

14. Upon acceptance of the article, no further changes are allowed, except with the permission of the editor. If the article has already been forwarded to our production department, any changes must be made on the hard copy of the original submitted manuscript and faxed to them.

Journal of Iranian Research and Analysis

ADDRESS FOR SUBMISSION:

Hamid Zangeneh, Editor
Journal of Iranian Research and Analysis
Widener University
Economics Department
One University Place
Chester, PA 19013
USA
Phone: 610-499-1140
Fax: 610-499-4614
E-Mail: hxz0001@widener.edu
Web:
Address May Change:

PUBLICATION GUIDELINES:

Manuscript Length: 16-20
Copies Required: Two
Computer Submission: Yes
Format: MS Word
Fees to Review: No Reply

Manuscript Style:
   Chicago Manual of Style

CIRCULATION DATA:

Reader: Academics, Government
Frequency of Issue: 2 Times/Year
Copies per Issue: Less than 1,000
Sponsor/Publisher: Center for Iranian
  Research and Analysis (CIR)
Subscribe Price: 45.00 US$

REVIEW INFORMATION:

Type of Review: Blind Review
No. of External Reviewers: 2
No. of In House Reviewers: 1
Acceptance Rate: 21-30%
Time to Review: 1 - 2 Months
Reviewers Comments: Yes
Invited Articles: 31-50%
Fees to Publish: No Reply

MANUSCRIPT TOPICS:

Econometrics; Economic Development; Economic History; Fiscal Policy; International Economics & Trade; International Finance; Macro Economics; Micro Economics; Monetary Policy; Political Economy; Public Policy Economics; Regional Economics

MANUSCRIPT GUIDELINES/COMMENTS:

Web. http://faculty.quinnipiac.edu/libarts/monshipouri/cira/

If a manuscript is accepted, a style sheet will be sent to the author(s).

Journal of Labor Economics

ADDRESS FOR SUBMISSION:

Derek A. Neal, Editor
Journal of Labor Economics
University of Chicago
1101 East 58th Street
Chicago, IL 60637
USA
Phone: 312-702-8607
Fax: 312-702-2699
E-Mail: jole@gsb.uchicago.edu
Web: www.journals.uchicago.edu/JOLE
Address May Change:

PUBLICATION GUIDELINES:

Manuscript Length: No Reply
Copies Required: One
Computer Submission: Yes
Format: N/A
Fees to Review: 0.00 US$

Manuscript Style:
    Chicago Manual of Style

CIRCULATION DATA:

Reader: Academics
Frequency of Issue: Quarterly
Copies per Issue: 1,001 - 2,000
Sponsor/Publisher: University of Chicago
    Press
Subscribe Price: 54.00 US$ Individual
    241.00 US$ Institution
    40.00 US$ Student with ID Copy

REVIEW INFORMATION:

Type of Review: Editorial Review
No. of External Reviewers: 1-2
No. of In House Reviewers: 1
Acceptance Rate: 15%
Time to Review: 4 - 6 Months
Reviewers Comments: Yes
Invited Articles: 0-5%
Fees to Publish: 0.00 US$

MANUSCRIPT TOPICS:
Industrial Organization; Labor Economics; Micro Economics

MANUSCRIPT GUIDELINES/COMMENTS:

Since 1983, the *Journal of Labor Economics* has presented international research that examines issues affecting the economy as well as social and private behavior. The *Journal* publishes both theoretical and applied research results relating to the U.S. and international data. And its contributors investigate various aspects of labor economics, including supply and demand of labor services, personnel economics, distribution of income, unions and collective bargaining, applied and policy issues in labor economics, and labor markets and demographics.

Send your submissions to the Editor, *Journal of Labor Economics*, 1101 East 58th Street, Chicago, IL 60637. There is no submission fee. Please send *one* copy of the manuscript and cover letter accompanied by a diskette containing a PDF file. You may email the electronic file and send the paper copy and cover letter by postal mail.

You will receive acknowledgment of receipt of the manuscript from the editorial office within one week. Your paper will be evaluated by an associate editor and at least one qualified referee. Please allow at least three months before expecting an editorial decision. If your paper is accepted for publication, you will be sent more detailed instructions for preparing your manuscript.

Journal of Law and Economics

ADDRESS FOR SUBMISSION:

Maureen Callahan, Managing Edtior
Journal of Law and Economics
University of Chicago Law School
1111 East 60th Street
Chicago, IL 60637
USA
Phone: 773-702-9603
Fax: 773-702-0730
E-Mail: m-callahan@uchicago.edu
Web: www.journals.uchicago.edu/JLE
Address May Change:

PUBLICATION GUIDELINES:

Manuscript Length: 20+
Copies Required: Three
Computer Submission: No
Format: Any Word Processing Format
Fees to Review: 0.00 US$

Manuscript Style:
    Uniform System of Citation (Harvard
    Blue Book), Chicago Manual of Style

CIRCULATION DATA:

Reader: Academics
Frequency of Issue: 2 Times/Year
Copies per Issue: 3,500-4,000
Sponsor/Publisher: University of Chicago
    Law School/University of Chicago Press
Subscribe Price: 30.00 US$ Individual
    45.00 US$ Institution
    16.00 US$ Student w/ID Copy

REVIEW INFORMATION:

Type of Review: Editorial Review
No. of External Reviewers: 1-2
No. of In House Reviewers: 0
Acceptance Rate: 10%
Time to Review: 2-4 Months
Reviewers Comments: Yes
Invited Articles: 0%
Fees to Publish: 0.00 US$

MANUSCRIPT TOPICS:

Corporate Finance; Financial Institutions & Markets; Industrial Organization; Public Policy Economics

MANUSCRIPT GUIDELINES/COMMENTS:

Description

Established in 1958, the *JLE* explores the complex relationships between law and economics, focusing on the influence of regulation and legal institutions on the operation of economic systems. Although topically varied, articles are most often concerned with how markets behave and with the actual effects of governmental institutions on markets. Many of the articles, therefore, provide the basis for an informed discussion of public policy.

Guidelines

Exclusive submission to the *Journal of Law and Economics* is required. There is no submission fee.

Three copies of the paper should be submitted to the address listed above. Manuscripts should be typewritten on one side of the paper only and double-spaced throughout. Please do not use decorative bindings. We do not accept electronic submissions, and submissions will not be returned. Please include contact information for all authors.

We do not publish notes, comments or book reviews.

General Specifications

Manuscripts should be typewritten on one side of the paper only and double-spaced in 12-point type throughout. All elements of the manuscript must be double-spaced! This includes the abstract, text, indented quotations, equations, appendixes, endnotes (including any indented quotations and equations in the endnotes), tables (tables may run more than one page), table notes, and figure legends. The manuscript must be arranged in the following order with no two elements appearing on the same page. For example, footnotes should appear as endnotes on a new page after the end of the text, and each figure or table should begin on a separate page. Please arrange your manuscript as follows:

- Title page
- Abstract (strict limit of 150 words)
- Text
- Appendixes
- Bibliography
- Endnotes
- Tables
- Figure legends
- Figures

Text

For general matters of style, the *JLE* follows *The Chicago Manual of Style*, 14th edition, published by The University of Chicago Press.

The *Journal of Law and Economics* uses the following subheadings (in this order):
I. ROMAN NUMERALS, ALL CAPS
B. Letters, Italic Font, Lower Case
3. Arabic Numbers, Lower Case
Run-in Text, Italic Font, Lower Case.

If only three levels of subheads are used, omit the third-level subhead (3. Arabic Numbers, Lower Case).

Equations are set from your hard copy, or printout, not from the disk. Therefore, when particularly complex or lengthy equations are involved, please provide extra space above and below the equation to facilitate the markup for the typesetter.

Each figure and table must be mentioned in the text in order of its appearance. All figures and tables, including those in appendixes, must be mentioned in the text.

Do not use "etc.," "e.g.," or "i.e." anywhere. Please spell these out as "and so on" or "and the like," "for example," and "namely" or "that is."

Latin phrases, such as ceteris paribus, res ipsa loquitur, in situ, and ex post, are not italicized. Titles of books, journals, and names of cases are italicized in the text (but not in endnotes). Case names are always italicized when only one party is mentioned (*Brown* for Brown v. Board of Education) in text and endnotes.

Appendixes

Endnotes in appendixes should be numbered consecutively with those in the rest of the text.

Numbering of equations, tables, and figures in appendixes should begin again with 1 (Equation A1, Table A1, Figure A1, and so on, for Appendix A; Equation B1, Table B1, Figure B1, and so on, for Appendix B).

Bibliography

Bibliographic style is the humanities style in *The Chicago Manual of Style*. See paragraphs 15.69-73 in chapter 15.

A bibliography is required for all *JLE* papers. Entries must contain authors' names as they appear in the publication, cities of publication for books, and inclusive page numbers for journal articles and chapters in books. Examples follow

Smith, John, Q. *Urban Turmoil: The Politics of Hope*. New York: Polis Publishing Co., 1986.

Priest, George. "Understanding the Liability Crisis." In *New Directions in Liability Law: Proceedings of the Academy of Political Science*. Vol. 37, No. 1, edited by Walter Olsen, pp. 196-211. New York: Academy of Political Science, 1988.

Bakos, Yannis; Brynjolfsson, Erik; and Lichtman, Douglas. "Shared Information Goods." *Journal of Law and Economics* 42 (1999): 117-55.

Hanssen, Andrew. "Judicial Selection and Political Independence: Analysis of State Supreme Court Decisions." Working paper. Bozeman: Montana State University, 1996.

Schmitt, Richard B. "As Legal Reform Legislation Heads for Senate, Trial Lawyers Lobby Is Likely to Play Key Role." *Wall Street Journal* (March 10, 1995), A16, col. 1.

Endnotes

An acknowledgment note should be included, marked with an asterisk, and placed at the beginning of the endnotes. The acknowledgement note should be keyed to the title of the article.

Papers with author/date citations will be returned for reformatting. Complete citations must be given in legal-style endnotes.

Endnotes follow a modified form of Harvard *Bluebook* style (except for the *Bluebook*'s typefaces) and conform in general to *The Bluebook: A Uniform System of Citation* (15th ed.). In conflicting cases, this style sheet supersedes the *Bluebook*.

The signals "e.g.," "i.e.," and "cf." should be spelled out as "for example," "that is" or "namely," and "compare."

Italicize *id.*, *et al.*, *et seq.*, *supra*, and *infra*. Use *et al.* for four or more authors.

Cross References

Use *supra* to refer to citations given in earlier notes. For cross-references to citations in later notes, use *infra*, not "cited in" or "see below." Examples follow:

[41] See note 34 *supra*.

[42] See also discussion in note 62 *infra*.

[43] See Section IID *infra*.

[44] See text around note 11 *supra*.

The short form for previously cited works consists of the author's last name, the note number of the first citation of the work, and a locating (page, section, paragraph) reference if desired (for example, "Coase, *supra* note 1, at 1"). For citations to notes in which more than one work by a particular author is cited, use a short form of the title as well (for example, "Coase, Social Cost, *supra* note 1, at 1"). Examples follow:

[21] Eckert, *supra* note 2, at 97-98.

[22] Smith & Jones, *supra* note 4, at 97 n.8.

[23] Coase, Social Cost, *supra* note 1, at 1. (In this example, more than one work by Coase is cited in note 1, so a shortened title must be included.)<ENDQUOTE< UL>

[24] Id. at 99 nn.9 & 10.

Books

William M. Landes & Richard A. Posner, The Economic Structure of Tort Law (1987)

F. M. Scherer, Industrial Market Structure and Economic Performance 329 (2d ed. 1970)

Livestock Futures Research Symposium (Raymond M. Leuthold & Perry Dixon eds., Chicago Mercantile Exchange 1980)

Cesare Bonesaria Beccaria, An Essay on Crimes and Punishments, chs. 9 & 10 (1st ed. London 1769)

William L. Prosser et al., Prosser and Keeton on Torts 218-19 (5th ed. 1984)

Articles in Periodicals

Note. Journal names are abbreviated according to the *Bluebook*. However, the *Journal of Law and Economics* is abbreviated J. Law & Econ. and the *Journal of Legal Studies* is abbreviated J. Legal Stud.

Dennis W. Carlton, The Rigidity of Prices, 76 Am. Econ. Rev. 637 (1986)

Martin B. Zimmerman, Learning Effect and the Commercialization of New Energy Technologies: The Case of Nuclear Power, 13 Bell J. Econ. 297, 301 (1982)

Sanford J. Grossman *et al.*, Clustering and Competition in Asset Markets, 40 J. Law & Econ. 23 (1997)

Note. Allocating the Costs of Hazardous Waste Disposal, 94 Harv. L. Rev. 584 (1981)

Cass R. Sunstein, Selective Fatalism, in this issue, at 799

Part of an Edited Volume

Fisher Black, Michael C. Jensen, & Myron Scholes, The Capital Asset Pricing Model: Some Empirical Tests, in Studies in the Theory of Capital Markets 79 (Michael C. Jensen ed. 1972)

Working and Discussion Papers

George L. Priest, The Invention of Enterprise Liability: A Critical History of the Intellectual Foundations of American Tort Law (Working paper, Yale Univ. Law School, June 1984)

Jonathan M. Karpoff, John R. Lott, Jr., & Graeme Rankine, Environmental Violations, Legal Penalties, and Reputation Costs (Working paper No. 71, Univ. Chicago Law School 1999)

C.M. Lindsay, Impurities in the Theory of Public Expenditure 34 (Discussion Paper No. 20, Univ. California, Los Angeles, Dept Economics 1974)

Newspapers

Richard Phillips, Shame as a Deterrent, Chi. Trib., July 27, 1988, at C20

Airline Industry Decontrol in First Year Boosts Competition, Fails to Slash Fares, Wall St. J., October 23, 1979, at 6, col. 1

Editorial, Chi. Trib., May 26, 1996, at 12

Unpublished Materials

Michael T. Maloney & Robert E. McCormick, Environmental Quality Regulation (unpublished manuscript, Univ. Rochester, Grad. School of Management, June 1980)

Richard Ruback, The Effect of Discretionary Price Control Decision on Equity Values 45-49 (unpublished Ph.D. dissertation, Univ. Rochester, June 1980)

Thomas W. Hazlett, Assigning Property Rights to Radio Spectrum Users: Why Did the FCC License Auctions Take 67 Years? (paper presented at the conference Law and Economics of Property Rights to Radio Spectrum, Tomales Bay, Cal., July 1996)

Interviews or Correspondence should be labeled as such, with the approximate date(s) given. Richard A. Epstein, telephone conversation with the author, May 3, 1998

Web Pages

Fred Mintzer, Jeffrey Lotspiech, & Norishige Morimoto, Safeguarding Digital Library Contents and Users, D-Lib. Mag., December 1997, http://www.dlib.org/dlib/december97/ibm/12lotspiech.html, visited April 17, 1999

Cases

Names of cases are not italicized in the endnotes (unless shortened in subsequent references or in discussion: for example, *Brown* for Brown v. Board of Education).

Do not italicize words or phrases relating to the history of a case: aff'd, cert. granted, denied, en banc.

Always spell out "United States" as a party to a case.

Cases should be cited in full (including name) in their initial citation in the endnotes, even if mentioned in the text. For example:

Nichols v. Universal Pictures Corp., 45 F.2d 1119 (2d Cir. 1930)
Palsgraf v. Long Island Railroad, 162 N.E. 99 (N.Y. 1928)
United States v. Socony-Vacuum, 310 U.S. 150 (1940)

Subsequent citations to cases:

Socony-Vacuum, *supra* note 1
Palsgraf, *supra* note 27, at 23 (footnotes omitted)
45 F.2d 1121-22
162 N.E. 101

Statutes

42 U.S.C. § 22 (1983)
Cal. Health & Safety Code § 7185
Securities Act of 1983, 15 U.S.C. §§ 77a-77b
Bankruptcy Act of 1898, 11 U.S.C. § 1 (repealed 1978)

Tables

Tables follow the style given in chapter 12 of *The Chicago Manual of Style*.

No more than one table should appear on a page. All elements of tables, including the notes, must be double-spaced; tables may run more than one page. (Tables are set from your paper copy, and the copy editors need room to write instructions to the typesetter. Single-spaced tables are difficult for the typesetter to read and result in typesetting errors.)

Tables should have brief titles. All explanatory material should be provided in notes at the bottom of the table.

Identify all quantities, units of measurement, and abbreviations for all entries. What is clear to you may not be clear to the general reader of the *JLE*.

Sources should be identified in full at the bottom of the each table. Do not give cross-references to endnotes elsewhere in the article.

Figures

Figures must be camera ready and professionally drawn or generated as high-quality computer graphics. No more than one table or figure should appear on a page.

Titles to figures should be placed together on a separate double-spaced page labeled Figure Legends.

Each figure should be identified by number, in pencil, on the back of the page.

Please delete any figure boxes or rules around the figures.

In general, finished figures can be only 4.5" wide. Keys to identifying items in the figure should be set within the figure or at the top or bottom to avoid having to reduce the figure.

Please use the Times Roman font if there is any lettering or text in your figure (for a better match to the text of the article). Type must not be smaller than 7 points.

Avoid the use of shading. If distinctions must be made visually, please use hatching and cross-hatching or another means of display. Shading is difficult to reproduce and often looks blotchy in the printed journal.

Journal of Legal Economics

ADDRESS FOR SUBMISSION:

Michael W. Butler, Editor
Journal of Legal Economics
University of North Alabama
PO Box 5077
Florence, AL 35632-0001
USA
Phone: 256-765-4144
Fax: 256-765-4170
E-Mail: leglecon@unanov.una.edu
Web: jlegalecon.com
Address May Change:

CIRCULATION DATA:

Reader: Academics, Attorneys, Expert
    Witnesses
Frequency of Issue: 3 Times/Year
Copies per Issue: Less than 1,000
Sponsor/Publisher: Toysan Reed
Subscribe Price: 60.00 US$ USA
    75.00 US$ Outside USA

PUBLICATION GUIDELINES:

Manuscript Length: 16-20+
Copies Required: Four
Computer Submission: Yes
Format: IBM Compatible/WordPerfect
Fees to Review: 25.00 US$

Manuscript Style:
    Chicago Manual of Style

REVIEW INFORMATION:

Type of Review: Blind Review
No. of External Reviewers: 4
No. of In House Reviewers: 1
Acceptance Rate: 38%
Time to Review: 2 - 3 Months
Reviewers Comments: Yes
Invited Articles: 0-5%
Fees to Publish: 0.00 US$

MANUSCRIPT TOPICS:

Econometrics; Employment Discrimination; Forensic Economics; Forensic Economics Case Studies; Macro Economics; Micro Economics; Pension Valuation

MANUSCRIPT GUIDELINES/COMMENTS:

1. Four copies of a manuscript must be submitted. Contributors must also submit manuscripts and tables on IBM compatible diskettes in WordPerfect. The program and version used should be designated on the diskette label.

2. A submission fee of $25 must accompany the manuscript. Payment should be made by check or money order made payable to the *Journal of Legal Economics*.

3. Manuscripts must be double spaced on 8½ x 11-inch paper, typed on one side of the page only, with a margin of at least one inch on all four sides.

4. In addition to the title of the article, the first page should include only the author's name, title, affiliation, complete mailing address, and telephone number, fax number, and email address.

5. Each table should be on a separate page and numbered consecutively. Each figure should be on a separate page and numbered consecutively. Headings and other textual material for tables and figures should be double spaced with only the first letter of a word capitalized.

6. References should be cited within the text using the author-date system. The last name of the author followed by the year of publication should be enclosed in parentheses and usually placed at the end of the sentence before the punctuation, i.e., (Smith 1981).

7. Bibliographic entries should be listed alphabetically at the end of the paper under the heading "References." The following formats for books and journals, respectively, should be employed (**italicize books and journals**).

Brown, Mark S. 1985. *New Economics*. New York: Harper and Row.
West, Paul J. 1987. "The Future Debt Crisis." *The Journal of Investments* 2:23-8.

Note. Each entry must have a year of publication, and all journal references should include volume and page numbers.

8. The use of endnotes is discouraged. However, if information cannot be incorporated in the main text, endnotes should be typed double spaced on a separate sheet of paper and numbered consecutively. Footnotes may not be used.

9. The use of first person should be avoided.

10. Unpublished papers should not be cited as references.

11. All matters of style should correspond to those prescribed by the *Chicago Manual of Style*, 13th ed. A guide for reference lists and author-date citations is available upon request.

References (italicize books and journals)

Anderson, Paul C. 1984. "The Psychology of Economics." *Journal of Business* Psychology 3:45-6.

Andrews, John T., and P.R. Swift. 1983. "Advantages of Historical Perspective." *Journal of Economic Literature* 4:14558.

Drucker, Peter. 1954. *The Practice of Management*. New York: Harper and Row.

Ford, Robert C., F.S. McLaughlin, and J. Nixdorf. 1980. "Ten Questions about MB0." *California Management Review* 23:88-94.

Killen, Robert T. 1988. *Managing Corporate Structure*. Edited by M.J. Simpson. San Francisco: Brighton Publications.

Landrum, Terry, ed. 1990. *Predicting Economic Trends*. Boston: Winter Street Press.

Martin, Jane S., Ida J. Froth, and C.P. Stowe. 1973. *Monetary Guidelines*. Chicago: Alwether and Cleve.

Proctor, Arthur, and Lila Proctor. 1989. "Value of Household Labor." *Journal of Managerial Issues* 2(3)(Fall): 21-2.

Roberts, Clifford, and Mark Bellows. 1987. *Corporate Managerial Styles*. Chicago: Winston Press.

_____, and Frances Simpson. 1989. "Theories of Regulation." *Law and Economics Quarterly*. 2:70-5.

Swanson, Beverly G. 1978. Marketing Decisions. Englewood Cliffs, New Jersey: Prentice-Hall.

United States Census Bureau. 1980. Growth Trends in the Southeastern Quadrant of the United States.

Vendex v. Arizona. 1982. 462 U.S. 523, 543-47.

Note. All entries must include the year of publication. For journals, volume and page numbers are required. Issue numbers and other date information may be indicated as in "Proctor" entry above; however, such facts are usually unnecessary, and therefore discouraged.

Sample Author-Date Citations
- One author: (Smith 1984)
- Two authors: (Lewis and Brown 1979)
- Three authors: (Winston, Black, and Termin 1988)
- Two authors with same last name: (Weinberg and Weinberg 1989)
- More than three authors: (Zimmerman et al. 1958)
- No individual author's name: (United States Census Bureau 1989)

Authors' names incorporated in text:
    Jones and Carter (1980) report findings...

Two or more references given together:
    (French 1972; Long and Harper 1975; King 1989)

Page number necessary for identification of reference:
    (Jasper 1980, 740)

Legal case: (Vendex v. Arizona 1982)

Note. Reference citations should usually appear at the end of a sentence before the punctuation.

Journal of Libertarian Studies

ADDRESS FOR SUBMISSION:

Hans-Hermann Hoppe, Editor
Journal of Libertarian Studies
Mises Institute
1594 Ottawa Drive
Las Vegas, NV 89109
USA
Phone: 705-369-6469
Fax: 702-369-9450
E-Mail: hoppeh@unlv.edu
Web: www.mises.org
Address May Change:

PUBLICATION GUIDELINES:

Manuscript Length: 16-25
Copies Required: Three
Computer Submission: Yes
Format: No Reply
Fees to Review: 0.00 US$

Manuscript Style:
    Chicago Manual of Style

CIRCULATION DATA:

Reader: Academics, Educated Laymen,
    Professionals
Frequency of Issue: Quarterly
Copies per Issue: 1,001 - 2,000
Sponsor/Publisher: Ludwig von Mises
    Institute
Subscribe Price: 29.00 US$

REVIEW INFORMATION:

Type of Review: Blind Review
No. of External Reviewers: 2
No. of In House Reviewers: 2
Acceptance Rate: 6-10%
Time to Review: 1 - 2 Months
Reviewers Comments: Yes if reviewers
    agree
Invited Articles: 0-5%
Fees to Publish: 0.00 US$

MANUSCRIPT TOPICS:

Economic Development; Economic History; Financial Institutions & Markets; History; Industrial Organization; International Economics & Trade; International Finance; Macro Economics; Micro Economics; Monetary Policy; Philosophy; Public Policy Economics

MANUSCRIPT GUIDELINES/COMMENTS:

Submissions

The *Journal of Libertarian Studies* publishes both solicited and unsolicited manuscripts. Authors submitting manuscripts should provide three clear copies, including abstracts of not more than 250 words, to assist the referees. The manuscript should be double-spaced. Please type on only one side of the page, using adequate margins. Manuscripts may also be submitted electronically. If an article is accepted, the author will be required to provide copies both in print and on disk, preferably in Microsoft Word. All manuscripts and correspondence should be addressed to the Editor. See additional information on book review submissions.

The *Journal of Libertarian Studies* edits for clarity, brevity, and in accordance with the *Chicago Manual of Style*. Authors should use footnotes, rather than endnotes or in-text references, and must include complete bibliographical information. Footnotes should be consecutively numbered. Notes must be formatted according to the *Chicago Manual of Style* or authors must resubmit them in correct form if the accepted manuscript is to be published. Authors are advised to examine the footnotes in this issue to see how the style is applied. In addition, in the interest of assisting researchers, a complete bibliography is to be included with the article.

Authors should include information on their titles and professional affiliations, along with mailing address, telephone number, and email address. Authors should also indicate if the manuscript has been or is to be published elsewhere or presented at a conference.

The *Journal of Libertarian Studies* is abstracted and indexed in *History and Life; Political Science Abstracts; The Philosopher's Index;* and *International Political Science Abstracts.*

Journal of Macroeconomics

ADDRESS FOR SUBMISSION:

W. Douglas McMillin, Co-Editor
Journal of Macroeconomics
Louisiana State University
E.J. Ourso College of
  Business Administration
2113 CEBA
Baton Rouge, LA 70803
USA
Phone: 225-388-5211
Fax: 225-578-3807
E-Mail: jmacro@isu.edu
Web: www.elsevier.com
Address May Change:

PUBLICATION GUIDELINES:

Manuscript Length: No Reply
Copies Required: Three
Computer Submission: No
Format: N/A
Fees to Review: 0.00 US$

Manuscript Style:
    See Manuscript Guidelines

CIRCULATION DATA:

Reader: Academics
Frequency of Issue: Quarterly
Copies per Issue: 1,001 - 2,000
Sponsor/Publisher: Elsevier Science
    Publishing Co.
Subscribe Price: 50.00 US$ Individual
    250.00 US$ Institution
    50.00 Euro Indv, 250 Euro Instn

REVIEW INFORMATION:

Type of Review: Blind Review
No. of External Reviewers: 2
No. of In House Reviewers: 0
Acceptance Rate: 11-20%
Time to Review: 2 - 3 Months
Reviewers Comments: Yes
Invited Articles: 0-5%
Fees to Publish: 0.00 US$

MANUSCRIPT TOPICS:
Econometrics; Economic Development; Economic History; Financial Institutions & Markets;
Fiscal Policy; International Finance; Macro Economics; Monetary Policy

MANUSCRIPT GUIDELINES/COMMENTS:

1. An abstract of not more than 100 words should accompany the manuscript. The entire paper
must be double-spaced. Paragraphs must be indented. American, rather than British, spelling
is preferred.

2. Footnotes should be numbered consecutively and typed double-spaced on a SEPARATE
page at the END of the paper. Institutional affiliations should not be included in the numbered
footnotes. Footnotes that are merely citations should be incorporated into the text (i.e., "...in
disequilibrium [see Samuelson (1947)]"). In general, keep footnotes to a minimum. In
indicating the placement of a footnote, use superscript numerals.

3. A list of references should be typed, double-spaced, on a separate page(s), and placed at the end of the manuscript. Book reference: Theil, H. 1971. Principles of Econometrics. John Wiley and Sons, New York. Journal sample: Cornell, B. 1983. The Money Supply Announcements Puzzle: Review and Interpretation. American Economic Review 73, 644-57. For other examples, consult a current issue of the *Journal of Macroeconomics* or contact Elsevier Science Publishing.

4. Where the paper is divided into sections, Arabic numerals should be used in numbering the sections. For example: 4. Conclusion.

5. Equation numbers should be given on the right-hand side of the page. It is not necessary, in a complicated model, to number the equations; only those equations that will be referred to later in the paper need have numbers.

6. Tables must be typed on **separate** sheets of paper.

7. Illustrations must be drawn **professionally**, in black ink on white paper, and must be ready for reproduction. Only those words and symbols explaining curves or labeling axes, for example, should appear in the figure. Illustrations should be in proportion to a 4½" x 7¾" page.

8. Stacked fractions should be set on one line whenever possible, e.g., (a/b).

9. In papers containing mathematical notation, the definitions of all the variables should be collected together in one place.

Journal of Mathematical Economics

ADDRESS FOR SUBMISSION:

Bernard Cornet, Editor
Journal of Mathematical Economics
Universite De Paris I
  Pantheon-Sorbonne
Maison des Sciences Economiques
106-112 Boulevard de l'hopital
Paris Cedex 13, 75647
France
Phone: +33 1 44-07-8300
Fax: +33 1 44-07-8301
E-Mail: cornet@univ-paris1.fr
Web: See Guidelines
Address May Change:

PUBLICATION GUIDELINES:

Manuscript Length: 26-30
Copies Required: Three
Computer Submission: Yes
Format: N/A
Fees to Review: 0.00 US$

Manuscript Style:
    See Manuscript Guidelines

CIRCULATION DATA:

Reader: Academics
Frequency of Issue: 8 Times/Year
Copies per Issue: No Reply
Sponsor/Publisher: Elsevier Science
    Publishing Co.
Subscribe Price: 115.00 US$ Individual
    1493.00 US$ Institution
    1334.00 Euro Institution

REVIEW INFORMATION:

Type of Review: Blind Review
No. of External Reviewers: 2
No. of In House Reviewers: 1
Acceptance Rate: 21-30%
Time to Review: 4 - 6 Months
Reviewers Comments: Yes
Invited Articles: 0-5%
Fees to Publish: 0.00 US$

MANUSCRIPT TOPICS:
Government & Non-Profit Accounting; International Economics & Trade; Mathematical
Economics

MANUSCRIPT GUIDELINES/COMMENTS:

Web. http://www.Elsevier.com/homepage/sae/econworld/econbase/mateco/frame.htm

Description
In the Editors view, the formal mathematical expression of economic ideas is of vital
importance to economics. Such an expression can determine whether a loose economic
intuition has a coherent, logical meaning. Also, a full formal development of economic ideas
can itself suggest new economic concepts and intuitions.

The primary objective of the *Journal* is to provide a forum for work in economic theory which
expresses economic ideas using formal mathematical reasoning. For work to add to this
primary objective, it is not sufficient that the mathematical reasoning be new and correct. The

work should have real economic content. The economic ideas should be interesting and important. These ideas may pertain to any field of economics or any school of economic thought. The economic ideas may be well known, provided they are expressed and developed in a novel way.

Guide for Authors

1. Papers must be in English.

2. Papers for publication should be sent in triplicate to the Editor. Authors are invited to submit, along with the hard copy, a PDF file that will be used to expedite the refereeing process.

Submission of a paper will be held to imply that it contains original unpublished work and is not being submitted for publication elsewhere. The Editor does not accept responsibility for damage or loss of papers submitted. Upon acceptance of an article, author(s) will be asked to transfer copyright of the article to the publisher. This transfer will ensure the widest possible dissemination of information.

3. Submission of accepted papers as electronic manuscripts, i.e., on disk with accompanying manuscript, is encouraged. Electronic manuscripts have the advantage that there is no need for rekeying of text, thereby avoiding the possibility of introducing errors and resulting in reliable and fast delivery of proofs. The preferred storage medium is a 5.25 or 3.5-inch disk in MS-DOS format, although other systems are welcome, e.g., Macintosh (in this case, save your file in the usual manner; do not use the option 'save in MS-DOS format'). Do not submit your original paper as electronic manuscript but hold on to the disk until asked for this by the Editor. You will be contacted to supply the electronic version should your paper be accepted. Make absolutely sure that the file on the disk and the printout are identical. Please use a new and correctly formatted disk and label this with your name; also specify the software and hardware used as well as the title of the file to be processed. Do not convert the file to plain ASCII. Ensure that the letter 'l' and digit '1', and also the letter 'O' and digit '0' are used properly, and format your article (tabs, indents, etc.) consistently. Characters not available on your word processor (Greek letters mathematical symbols, etc.) should not be left open but indicated by a unique code (e.g. gralpha, alpha, @, etc., for the Greek letter α). Such codes should be used consistently throughout the entire text; a list of codes used should accompany the electronic manuscript. Do not allow your word processor to introduce word breaks and do not use a justified layout. Please adhere strictly to the general instructions below on style, arrangement and, in particular, the reference style of the *Journal*.

4. Manuscripts should be double spaced, with wide margins, and printed on one side of the paper only. All pages should be numbered consecutively. Titles and subtitles should be short. References, tables, and legends for the figures should be printed on separate pages. The legends and titles on tables and figures must be sufficiently descriptive such that they are understandable without reference to the text. The dimensions of figure axes and the body of tables must be clearly labeled in English.

5. The first page of the manuscript should contain the following information: (i) the title; (ii) the name(s) and institutional affiliation(s) of the author(s); (iii) an abstract of not more than

100 words. A footnote on the same sheet should give the name, address, and telephone and fax numbers of the corresponding author [as well as an e-mail address].

6. The first page of the manuscript should also contain at least one classification code according to the Classification System for Journal Articles as used by the *Journal of Economic Literature*; in addition, up to five key words should be supplied.

7. Acknowledgements and information on grants received can be given in a first footnote, which should not be included in the consecutive numbering of footnotes.

8. Footnotes should be kept to a minimum and numbered consecutively throughout the text with superscript Arabic numerals.

9. Displayed formulae should be numbered consecutively throughout the manuscript as (1), (2), etc. against the right-hand margin of the page. In cases where the derivation of formulae has been abbreviated, it is of great help to the referees if the full derivation can be presented on a separate sheet (not to be published).

10. References to publications should be as follows: 'Smith (1992) reported that...' or 'This problem has been studied previously (e.g., Smith et al., 1969)'. The author should make sure that there is a strict one-to-one correspondence between the names and years in the text and those on the list. The list of references should appear at the end of the main text (after any appendices, but before tables and legends for figures). It should be double spaced and listed in alphabetical order by author's name. References should appear as follows:

For Monographs
Hawawini, G. and I. Swary, 1990, Mergers and acquisitions in the U.S. banking industry: Evidence from the capital markets (North-Holland, Amsterdam).

For Contributions to Collective Works
Brunner, K. and A.H. Meltzer, 1990, Money supply, in: B.M. Friedman and F.H. Hahn, eds., Handbook of monetary economics, Vol. 1 (North- Holland, Amsterdam) 357-396.

For Periodicals
Griffiths, W. and G. Judge, 1992, Testing and estimating location vectors when the error covariance matrix is unknown, Journal of Econometrics 54, 121-138.

Note that journal titles should not be abbreviated.

11. Illustrations will be reproduced photographically from originals supplied by the author; they will not be redrawn by the publisher. Please provide all illustrations in quadruplicate (one high-contrast original and three photocopies). Care should be taken that lettering and symbols are of a comparable size. The illustrations should not be inserted in the text, and should be marked on the back with figure number, title of paper, and author's name. All graphs and diagrams should be referred to as figures, and should be numbered consecutively in the text in Arabic numerals. Illustration for papers submitted as electronic manuscripts should be in traditional form.

894

Papers that were received by Elsevier after mid January 2004 for this *Journal* will appear in colour on Science Direct in this new programme. For those papers which contain a mixture of colour and black & white illustrations, some of the figures that appear in black and white in the printed version of the *Journal* will appear in colour, online, in ScienceDirect. There are no extra charges for authors who participate in this new facility. Further information on electronic artwork can be found at http://authors.elsevier.com/artwork.

12. Tables should be numbered consecutively in the text in Arabic numerals and printed on separate sheets.

Any manuscript which does not conform to the above instructions may be returned for the necessary revision before publication.

Page proofs will be sent to the corresponding author. Proofs should be corrected carefully; the responsibility for detecting errors lies with the author. Corrections should be restricted to instances in which the proof is at variance with the manuscript. No deviations from the version accepted by the Editors are permissible without the prior and explicit approval by the Editors; these alterations will be charged. Fifty reprints of each paper are supplied free of charge to the corresponding author; additional reprints are available at cost if they are ordered when the proof is returned.

Journal of Monetary Economics

ADDRESS FOR SUBMISSION:

Susan L. North, Editorial Assistant
Journal of Monetary Economics
University of Rochester
W.E. Simon Graduate School of Business
Rochester, NY 14627
USA
Phone: 716-275-2523
Fax: 716-442-7069
E-Mail: north@simon.rochester.edu
Web: www.elsevier.nl
Address May Change:

PUBLICATION GUIDELINES:

Manuscript Length: 30 Pages
Copies Required: Four
Computer Submission: Yes + Original
Format: N/A
Fees to Review: 100.00 US$ Subscriber
    175.00 US$ Non Subscriber

Manuscript Style:
    See Manuscript Guidelines

CIRCULATION DATA:

Reader: Academics
Frequency of Issue: Bi-Monthly
Copies per Issue: 2,001 - 3,000
Sponsor/Publisher: University of Rochester/
    Elsevier Science
Subscribe Price: 95.00 US$ Individual
    1634.00 US$ Institution
    60.00 US$ Student

REVIEW INFORMATION:

Type of Review: Editorial Review
No. of External Reviewers: 3
No. of In House Reviewers: No Reply
Acceptance Rate: 6-10%
Time to Review: 2 - 3 Months
Reviewers Comments: Yes
Invited Articles: 0-5%
Fees to Publish: 0.00 US$

MANUSCRIPT TOPICS:
Industrial Organization; International Economics & Trade; International Finance; Macro Economics; Monetary Policy

MANUSCRIPT GUIDELINES/COMMENTS:

Description
The profession has witnessed over the past twenty years a remarkable expansion of research activities bearing on problems in the broader field of monetary economics. The strong interest in monetary analysis has been increasingly matched in recent years by the growing attention to the working and structure of financial institutions. The role of various institutional arrangements, the consequences of specific changes in banking structure and the welfare aspects of structural policies have attracted an increasing interest in the profession. There has also been a growing attention to the operation of credit markets and to various aspects in the behavior of rates of return on assets. The *Journal of Monetary Economics* provides a specialized forum for the publication of this research.

Guide for Authors
1. Papers must be in English.

2. Papers for publication should be sent in quadruplicate (with one copy not stapled) to:
Editorial Office, Journal of Monetary Economics
William E. Simon Graduate School of Business Administration
University of Rochester, Rochester, NY 14627, USA

There is a standard submission fee of US$175.00 for all unsolicited manuscripts submitted for publication. There are reduced fees for subscribers to the *Journal* (US$100.00), students (US$75.00), and student subscribers (US$50.00). To encourage quicker response referees will be paid a nominal fee and the submission fee will be used to cover these refereeing expenses. There are no page charges. Cheques should be made payable to the *Journal of Monetary Economics*. When a paper is accepted the fee will be reimbursed.

Submission of a paper will be held to imply that it contains original unpublished work and is not being submitted for publication elsewhere. The Editor does not accept responsibility for damage or loss of papers submitted. Upon acceptance of an article, author(s) will be asked to transfer copyright of the article to the publisher. This transfer will ensure the widest possible dissemination of information.

3. Submission of accepted papers as electronic manuscripts, i.e., on disk with accompanying manuscript, is encouraged. Electronic manuscripts have the advantage that there is no need for rekeying of text, thereby avoiding the possibility of introducing errors and resulting in reliable and fast delivery of proofs. The preferred storage medium is a 5.25 or 3.5-inch disk in MS-DOS format, although other systems are welcome, e.g., Macintosh (in this case, save your file in the usual manner; do not use the option 'save in MS-DOS format"). Do not submit your original paper as electronic manuscript but hold on to disk until asked for this by the Editor (in case your paper is accepted without revisions). Do submit the accepted version of your paper as electronic manuscript. Make absolutely sure that the file on the disk and the printout are identical. Please use a new and correctly formatted disk and label this with your name; also specify the software and hardware used as well as the title of the file to be processed. Do not convert the file to plain ASCII. Ensure that the letter 'l' and digit'1', and also the letter 'O' and digit '0' are used properly, and format your article (tabs, indents, etc.) consistently. Characters not available on your word processor (Greek letters mathematical symbols, etc.) should not be left open but indicated by a unique code (e.g. gralpha, alpha, etc., for the Greek letter α). Such codes should be used consistently throughout the entire text; a list of codes used should accompany the electronic manuscript. Do not allow your word processor to introduce word breaks and do not use a justified layout. Please adhere strictly to the general instructions below on style, arrangement and, in particular, the reference style of the *Journal*.

4. Manuscripts should be double spaced, with wide margins, and printed on one side of the paper only. All pages should be numbered consequently. Titles and subtitles should be short. References, tables, and legends for the figures should be printed on separate pages.

5. The first page of the manuscript should contain the following information: (i) the title; (ii) the name(s) and institutional affiliation(s)of the author(s); (iii) an abstract of not more than 100 words. A footnote on the same sheet should give the name, address, and telephone and fax numbers of the corresponding author [as well as an e-mail address].

6. The first page of the manuscript should also contain at least one classification code according to the *Classification System for Journal Articles* as used by the *Journal of Economic Literature*; in addition, up to five key words should be supplied.

7. Acknowledgements and information on grants received can be given in a first footnote, which should not be included in the consecutive numbering of footnotes.

8. Footnotes should be kept to a minimum and numbered consecutively throughout the text with superscript Arabic numerals.

9. Displayed formulae should be numbered consecutively throughout the manuscript as (1), (2), etc. against the right-hand margin of the page. In cases where the derivation of formulae has been abbreviated, it is of great help to the referees if the full derivation can be presented on a separate sheet (not to be published).

10. References to publications should be as follows: 'Smith (1992) reported that...' or 'This problem has been studied previously (e.g., Smith et al., 1969)'. The author should make sure that there is a strict one-to-one correspondence between the names and years in the text and those on the list. The list of references should appear at the end of the main text (after any appendices, but before tables and legends for figures). It should be double spaced and listed in alphabetical order by author's name. References should appear as follows:

For Monograph
Hawawini, G. and I. Swary, 1990, Mergers and acquisitions in the U.S. banking industry: Evidence from the capital markets (North-Holland, Amsterdam).

For Contributions to Collective Works
Brunner, K. and A.H. Meltzer, 1990, Money supply, in: B.M. Friedman and F.H. Hahn, eds., Handbook of monetary economics, Vol. 1 (North-Holland, Amsterdam) 357-396.

For Periodical
Griffiths, W. and G. Judge, 1992, Testing and estimating location vectors when the error covariance matrix is unknown, Journal of Econometrics 54, 121-138.

Note that journal titles should not be abbreviated.

11. Illustrations will be reproduced photographically from originals supplied by the author; they will not be redrawn by the publisher. Please provide all illustrations in quadruplicate (one high-contrast original and three photocopies). Care should be taken that lettering and symbols are of a comparable size. The illustrations should not be inserted in the text, and should be marked on the back with figure number, title of paper, and author's name. All graphs and diagrams should be referred to as figures, and should be numbered consecutively in the text in Arabic numerals. Illustration for papers submitted as electronic manuscripts should be in traditional form.

12. Tables should be numbered consecutively in the text in Arabic numerals and printed on separate sheets.

Any manuscript which does not conform to the above instructions may be returned for the necessary revision before publication.

Page proofs will be sent to the corresponding author. Proofs should be corrected carefully; the responsibility for detecting errors lies with the author. Corrections should be restricted to instances in which the proof is at variance with the manuscript. No deviations from the version accepted by the Editors are permissible without the prior and explicit approval by the Editors; these alterations will be charged. Fifty reprints of each paper are supplied free of charge to the corresponding author; additional reprints are available at cost if they are ordered when the proof is returned.

For complete, up-to-date addresses of Editors please check the Website.

Journal of Money Laundering Control

ADDRESS FOR SUBMISSION:

Daryn Moody, Editor
Journal of Money Laundering Control
Henry Stewart Publications
Museum House
25 Museum Street
London, WC1A 1JT
UK
Phone: 44 20 7323 2916
Fax: 44 20 7323 2918
E-Mail: daryn@hspublications.co.uk
Web: www.henrystewart.co.uk
Address May Change:

PUBLICATION GUIDELINES:

Manuscript Length: 11-30
Copies Required: Three
Computer Submission: Yes
Format: MS Word
Fees to Review: 0.00 US$

Manuscript Style:
    See Manuscript Guidelines

CIRCULATION DATA:

Reader: Academics, Business Persons
Frequency of Issue: Quarterly
Copies per Issue: 1,001 - 2,000
Sponsor/Publisher: Henry Stewart
    Publications
Subscribe Price: 120.00 US$ Individual
    385.00 US$ Institution
    80.00 Pounds Indv, 255 Pounds Instn

REVIEW INFORMATION:

Type of Review: Blind Review
No. of External Reviewers: 2
No. of In House Reviewers: 1
Acceptance Rate: 21-30%
Time to Review: 1 - 2 Months
Reviewers Comments: Yes
Invited Articles: 6-10%
Fees to Publish: 0.00 US$

MANUSCRIPT TOPICS:
Financial Crime; International Economics & Trade; International Finance; Money
Laundering; Public Policy Economics; Regional Economics

MANUSCRIPT GUIDELINES/COMMENTS:

1. Papers should be between 2,000 and 6,000 words in length. They should be typewritten, double-spaced, on A4 or US letter-sized paper. A copy should also be submitted on disk with a note of the hardware and software used.

2. All papers should be accompanied by a short abstract, outlining the aims and subject matter.

3. All papers should be accompanied by a short (about 80 words) description of the author(s) and, if appropriate, the organization of which he or she is a member.

4. Papers should be supported by actual or hypothetical examples, wherever possible and appropriate. Authors should not seek to use the *Journal* as a vehicle for marketing any specific product or service.

5. Authors should avoid the use of language or slang which is not in keeping with the academic and professional style of the *Journal*.

6. Titles of organizations etc., should be written out first, in full, followed by the organization's initials in brackets; and thereafter, the initials only should be used.

7. Papers should be supported by references. These should be set out in accordance with the Vancouver style—that is, they should be referred to by number in the text and set out in full in numerical order at the end of the text.

8. Photographs and illustrations supporting papers should be submitted where appropriate. Photographs should be good quality positives, printed from the original negatives, and in black and white only. Figures and other line illustrations should be submitted in good quality originals, and a copy of the data should also be included.

9. Authors are asked to ensure the references to named people and/or organizations are accurate and without libelous implications.

10. All contributions sent to the Publisher; whether they are invited or not, will be sent to the Editor and also submitted to two members of the Editorial Board for double-blind peer review. Any such contribution must bear the author's full name and address, even if this is not for publication. Contributions, whether published pseudonymously or not, are accepted on the strict understanding that the author is responsible for the accuracy of all opinion, technical comment, factual report, data figures, illustrations, and photographs. Publication does not necessarily imply that these are the opinions of the Editors, Editorial Board or the Publisher, nor does the Board accept any liability for the accuracy of such comment, report, and other technical and factual information. The Publisher will, however, strive to ensure that all opinion, comments, reports, data, figures, illustrations, and photographs are accurate, insofar as it is within its abilities to do so. The Publisher reserves the right to edit, abridge or omit material submitted for publication.

11. The author bears the responsibility for checking whether material submitted is subject to copyright or ownership rights, e.g., photographs, illustrations, trade literature, and data. Where use is so restricted, the Publisher must be informed with the submission of the material.

12. No contribution will be accepted which has been published elsewhere, unless it is expressly invited or agreed by the Editors and the Publisher. Papers and contributions published become the copyright of the Publisher, unless otherwise stated.

13. All reasonable efforts are made to ensure accurate reproduction of text, photographs and illustrations. The Publisher does not accept responsibility for mistakes, be they editorial or typographical, nor for consequences resulting from them.

Journal of Money, Credit and Banking

ADDRESS FOR SUBMISSION:

Paul Evans, Editor
Journal of Money, Credit and Banking
The Ohio State University
#410 Arps Hall
Department of Economics
1945 North High Street
Columbus, OH 43210-1172
USA
Phone: 614-292-7834
Fax: 614-292-3906
E-Mail: evans.21@osu.edu
Web: www.econ.ohio-state.edu/jmcb.htm
Address May Change:

PUBLICATION GUIDELINES:

Manuscript Length: 0-30
Copies Required: One
Computer Submission: Yes
Format: No Reply
Fees to Review:
    See Web Site

Manuscript Style:
    Chicago Manual of Style

CIRCULATION DATA:

Reader: Academics
Frequency of Issue: Bi-Monthly
Copies per Issue: 3,001 - 4,000
Sponsor/Publisher: Ohio State University
    Press
Subscribe Price: 38.00 US$ Student-Ppr
    75.00 US$ Individual-Paper
    210.00 US$ /$235 Inst-Paper/Electronic

REVIEW INFORMATION:

Type of Review: Editorial Review
No. of External Reviewers: 2
No. of In House Reviewers: 1
Acceptance Rate: 10-15%
Time to Review: 4 - 6 Months
Reviewers Comments: Yes
Invited Articles: 0-5%
Fees to Publish: 0.00 US$

MANUSCRIPT TOPICS:

Econometrics; Economic History; International Finance; Macro Economics; Monetary Policy

MANUSCRIPT GUIDELINES/COMMENTS:

Web

http://www.econ.ohio-state.edu/jmcb.html – or – https://Gemini.econ.umd.edu/jmcb

Manuscript Guidelines

1. Manuscripts should be submitted to the Editors. They can be via email, on the secure Website or as a hard copy.

2. Manuscripts must be in English, must contain original unpublished work, must not be under consideration for publication elsewhere, and should not exceed 30 pages in overall length.

3. Manuscripts should be typewritten, double-spaced, on one side only of white bond paper, 8½ x 11 inches in size, with margins at least one inch wide. An abstract, double-spaced, must

902

accompany the article. It should summarize the main points of the paper in no more than 100 words. Authors must supply their professional title, department, and the name of the institutions with which they are affiliated on both the title page and the abstract.

4. Literature Cited. All works cited should be listed alphabetically by author, in a double-spaced list, at the end of the manuscript. **Use full first and last names. Do NOT use em spaces**. *Example:*

Rudenbusch, Glenn D., and Lars E.O. Svensson. (1999) "Policy roles for Inflation Targeting." In *Monetary Policy Rules*, edited by John B. Taylor, pp. 205-46. Chicago: University of Chicago Press.

Stigum, Marcia. (1990) *The Money Market*, 3rd ed. Homewood, IL: Dow Jones-Irwin.

Glaeser, Edward L., Bruce Sacerdote, and Jose A. Scheinkman. (1996) "Crime and Social Interactions." *Quarterly Journal of Economics*, 111, 507-48.

Spindt, Paul A. and Ronald J. Hoffmeister. (1998a) "The Micromechanics of the Federal funds market: Implications for Day-of-the-Week Effects in funds Rate Variability." *Journal of Financial and Quantitative Analysis*, 23:4, 401-16.

Spindt, Paul A. and Ronald J. Hoffmeister. (1998b) "The Micromechanics of the Federal funds market: Implications for Day-of-the-Week Effects in funds Rate Variability." *Journal of Financial and Quantitative Analysis*, 23:4, 401-16.

5. Footnotes should not be used for the purpose of citation. In the final draft, footnotes must be converted to endnotes.

6. Mathematics. Equations must be typed and important displayed equations identified by consecutive Arabic numbers in parentheses on the right. Expressions should be aligned and compound subscripts and superscripts clearly marked if there is any potential for confusion. Handwritten symbols should be identified in the margin the first time they appear. Equations should not be unnecessarily numerous or complex. A slash (/) should be used to separate the numerator and denominator of all in-text fractions and short displayed fractions. Multiple dots and bars over expressions should be avoided where primes can be used. Indicate boldface characters by drawing a wavy line under them; a single underlined (a) means italic to a printer.

7. Illustrations submitted with the final draft must be of professional quality, ready for reproduction, executed on white paper or vellum, in black ink, with clear, medium weight, black lines and figures. All lettering on figures should be executed by an artist in pen and ink, by means of dry transfer letters, or by applying typeset material to the prepared artwork. Typewritten lettering should not appear in illustrations. Figures should be capable of legible reduction to a size no larger than 4½ x 7 inches (full page) and preferably no larger than 4½ x 3½ inches (half page); they should be numbered consecutively, and the number and author's name should be penciled lightly on the back of each. All illustrations must have captions, which should not appear on the artwork, but should be typed, double-spaced on a sheet at the end of the manuscript. If there is any potential for doubt, the word "top" should be written on the back of the illustration.

8. **Tables**. Tables should be numbered consecutively throughout the article and typed on separate sheets at the end of the manuscript. Each table must include a descriptive title and headings to columns. Gather general footnotes to tables as "Note:" or "Notes:", and use "a, b, c, etc.", for specific footnotes. Asterisks * and/or ** indicate significance at the 5% and 1% levels, respectively.

9. **Copyrighted Material**. Permission to reprint any previously published material (e.g., tables, illustrations, text extracts) must be obtained by the author from the copyright holder and copies of the grants of permission must be submitted to the editors with the final draft of the manuscript.

List of Citations

10. Citations are made by the author's last name and date of publications enclosed in parentheses without punctuations. Example: (Barro 1981), (Hopewell and Kaufman 1974a), Glaeser et al 1992)

11. When a reference must be made to a particular page, selection, or equation, it should be placed within the parentheses. Example: (Box and Jenkins 1976, p. 361), (Box and Jenkins 1976, eq.4)

12. References to periodicals must include the author's full name, article title (with the first letter of all significant words capitalized—complete unabbreviated name of the periodical, volume number (delete "Vol."), month and year, and page numbers:

Dwyer, Gerald P., Jr. "Inflation and Government Deficits". Economic Inquiry 20 (July 1982), 315-29.

13. Reference to books or article in books must list in order the author's name, book title, edition or volume number (if any), editor (if any), page numbers (where relevant), place of publication, name of publisher, and year:

Barro, Robert J. "Unanticipated Money Growth and Economic Activity in the U.S." In Money, Expectations, and Business Cycles, edited by Robert J. Barro, pp. 137-69. New York: Academic Press, 1981.

Box, George E., and Gwylim M. Jenkins. Time Series Analysis: Forecasts and Control, 2nd ed. San Francisco: Holden Day, 1976.

14. If an author or team of authors appears more than once, substitute a short rule for the name or names in successive citations:

Sargent, Thomas J., and Neil Wallace. "Rational Expectations, the Optimal Money Instrument and the Optimal Money Supply Rule." Journal of Political Economy 83 (April 1975), 241-54.

_____. "Rational Expectations and the Theory of Economic Policy". Journal of Monetary Economics 2 (April 1976), 169-83.

15. If two or more works by the same author bear the same publication date, they should be distinguished by lower case letters after the citations:

Juster, F. Thomas, and Paul Wachtel. "Inflation and the Consumer". Brookings Papers of Economic Activity 1 (1972), 71-121(a).

_____. "A Note on Inflation and the Saving Rate". Brookings Papers on Economic Activity 3 (1972), 765-78(b).

The letter should also appear in the citation in the text. For example: (1972a), (1972b), etc.

15. Citations are made by the author's last name and date of publications enclosed in parentheses without punctuations. Example: (Barro 1981), Hopewell and Kaufman 1974a), Glaeser et al 1992)

If the author's name has just been mentioned, it is not necessary to repeat the name in the citation. For example: "Information of the type developed by Barro (1981)..."

When a reference must be made to a particular page, section, or equation, it should be placed within the parentheses. For example: (Box and Jenkins 1976, p. 361), (Box and Jenkins 1976, eq. 4), etc.

Journal of Multinational Financial Management

ADDRESS FOR SUBMISSION:

Ike Mathur, Co-Editor
Journal of Multinational Financial
    Management
Southern Illinois University
c/o College of Business & Administration
Carbondale, IL 62901-4626
USA
Phone: 618-453-1421
Fax: 618-453-5626
E-Mail: imathur@cba.siu.edu
Web: www.elsevier.nl/inca/publications
Address May Change:

PUBLICATION GUIDELINES:

Manuscript Length: 21-25
Copies Required: Three
Computer Submission: No
Format: N/A
Fees to Review: 50.00 US$

Manuscript Style:
  , Journal of Economic Literature

CIRCULATION DATA:

Reader: Academics
Frequency of Issue: Quarterly
Copies per Issue: Less than 1,000
Sponsor/Publisher: Elsevier Science
    Publishing Co.
Subscribe Price: 50.00 US$ Individual
    216.00 US$ Institution
    44.92 Euro Indv., 192.86 Euro Inst.

REVIEW INFORMATION:

Type of Review: Blind Review
No. of External Reviewers: 1
No. of In House Reviewers: 1
Acceptance Rate: 11-20%
Time to Review: 2 - 3 Months
Reviewers Comments: Yes
Invited Articles: 6-10%
Fees to Publish: 0.00 US$

MANUSCRIPT TOPICS:
Corporate Finance; International Finance; Portfolio & Security Analysis

MANUSCRIPT GUIDELINES/COMMENTS:

Web
http://www.elsevier.nl/inca/publications/store/6/0/0/1/1/2/

Editors
G. Booth, Michigan State Univ., East Langsing, Michigan, USA
Ike Mathur, Southern Illinois Univ., Carbondale, Illinois USA

Aims and Scope
International trade, financing and investments have grown at an extremely rapid pace in recent years, and the operations of corporations have become increasingly multinationalized. Corporate executives buying and selling goods and services, and making financing and investment decisions across national boundaries, have developed policies and procedures for managing cash flows denominated in foreign currencies. These policies and procedures, and

the related managerial actions of executives, change as new relevant information becomes available.

The purpose of the *Journal of Multinational Financial Management* is to publish rigorous, original articles dealing with the management of the multinational enterprise. Theoretical, conceptual, and empirical papers providing meaningful insights into the subject areas will be considered.

The following topic areas, although not exhaustive, are representative of the coverage in this *Journal*.
- Foreign exchange risk management
- International capital budgeting
- Forecasting exchange rates
- Foreign direct investment
- Hedging strategies
- Cost of capital
- Managing transaction exposure
- Political risk assessment
- International working capital management
- International financial planning
- International tax management
- International diversification
- Transfer pricing strategies
- International liability management
- International mergers

Guide for Authors
1. Papers must be in English.

2. Papers for publication should be sent in triplicate to Professor Ike Mathur, Editor, accompanied by a submission fee of US$50.00. Payments are by credit card by printing, completing the manuscript transmittal form (found on Web) and attaching it to the submitted paper. There are no page charges. Submission of a paper will be held to imply that it contains original unpublished work and is not being submitted for publication elsewhere. The Editor does not accept responsibility for damage or loss of papers submitted. Upon acceptance of an article, author(s) will be asked to transfer copyright of the article to the publisher. This transfer will ensure the widest possible dissemination of information.

3. Submission of accepted papers as electronic manuscripts, i.e., on disk with accompanying manuscript, is encouraged. Electronic manuscripts have the advantage that there is no need for rekeying of text, thereby avoiding the possibility of introducing errors and resulting in reliable and fast delivery of proofs. The preferred storage medium is a 5.25 or 3.5-inch disk in MS-DOS format, although other systems are welcome, e.g., Macintosh (in this case, save your file in the usual manner; do not use the option "save in MS-DOS format"). Do not submit your original paper as electronic manuscript but hold on to disk until asked for this by the Editor (in case your paper is accepted without revisions). Do submit the accepted version of your paper

as electronic manuscript. Make absolutely sure that the file on the disk and the printout are identical. Please use a new and correctly formatted disk and label this with your name; also specify the software and hardware used as well as the title of the file to be processed. Do not convert the file to plain ASCII. Ensure that the letter 'l' and digit '1', and also the letter 'O' and digit '0' are used properly, and format your article (tabs, indents, etc.) consistently. Characters not available on your word processor (Greek letters mathematical symbols, etc.) should not be left open but indicated by a unique code (e.g. gralpha, alpha, etc., for the Greek letter α). Such codes should be used consistently throughout the entire text; a list of codes used should accompany the electronic manuscript. Do not allow your word processor to introduce word breaks and do not use a justified layout. Please adhere strictly to the general instructions below on style, arrangement and, in particular, the reference style of the *Journal*.

4. Manuscripts should be double spaced, with wide margins, and printed on one side of the paper only. All pages should be numbered consequently. Titles and subtitles should be short. References, tables, and legends for the figures should be printed on separate pages.

5. The first page of the manuscript should contain the following information: (i) the title; (ii) the name(s) and institutional affiliation(s) of the author(s); (iii) an abstract of not more than 100 words. A footnote on the same sheet should give the name, address, telephone and fax numbers and e-mail address of the corresponding author.

6. The first page of the manuscript should also contain at least one classification code according to the Classification System for Journal Articles as used by the *Journal of Economic Literature*; in addition, up to five key words should be supplied.

7. Acknowledgements and information on grants received can be given in a first footnote, which should not be included in the consecutive numbering of footnotes.

8. Footnotes should be kept to a minimum and numbered consecutively throughout the text with superscript Arabic numerals.

9. Displayed formulae should be numbered consecutively throughout the manuscript as (1), (2), etc. against the right-hand margin of the page. In cases where the derivation of formulae has been abbreviated, it is of great help to the referees if the full derivation can be presented on a separate sheet (not to be published).

10. References to publications should be as follows: 'Smith (1992) reported that...' or 'This problem has been studied previously (e.g., Smith et al., 1969)'. The author should make sure that there is a strict one-to-one correspondence between the names and years in the text and those on the list. The list of references should appear at the end of the main text (after any appendices, but before tables and legends for figures). It should be double spaced and listed in alphabetical order by author's name. References should appear as follows:

For monographs
Hawawini, G. and I. Swary, 1990, Mergers and acquisitions in the U.S. banking industry: Evidence from the capital markets (North-Holland, Amsterdam).

908

For contributions to collective works
Brunner, K. and A.H. Meltzer, 1990, Money supply, in: B.M. Friedman and F.H. Hahn, eds., Handbook of monetary economics, Vol. 1 (North-Holland, Amsterdam) 357-396.

For periodicals
Griffiths, W. and G. Judge, 1992, Testing and estimating location vectors when the error covariance matrix is unknown, Journal of Econometrics 54, 121- 138.
Note that journal titles should not be abbreviated.

11. Illustrations will be reproduced photographically from originals supplied by the author; they will not be redrawn by the publisher. Please provide all illustrations in quadruplicate (one high-contrast original and three photocopies). Care should be taken that lettering and symbols are of a comparable size. The illustrations should not be inserted in the text, and should be marked on the back with figure number, title of paper, and author's name. All graphs and diagrams should be referred to as figures, and should be numbered consecutively in the text in Arabic numerals. Illustration for papers submitted as electronic manuscripts should be in traditional form.

12. Tables should be numbered consecutively in the text in Arabic numerals and printed on separate sheets.

Any manuscript which does not conform to the above instructions may be returned for the necessary revision before publication.

13. Page proofs will be sent to the corresponding author. Proofs should be corrected carefully; the responsibility for detecting errors lies with the author. Corrections should be restricted to instances in which the proof is at variance with the manuscript. Extensive alterations will be charged. Fifty reprints of each paper are supplied free of charge to the corresponding author; additional reprints are available at cost if they are ordered when the proof is returned.

Journal of Pension Planning and Compliance

ADDRESS FOR SUBMISSION:

Bruce J. McNeil, Editor-in-Chief
Journal of Pension Planning and
    Compliance
Dorsey & Whitney, LLP
50 South Sixth Street, Suite 1500
Minneapolis, MN 55402-1498
USA
Phone: 612-340-5640
Fax: 612-340-2777
E-Mail: mcneil.bruce@dorseylaw.com
Web:
Address May Change:

PUBLICATION GUIDELINES:

Manuscript Length: 21-25
Copies Required: Two
Computer Submission: Yes
Format: MS Word
Fees to Review: 0.00 US$

Manuscript Style:
    See Manuscript Guidelines

CIRCULATION DATA:

Reader: Business Persons
Frequency of Issue: Quarterly
Copies per Issue: 1,001 - 2,000
Sponsor/Publisher: Aspen Publishers, Inc.
Subscribe Price: 265.00 US$

REVIEW INFORMATION:

Type of Review: Editorial Review
No. of External Reviewers: 2
No. of In House Reviewers: No Reply
Acceptance Rate: 60%
Time to Review: 1 Month or Less
Reviewers Comments: Yes
Invited Articles: No Reply
Fees to Publish: 0.00 US$

MANUSCRIPT TOPICS:

Auditing; Employee Benefits; Government & Non-Profit Accounting; Insurance; Portfolio & Security Analysis; Tax Issues Related to Employee Benefits

MANUSCRIPT GUIDELINES/COMMENTS:

Publication Policies for Authors

Journal of Pension Planning & Compliance is devoted to providing practical information and ideas on matters of importance to professionals who deal with tax legal and business planning aspects of pensions and related benefits in their practices. The Journal encourages contributions from lawyers accountants, benefits administrators the academic community and others interested in the field of pension planning and compliance.

Journal of Pension Planning & Compliance emphasizes quality and clarity of exposition. Reviewers consider the following criteria in assessing submissions: value of thee information to the Journal's audience substantive contribution to thee broadly defined field of pensions planning and compliance an overall quality of manuscripts The decision to publish a given manuscript is made by the Editor-in-Chief relying on the recommendations of the reviewers.

Submission of a manuscript clearly implies commitment to publish in the *Journal*. Papers previously published or under review by other journals are unacceptable articles adapted from book-length works-in-progress will be considered under acceptable copyright arrangements.

Manuscript Specifications
Manuscripts submitted for publication should not exceed 40 typewritten papers; the publisher encourages submission of shorter papers. All textual material—including notes and references—must be double-spaced in a full-size, non-proportional typeface (e.g., 12-pt. Courier), on one side only of 8½" x 11" good-quality paper, with 1½" margins all around. All pages must be numbered. Notes and references must be placed separately, double-spaced, as endnotes; footnote format is unacceptable. Improperly prepared manuscripts will be returned for re-preparation.

Within the article, use short subheadings for organization and emphasis. Include a cover sheet with the author's address and affiliations, mailing address, and phone and fax numbers. To ensure anonymity in the review process, the first page of the text should show only the title of the submission.

Artwork, including tables, charts, and graphs, must be of camera-ready quality. Each should be on a separate page placed at the end of the text, with proper placement indicated within text (e.g., "Insert Table 2 here").

Three high-quality copies of the manuscript should be submitted to the Editor-in-Chief. Include an abstract of 125 to 150 words and a biographical statement of 50 words or less.

Acceptance
Once an article has been formally accepted, the author must submit the article to the publisher in two formats: three high-quality manuscript copies and a WordPerfect or ASCII computer file, on 3½" floppy diskette, labeled with file type, name of software version, article title, and author's name.

Copyright is retained by the publisher, and articles are subject to editorial revision. There is no payment for articles; authors receive ten copies of the issue in which the article is published. Manuscripts not accepted for publication are not returned. Authors should keep a copy of any submission for their files.

Manuscript submissions and inquiries should be directed to Editor-in-Chief.

For business and production matters contact *Journal of Pension Planning & Compliance*, Panel Publishers, 36 West 44th Street, New York, NY 10036 USA, 212-790-2041.

Journal of Pharmaceutical Finance, Economics & Policy

ADDRESS FOR SUBMISSION:

Albert I. Wertheimer, Editor
Journal of Pharmaceutical Finance,
    Economics & Policy
Temple University
School of Pharmacy/Center for
  Pharmaceutical Health Services Resch.
3307 N Broad Street
Philadephia, PA 19140
USA
Phone: 215-707-1291
Fax: 215-707-8188
E-Mail: albert.wertheimer@temple.edu
Web: www.haworthpressinc.com
Address May Change:

PUBLICATION GUIDELINES:

Manuscript Length: 11-15
Copies Required: Three
Computer Submission: Yes
Format: Open
Fees to Review: 0.00 US$

Manuscript Style:
    See Manuscript Guidelines

CIRCULATION DATA:

Reader: Business Persons
Frequency of Issue: Quarterly
Copies per Issue: Less than 1,000
Sponsor/Publisher: Profit Oriented Group
Subscribe Price: 60.00 US$ Individual
      120.00 US$ Institution
      365.00 US$ Agency / Library

REVIEW INFORMATION:

Type of Review: Blind Review
No. of External Reviewers: 2
No. of In House Reviewers: 1
Acceptance Rate: 50%
Time to Review: 6 Weeks or Less
Reviewers Comments: Yes
Invited Articles: 6-10%
Fees to Publish: 0.00 US$

MANUSCRIPT TOPICS:
Drug Finance; Drug Policy; Econometrics; Health Economics; Pharmaco Economics

MANUSCRIPT GUIDELINES/COMMENTS:

About the Journal
Beginning in 2003, the *Journal of Research in Pharmaceutical Economics* and the *Journal of Managed Pharmaceutical Care* merge to become the *Journal of Pharmaceutical Finance, Economics & Policy*, a unique new forum where top researchers in pharmaco-economics, finance, and public policy come together to share their research findings with their colleagues.

The *Journal of Pharmaceutical Finance, Economics & Policy* will bring you original articles, research reports, and reviews of the current literature on:
- Pharmaco-economics
- Outcomes research
- Patient satisfaction

- Quality-of-life issues
- Policy analysis
- Financing
- Pricing
- And more!

The peer-reviewed, refereed Journal of Pharmaceutical Finance, Economics & Policy is co-edited by the men who led the previous publications. Mickey C. Smith, PhD, is Director of the Center for Pharmaceutical Marketing and Management at the University of Mississippi School of Pharmacy and Albert I. Wertheimer, PhD, is Director of the Center for Pharmaceutical Health Services Research at the Temple University School of Pharmacy. The editors recognize that the importance of these three fields grows by the day and are dedicated to publishing the most reliable, up-to-date information possible.

INSTRUCTIONS FOR AUTHORS

1. **Original Articles Only**. Submission of a manuscript to this Journal represents a certification on the part of the author(s) that it is an original work, and that neither this manuscript nor a version of it has been published elsewhere nor is being considered for publication elsewhere.

2. **Manuscript Length**. Each journal has different manuscript length. To obtain manuscript length submission information, please search our special manuscript submissions form.

3. **Manuscript Style**. Each journal has different manuscript style. To obtain manuscript style submission information, please search our special manuscript submissions form.

If an author wishes to submit a paper that has been already prepared in another style, he or she may do so. However, if the paper is accepted (with or without reviewer's alterations), the author is fully responsible for retyping the manuscript in the correct style as indicated above. Neither the Editor nor the Publisher is responsible for re-preparing manuscript copy to adhere to the Journal's style.

4. **Manuscript Preparation**
Margins. Leave at least a 1" margin on all four sides.
Paper. Use clean, white 8½" x 11" bond paper.
Number of Copies. 4 (the original plus three photocopies)

Cover Page. **Important**—Staple a cover page to the manuscript, indicating only the article title (this is used for anonymous refereeing).

Second "Title Page". Enclose a regular title page but do not staple it to the manuscript. Include the title again, plus:
- Full authorship
- An ABSTRACT of about 100 words. (Below the abstract provide 3–10 key words for index purposes).

- A header or footer on each page with abbreviated title and pg number of total (e.g., pg 2 of 7)
- An introductory footnote with authors' academic degrees, professional titles, affiliations, mailing and e-mail addresses, and any desired acknowledgment of research support or other credit.

5. **Return Envelopes**. When you submit your four manuscript copies, also include:
- A 9" x 12" envelope, self-addressed and stamped (with sufficient postage to ensure return of your manuscript);
- A regular envelope, stamped and self-addressed. This is for the Editor to send you an "acknowledgement of receipt" letter.

6. **Spelling, Grammar, and Punctuation**. You are responsible for preparing manuscript copy which is clearly written in acceptable, scholarly English and which contains no errors of spelling, grammar, or punctuation. Neither the Editor nor the Publisher is responsible for correcting errors of spelling and grammar. The manuscript, after acceptance by the Editor, must be immediately ready for typesetting as it is finally submitted by the author(s).

Check your paper for the following common errors:
- Dangling modifiers
- Misplaced modifiers
- Unclear antecedents
- Incorrect or inconsistent abbreviations

Also, check the accuracy of all arithmetic calculations, statistics, numerical data, text citations, and references.

7. **Inconsistencies Must Be Avoided**. Be sure you are consistent in your use of abbreviations, terminology, and in citing references, from one part of your paper to another.

8. **Preparation of Tables, Figures, and Illustrations**. Any material that is not textual is considered artwork. This includes tables, figures, diagrams, charts, graphs, illustrations, appendices, screen captures, and photos. Tables and figures (including legend, notes, and sources) should be no larger than 4½ x 6½". Type styles should be Helvetica (or Helvetica narrow if necessary) and no smaller than 8 point. We request that computer-generated figures be in black and white and/or shades of gray (preferably no color, for it does not reproduce well). Camera-ready art must contain no grammatical, typographical, or format errors and must reproduce sharply and clearly in the dimensions of the final printed page (4½ x 6½"). Photos and screen captures must be on disk as a TIF file, or other graphic file format such as JPEG or BMP. For rapid publication we must receive black-and-white glossy or matte positives (white background with black images and/or wording) in addition to files on disk. Tables should be created in the text document file using the software's Table feature.

9. **Submitting Art**. Both a printed hard copy and a disk copy of the art must be provided. We request that each piece of art be sent in its own file, on a disk separate from the disk containing the manuscript text file(s), and be clearly labeled. We reserve the right to (if

necessary) request new art, alter art, or if all else has failed in achieving art that is presentable, delete art. If submitted art cannot be used, the Publisher reserves the right to redo the art and to change the author for a fee of $35.00 per hour for this service. The Haworth Press, Inc. is not responsible for errors incurred in the preparation of new artwork. Camera-ready artwork must be prepared on separate sheets of paper. Always use black ink and professional drawing instruments. On the back of these items, write your article title and the journal title lightly in soft-lead pencil (please do not write on the face of art). In the text file, skip extra lines and indicate where these figures are placed. Photos are considered part of the acceptable manuscript and remain with the Publisher for use in additional printings.

10. **Electronic Media**. Haworth's in-house typesetting unit is able to utilize your final manuscript material as prepared on most personal computers and word processors. This will minimize typographical errors and decrease overall production time. Please send the first draft and final draft copies of your manuscript to the journal Editor in print format for his/her final review and approval. After approval of your final manuscript, please submit the final approved version both on printed format ("hard copy") and floppy diskette. On the outside of the diskette package write:

1. The brand name of your computer or word processor
2. The word processing program and version that you used
3. The title of your article
4. The file name

Note. Disk and hard copy must agree. In case of discrepancies, it is The Haworth Press' policy to follow hard copy. Authors are advised that no revisions of the manuscript can be made after acceptance by the Editor for publication. The benefits of this procedure are many with speed and accuracy being the most obvious. We look forward to working with your electronic submission which will allow us to serve you more efficiently.

11. **Alterations Required by Referees and Reviewers**. Many times a paper is accepted by the Editor contingent upon changes that are mandated by anonymous specialist referees and members of the Editorial Board. If the Editor returns your manuscript for revisions, you are responsible for retyping any sections of the paper to incorporate these revisions (if applicable, revisions should also be put on disk).

12. **Typesetting**. You will not be receiving galley proofs of your article. Editorial revisions, if any, must therefore be made while your article is still in manuscript. The final version of the manuscript will be the version you see published. Typesetter's errors will be corrected by the production staff of The Haworth Press. Authors are expected to submit manuscripts, disks, and art that are free from error.

13. **Reprints**. The senior author will receive two copies of the journal issue and complimentary reprints of his or her article. The junior author will receive two copies of the journal issue. These are sent several weeks after the journal issue is published and in circulation. An order form for the purchase of additional reprints will also be sent to all authors at this time. (Approximately 4–6 weeks is necessary for the preparation of reprints.) Please do not query the Journal's Editor about reprints. All such questions should be sent

directly to The Haworth Press, Inc., Production Department, 37 West Broad Street, West Hazleton, PA 18202. To order additional reprints (minimum: 50 copies), please contact The Haworth Document Delivery Center, 10 Alice Street, Binghamton, NY 13904-1580; 1-800-342-9678 or Fax (607) 722-6362.

14. **Copyright**. Copyright ownership of your manuscript must be transferred officially to The Haworth Press, Inc. before we can begin the peer-review process. The Editor's letter acknowledging receipt of the manuscript will be accompanied by a form fully explaining this. All authors must sign the form and return the original to the Editor as soon as possible. Failure to return the copyright form in a timely fashion will result in a delay in review and subsequent publication.

Journal of Policy Analysis and Management

ADDRESS FOR SUBMISSION:

Peter Reuter, Editor
Journal of Policy Analysis and Management
University of Maryland
School of Public Affairs
2101 Van Munching Hall
College Park, MD 20742
USA
Phone: 301-405-6367
Fax: 301-403-4675
E-Mail: preuter@umd.edu
Web: www3.interscience.wiley.com/
Address May Change:

PUBLICATION GUIDELINES:

Manuscript Length: 20+
Copies Required: Three
Computer Submission: Yes - Required
Format: N/A
Fees to Review: 0.00 US$

Manuscript Style:
    See Manuscript Guidelines

CIRCULATION DATA:

Reader: Academics
Frequency of Issue: Quarterly
Copies per Issue: 3,001 - 4,000
Sponsor/Publisher: University of Maryland,
    School of Public Affairs/Wiley
    InterScience
Subscribe Price: 350.00 US$ Indv-N Amer
    799.00 US$ Institution-USA
    823.00 US$ Inst-ROW;
    $839Canada/Mexico

REVIEW INFORMATION:

Type of Review: Blind Review
No. of External Reviewers: 2-4
No. of In House Reviewers: 1
Acceptance Rate: 11-20%
Time to Review: 3-6 Months
Reviewers Comments: Yes
Invited Articles: 0-5%
Fees to Publish: 0.00 US$

MANUSCRIPT TOPICS:
Public Policy Economics

MANUSCRIPT GUIDELINES/COMMENTS:

JPAM welcomes unsolicited manuscripts from all sources. Potential contributors should prepare manuscripts with an awareness of the substantive goals and presentational styles of the following sections.

Feature Articles
JPAM strives for quality, relevance, and originality. The editors give priority to articles that relate their conclusions broadly to a number of substantive fields of public policy or that deal with issues of professional practice in policy analysis and public management. Although an interdisciplinary perspective is usually most appropriate, articles that employ the tools of a single discipline are welcome if they have substantive relevance and if they are written for a general rather than disciplinary audience. The editors welcome proposals for articles that review the state of knowledge in particular policy areas.

Insights

The editors seek short articles of no more than 2,000 words that present novel policy ideas, challenge common wisdom, report surprising research findings, draw lessons from experience, or illustrate the application of an analytical or managerial method. Each article should develop a single idea with clarity and precision. Wit and verve, and occasionally irreverence, are welcome.

Curriculum and Case Notes

The editors believe that *JPAM* should play a role in improving professional education in policy analysis and public management and therefore welcome short articles that deal with broad issues of curriculum or specific aspects of pedagogy. The latter includes descriptions of particularly valuable exercises and cases.

Notes on Style

The editors hope to preserve each author's distinctive style of presentation in the final edited version of any piece. Bear in mind, however, that *JPAM*'s fundamental purpose is to promote more effective communication among those interested in policy analysis and public management.

The substantive interests of our readers are wide ranging. We encourage you to develop and apply your ideas in a way that will interest the greatest number of readers. Try to avoid the shorthand and jargon understood exclusively by specialists operating in narrow fields.

1. **Manuscripts**. Send all manuscripts and correspondence on editorial the editor. Submissions to Insights and Curriculum and Case Notes should be sent to the respective section editors. Send any other correspondence to the publisher.
- Submit manuscripts in triplicate, double- or triple-spaced on standard 8½ x 11 inch paper, printed on one side only.
- Leave generous margins and avoid small typefaces, faded ribbons, and faulty copy machines.
- Cover sheet should contain the manuscript title and author(s)' name(s). Include affiliation, address, and telephone number of corresponding author on the cover sheet.
- Include on cover sheet a short bio line giving your name, title, and affiliation.
- Second page should include the manuscript title and abstract. To comply with *JPAM*'s "double blind" policy for author/referee anonymity, the second page should not contain the author(s) name(s) or affiliation. The abstract should be about 125 words summarizing the content of the article.

2. **Tables**. Be parsimonious in the use and design of tables. Provide only data relevant to the textual argument. Create headings that communicate the argument under discussion. Avoid designing tables so wide that they must be printed at right angles to the normal reading position. Tables must be numbered and titled.

3. **Figures**. Rough drawings of figures are acceptable upon submission. All illustrations and figures in accepted manuscripts must be provided to us camera-ready.

4. **Headings**. Try to avoid more than three levels of heading. Type major headings in bold or all capitals at the left margin (rather than centered). Type important subheadings with initial capitals, also at the left margin. Underline and indent minor subheadings to begin a paragraph. Do not use numbers or letters to identify sections.

5. **Footnotes**. A substantive idea that seems worth presenting in a footnote is usually worth presenting in the text. When inclusion in the text proves difficult, that indicates a strong argument for dropping the point. If you decide that you must include certain ideas as notes, number them consecutively and place them at the bottom of the page.

6. **References**. Include at the end of your manuscript a complete list of references in the following format:

Borrus, Michael (in press), "The Regional Architecture of Global Electronics: Trajectories, Linkages and Access in Technology," in Peter Gourevitch and Paolo Guerrieri (eds.), New Challenges to International Cooperation: Adjustment of Firms, Policies, and Organizations to Global Competition (La Jolla, CA: University of California at San Diego).

Feuer, Michael and Henry Glick (1987), "Is Firm-Sponsored Education Viable?" Journal of Economic Behavior and Organization 8, pp. 121-136.

Mullis, I., J. Dossey, M. Foertsch, L. Jones, and C. Gentile (1991), Trends in Academic Progress (Washington, DC: U.S. Department of Education).

Arrange the list in alphabetical order by author; for more than one publication by an author (or coauthors), arrange by publication date with the earliest publication first.

Citations in the text and in notes should be bracketed and contain author name(s), year of publication, and page number (where quoted or more specific reference):

[Smith, 1949, p. 385].

7. **Bio-Line**. Please include a "bio" line at the end of your text with your name, title, affiliation, e.g., Janet Rothenberg Pack, Professor of Public Policy and Management, The Wharton School, University of Pennsylvania; Victoria Heid, Budget Analyst, Fiscal Research Division, Maryland General Assembly.

Copyright Information

Since a new U.S. copyright law became effective January 1978, the transfer of copyright from author to publisher, heretofore implicit in the submission of a manuscript, must now be explicitly transferred to enable the publisher to assure maximum dissemination of the author's work. A copy of the agreement, executed and signed by the author, is required with each manuscript submission. (If the article is a "work made for hire," the agreement must be signed by the employer.) Copies of the form to be used appear in the first and last issues of each volume and are also available from the editor. No manuscript can be considered accepted until a signed copyright transfer agreement has been received. It is the author's responsibility to obtain written permission to reproduce material that has appeared in another publication.

Journal of Political Economy

ADDRESS FOR SUBMISSION:

The Editors
Journal of Political Economy
University of Chicago
1126 East 59th Street
Chicago, IL 60637
USA
Phone: 773-702-8241
Fax: 773-702-8490
E-Mail: jpe-office@uchicago.edu
Web: www.journals.uchicago.edu/JPE/
Address May Change:

PUBLICATION GUIDELINES:

Manuscript Length: Any
Copies Required: Three
Computer Submission: No
Format: N/A
Fees to Review: 50.00 US$

Manuscript Style:
    Chicago Manual of Style

CIRCULATION DATA:

Reader: Academics
Frequency of Issue: Bi-Monthly
Copies per Issue: 5,001 - 10,000
Sponsor/Publisher: University of Chicago
    Press
Subscribe Price: 50.00 US$ Individual
    248.00 US$ Institution
    32.00 US$ Student

REVIEW INFORMATION:

Type of Review: Editorial Review
No. of External Reviewers: 1-2
No. of In House Reviewers: 1
Acceptance Rate: 6-10%
Time to Review: 4 - 6 Months
Reviewers Comments: Yes
Invited Articles: 0-5%
Fees to Publish: 0.00 US$

MANUSCRIPT TOPICS:

Agricultural Economics; Econometrics; Economic History; Industrial Organization;
International Economics & Trade; International Finance; Labor Economics; Law &
Economics; Public Policy Economics; Urban & Rural Economics

MANUSCRIPT GUIDELINES/COMMENTS:

Instructions to Contributors
The following guidelines are not necessary for submission. These are only for accepted
papers.

Note. We publish theoretical and empirical research in virtually every field of economics, but
the research must be of interest to a wide, general audience.

Please prepare one hard copy and two photocopies of the manuscript. Also include a computer
disk prepared according to the following guidelines.

Disk Formats and Word Processing Programs

Journal of Political Economy (*JPE*) is currently equipped to accept double-density or high-density 3½-inch disks prepared with a Macintosh or an IBM-compatible computer. The programs we currently accept are LaTeX, Microsoft Word (all versions), Scientific Word, and WordPerfect (all versions). If you have used something else, please submit the disk anyway. If we are not able to translate the WordPerfect (all versions) file, we will have your paper rekeyed. Please specify which program and version you have used on the disk label.

We use Epic, a program that adds SGML codes that will be used, not only to typeset articles for the print version, but also to post the articles on the Internet.

The Text File Itself

The entire article should be submitted on disk as a single text file. The elements of the manuscript in the text file should be ordered according to the checklist (shown later in these instructions). Tables should be included in the same file on the disk at the end of the text. Figures (if possible) should be included on the disk as a separate file. **Do not** put complicated in-line equations, such as built-up fractions, in the text. They should be displayed.

To facilitate preparing your file for typesetting, please keep it as free of formatting codes as possible: unnecessary line spacing, style codes, font codes, etc. Stick with the default settings of whatever word processing program you are using if you can. Use hard returns only at the ends of paragraphs or between sections of the manuscript. Don't insert them in the middle of a paragraph when you are dissatisfied with the way a line breaks. Use tabs to indent at the beginnings of paragraphs. Do not use automatic numbering for sections or lists. Any numbers must be explicitly typed in.

Please be consistent. If you use two hyphens to stand for a long dash or a superscript letter "0" for a degree sign, do it that way throughout the manuscript. Then if we have to change it we can do it all at once with a search and replace rather than one at a time.

Instructions for Math

To produce display equations—equations that are centered on a separate line—use the Equation Editor included with your program. Single characters in the text (e.g., "time t") may be inserted like other normal text. For individual math symbols, Greek letters, and other special characters for which there is no keyboard shortcut, each version of Word or WordPerfect has an "Insert > Symbol" or "Insert > Character" command, which produces a chart of symbols from which you can choose.

Instructions for Tables

Each table should be typed on a separate page after the article. Each table should be numbered and should be referred to in order in the text. (Appendix tables should be numbered A1, etc.) You must use your program's table editor to create tables. Do not create tables by typing single lines of text followed by a hard return, with spaces or tabs used to align columns. Such tables will have to be rekeyed, causing an increased probability of error in the rekeyed data.

All the content of a table, including column heads and subheads, must be in a single table. Do not break large tables into smaller ones merely to accommodate page breaks. Each row of data must be in a separate row of table cells. Use no vertical lines and a minimum of horizontal lines: a double line at the top, a single line after the column headings, and a single line at the bottom. If the table is divided into panels, place a single line after the panels:

TABLE 1

Year	Regression		
	A	B	C
	Panel A		
1997	.01	.02	.03
1998	.03	.04	.05
	Panel B		
1997	.01	.02	.03
1998	.03	.04	.05

Hard Copy

The hard copy must match the disk copy exactly and must follow the format instructions below. This copy is our backup: If for some reason we can't set your article from the machine-readable file, we will have it rekeyed by a typing service. It also serves as a reference if we need to see how you intend for something to look that isn't self-evident on the disk. Please label any rare or ambiguous special characters on the hard copy because we may not be able to identify them in the text file.

Checklist—Hard Copy

☐ Title page, with affiliation (institutions and research centers, such as NBER, but not departments or positions)
☐ Abstract of less than 100 words (for articles only)
☐ Text double-spaced
☐ Appendices (if applicable)
☐ References
☐ Tables (each separate page)
☐ Figures (camera-ready)

- **All manuscripts must be double-spaced**, including References. Footnotes at the bottom of pages may be single-spaced. Allow right- and left-hand margins of no less than 1 inch each. Use a typeface of no less than 12-point type.
- **First Pages of Manuscript**. The title should be at least 2 inches from the top edge of the page. Allow a 1-inch space and, on a separate line, type the name(s) of the author(s). One inch below this, on a separate line, type the author's affiliation. Coauthors with different affiliations should be on separate lines. Begin the abstract on the second page (abstracts are not needed for comments or miscellanies). The text of the article begins on the third page.
- **References**. The references follow the text (and the appendix if there is one) on a new page. They should be typed in alphabetical order by authors' last names and then by date

of publication. Do not number them. Each runover line should be indented one-half inch. All references listed must be referred to in the text by last name and year. All sources mentioned in the text must be listed in the reference list. Examples of reference style follow.

Journal Article
> Smith, John D. "Economics Today." *Journal of Political Economy* 68 (October 1960): 126-42. BOOK:
> Smith, John D. *Economics Today.* 2 vols. New York: Oxford University Press, 1965.

Unpublished Manuscript
> Smith, John D. "Economics Today." Manuscript. Chicago: University of Chicago, Department of Economics, 1963.

If there are two separate references to different works by the same author published in the same year, alphabetize them by article title, and put *(a)* after the first reference and *(b)* after the second. Refer to them in the text as Smith *(1964a, 1964b)*.

- **Footnotes.** The acknowledgment note should be unnumbered and should precede any numbered notes. Other notes should be numbered in order and should correspond with the numbers in the text. In both places, note numbers should be shown as superscripts.
  Examples
  In the text: ...in that study4
  In the note: 4J.P. Jones claims that...

Notes are not necessary if only to refer to a work cited. In this case, the information should be placed in the text in parentheses. Example: ...in that study (Jones 1956, pp. 8-14). Notes are necessary only for further explanation of something within the text.

- **Figures.** Each figure should be on a separate sheet of paper. All figures must be camera-ready (very neatly and accurately drawn). Use shading only if absolutely necessary, for example, to distinguish bars in a bar graph. All figures should be numbered and referred to in order in the text as figure 1, figure 2, etc. Do not use boxes around figures unless they are integral parts of the axes. Figure legends (titles) should not appear on the actual figure. They should be typed on the final page of the manuscript in order, even if the legend is nothing more than the figure number. If a figure is divided into parts (e.g., fig. *la, Ib.)*, center the label a, b, etc., at the top of each part. Any text explaining what is in the part should go in the legend. Please note that a journal page is 6 x 9 inches and the space for text is 4¼ x 7¼ inches. Very large figures will need to fit those dimensions. They will be photographically reduced, but may become too small. Please take this into consideration when preparing final figures.

- **Miscellaneous.** Any unusual symbols or abbreviations in the text should be identified in the margin in pencil. Vectors or matrices (which will be set in boldface type) should be clearly specified.

Journal of Portfolio Management

ADDRESS FOR SUBMISSION:

Frank J. Fabozzi, Editor
Journal of Portfolio Management
858 Tower View Circle
New Hope, PA 18938
USA
Phone: 215-598-8924
Fax: 215-598-8932
E-Mail: fabozzi321@aol.com
Web:
Address May Change:

PUBLICATION GUIDELINES:

Manuscript Length: 16-20
Copies Required: Three
Computer Submission: Yes
Format: Word, PDF, Excel-Graphic Elmnts
Fees to Review: 0.00 US$

Manuscript Style:
   See Manuscript Guidelines

CIRCULATION DATA:

Reader: Business Persons
Frequency of Issue: Quarterly
Copies per Issue: 3,500-4,000
Sponsor/Publisher: Institutional Investor,
   Inc.
Subscribe Price: 410.00 US$
   205.00 US$ Academics

REVIEW INFORMATION:

Type of Review: Blind Review
No. of External Reviewers: 1
No. of In House Reviewers: 1
Acceptance Rate: 6-10%
Time to Review: 10 Weeks
Reviewers Comments: No
Invited Articles: 0-5%
Fees to Publish: 0.00 US$

MANUSCRIPT TOPICS:
Portfolio & Security Analysis

MANUSCRIPT GUIDELINES/COMMENTS:

We publish this *Journal* so that its subscribers will read the articles that we select. To that end, the editors place strong emphasis on the literary quality of the *Journal*'s contents. We aim for simple sentences and a minimal number of syllables per word.

We agree with Polonius that brevity is the soul of wit. Therefore, we accept manuscripts that exceed twenty double-spaced pages in only the most exceptional circumstances.

The editors have a passionate and well-known abhorrence of passive sentences as well as a long-standing dislike of extensive summaries of the literature. Lively and succinct introductions and carefully crafted summaries are essential. Follow equations with English translations.

Please follow our guidelines in the interests of uniformity and to accelerate both reviewing and editing for publication. We will return to the author for revision any paper, including an accepted paper, that deviates in large part from these style instructions. Meanwhile, the editors reserve the right to make further changes for clarity and consistency.

1. Authors should submit three copies of the manuscript, double-spaced with wide margins, and with pages numbered consecutively. The front page should include the authors' full titles as well as their complete addresses, phone numbers, fax numbers, and e-mail addresses. Authors **must** include an e-mail address or a fax number as well, preferably e-mail. If authors provide neither and want confirmation by mail, they must provide a stamped self-addressed envelope; confirmation of receipt will not be provided otherwise. Please include a copy of the manuscript on a diskette with the authors' names, addresses, and article title securely attached. Please note the type of word processing software used. The disk should be saved in the lowest version of the format possible, while retaining emphasis such as bold or italic. If possible, please include on the disk all tables and graphs as well.

2. References, endnotes, tables, and figures should appear on separate pages at the end of the text. Double-space all textual material.

3. Limit references to works cited in the text and list them in alphabetical order, not numbered. Citations in the text should appear as: "Jones [1983] concludes that..." with page numbers of quotations, as [1983, p. 125].

   References to a book: Jones, Mary. Portfolio Management. Boston: XYZ Publishers, 1983.

   References to a periodical and references with more than one author: Jones, Mary, and John Smith. "Inflation and Strategy." Journal of Portfolio Management, Winter 1983, pp. 32-40.

4. Endnotes should be few and far between as well as brief. Endnotes should contain commas rather than periods between authors' names and titles of works and sources. Use superscript Arabic numbers in the text and on the endnote page.

5. Number and title all tables and figures, using Arabic numerals, with one table or figure to a page. Write out column headings, stubs, and legends, which should be understandable without reference to the text. Graphs must be submitted in camera-ready form, and the graphs and the labels should be as large as possible for maximum clarity during reproduction. We cannot draw charts for you.

6. Center equations, except for short mathematical expressions, on a separate line and number them consecutively with Arabic numerals in parentheses in the right-hand margin. Identify Greek letters in the margin for the typesetter. Authors are responsible for the location of superscripts and subscripts, length of fraction lines, placement of brackets and function signs, and differentiation between the numeral zero and the letter o.

7. The manuscript should include a nontechnical abstract. No references should be included in the abstract.

8. The *Journal of Portfolio Management's* copyright agreement form must be signed prior to publication. Only one author's signature is necessary.

9. Acknowledgment of receipt of a manuscript will be provided by e-mail. If an e-mail address is not provided, confirmation will be by fax. If neither an e-mail address nor a fax number are provided, you will only receive a confirmation if you provide a stamped self-addressed envelope. The review process takes approximately ten weeks.

Journal of Poverty

ADDRESS FOR SUBMISSION:

Keith Kilty/Elizabeth Segal, Co-Editors
Journal of Poverty
PO Box 3613
Columbus, OH 43210-3613
USA
Phone: 614-292-7181
Fax: 614-292-6940
E-Mail: kilty.1@osu.edu
Web: www.journalofpoverty.org
Address May Change:

PUBLICATION GUIDELINES:

Manuscript Length: 5-30 Typed Pages
Copies Required: Five
Computer Submission: No
Format: N/A
Fees to Review: 0.00 US$

Manuscript Style:
    American Psychological Association

CIRCULATION DATA:

Reader: Academics
Frequency of Issue: Quarterly
Copies per Issue: 2,001 - 3,000
Sponsor/Publisher: Haworth Press, Inc.
Subscribe Price: 50.00 US$ Individual
    75.00 US$ Institution
    185.00 US$ Library

REVIEW INFORMATION:

Type of Review: Blind Review
No. of External Reviewers: 3
No. of In House Reviewers: 1
Acceptance Rate: 20%
Time to Review: 2 - 3 Months
Reviewers Comments: Yes
Invited Articles: No Reply
Fees to Publish: 0.00 US$

MANUSCRIPT TOPICS:

Economic History; Fiscal Policy; Macro Economics; Political & Economic Inequalities;
Poverty; Public Policy Economics

MANUSCRIPT GUIDELINES/COMMENTS:

About the Journal

Poverty is more than just the state of being "poor." Millions of Americans suffer financial
hardships and economic disadvantages that leave them socially and politically impoverished
as well. But most journal articles ignore how people are marginalized by poverty and don't
reflect the social, emotional, or broader economic needs of those receiving public assistance.
The *Journal of Poverty* is the first refereed journal to recognize the inequalities in our social,
political, and economic structures, presenting progressing strategies that expand society's
increasingly narrow notions of poverty and inequality.

The *Journal*'s broad understanding of poverty—more inclusive than the traditional view—
keeps the focus on people's need for education, employment, safe and affordable housing,
nutrition, and adequate medical care, and on interventions that range from direct practice to
community organization to social policy analysis. The *Journal*'s articles will increase your
knowledge and awareness of oppressive forces such as racism, sexism, classism, and

homophobia that contribute to the maintenance of poverty and inequality. Contributing authors present effective strategies for change through conceptual analyses involving quantitative and qualitative methods as they address such topics as:

- Welfare policy and reform
- Race and welfare
- Immigrants' rights to welfare
- Welfare-to-work transitions
- Managed healthcare
- Child support agencies
- Class differences
- Disability
- Academic achievement
- Affirmative action
- Domestic violence
- Local food system projects
- Temporary Assistance for Needy Families (TANF)

Visit the *Journal*'s Web site at www.journalofpoverty.org.

INSTRUCTIONS FOR AUTHORS

1. **Original Articles Only**. Submission of a manuscript to this *Journal* represents a certification on the part of the author(s) that it is an original work, and that neither this manuscript nor a version of it has been published elsewhere nor is being considered for publication elsewhere.

2. **Manuscript Length**. Your manuscript may be approximately **5-30** typed pages, double-spaced (including references and abstract). Lengthier manuscripts may be considered, but only at the discretion of the Editor. Sometimes, lengthier manuscripts may be considered if they can be divided up into sections for publication in successive *Journal* issues.

4. **Manuscript Style**. References, citations, and general style of manuscripts for this *Journal* should follow the APA style (as outlined in the latest edition of the *Publication Manual of the American Psychological Association*). References should be double-spaced and placed in alphabetical order.

If an author wishes to submit a paper that has been already prepared in another style, he or she may do so. However, if the paper is accepted (with or without reviewer's alterations), the author is fully responsible for retyping the manuscript in the correct style as indicated above. Neither the Editor nor the Publisher is responsible for re-preparing manuscript copy to adhere to the *Journal*'s style.

4. **Manuscript Preparation**
Margins. leave at least a 1" margin on all four sides.
Paper. Use clean, white 8½" x 11" bond paper.
Number of Copies. 4 (the original plus three photocopies)

Cover Page. **Important**—Staple a cover page to the manuscript, indicating only the article title (this is used for anonymous refereeing).

Second "Title Page". Enclose a regular title page but do not staple it to the manuscript. Include the title again, plus:

- Full authorship
- An ABSTRACT of about 100 words. (Below the abstract provide 3-10 key words for index purposes).
- A header or footer on each page with abbreviated title and pg number of total (e.g., pg 2 of 7)
- An introductory footnote with authors' academic degrees, professional titles, affiliations, mailing and e-mail addresses, and any desired acknowledgment of research support or other credit.

5. **Return Envelopes**. When you submit your four manuscript copies, also include:

- A 9" x 12" envelope, self-addressed and stamped (with sufficient postage to ensure return of your manuscript);
- A regular envelope, stamped and self-addressed. This is for the Editor to send you an "acknowledgement of receipt" letter.

6. **Spelling, Grammar, and Punctuation**. You are responsible for preparing manuscript copy which is clearly written in acceptable, scholarly English and which contains no errors of spelling, grammar, or punctuation. Neither the Editor nor the Publisher is responsible for correcting errors of spelling and grammar. The manuscript, after acceptance by the Editor, must be immediately ready for typesetting as it is finally submitted by the author(s).

Check your paper for the following common errors:

- Dangling modifiers
- Misplaced modifiers
- Unclear antecedents
- Incorrect or inconsistent abbreviations

Also, check the accuracy of all arithmetic calculations, statistics, numerical data, text citations, and references.

7. **Inconsistencies Must Be Avoided**. Be sure you are consistent in your use of abbreviations, terminology, and in citing references, from one part of your paper to another.

8. **Preparation of Tables, Figures, and Illustrations**. Any material that is not textual is considered artwork. This includes tables, figures, diagrams, charts, graphs, illustrations, appendices, screen captures, and photos. Tables and figures (including legend, notes, and sources) should be no larger than 4½ x 6½". Type styles should be Helvetica (or Helvetica narrow if necessary) and no smaller than 8 point. We request that computer-generated figures be in black and white and/or shades of gray (preferably no color, for it does not reproduce well). Camera-ready art must contain no grammatical, typographical, or format errors and must reproduce sharply and clearly in the dimensions of the final printed page (4½ x 6½"). Photos and screen captures must be on disk as a TIF file, or other graphic file format such as

JPEG or BMP. For rapid publication we must receive black-and-white glossy or matte positives (white background with black images and/or wording) in addition to files on disk. Tables should be created in the text document file using the software's Table feature.

9. **Submitting Art**. Both a printed hard copy and a disk copy of the art must be provided. We request that each piece of art be sent in its own file, on a disk separate from the disk containing the manuscript text file(s), and be clearly labeled. We reserve the right to (if necessary) request new art, alter art, or if all else has failed in achieving art that is presentable, delete art. If submitted art cannot be used, the Publisher reserves the right to redo the art and to change the author for a fee of $35.00 per hour for this service. The Haworth Press, Inc. is not responsible for errors incurred in the preparation of new artwork. Camera-ready artwork must be prepared on separate sheets of paper. Always use black ink and professional drawing instruments. On the back of these items, write your article title and the journal title lightly in soft-lead pencil (please do not write on the face of art). In the text file, skip extra lines and indicate where these figures are placed. Photos are considered part of the acceptable manuscript and remain with the Publisher for use in additional printings.

10. **Electronic Media**. Haworth's in-house typesetting unit is able to utilize your final manuscript material as prepared on most personal computers and word processors. This will minimize typographical errors and decrease overall production time. Please send the first draft and final draft copies of your manuscript to the journal Editor in print format for his/her final review and approval. After approval of your final manuscript, please submit the final approved version both on printed format ("hard copy") and floppy diskette. On the outside of the diskette package write:
1. The brand name of your computer or word processor
2. The word processing program and version that you used
3. The title of your article
4. The file name

NOTE. Disk and hard copy must agree. In case of discrepancies, it is The Haworth Press' policy to follow hard copy. Authors are advised that no revisions of the manuscript can be made after acceptance by the Editor for publication. The benefits of this procedure are many with speed and accuracy being the most obvious. We look forward to working with your electronic submission which will allow us to serve you more efficiently.

11. **Alterations Required by Referees and Reviewers**. Many times a paper is accepted by the Editor contingent upon changes that are mandated by anonymous specialist referees and members of the Editorial Board. If the Editor returns your manuscript for revisions, you are responsible for retyping any sections of the paper to incorporate these revisions (if applicable, revisions should also be put on disk).

12. **Typesetting**. You will not be receiving galley proofs of your article. Editorial revisions, if any, must therefore be made while your article is still in manuscript. The final version of the manuscript will be the version you see published. Typesetter's errors will be corrected by the production staff of The Haworth Press. Authors are expected to submit manuscripts, disks, and art that are free from error.

13. **Reprints**. The senior author will receive two copies of the *Journal* issue and complimentary reprints of his or her article. The junior author will receive two copies of the *Journal* issue. These are sent several weeks after the *Journal* issue is published and in circulation. An order form for the purchase of additional reprints will also be sent to all authors at this time. (Approximately 4-6 weeks is necessary for the preparation of reprints.) Please do not query the *Journal*'s Editor about reprints. All such questions should be sent directly to The Haworth Press, Inc., Production Department, 37 West Broad Street, West Hazleton, PA 18202. To order additional reprints (minimum 50 copies), please contact The Haworth Document Delivery Center, 10 Alice Street, Binghamton, NY 13904-1580; 1-800-429-6784 or Fax (607) 722-6362.

14. **Copyright**. Copyright ownership of your manuscript must be transferred officially to The Haworth Press, Inc. before we can begin the peer-review process. The Editor's letter acknowledging receipt of the manuscript will be accompanied by a form fully explaining this. All authors must sign the form and return the original to the Editor as soon as possible. Failure to return the copyright form in a timely fashion will result in a delay in review and subsequent publication.

Journal of Private Enterprise

ADDRESS FOR SUBMISSION:

Gerald Gunderson, Editor
Journal of Private Enterprise
Trinity College
Box 702533
300 Summit Street
Hartford, CT 06106
USA
Phone: 860-297-2395
Fax: 860-987-6261
E-Mail: gerald.gunderson@trincoll.edu
Web: N/A
Address May Change:

PUBLICATION GUIDELINES:

Manuscript Length: 10-12+
Copies Required: Three
Computer Submission: Yes - Preferred
Format: MS Word, WordPerfect
Fees to Review: 45.00 US$ APEE Member
    65.00 US$ Non-Member

Manuscript Style:
    Chicago Manual of Style, Webster's
    Collegiate Dictionary

CIRCULATION DATA:

Reader: Academics
Frequency of Issue: 2 Times/Year
Copies per Issue: Less than 1,000
Sponsor/Publisher: Association of Private
    Enterprise Education
Subscribe Price: 0.00 US$ APE Member
    55.00 US$ Membership

REVIEW INFORMATION:

Type of Review: Blind Review
No. of External Reviewers: 2
No. of In House Reviewers: 1
Acceptance Rate: 21-30%
Time to Review: 2 - 3 Months
Reviewers Comments: Yes Often
Invited Articles: 6-10%
Fees to Publish: 0.00 US$

MANUSCRIPT TOPICS:

Accounting Theory & Practice; Econometrics; Economic Development; Economic History; Fiscal Policy; Industrial Organization; International Economics & Trade; International Finance; Macro Economics; Micro Economics; Monetary Policy; Private Enterprise; Public Policy Economics; Regional Economics

MANUSCRIPT GUIDELINES/COMMENTS:

The Journal of Private Enterprise is published by The Association of Private Enterprise Education (APEE). This journal brings together scholars in such fields as Economics, Management, Entrepreneurship, Marketing, Finance, Ethics, Religion and Education who have done significant research on topics pertaining to systems of private enterprise worldwide. Most of these papers are originally presented at the Annual Conference of The Association of Private Enterprise Education. (Papers may also be submitted if nominated by a member of the editorial board, or by a submission fee of $45 plus the annual APEE membership fee of $55 if not currently a member.) Each presentation at a conference is evaluated by members of the Editorial Board. The Journal publishes only full papers, no abstracts or book reviews. There is also a popular, regular section of the Journal devoted to educational notes; short accounts of innovations in teaching topics in private enterprise of interest to Journal readers. Those interested in particular educational notes should contact the authors directly. The *Journal* is currently published twice annually with additional special issues.

Before publication, articles in the *Journal* must conform to stylistic guidelines based on the current editions of the *Chicago Manual of Style* and *Merriam-Webster's Collegiate Dictionary*. Please cite sources by the author's name and year of publication immediately in the text, for example (Smith, 1996). Only notes which add comments beyond the citation require a separate footnote. Submitting the paper on a 3.5 computer disk which employs a common language such as WordPerfect or Microsoft Word is very much appreciated.

Journal of Private Equity (The)

ADDRESS FOR SUBMISSION:

James E. Schrager, Editor
Journal of Private Equity (The)
Great Lakes Consulting Group
Kokoku Wire Building
1217 South Walnut
South Bend, IN 46619
USA
Phone: 574-287-4500
Fax: 574-234-8207
E-Mail: james.schrager@gsb.uchicago.edu
Web: www.iijpe.com
Address May Change:

PUBLICATION GUIDELINES:

Manuscript Length: 16-25
Copies Required: Two
Computer Submission: Yes
Format: MS Word
Fees to Review: 0.00 US$

Manuscript Style:
   No Reply

CIRCULATION DATA:

Reader: Academics, Business Persons
Frequency of Issue: Quarterly
Copies per Issue: Less than 1,000
Sponsor/Publisher: Institutional Investor,
   Inc.
Subscribe Price: 450.00 US$

REVIEW INFORMATION:

Type of Review: Editorial Review
No. of External Reviewers: 2
No. of In House Reviewers: 0
Acceptance Rate: 21-30%
Time to Review: 2 - 3 Months
Reviewers Comments: Yes
Invited Articles: 0-5%
Fees to Publish: 0.00 US$

MANUSCRIPT TOPICS:

Financial Institutions & Markets; Financial Services; International Finance; Macro
Economics; Portfolio & Security Analysis; Real Estate; Tax Accounting

MANUSCRIPT GUIDELINES/COMMENTS:

Topics

Practical research and analysis for the venture capital and private equity markets. Submissions
on these topics is particularly encouraged:
- Valuation models, exit strategies, performance analysis
- Global opportunities and specific industry prospects
- Regulatory and tax issues
- Management-related concerns such as compensation and incentive structures

Please follow the guidelines below when you prepare a manuscript for submission. The
editors will edit and copyedit articles for clarity and consistency. *Please note that we reserve
the right to return to an author any paper accepted for publication that is not prepared
according to these instructions.*

1. **Article Submission**. Please submit 2 copies double-spaced sized on an 8.5"x11" page with 1.5"-2" margins and numbered pages. Include on the title page the authors' names and titles as they are to appear, including affiliation, mailing address, telephone and fax numbers, and e-mail address. Also submit an electronic file. Text should be formatted in 12 point type. If submitting a pdf file, please prepare with all fonts embedded and, if possible, include an accompanying Word file which would include the running text. We do not support articles submitted in WordPerfect. Please save any WordPerfect files as a text document and please provide separate eps files for any graphic elements. **All manuscripts are expected to be submitted in final form.** We reserve the right to limit any changes following article formatting based upon content, not style.

2. **Abstract**. On the page after the title page, please provide a brief article summary or abstract suitable for the table of contents. Do not begin the paper with a heading such as "introduction." Do not number section or subsection headings.

3. Do not asterisk or footnote any authors' names listed as bylines. Footnoting should only begin in the body of the article.

4. **Exhibits**. Please put tables and graphs on separate individual pages at the end of the paper. Do not integrate them with the text; do not call them table 1 and figure 1. Please call any tabular or graphical material Exhibits, numbered in Arabic numbers consecutively in order of appearance in the text. We reserve the right to return to an author for reformatting any paper accepted for publication that does not conform to this style.

5. **Exhibit Presentation**. Please organize and present tables consistently throughout a paper, because we will print them the way they are presented to us. **Exhibits should be created as grayscale, as opposed to color, since the journal is printed in black and white. Please make sure that all categories in an exhibit can be distinguished from each other.** Align numbers correctly by decimal points; use the same number of decimal points for the same sorts of numbers; center headings, columns, and numbers correctly; use the exact same language in successive appearances; identify any bold-faced or italicized entries in exhibits; and provide any source notes necessary.

6. **Graphs**. Please submit graphs for accepted papers in electronic form. We cannot produce graphs for authors. Graphs will appear the way you submit them. Please be consistent as to fonts, capitalization, and abbreviations in graphs throughout the paper, and label all axes and lines in graphs clearly and absolutely consistently. When pasting graphs into Word, paste as an object, not as a picture, so we will be able to have access to original graph.

7. **Equations**. Please display called-out equations on separate lines, aligned on the exact same indents as the text paragraphs and with no punctuation following. Number equations consecutively throughout the paper in Arabic numbers at the right-hand margin. Clarify in handwriting any operations signs or Greek letters or any notation that may be unclear. Leave space around operations signs like plus and minus everywhere. We reserve the right to return for resubmission any accepted article that prepares equations in any other way. It would be

preferable if manuscripts containing mathematical equations be submitted in Microsoft Word using either Equation Editor or MathType.

8. **Reference Citations**. In the text, please refer to authors and works as: Smith [2000]. Use brackets for the year, not parentheses. The same is true for references within parentheses, such as: "(see also Smith [2000])."

9. **Reference Styles**

Brokerage house internal publications	Askin, D.J., and S.D. Meyer. "Dollar Rolls: A LowCost Financing Technique." Mortgage-Backed Securities Research, Drexel Burnham Lambert, 1986.
Journal articles	Batlin, C.A. "Hedging Mortgage-Backed Securities with Treasury Bond Futures." *Journal of Futures Markets,* 7 (1987), pp. 675-693.
——. "Trading Mortgage-Backed Securities with Treasury Bond Futures." Journal of Futures Markets, 7 (1987), pp. 675-693.	Same author, alphabetized by title, two em-dashes instead of repeating name
Working papers	Boudoukh, J.,M. Richardson, R. Stanton, and R.F. Whitelaw. "Pricing Mortgage-Backed Securities in a Multifactor Interest Rate Environment: A Multivariate Density Estimation Approach." Working Paper, New York University, 1995.
Sections of books	Breeden, D.T., and M.J. Giarla. "Hedging Interest Rate Risk with Futures, Swaps, and Options." In F. Fabozzi, ed., *The Handbook of Mortgage-Backed Securities.* Chicago: Probus Publishing, 1992, 3rd edition, pp. 847-960.
Books	Hull, J., ed. *Options, Futures and Other Derivative Securities.* Englewood Cliffs, NJ: Prentice-Hall, 1993, 2nd edition.

10. **Endnotes**. Please put in endnotes only material that is not essential to the understanding of an article. If it is essential, it belongs in the text. Do not place a footnote by the authors' names. Any biographical information can be indicated in a separate section and will not be footnoted. Authors' bio information appearing in the article will be limited to their titles, current affiliations, and locations. Do not include in endnotes full reference details; these belong in a separate references list; see below. We will delete non-essential endnotes in the interest of minimizing distraction and enhancing clarity. We also reserve the right to return to an author any article accepted for publication that includes endnotes with embedded reference detail and no separate references list in exchange for preparation of a paper with the appropriate endnotes and a separate references list.

11. **References lists**. Please list only those articles cited in a separate alphabetical references list at the end of the paper. Please follow absolutely the style you see in this journal. We reserve the right to return any accepted article for preparation of a references list according to this style.

12. **Electronic Files**. Word documents are preferred for the articles themselves. Excel can be used for the preparation of graphic elements, making sure that they are embedded in the Word document prior to submission. <u>For those working with .tek or LaTeX files</u>: *PDF files of the articles must be submitted*, making sure to embed all fonts when the PDF file is prepared. Please also include a Word file which contains the text of the article.

13. **Copyright Agreement**: Institutional Investor Inc.'s copyright agreement form - giving us non-exclusive rights to publish the material in all media - must be signed prior to publication.

14. Upon acceptance of the article, no further changes are allowed, except with the permission of the editor. If the article has already been forwarded to our production department, any changes must be made on the hard copy of the original submitted manuscript and faxed to them.

Journal of Productivity Analysis

ADDRESS FOR SUBMISSION:

Robin C. Sickles, Editor-in-Chief
Journal of Productivity Analysis
Rice University
Department of Economics
Houston, TX 77005-1892
USA
Phone: +1-713-348-3322
Fax: +1-713-348-5278
E-Mail: rsickles@rice.edu
Web: www.kluwer.com
Address May Change:

PUBLICATION GUIDELINES:

Manuscript Length: 26-30
Copies Required: Four
Computer Submission: Yes - Preferred
Format: PDF
Fees to Review: 0.00 US$

Manuscript Style:
    , Kluwer

CIRCULATION DATA:

Reader: Academics
Frequency of Issue: Bi-Monthly
Copies per Issue: Less than 1,000
Sponsor/Publisher: Kluwer Academic
    Publishers
Subscribe Price: 139.00 US$ Individual
    563.00 US$ Institution

REVIEW INFORMATION:

Type of Review: Editorial Review
No. of External Reviewers: 3
No. of In House Reviewers: 1
Acceptance Rate: 21-30%
Time to Review: 4 - 6 Months
Reviewers Comments: Yes
Invited Articles: 0-5%
Fees to Publish: 0.00 US$

MANUSCRIPT TOPICS:
Cost Accounting; Econometrics; Economic Development; Financial Institutions & Markets;
Financial Services; Industrial Organization; International Economics & Trade; Micro
Economics; Productivity; Public Policy Economics

MANUSCRIPT GUIDELINES/COMMENTS:

Aims & Scope
The *Journal of Productivity Analysis* publishes theoretical and applied research that addresses
issues involving the measurement, explanation, and improvement of productivity. The broad
scope of the journal encompasses productivity-related developments spanning the disciplines
of economics, the management sciences, operations research, and business and public
administration. Topics covered in the journal include, but are not limited to, productivity
theory, organizational design, index number theory, and related foundations of productivity
analysis. The journal also publishes research on computational methods that are employed in
productivity analysis, including econometric and mathematical programming techniques, and
empirical research based on data at all levels of aggregation, ranging from aggregate
macroeconomic data to disaggregate microeconomic data. The empirical research illustrates

938

the application of theory and techniques to the measurement of productivity, and develops implications for the design of managerial strategies and public policy to enhance productivity.

Manuscript Submission
Submissions (manuscript and cover letter) should be sent electronically as PDF files to the Editor-in-Chief.

Papers submitted to the *Journal* will be directed through the review process by the editor-in-chief to one of the editors, who will handle the paper from submission through final recommendation and decision. Contributors are invited to nominate an editor to handle their paper when they submit it to the *Journal*.

Manuscript Preparation
Submitted papers should typically be less than 20 double-spaced typewritten pages, and should in no event exceed 40 pages. Final versions of accepted manuscripts (including notes, references, tables, and legends) should be typed double-spaced on 8½ x 11" (22cm x 29cm) white paper with 1" (2.5cm) margins on all sides. Sections should appear in the following order: title page, abstract, text, notes, references, tables, figure legends, and figures. Comments or replies to previously published articles should also follow this format with the exception of abstracts, which are not required.

Title Page. The title page should include the article title, authors' names and permanent affiliations, and the name, current address, e-mail address and telephone number of the person to whom page proofs and offprints should be sent.

Abstract. The following page should include an abstract of not more than 100 words and a list of two to six keywords.

Text. The text of the article should begin on a new page. The introduction should have no heading or number. Subsequent section headings (including appendices) should be designated by Arabic numerals (1, 2, etc.), and subsection headings should be numbered 1.1, 1.2, etc. Figures, tables, and displayed equations should be numbered consecutively throughout the text (1, 2, etc.). Equation numbers should appear flush left in parentheses and running variables for equations (e.g., $i = 1,..., n$) flush right in parentheses.

Notes. Acknowledgments and related information should appear in a note designated by an asterisk after the last author's name, and subsequent notes should be numbered consecutively and designated by superscripts in the text. All notes should be typed double-spaced beginning on a separate page following the text.

References. References in the text should follow the author-date format (e.g., Brown (1986), Jones (1978a, 1978b), Smith and Johnson (1983)). References should be typed double-spaced beginning on a separate page following the notes, according to the following samples (journal and book titles may be underlined rather than italicized). References with up to three authors should include the names of each author; references with four or more authors should cite the first author and add "et al." It is the responsibility of the authors to verify all references.

Sample References

Becker, Gordon, Morris DeGroot, and Jacob Marschak. (1964). "Measuring Utility by a Single-Response Sequential Method." Behavioral Science 9, 226--232.

Schoemaker, Paul. (1980). Experiments in Decisions Under Risk: The Expected Utility Hypothesis. Boston:Kluwer-Nijhoff Publishing.

Smith, V. Kerry. (1986). A Conceptual Overview of the Foundations of Benefit-Cost Analysis. In Bentkover, Vincent Covello, and Jeryl Mumpower (eds.), Benefits Assessment: The State of the Art. Dordrecht: D.Reidel Publishing Co.

Tables. Tables should be titled and typed double-spaced, each on a separate sheet, following the references. Notes to tables should be designated by superscripted letters (a, b, etc.) within each table and typed double-spaced on the same page as the table. Use descriptive labels rather than computer acronyms, and explain all abbreviations. When tables are typed on oversized paper, please submit both the original and a reduced copy.

Illustration Style
1. Originals for illustrations should be sharp, noise-free, and of good contrast. We regret that we cannot provide drafting or art service.
2. Each figure should be mentioned in the text and numbered consecutively using Arabic numerals. Specify the desired location of each figure in the text. Each figure must have a caption. Proper style for captions, e.g., "Figure 1. Buffer occupancy for various bit rates."
3. Number each table consecutively using Arabic numerals. Please label any material that can be typeset as a table, reserving the term "figure" for material that has been drawn. Specify the desired location of each table in the text. Type a brief title above each table.
4. All lettering should be large enough to permit legible reduction.
5. Suggested figure formats: TIFF, GIF, EPS, PPT, and Postscript. Files should be at least 300 dpi.

Electronic Delivery of Accepted Papers
Important. After your paper has been ACCEPTED, please send the electronic version via one of the methods listed below. Note: in the event of minor discrepancies between the electronic version and hard copy, the electronic file will be used as the final version.

Kluwer accepts a wide range of file formats. For manuscripts: Word, WordPerfect, RTF, TXT, and LaTex. For figures: TIFF, GIF, EPS, PPT, and Postscript. PDF is not an acceptable format.

Via Electronic Mail
1. Please e-mail electronic version to AuthorFiles@wkap.com.
2. Recommended formats for sending large files via e-mail:
   - Compression—.zip or .sit
   - Collecting files—.tar
3. The e-mail message should include the author's last name, the name of the journal to which the paper has been accepted, and the type of file. Our e-mail system can handle a maximum of 20 MB per e-mail. Please send larger files via FTP.

Via Anonymous FTP
ftp: ftp.wkap.com
cd: /incoming/production

Send an e-mail to AuthorFiles@wkap.com to inform Kluwer that your files have been uploaded to this FTP site.

Via Disk
4. Label a disk with the names of the operating system and file types, along with the authors' names, manuscript title, and name of journal to which the paper has been accepted.
5. Mail disk to Kluwer Academic Publishers, Desktop Department, 101 Philip Drive, Assinippi Park, Norwell, MA 02061, USA

Questions about the above procedures can be e-mailed to AuthorSupport@wkap.com.

Proofing
Please be sure to include your e-mail address on your paper. If your paper is accepted, we will provide proofs electronically. Your cooperation is appreciated. The proofread copy should be returned to the Publisher within 72 hours.

Copyright
It is the policy of Kluwer Academic Publishers to own the copyright of all contributions it publishes. To comply with U.S. Copyright Law, authors are required to sign a copyright transfer form before publication. This form returns to authors and their employers' full rights to reuse their material for their own purposes. Authors must submit a signed copy of this form with their manuscript.

Offprints
Each group of authors is entitled to 50 free offprints of their paper. Additional offprints may be ordered through the offprint form provided with the proofs.

Journal of Property Investment & Finance

ADDRESS FOR SUBMISSION:

Nick French, Editor
Journal of Property Investment & Finance
1 Laurel Bank Cottages
Pot Kiln Lane
Frilsham Common, Frilsham
Berkshire, RG18 9XQ
UK
Phone: 44 (0)118-378-6336
Fax: 44 (0)118-378-8172
E-Mail: jpif@nickfrench.org.uk
Web: www.emeraldinsight.com/jpif.htm
Address May Change:

PUBLICATION GUIDELINES:

Manuscript Length: 16-20
Copies Required: Three
Computer Submission: Yes
Format: MS Word, WordPerfect
Fees to Review: 0.00 US$

Manuscript Style:
    Uniform System of Citation (Harvard
    Blue Book)

CIRCULATION DATA:

Reader: Academics, Business Persons
Frequency of Issue: 5 Times/Year
Copies per Issue: No Reply
Sponsor/Publisher: Emerald Group
    Publishing Ltd.
Subscribe Price: 2379.00 US$
    1509.00 Pounds /2409 Euro +VAT
    2819.00 AUS$

REVIEW INFORMATION:

Type of Review: Blind Review
No. of External Reviewers: 2
No. of In House Reviewers: 1
Acceptance Rate: 50%
Time to Review: 2 - 3 Months
Reviewers Comments: Yes
Invited Articles: 11-20%
Fees to Publish: 0.00 US$

MANUSCRIPT TOPICS:
Real Estate

MANUSCRIPT GUIDELINES/COMMENTS:

Unique Attributes
The *Journal of Property Investment & Finance* aims to provide an international forum for the interchange of information and ideas relating to property valuation and investment. Explores the interface between academic research and practical application by disseminating new research findings alongside articles related to everyday professional practice. Papers are published in two sections—Academic Papers and Practice Papers. Academic papers are refereed to the highest academic standard through double-blind refereeing procedures. The practice papers are more pragmatic in their subject approach and are refereed on this basis.

Topicality
Recent changes in the property market have already forced major rethinking within the industry. Practitioners are under great pressure to improve professional education and policing standards, and separate transaction and advisory business, to prevent property advice falling

outside the mandate of chartered surveyors into less well regulated hands. The *Journal* tackles central issues such as this to keep industry practitioners informed on current thinking and developments.

Key Benefits

The *Journal* is published under the guidance of an expert international board and presents fully refereed papers on practice and methodology in the field. It is widely regarded as essential reading for industry practitioners, with its authoritative content and internationally respected contributors.

Key Journal Audiences

Academics and practitioners in all areas of the property industry

Coverage

Fully refereed papers on practice and methodology in the UK, France, Germany, USA and other countries, in the following areas:

- Academic papers on the latest research, thinking and developments
- Computer briefings covering the latest information technology
- Law reports assessing new legislation
- Market data for a comprehensive review of current research
- Practice papers—a forum for the exchange of ideas and experiences

Notes for Contributors

Three copies of the manuscript should be submitted in double line spacing with wide margins. All authors should be shown and author's details must be printed on a separate front sheet and the author should not be identified anywhere else in the article.

The submission must be provided with a disk copy of the same version labelled with: disk format; author name(s); title of article; journal title; file name.

In preparing the disk, please use one of the following formats: Word, WordPerfect, Rich Text Format or TeX/LaTeX. Figures that are provided electronically must be in tif, gif or pic file extensions. All figures and graphics must also be supplied as good quality originals.

Copyright

Articles submitted to the *Journal* should be original contributions and should not be under consideration for any other publication at the same time. Authors submitting articles for publication warrant that the work is not an infringement of any existing copyright and will indemnify the publisher against any breach of such warranty. For ease of dissemination and to ensure proper policing of use, papers and contributions become the legal copyright of the publisher unless otherwise agreed. Submissions should be sent to:

Editorial Objectives

Journal of Property Investment & Finance aims to provide an international forum for the interchange of information and ideas relating to COMMERCIAL property investment and finance.

The *Journal* seeks to:

- Publish well-written, readable articles of intellectual rigour with a theoretical and practical relevance to the real estate profession;
- Address subjects of major interest and practical importance to the real estate profession;
- Improve property appraisal, finance and investment skills by promoting awareness of new theories, applications and related concepts and their implications to market conditions;
- Assist the property professional to keep up-to-date with developments in real estate law, Internet sites and recent publications;
- Provide a cumulative source of reference material.

Editorial Scope

Journal of Property Investment & Finance covers the full range of professional activities relating to property appraisal, investment and finance. This includes micro and macroeconomics issues; appraisal methods; capital market and portfolio theory; property financing issues and all matters which directly or indirectly affect the attractiveness of property as an investment.

Reviewing Process

Each paper submitted is subject to the following review procedure. The editor will review the paper for general suitability for the *Journal*. Subject to the exact reviewing criteria noted below, a double blind review process will be operated.

Emerald Literati Editing Service

The Literati Club can recommend the services of a number of freelance copy editors, all themselves experienced authors, to contributors who wish to improve the standard of English in their paper before submission. This is particularly useful for those whose first language is not English. http://www.emeraldinsight.com/literaticlub/editingservice.htm

Due to the practical nature of articles submitted for inclusion the Practice Briefing; contributions for this section will be considered by a member of the editorial board and one external referee.

The editorial board reserves the right to suspend the above criteria in the case of special issues, any such suspension of refereeing standards being duly noted at the time of publication.

Manuscript Requirements

As a guide, articles should be between 2,000 and 4,000 words in length. A title of not more than eight words should be provided. A brief **autobiographical note** should be supplied including full name, affiliation, e-mail address and full international contact details. Authors must supply an **abstract** of 100-150 words. Up to six **keywords** should be included which encapsulate the principal subjects covered by the article.

Where there is a **methodology**, it should be clearly described under a separate heading. **Headings** must be short, clearly defined and not numbered.

Notes and **endnotes** should be used only if absolutely necessary. They should, however, always be used for citing Web sites. They should be identified in the text by consecutive numbers enclosed in square brackets and listed at the end of the article. Please then provide full Web site addresses in the end list.

Figures, charts and **diagrams** should be kept to a minimum. They must be black and white with minimum shading and numbered consecutively using Arabic numerals with a brief title and labelled axes. In the text, the position of the figure should be shown by typing on a separate line the words "take in Figure 2". Good quality originals must be provided.

Tables should be kept to a minimum. They must be numbered consecutively with roman numerals and a brief title. In the text, the position of the table should be shown by typing on a separate line the words "take in Table IV".

Photos and **illustrations** must be supplied as good quality black and white original half tones with captions. Their position should be shown in the text by typing on a separate line the words "take in Plate 2".

References to other publications should be complete and in Harvard style. They should contain full bibliographical details and *Journal* titles should not be abbreviated. For multiple citations in the same year use a, b, c immediately following the year of publication. References should be shown within the text by giving the author's last name followed by a comma and year of publication all in round brackets, e.g. (Fox, 1994). At the end of the article should be a reference list in alphabetical order as follows:

a) *For Book*
Surname, initials and year of publication, title, publisher, place of publication, e.g. Casson, M. (1979), Alternatives to the Multinational Enterprise, Macmillan, London.

b) *For Chapter in Edited Book*
Surname, initials and year, "title", editor's surname, initials, title, publisher, place, pages, e.g. Bessley, M. and Wilson, P. (1984), "Public policy and small firms in Britain", in Levicki, C. (Ed.), Small Business Theory and Policy, Croom Helm, London, pp. 111-26. Please note that the chapter title must be underlined.

c) *For Article*
Surname, initials, year "title", journal, volume, number, pages, e.g. Fox, S. (1994) "Empowerment as a catalyst for change: an example from the food industry", Supply Chain Management, Vol 2 No 3, pp. 29-33

If there is more than one author list surnames followed by initials. All authors should be shown.

Electronic sources should include the URL of the electronic site at which they may be found, as follows: Neuman, B.C. (1995), "Security, payment, and privacy for network commerce",

IEEE Journal on Selected Areas in Communications, Vol. 13 No.8, October, pp. 1523-31. Available (IEEE SEPTEMBER) http://www.research.att.com/jsac/

Final Submission of the Article

Once accepted for publication, each article must be accompanied by a completed and signed **Journal Article Record Form** available from the Editor.

The manuscript will be considered to be the definitive version of the article. The author must ensure that it is complete, grammatically correct and without spelling or typographical errors.

Final Submission Requirements

Manuscripts must be clean, good quality hard copy and; include an abstract and keywords have Harvard style references include any figures, photos and graphics as good quality originals be accompanied by a labelled disk be accompanied by a completed Journal Article Record Form.

Journal of Property Management

ADDRESS FOR SUBMISSION:

Amanda Druckman, Associate Editor
Journal of Property Management
Institute of Real Estate Management
430 North Michigan Avenue
Chicago, IL 60611-4090
USA
Phone: 312-329-6058
Fax: 312-410-7958
E-Mail: adruckman@irem.org
Web:
Address May Change:

PUBLICATION GUIDELINES:

Manuscript Length: 5-10
Copies Required: One
Computer Submission: Yes
Format: IBM
Fees to Review: 0.00 US$

Manuscript Style:
    Chicago Manual of Style

CIRCULATION DATA:

Reader: , Real Estate Professionals
Frequency of Issue: Bi-Monthly
Copies per Issue: 20,000
Sponsor/Publisher: Institute of Real Estate
    Management
Subscribe Price: 56.95 US$ USA
    65.74 US$ Canada
    100.90 US$ Foreign - Airmail

REVIEW INFORMATION:

Type of Review: Blind Review
No. of External Reviewers: 3
No. of In House Reviewers: 2
Acceptance Rate: 21-30%
Time to Review: 2 - 3 Months
Reviewers Comments: Yes
Invited Articles: 31-50%
Fees to Publish: 0.00 US$

MANUSCRIPT TOPICS:
Real Estate; Tax Accounting

MANUSCRIPT GUIDELINES/COMMENTS:

Focus
1. The *Journal of Property Management (JPM)* is published bi-monthly by the Institute of Real Estate Management (IREM) of the National Association of Realtors. Founded in 1934, IREM is a national professional organization of asset and property managers. Only those who have met the stringent qualifying standards that earn them the Certified Property Manager designation may become members of the association.

The *Journal* provides a forum for sharing ideas and discussing new trends that affect the management of investment real estate. Articles may address the management of apartments, office buildings, shopping and strip centers, mixed-use properties, office/industrial properties, condominiums, and special-purpose real estate.

Contents
2. Each issue of *JPM* includes most or all of the following sections:

- Main Features Section—bylined articles on trends, property types, maintenance, business operations, and case studies of property management and related topics.
- *JPM* Columns—bylined short articles on legal, tax, investment, and insurance issues that directly relate to real estate.
- Other Sections—new products and publications, industry news, legislative news, and coming events.

To help you select a topic, *JPM* publishes an annual editorial calendar for its feature departments and sections. The editorial staff also prepares topic lists for *JPM* Departments and OTB sections. Articles on other real estate-related topics are also welcomed.

Specific examples, actual figures, and other information drawn from your practical experience should be an essential part of your article. However, articles which primarily promote a firm and its officers or a particular property or product are not acceptable.

Please feel free to contact the *JPM* editorial staff at 312-661-1930 to discuss specific article ideas. The staff will also be happy to send you a sample case study article outline or to assist you in preparing an outline for your topic.

Readership
3. *JPM*'s readers are members of the Institute of Real Estate Management and others experienced in property and asset management or related real estate fields. In writing your article, keep in mind that these readers are familiar with the fundamentals of real estate and with basic terms and practices in the industry. However, when in doubt, define your terms.

Article Preparation and Production

Physical Preparation of the Manuscript
4. All articles should be typed, double-spaced on clean, white paper (8½" x 11") with few, if any, handwritten corrections. Also submit a disk. Also include a short biography with company, title, professional background, etc.

Graphics
5. Charts, graphs, diagrams, and color or black-and-white photographs help clarify information and add visual interest to your article. Please enclose any available artwork along with your article. When submitting artwork, keep the following points in mind.

- Photographs should be either glossy prints, 35 mm slides, or color transparencies (preferably duplicates). Preprinted material and Polaroids are not acceptable for reproduction.
- Be certain that all illustrations and photographs are clearly labeled with descriptions and any required credit lines. Do not write directly on the back of photographs; instead attach a separate label to the back or edge.
- Unless specifically requested, artwork will not be returned.

Copyright

6. *JPM* is primarily interested in publishing original articles which have not appeared in other publications. In general, the Institute of Real Estate Management holds the exclusive copyright to all articles published in *JPM*, although special arrangements may be negotiated with specific authors.

If your manuscript has appeared in or been accepted by another publication, send a copy of the printed article and/or letter of acceptance with your submission. The *JPM* staff will secure permission to reprint. If your article has been submitted to other publications, you should note that fact when submitting your article to *JPM*.

Once your article has been published in *JPM*, the article may generally not be reprinted without permission form *JPM*. In almost every case this permission is granted, but a request in writing must be made to the *JPM* staff prior to reprinting.

The Review Process

7. All articles submitted to *JPM* must be reviewed and accepted by members of the *JPM* editorial review board or by the section coordinator prior to acceptance and publication.

Scheduling Publication

8. *JPM* is published bimonthly and operates on a three month lead time. This means that articles must be received a minimum of three months prior to publication. When combined with the length of time needed to review articles, it is not unusual for 6 to 9 months to elapse between the time an article is received in the *JPM* office and the time it is printed in the *Journal*.

Other factors may also influence publication dates, including the existing backlog of articles, the recent publication of an article on a similar topic, or the delaying of an article for publication in an issue pertinent to its topic. When an article is accepted, the *JPM* staff will try to give a realistic date for publication.

Payment

It is not *JPM*'s usual policy to pay an author for manuscripts. However, fees for professional writers are subject to negotiation.

Journal of Property Research

ADDRESS FOR SUBMISSION:

Bryan D. MacGregor, Editor
Journal of Property Research
University of Aberdeen
Business School
Department of Property
Old Aberdeen, Scotland, AB24 3QY
UK
Phone: +44 (0) 1224-272-356
Fax: +44 (0) 1224-272-214
E-Mail: jpr@abdn.ac.uk
Web: www.tandf.co.uk/journals/
Address May Change:

PUBLICATION GUIDELINES:

Manuscript Length: 26-30+
Copies Required: Three
Computer Submission: Yes - or Hard Copy
Format: MS Word
Fees to Review: 0.00 US$

Manuscript Style:
    See Manuscript Guidelines

CIRCULATION DATA:

Reader: Academics
Frequency of Issue: Quarterly
Copies per Issue: Less than 1,000
Sponsor/Publisher: Spon Press / Taylor &
    Francis
Subscribe Price: 193.00 US$ Individual
    627.00 US$ Institution
    117.00 Pounds Indv, 380 Pounds Inst

REVIEW INFORMATION:

Type of Review: Blind Review
No. of External Reviewers: 3
No. of In House Reviewers: 0
Acceptance Rate: 60%
Time to Review: 1 - 2 Months
Reviewers Comments: Yes
Invited Articles: 0-5%
Fees to Publish: 0.00 US$

MANUSCRIPT TOPICS:
Real Estate

MANUSCRIPT GUIDELINES/COMMENTS:

Aims and Scope
Journal of Property Research is an international journal with double-blind refereeing. It publishes papers in all areas of property economics, but particularly investment, finance, development, and occupier markets. Papers may be empirical or theoretical or may address issues of public policy and regulation.

Notes for Contributors
1. Submission
1.1 Authors should submit either by post or by email to the Editor. Postal submissions should be made in triplicate. Email submissions of Word or pdf files should be sent to jpr@abdn.ac.uk.

1.2 The refereeing process is double-blind, and all submitted papers will be referred to at least two reviewers.

2. Manuscript

2.1 Although there is no fixed limit on the length of articles, but concise presentation is encouraged, it would be appreciated if contributors keep their manuscripts within the range of 5,000-10,000 words. The manuscript must be in English, typed in double spacing on one side of A4 paper only, with a 4cm margin on the left-hand side.

2.2 The pages should be numbered consecutively. There should be no loose addenda or notes or other explanatory material. The manuscript should be arranged under numbered headings and subheadings, for example 1, 2, 2.1, 2.2, 2.2.1, etc.

Title Page

2.3 The first page of the manuscript must contain the full title—the name(s), affiliation(s), address(es) of the author(s), a running title of not more than 75 characters and spaces, and five key words for the purpose of indexing. If there is more than one author, the corresponding author should be indicated.

Abstract

2.4 The second page should contain the title and an abstract. It should not contain the name(s) of the author(s). The abstract should not exceed 200 words and must be a clear summary of the contents of the manuscript

Illustrations

2.5 Any illustrations must accompany the manuscript but should not be included in the text. Diagrams, charts, photographs and maps should be referred to as 'Fig. 1', 'Fig. 2', and so on. They should be numbered in the order in which they are referred to in the text.

2.6 Illustrations should be submitted in a form ready for reproduction. They will normally be reduced in size on reproduction, and authors should bear this in mind. Appropriate electronic submission is permissible.

Measurements

2.7 All measurements should be given in metric units.

References

2.8 The Harvard system is used. References in the text should be quoted in the following manner: Smith (1999) or (Brown and Green, 2001) or, if there are more than two authors ...Jones *et al.* (2002). If there is a citation of a page number or numbers, the format should, as appropriate, be Smith (1999, 20), smith (1999, 20-5), (Smith, 1999, 20) or (Smith, 1999, 20-5).

2.9 References should be collected at the end of the paper in alphabetical order by the first author's surname. If references to the same author have the same year, they should be differentiated by using 1998a and 1998b, and so on. The style should follow the examples below:

Chau, K.W., MacGregor, B.D. and Schwann, G. (2001) Price discovery in the Hong Kong real estate market, *Journal of Property Research*, 18(3), 187-216.

Brown, G.R. and Matysiak, G.A. (2000) *Real estate investment—a capital markets approach*, Financial Times Prentice Hall, Harlow.

Barrett, S. (1981) Implementation of public policy, in *Policy and Action* (edited by S. Barrett and C. Fudge), Chapman & Hall, London, pp. 1-33.

If no person is named as the author the body should be used. For example:
Royal Institution of Chartered Surveyors (1994) *Understanding the property cycle*. London.

Notes
2.10 A limited number of explanatory endnotes are permissible. These should be numbered 1, 2, 3, consecutively in the text, and denoted by superscripts.

3. **Proofs**
3.1 Proofs will be sent to the corresponding author for correction. The difficulty and expense involved in making amendments at proof stage make it essential for authors to prepare their manuscripts carefully—any alterations to the original text are strongly discouraged. Our aim is rapid publication; this will be helped if authors provide good copy following the above instructions, and return their proofs as quickly as possible.

4. **Offprints**
4.1 Each corresponding author will receive 25 free offprints and one bound copy of the *Journal*.

5. **Copyright**
5.1 Submission of an article to *Journal of Property Research* is taken to imply that it represents original, unpublished work, not under consideration for publication elsewhere.

5.2 When submitting a manuscript, authors will be asked to transfer the copyright for their articles to the Spon Press, if and when the article is accepted for publication. The copyright covers the exclusive rights to reproduce and distribute the article, including reprints, photographic reproductions, microfilm or any reproduction of a similar nature, and translations.

5.3 Permission to publish illustrations must be obtained by the author before submission and any acknowledgements should be included in the figure captions.

Journal of Public Economic Theory

ADDRESS FOR SUBMISSION:

John P Conley/Myrna H Wooders, Editors
Journal of Public Economic Theory
Vanderbilt University
Editorial Office
Department of Economics
415 Calhoun Hall
Nashville, TN 37235
USA
Phone: 615-322-2920
Fax: 615-343-8495
E-Mail: j.p.conley@vanderbilt.edu
Web: www.blackwellpublishing.com
Address May Change:

PUBLICATION GUIDELINES:

Manuscript Length: 1-30+
Copies Required: Four
Computer Submission: Yes - Preferred
Format: PDF - Preferred
Fees to Review: 0.00 US$

Manuscript Style:
, A Manual for Authors

CIRCULATION DATA:

Reader: Academics
Frequency of Issue: 5 Times/Year
Copies per Issue: Less than 1,000
Sponsor/Publisher: Assn. for Public
 Economic Theory/Blackwell Publishing
Subscribe Price: 34.00 US$ AHA/APS
 Mem
  28.00 US$ Student
  528.00 US$ Inst-Print/Premium Online

REVIEW INFORMATION:

Type of Review: Editorial Review
No. of External Reviewers: 2
No. of In House Reviewers: 1
Acceptance Rate: 21-30%
Time to Review: 2 - 6 Months
Reviewers Comments: Yes
Invited Articles: 11-20%
Fees to Publish: 0.00 US$

MANUSCRIPT TOPICS:

Fiscal Policy; Micro Economics; Public Economics; Public Policy Economics; Regional Economics

MANUSCRIPT GUIDELINES/COMMENTS:

The *Journal of Public Economic Theory* (*JPET*) publishes theoretical papers in all areas of public economics. *JPET* will consider survey articles notes, comments, exposita, and retrospectives as well as original research papers. In the interest of speeding the editorial process we strongly encourage electronic submissions. Please attach your cover letter along with your manuscript, both in PDF format, and send to j.p.conley@vanderbilt.edu. Alternatively, you may send four copies of your manuscript to the editorial office, *Journal of Public Economic Theory*.

The *Journal of Public Economic Theory* will consider only original papers for publication. Submission of a manuscript is taken to imply that to the best of the author's knowledge, the manuscript is not under consideration for publication elsewhere, that the same work has not been already been published, and that all of the authors as well as the institutions at which the work was carried out approve of its submission. While the manuscript is under editorial review, it is the responsibility of the authors to keep the Editors informed about submissions, publication plans, and publication of related research (or abstracts thereof) in other outlets, including letters journals, journals in other disciplines, collections of articles, and published dissertations. It is understood that submission of the paper for publication has been approved by all of the authors and by the institution where the work was carried out.

Articles and any other materials published in the *Journal of Public Economic Theory* represent the opinions of the author(s) and should not be construed to reflect the opinion of the Editorial Board or the Publisher of the *Journal*.

Authors submitting a manuscript do so on the understanding that if it is accepted for publication, copyright in the article, including the right to reproduce the article in all forms and media shall be assigned exclusively to the Publisher. The Publisher will not refuse any reasonable request by the author for permission to reproduce any of his or her contributions to the *Journal*.

First Submissions
Manuscripts must be in English and the main text should be double-spaced and printed on only one side. Footnotes and references may be single-spaced. For a first submission via hardcopy, any reasonable typed or computer-printed format meeting these requirements is acceptable. For electronic submission, the *Journal* requires that manuscripts be converted to PDF format.

General Formatting Conventions
Style. In general, authors should be guided by *A Manual for Authors* published in 1962 (and revised in 1980) by the American Mathematical Society, P.O. Box 6248, Providence, RI 02904.

Equations. All equations should be typewritten and the numbers for displayed equations should be placed in parentheses at the right margin. References to equations should use the form "(3)".

Footnotes. Footnotes should be used sparingly and should be identified by superscripted Arabic numerals in order of their appearance.

Figures. Figures should be numbered consecutively with Arabic numerals. Type sizes below 4 points should not be used. While there are exceptions, generally titles will be incorporated into the caption and will appear outside and below the illustration. Currently, *JPET* provides an image area of 5 1/8 inches horizontally by 7 3/4 inches vertically. All of an illustration, including the caption, must fit within that area. However, space is at a premium and in many cases half-page size may be appropriate.

Tables. Number tables consecutively with Roman numerals in order of appearance in the text. Each table should be typed double-spaced on a separate page. A short descriptive caption should be typed directly above each table.

954

References. Cite references in the text by author's surname and date of publication. The text citations can be given in the form "Tiebout (1956) claims that…"or "This casts doubt on the existence of equilibrium (see also Aivazian *et al.* 1987, and Harrison and McKee 1980)." References should be listed in alphabetical order and in descending order of date. Type the references double-spaced throughout. Style and punctuate references according to the following examples.

Arrow, K. (1970) "The Organization of Economic Activity: Issues Pertinent to the Choice of Market Versus Non-market Allocations" in *Public Expenditure and Policy Analysis* by R.H. Havenman and J. Margolis, Eds., Markham: Chicago, 67-81

Benabou, Roland (1994) "Education, Income Distribution, and Growth: The Local Connection" NBER working paper number 4798

Berglas, E. (1976) "Distribution of tastes and skills and the provision of local public goods" *Journal of Public Economics* 6, 409-423.

Cartwright, E. (2000) "Firm formation, the theory of equalizing differences and payoff monotonicity," University of Warwick, Department of Economics MSc Dissertation.

Mas-Colell, A and J. Silvestre (1991) "A Note on Cost-Share Equilibrium and Owner-Consumers" *Journal of Economic Theory* **54**, 204-14.

Edgeworth, F.Y. (1881) *Mathematical Psychics*, Kegan Paul: London.

Citations of Unpublished Work. Only articles and books that have been published, are in press or have been published and archived in a working paper (discussion paper or preprint) series, and MSc or PhD dissertation should be included in the references. Citation of working papers should include the number of the paper. Other unpublished results or personal communications may be cited in the text either in the body of the paper or as footnotes. The corresponding author should have the permission of the author of such unpublished work to before such citations are made. Any person cited as a source of personal communications has approved such citation. Written authorization may be required at the Editor's discretion.

Accepted Manuscripts
On acceptance, a final copy of the manuscript should be submitted that conforms to the following guidelines. The manuscript should be double-spaced and printed on only one side of letter size or A4 white paper. Pages should be numbered consecutively. Page 1 should contain the article, title, author(s) name(s) and complete affiliation(s), (name of institution, city, state, country and postal code, and email address, if available). At the bottom of page 1 place any footnotes to the title (indicated by superscript *, or other non-alphanumeric character). Page 2 should contain a proposed running head (abbreviated form of the title) of less than 40 characters including letters and spaces, the name and mailing address of the author to whom proofs should be sent, and an abstract of no more than 100 words. The abstract will appear at the beginning of the article in the *Journal*; use the abstract format, which is required by the *Journal of Economic Literature*, including the appropriate classification number(s).

Final drafts may be submitted either physically or via email. We strongly prefer electronic submissions. We will need one version in PDF format for the typesetter to use a guide for how you wish your paper to appear in addition to an editable version (for example, Word, or TeX format). This speeds typesetting and reduces errors in rekeying. Please include both files in an email indicating this is a final draft. In you prefer to submit your final draft via hard copy, please include two printed copies and a disk with an editable version as described above.

Graphics

Graphs and photographs may be sent in either camera-ready black and white copy, film negatives, or in digital format. Better printing quality can be achieved for figures that incorporate screen tints by submitting them in a digital format. Illustrations that utilize fine screens (i.e., those with a pattern that is not really noticeable under normal viewing and appear more like an even tone), may not photograph well and should be sent in digital form. Xeroxed copy will not reproduce well at all. Providing EPS or TIFF files for artwork along with hard copy will ensure a quality reproduction of any questionable art originals.

Anyone submitting artwork in a digital format must also have a hardcopy produced locally before submitting the material. Often what is seen on a computer screen is not what is rendered by an image setter. For example, because a monitor has a coarse resolution, the finest line will be visible. But when the illustration is printed on an image setter the line will disappear due to the much higher resolution of that device. These copies should be labeled with the article title and figure number and submitted with the digital copy.

Material may be submitted in graphic formats common to major graphics packages such as CorelDraw, Adobe Illustrator, Freehand, or in more generic formats such as EPS, PICT, or TIFF.

Journal of Quantitative Economics

ADDRESS FOR SUBMISSION:

Dr. D.M. Nachane, Managing Editor
Journal of Quantitative Economics
University of Mumbai
c/o Department of Economics
Vidyanagari
Mumbai, 400 098
India
Phone: 91-22-2840-0919
Fax:
E-Mail: nachame@igidr.ac.in
Web:
Address May Change:

PUBLICATION GUIDELINES:

Manuscript Length: 21-25
Copies Required: Two
Computer Submission: Yes Disk, Email
Format: Word 97
Fees to Review: 0.00 US$

Manuscript Style:
    See Manuscript Guidelines

CIRCULATION DATA:

Reader: Academics, Policy Makers
Frequency of Issue: Bi-Monthly
Copies per Issue: Less than 1,000
Sponsor/Publisher: Indian Econometric
    Society
Subscribe Price: 50.00 US$

REVIEW INFORMATION:

Type of Review: Blind Review
No. of External Reviewers: 1
No. of In House Reviewers: 1
Acceptance Rate: 21-30%
Time to Review: 4 - 6 Months
Reviewers Comments: Yes
Invited Articles: 0-5%
Fees to Publish: 0.00 US$

MANUSCRIPT TOPICS:

Econometrics; Economic Development; Fiscal Policy; International Economics & Trade;
International Finance; Macro Economics; Micro Economics; Monetary Policy

MANUSCRIPT GUIDELINES/COMMENTS:

Manuscripts, editorial communications and books for review should be sent to D.M. Nachane
or M.J. Manohar Rao, Managing Editors, *Journal of Quantitative Economics*, Department of
Economics, University of Mumbai, Vidyanagari, Kalina, Mumbai 400 098, India. Authors
residing outside India may send the manuscripts of papers either to the Managing Editors in
India or to one of the Associate Editors located in their regions, as indicated below.

USA and Canada

Professor David E.A. Giles, Department of Economics, University of Victoria, P.O. Box
    3050, Victoria B.S., Canada V8W 3P5

Professor Amartya Sen, The Master's Lodge, Trinity College, Cambridge CB2, 1TQ, England

Professor T.N. Srinivasan, Department of Economics, Yale University, Box 1987, Yale Station, New Haven, Connecticut 06520 USA

Professor Aman Ullah, Graduate School of Management, University of California at Riverside, Riverside, California 92521, USA

East Asia, Australia and New Zealand
Professor Maxwell King, Department of Econometrics, Monash University, Clayton, Victoria, Australia

The following rules are designed to expedite the processing of papers and to reduce printing costs.

1. Manuscript should be clearly typed, double-spaced with wide left hand margins. Two copies should be submitted.

2. Brevity in the presentation of the material will be appreciated. Authors should ensure that the paper, including graphs, tables, figures, and references, do not exceed 25 printed pages—A4 size in double space.

3. The first page should have the following information in this order:
   a) Title of the paper
   b) Name(s) of author(s)
   c) Institutional affiliations and full addresses
   d) Abstract not exceeding 100 words
   e) A starred footnote on the same page should state acknowledgements, sources of funds, etc., if any

4. All the notes should be typed consecutively and presented at the end of the paper.

5. To avoid delay and to reduce costs, proofreading is arranged by the office of the Managing Editors.

6. Two copies of the *Journal* will be sent to the authors.

Journal of Real Estate Finance and Economics

ADDRESS FOR SUBMISSION:

James B. Kau, Co-Editor
Journal of Real Estate Finance and
    Economics
University of Georgia
Terry College of Business
 & Administration
314 Brooks Hall
Athens, GA 30602
USA
Phone: 706-562-3805 or -4290
Fax: 706-542-4295
E-Mail: ekittle@terry.uga.edu
Web: jrefe.org
Address May Change:

PUBLICATION GUIDELINES:

Manuscript Length: 21-25
Copies Required: Three
Computer Submission: No
Format: N/A
Fees to Review: 0.00 US$ Subscriber
    50.00 US$ Non-Subscriber

Manuscript Style:
    See Manuscript Guidelines

CIRCULATION DATA:

Reader: Academics
Frequency of Issue: Bi-Monthly
Copies per Issue: 1,001 - 2,000
Sponsor/Publisher: Kluwer Academic
    Publishers
Subscribe Price: 264.00 US$ Individual
    782.00 US$ Institution
    60.00 US$ AREUEA

REVIEW INFORMATION:

Type of Review: Blind Review
No. of External Reviewers: 2
No. of In House Reviewers: 0
Acceptance Rate: 11-20%
Time to Review: 1 - 2 Months
Reviewers Comments: Yes
Invited Articles: 11-20%
Fees to Publish: 0.00 US$

MANUSCRIPT TOPICS:

Behavioral Economics; Corporate Finance; Econometrics; Economic Development;
Insurance; Micro Economics; Public Policy Economics; Real Estate; Regional Economics

MANUSCRIPT GUIDELINES/COMMENTS:

Editors
Steven Grenadier, *Stanford University, CA, USA*

James B. Kau, *College of Business Administration, The University of Georgia, USA*

C.F. Sirmans, *Center for Real Estate and Urban Economic Studies, The University of Connecticut, Storrs, USA*

There has been an expansion of theoretical and empirical research on real estate using the paradigms and methodologies of finance and economics. Examples of this research include the working and structure of markets, the role of various institutional arrangements, the attention given mortgages and asset securitization, risk management and valuation, and public policy and regulation. The *Journal of Real Estate Finance and Economics* provides a forum for the publication of this research. The subject areas in which the papers published in the journal include urban economics, housing, regional science and public policy.

Guide for Authors

There is no fixed limit on the length of the articles, though concise presentation is encouraged. All articles will be refereed. The journal welcomes comments dealing with material that has previously appeared in the journal. The journal will also publish longer articles of opinion or speculation and review articles on selected topics; these will normally be by invitation, but interested persons are invited to contact the editors. Manuscripts submitted to the journal must not be under simultaneous consideration by any other journal and should not have been published elsewhere in a substantially similar form. Unsolicited manuscripts are to be charged a submissions fee of US$50 for nonsubscribers; there is no submissions fee payable for current subscribers. Payment of subscription may accompany submissions; in this case, payment of an annual individual subscription should accompany the submitted manuscript. All payments should be remitted payable to the Editor. No part of a paper that has been published in *The Journal of Real Estate Finance and Economics* may be reproduced elsewhere without the written permission of the publisher.

Four copies of each manuscript must be submitted in English and typed double-spaced on 22 x 29 cm (8½ x 11 in) white bond paper. On a separate sheet of paper please include complete contact information for the corresponding author (mailing address, e-mail address, telephone and fax numbers). Please send submission to James B. Kau, Co-Editor.

Electronic Delivery of Accepted Papers

IMPORTANT. Send hard copy (of ACCEPTED paper) via one of the methods listed above. Note, in the event of minor discrepancies between the electronic version and the hard copy, the electronic file will be used as the final version.

Kluwer accepts a wide range of file formats: for manuscripts—Word, WordPerfect, RTF, TXT, and LaTex; for figures—TIFF, GIF, JPEG, EPS, PPT, and PostScript. PDF is not an acceptable format.

Via Electronic Mail

1. Please e-mail ACCEPTED, FINAL papers to: KAPfiles@wkap.com

2. Recommended formats for sending files via e-mail:
   - Binary files—uuencode or binhex
   - Compressing files—compress, pkzip, or gzip
   - Collecting files—tar

3. The e-mail message should include the author's last name, the name of the journal to which the paper has been accepted, and the type of file. Our e-mail system can handle maximum file size of 20 MB. Please FTP larger files.

Via Anonymous FTP
ftp: ftp.wkap.com
cd: /incoming/production

Send e-mail to KAPfiles@wkap.com to inform Kluwer electronic version is at this FTP site.

Via Disk
1. Label a disk with the operating system and word processing program along with the authors' names, manuscript title, and name of journal to which the paper has been accepted.

2. Mail disk to: Kluwer Academic Publishers, Desktop Department, 101 Philip Drive, Assinippi Park, Norwell, MA 02061, USA

Any questions about the above procedures please send e-mail to: dthelp@wkap.com.

Proofing
Please be sure to include your e-mail address on your paper. If your paper is accepted, we will be forwarding your page proofs via e-mail. Your cooperation is appreciated. The proofread copy should be received back by the Publisher within 72 hours.

Copyright
It is the policy of Kluwer Academic Publishers to own the copyright of all contributions it publishes. To comply with the U.S. Copyright Law, authors are required to sign a copyright transfer form before publication. This form returns to authors and their employers full rights to reuse their material for their own purposes. Authors must submit a signed copy of this form with their manuscript.

Offprints
Each group of authors will be entitled to 50 free reprints of their paper.

Journal of Real Estate Literature

ADDRESS FOR SUBMISSION:

Karl L. Guntermann, Editor
Journal of Real Estate Literature
Arizona State University
W.P. Carey School of Business
Department of Supply Chain Management
Box 874706
Temple, AZ 85287
USA
Phone: 480-965-7206
Fax: 480-965-8629
E-Mail: karl.guntermann@asu.edu
Web: www.aresnet.org
Address May Change:

PUBLICATION GUIDELINES:

Manuscript Length: 16-20
Copies Required: Four
Computer Submission: Yes
Format: N/A
Fees to Review: 0.00 US$ Member
    110.00 US$ Non-Member

Manuscript Style:
    See Manuscript Guidelines

CIRCULATION DATA:

Reader: Academics, Business Persons
Frequency of Issue: Quarterly 3 Times/Year
Copies per Issue: Less Than 1,500
Sponsor/Publisher: American Real Estate
   Society
Subscribe Price: 110.00 US$ Academic
   225.00 US$ Professional
   350.00 US$ -$450 Library

REVIEW INFORMATION:

Type of Review: Blind Review
No. of External Reviewers: 2
No. of In House Reviewers: 0
Acceptance Rate: 11-20%
Time to Review: 1 - 2 Months
Reviewers Comments: Yes
Invited Articles: 0-5%
Fees to Publish: 0.00 US$

MANUSCRIPT TOPICS:

Behavioral Economics; Financial Institutions & Markets; International Finance; Portfolio & Security Analysis; Real Estate; Regional Economics; Tax Accounting

MANUSCRIPT GUIDELINES/COMMENTS:

Editor
Karl L. Guntermann, Arizona State University (address above)

Co-Editors
Review Articles—John F. McDonald, (University of Illinois-Chicago
International Articles—Arthur L. Schwartz, Jr., University of South Florida
Current Journals—James E. Larsen, Wright State University
REI Tech—Grant Thrall, University of Florida
Book Reviews—James Frew, Willamette University
Doctoral Dissertations—Randy I Anderson, Baruch College
Working Papers—Jack Harris, Texas A & M University

The *Journal of Real Estate Literature* is a publication of the American Real Estate Society. The purpose of this journal is to provide a source of information to encourage academic research and teaching in the field of real estate. Our scope includes, but goes beyond that of the traditional literature journal listing published research, dissertations, and work in progress.

Correspondence relating to the sections should be sent to the appropriate co-editor. Further information is contained in the introduction to each section and at the Web address.

Journal of Real Estate Research

ADDRESS FOR SUBMISSION:

Ko Wang, Editor
Journal of Real Estate Research
California State University, Fullerton
School of Business
  Administration & Economics
Department of Finance
Fullerton, CA 92834-6848
USA
Phone: 714-278-4363
Fax: 714-278-2161
E-Mail: kwang@fullerton.edu
Web: business.fullerton.edu/journal
Address May Change:

PUBLICATION GUIDELINES:

Manuscript Length: 16-20
Copies Required: Four
Computer Submission: Yes
Format: Word, WordPerfect, PDF, English
Fees to Review: 0.00 US$ ARES Member
  110.00 US$ Non-Members

Manuscript Style:
  See Manuscript Guidelines

CIRCULATION DATA:

Reader: Academics
Frequency of Issue: Quarterly
Copies per Issue: 1,001 - 2,000
Sponsor/Publisher: American Real Estate
  Association
Subscribe Price: 110.00 US$

REVIEW INFORMATION:

Type of Review: Blind Review
No. of External Reviewers: 3
No. of In House Reviewers: 0
Acceptance Rate: 11-20%
Time to Review: 1 - 2 Months
Reviewers Comments: Yes
Invited Articles: 11-20%
Fees to Publish: 0.00 US$

MANUSCRIPT TOPICS:
Real Estate

MANUSCRIPT GUIDELINES/COMMENTS:

Journal Objectives
The *Journal of Real Estate Research* (*JRER*) is an official publication of the American Real Estate Society. *JRER* is committed to publishing the highest quality analytical, empirical and clinical research that are useful to business decision-makers in the fields of real estate development, economics, finance, investment, law, management, marketing, secondary markets and valuation. Theoretical papers that fail to provide testable or policy implications and empirical papers that cannot be replicated are discouraged. The Editorial Board of *JRER* is interested in expanding the frontiers of scholarly real estate research and is willing to work with any potential author who is developing new and exciting ideas.

Review and Publication Policies

The Editor reads each submitted manuscript to decide if the topic and content of the paper fit the objectives of *JRER*. Manuscripts that are appropriate are assigned anonymously by the Editor to one member of the Editorial Board and at least one other reviewer. The Editor makes an editorial decision upon receiving recommendations from the referees.

When a referee decides to reject a manuscript, the referee presents a critique to the Editor who then forwards it to the author. Each detailed critique includes a specific recommendation from the referee indicating whether or not the author should be encouraged to resubmit the manuscript for publication consideration. The Editor makes the final decision regarding re-submissions. Upon receiving a re-submission, the Editor determines whether or not the manuscript should re-enter the reviewing process, be accepted or simply be returned.

The Editor determines the publication dates for accepted manuscripts. As a general rule, the Editor attempts to "balance" the topics covered in any one issue. Consequently, in an effort to balance the coverage of topics, the Editor may choose the articles to be included in a given issue from among those already accepted for publication. This general rule will be set aside should the Board of Directors decide to do so, such as in the case of a special issue devoted to a single topic.

Submission via email is strongly encouraged. Except for the final version, manuscripts can be submitted via email in Word®, PDF® or WordPerfect® file formats to jrer@fullerton.edu. Articles and correspondence can also be directed to the Editor.

If you would like to discuss the editorial policy and research interests of the *JRER*, please feel free to email Ko Wang, Editor of the *Journal*.

Submission Requirements

Authors should submit four hard copies of the manuscript that is double-spaced and paginated. The cover page, which will be removed before the manuscript is sent to a referee, should contain: the title, all authors and their affiliations (mailing addresses), phone and fax numbers, and email addresses. Except for the cover page, all pages should be numbered consecutively. Upon acceptance, authors will have to submit an IBM-compatible disk containing the file of the manuscript and four style-correct copies of the manuscript. The Editor does not accept responsibility for damage or loss of papers submitted.

Submitted manuscripts should be original research, and the names appearing on the article should be that of the individuals who conducted the research. The article should not be under review simultaneously at another journal nor substantially resemble articles that are under review at another journal. Upon acceptance, ARES automatically owns the copyright of the article. The transfer of copyright will ensure the widest possible dissemination of information.

Submission via email is strongly encouraged. Except for the final version, manuscripts can be submitted via email in Word®, PDF® or WordPerfect® file formats to jrer@fullerton.edu. Articles and correspondence can also be directed to the Editor.

STYLE GUIDELINES

Abstracts

An abstract of no more than 100 words, summarizing the research purpose, method and findings, is required.

Headings

Headings should be numbered consecutively as 1, 2, etc. Subheadings should be numbered as 1.1, 1.2, etc. Heading numbers are for editorial purposes only and will be removed before printing. Do not include references to section numbers in the text.

Exhibits

Tables and figures should be numbered consecutively in the text in Arabic numbers and printed on separate pages. Tables and figures should be self-explanatory and labeled clearly (such as Table 1 and Figure 1). Explanatory paragraphs should be offered to fully explain the table or figure so that the reader does not need to refer to the text. Significant digits should be rounded to no more than two or three numbers. All figures need to be sharp, clear and camera-ready.

Mathematical Proofs and Equations

Lengthy mathematical proofs and extensively detailed mathematical tables should be placed in an appendix. Equations should be placed on a separate line, centered and numbered consecutively at the right margin.

Endnotes

Endnotes in the text must be cited consecutively. They should be double-spaced and appear on a separate page. Avoid numerous and lengthy endnotes. Do not use notes if they can be readily included in the text.

References

References must be presented alphabetically by the last name of the author and be double-spaced. References must be dated, and the citations in the text must agree. Only those references cited within the text should be included. The references must fit the following format:

Judge, G.G., W.E. Griffiths, R.C. Hill, H. Lutkepohl and T.C. Lee, *The Theory and Practice of Econometrics*, second edition, New York: John Wiley, 1985.

Kinnard, W.N., Tools and Techniques for Measuring the Effects of Proximity to Radioactive Contamination of Soil on Single-Family Residential Sales Prices, Paper presented at the Appraisal Institute Symposium, 1991.

Mills, E.S., The Value of Urban Land, In H.S. Perloft, (ed.), *The Quality of the Urban Environment*, Baltimore: Johns Hopkins University, 1971.

Shilton, L., W. O'Connor, K. Teall and J.R. Webb, Real Estate Taxation and Commercial Loan Underwriting, *Decision Sciences*, 1992, 23, 1162–73.

Acknowledgment
Authors may include a brief acknowledgment. It should appear after the references.

Keywords
Authors should provide one to six keywords that clearly indicate the subject mater of the paper for indexing.

Page Proofs
Page proofs will be sent to the corresponding author. Proofs should be reviewed carefully. The Editor views the last submitted version as the final copy. No rewrites of any kind are permitted at the page proof stage. Corrections are permitted for errors that occurred as a result of editing or typesetting only. The responsibility for detecting errors lies with the author.

Journal of Regional Analysis and Policy

ADDRESS FOR SUBMISSION:

S. Deller, D. Marcouiller, Co-Editors
Journal of Regional Analysis and Policy
University of Wisconsin-Extension
Center for Community Economic
  Development
610 Langdon Street
Madison, WI 53703-1104
USA
Phone: 608-263-6251
Fax: 608-263-6251
E-Mail: deller@aae.wisc.edu
Web: See Guidelines
Address May Change:

PUBLICATION GUIDELINES:

Manuscript Length: 26-30
Copies Required: Four
Computer Submission: Yes Email
Format: MS Word
Fees to Review: 0.00 US$

Manuscript Style:
  Chicago Manual of Style

CIRCULATION DATA:

Reader: Academics
Frequency of Issue: 2 Times/Year
Copies per Issue: Less than 1,000
Sponsor/Publisher: Mid-Continent Regional
  Science Association
Subscribe Price: 45.00 US$

REVIEW INFORMATION:

Type of Review: Blind Review
No. of External Reviewers: 2
No. of In House Reviewers: 1
Acceptance Rate: 21-30%
Time to Review: 4 - 6 Months
Reviewers Comments: Yes
Invited Articles: 21-30%
Fees to Publish: 0.00 US$

MANUSCRIPT TOPICS:
Economic Development; Fiscal Policy; Public Policy Economics; Regional Economics

MANUSCRIPT GUIDELINES/COMMENTS:

Editors. Steven Deller, David Marcouiller
Web. http://www.uwex.edu/ces/cced/jrap/frontpage.html

1. **Conditions of Manuscripts**. Manuscripts accepted for publication will be edited and typeset using IBM Microsoft Word 6.0. Articles must be submitted on a 3.5-inch disk in this format (or compatible software).

2. **Citations**. All works cited should be listed alphabetically by author in a numbered list at the end of the manuscript. Data must include the author's full name, title of the work, and (in the case of books) the place of publication, publisher, and date or (*in the case of articles) the periodical, volume number, date, and inclusive pages. Citations in the text should include author and year and should be enclosed in parentheses.

3. **Footnotes**. Footnotes may be used for comments, explanations, and the like. Their length should be minimal.

4. **Illustrations**. Illustrations must be of professional quality and camera ready. Illustrations should be no more than 4.75 x 7.25 inches. All illustrations must have captions.

5. **Mathematics**. Equations should be identified by consecutive Arabic numbers in parentheses on the right.

6. **Tables**. Tables should be numbered consecutively throughout the article. Each table should have a descriptive heading as well as a number.

7. **Number of copies**. Four (4) copies of the manuscript are required.

8. **Pedagogy**. The editors of *The Journal of Regional Analysis & Policy* wish to encourage our readers to submit their suggestions/techniques for improving the teaching and learning environment in courses devoted to regional analysis and policy. Papers submitted may describe new data sources appropriate for class exercises, applied techniques designed to illustrate facets of our discipline, new software utilized in the classroom environment, or, simply, new perspectives on presenting the core concepts of our courses. While not undergoing the usual blind review process, the editors and editorial board will try to maintain a level of utility and clarity as well as a lack of redundancy in publishing submissions. We hope this section of *JRAP* becomes a regular feature for the exchange of pedagogic techniques designed to stimulate nascent scholars in our discipline.

Journal of Regional Science

ADDRESS FOR SUBMISSION:

Marlon Boarnet, Andrew Haughwout-
    Editors
Journal of Regional Science
University of California, Irvine
School of Social Ecology
Dept of Urban and Regional Planning
Irvine, CA 92697-7075
USA
Phone: 949-824-3181
Fax: 949-824-8566
E-Mail: jregsci@uci.edu
Web: www.blackwellpublishing.com
Address May Change:

PUBLICATION GUIDELINES:

Manuscript Length: 20-30
Copies Required: Four
Computer Submission: No
Format: N/A
Fees to Review: 0.00 US$

Manuscript Style:
    Chicago Manual of Style

CIRCULATION DATA:

Reader: Academics
Frequency of Issue: Quarterly
Copies per Issue: 1,001 - 2,000
Sponsor/Publisher: Blackwell Publishing
Subscribe Price:
    See Web Site

REVIEW INFORMATION:

Type of Review: Editorial Review
No. of External Reviewers: 3
No. of In House Reviewers: 1
Acceptance Rate: 21-30%
Time to Review: 2 - 3 Months
Reviewers Comments: Yes
Invited Articles: 0-5%
Fees to Publish: 0.00 US$

MANUSCRIPT TOPICS:
Economic Development; Fiscal Policy; International Economics & Trade; Public Policy
Economics; Real Estate; Regional Economics

MANUSCRIPT GUIDELINES/COMMENTS:

Description
This prestigious *Journal* publishes original articles at the cutting edge of regional science.
Combining theoretical, methodological, and empirical research with a consistent editorial
focus, the *Journal of Regional Science* is one of the most highly cited journals in the field,
bringing to regional and urban analysis the most useful techniques from other disciplines.

Submission
Manuscripts are assumed to be submitted for the exclusive consideration of the *Journal of
Regional Science*. The style of the *Journal* should be followed as closely as possible. Style
guidelines are available upon request.

The *Journal* uses a double-blind review process. Referees are not identified to authors, and authors' names are not known to reviewers. The Editors strive to obtain three reviews of each manuscript submitted.

Manuscript

1. Submit **four** copies of the manuscript. It must be typewritten and double-spaced, and should not exceed 30 pages, including tables and references.

2. Title of paper, name of author, author's position, E-mail address and affiliation should be noted on the **first page** of the manuscript.

3. **Major subsections** should be identified by Arabic numerals and capitalized headings.

4. **Equations** should be clearly separated from the text and numbered (if referred to in the text), in parentheses, at the left-hand side. The numbering should be continuous throughout the paper.

5. **References**. All reference works should be arranged alphabetically by author (or title if there is no author), and grouped at the end of the article as **References**. Reference to a work in the text or in footnotes should be by author's surname and the year of publication of the work cited, in parentheses. General reference to works should appear in the text and not as a footnote. For example: "The papers by Beckmann (1978) and Isard (1958) emphasize this locational aspect." More detailed references to works appear as footnotes. For example, a footnote might read: "See Intriligator (1971, Chap. 5) and Vajda (1961) or any other standard work on linear programming, for specific details of the calculations employed here."

Reference works, listed at the end of the article, should have the following form:
- **Articles**. Surname, First Name and Initial. Year. "Title of Article," Journal, Volume, inclusive pages. For example: Isard, Walter. 1958. "Interregional Linear Programming: An Elementary Presentation and a General Model," *Journal of Regional Science*, 1, 1-59.
- **Books**. Surname, First Name and Initial, Year. Title of Book, City of Publication: Publisher. For example: Hartshorn, Truman A. 1980. Interpreting the City. An Urban Geography. New York: Wiley.

6. **Figures** must be drawn in black ink on white paper, suitable for direct photographic reproduction with reduction if necessary. Titles and other explanatory material for figures should appear on a separate page, not on the figures themselves.

7. **Footnotes** should be listed at the end of the text, on a separate sheet of paper, double-spaced throughout.

8. An **Abstract** of no more than 100 words should be submitted with the manuscript.

Journal of Regulatory Economics

ADDRESS FOR SUBMISSION:

Michael A. Crew, Editor
Journal of Regulatory Economics
Rutgers University
Rutgers Business School
Ctr for Research in Regulated Industries
180 University Avenue
Newark, NJ 0710201897
USA
Phone: 973-353-5049
Fax: 973-353-1348
E-Mail: crri@andromeda.rutgers.edu
Web: www.crri.rutgers.edu
Address May Change:

PUBLICATION GUIDELINES:

Manuscript Length: 26-30
Copies Required: Three
Computer Submission: Yes
Format: See Manuscript Guidelines
Fees to Review: 0.00 US$

Manuscript Style:
    Chicago Manual of Style

CIRCULATION DATA:

Reader: Academics
Frequency of Issue: Bi-Monthly
Copies per Issue: Less than 1,000
Sponsor/Publisher: Kluwer Academic
    Publishers
Subscribe Price: 230.00 US$ Individual
    460.00 US$ Institution

REVIEW INFORMATION:

Type of Review: Editorial Review
No. of External Reviewers: 2
No. of In House Reviewers: 0
Acceptance Rate: 21-30%
Time to Review: 1 - 2 Months
Reviewers Comments: Yes
Invited Articles: 0-5%
Fees to Publish: 56.00 US$ Pg. over 16

MANUSCRIPT TOPICS:
Micro Economics; Public Policy Economics; Regulatory Economics

MANUSCRIPT GUIDELINES/COMMENTS:

AIMS & SCOPE
Recent legislative and policy reforms have changed the nature of regulation. Partial deregulation has created a new dimension to regulatory problems, as the debate is extended to include diversification and new forms of regulation. The introduction of incentive-based rate schedules and ratemaking procedures, the integration of demand-side programs with planning for capital expansion, and other developments, raise a host of theoretical and empirical questions. The *Journal of Regulatory Economics* serves as a highly quality forum for the analysis of regulatory theories and institutions by developing the rigorous foundations of regulation. Both theoretical and applied papers are published, including those describing experimental research. Papers on all aspects of regulation are published, including the traditional problems of natural monopoly, deregulation and new policy instruments, insurance and financial regulation, health and safety regulation, environmental regulation, hazardous and

solid waste regulation, and consumer product regulation. The *Journal of Regulatory Economics* provides researchers, policy makers and institutions with current perspectives on the theory and practice of the economics of regulation. While there are a number of journals and magazines that include the study of regulation, *JRE* is unique in that it fills a gap in the market for a high-quality journal dealing solely with the economics of regulation.

MANUSCRIPT SUBMISSION

JRE is published bimonthly. It offers expedited handling and publication of manuscripts. Every effort is made to provide decisions within two months of receipt of manuscripts. The publication schedule for articles is expedited by the submission of accepted articles on electronic media, which is then forwarded to the Kluwer Academic Publishers for typesetting.

Submissions should be mailed to the Editor. Submissions (three copies) should be typed, double-spaced, and single-sided. An abstract (not to exceed 100 words) should be included at the beginning of the paper. Authors should include an email address for immediate acknowledgment of receipt.

There is no submission fee. For articles that are accepted for publication, there is no page charge for articles which are submitted on electronic media according to the JRE instructions and which do not exceed sixteen typeset pages.

FEES

Charge for Excess Pages. Accepted papers, which are in excess of sixteen typeset pages, will incur a page charge of US$56 per typeset page to the nearest quarter page for all pages over sixteen. (This is approximately US$30 per typed manuscript page for pages in excess of thirty.)

Retyping Fee. Accepted papers not provided on electronic media will incur a retyping fee of US$10 per typeset page to defray partially the cost of retyping.

Math Conversion Fee. Accepted articles containing mathematical text, which is not prepared in an acceptable format will be charged a fee to have the journal staff convert the paper. The amount of the conversion fee is dependent on the amount of additional work required by the journal staff. An estimate for the amount will be given to the author on request. In the case of articles that are not submitted on electronic media, this fee is in addition to the retyping fee.

MANUSCRIPT STYLE

Upon acceptance for publication, please provide, for copy-editing, one double-spaced, single-sided copy of the paper, prepared according to the following "style" instructions.

Upon acceptance for publication, please provide, for copyediting, one double-spaced, single-sided copy of the paper and a diskette, prepared according to the following *Style Instructions*. The increase in the number of submissions and accepted papers has made the production of the *JRE* a major task. In an attempt to achieve to make the task of production more manageable and to achieve speedy publication of articles we have been obliged to revise the *Style Instructions*. It is essential that authors follow precisely the instructions given below.

Failure to do so could delay the publication of the article. The instructions fall into format, style and documentation preparation.

Please provide, for copyediting, one double-spaced, single-sided copy of the paper, prepared according to the following "style" instructions.

Cover Page. Do not include a cover page. Give the paper title, followed by the authors, including each author's name, affiliation and complete mailing address. Any explanations or thanks should be put in an acknowledgment footnote (with asterisk as follows). Delete all extraneous information (e.g., version date, etc.), for example:

Title of article:
Subtitle of Article*

John J. Smith
Affiliation
Mailing Address
your@email.account

Abstract. Begin the paper with the abstract, not to exceed 100 words.

Figures and Tables. Please indicate on the hard copy and electronic copies where you would like the figures and tables placed. All diagrams, figures, and tables that are contained within the document and not sent separately should be made to fit within the page margins. Make sure all figures and tables are titled and numbered (with Arabic numerals) and are referred to as such in the text. Do not capitalize the words "figure" and "table" in references which appear in the text, for example "see figure 1" or "as shown in table 7". If the diagrams are too large to be displayed in Portrait and must be in Landscape then they should be placed at the end of the document or in a separate file to be inserted at time of typesetting.

Suggested figure formats are TIFF, GIF, EPS, PPT and Postscript. Files should be at least 300 dpi.

Originals for illustrations should be sharp, noise-free, and of good contrast. We regret that we cannot provide drafting or art service.

Titles of all diagrams, figures, and tables should be read as follows: the item (table or figure), its numbers, colon, and the title of that item. Examples:

Table 1: Title
Figure 1: Title

Headings. Use Arabic numbering for sections and subsections. Headings for sections will be in CAPS. Subheadings are to be in Title Caps. For example:

2. TRANSPORTATION
2.1. Surface
2.1.1. Truck

Italics and Boldface. You may use the italics and boldface features of a compatible word-processing package.

Hyphenation. Do not hyphenate words at the end of lines.

Underlining. Use italics for emphasis or to indicate titles of published material; do not use underlining in your text.

Equations. Equation numbers should be in parentheses and should follow displayed equations. There is not need to number equations which will not be referred to later in the text (although you may number such equations if you choose). Equations contained within the text that are not done with an equation editor should be *italicized* where applicable.

Footnotes. All notes should appear as footnotes. The footnote numbers in the text should be superscripted. If a footnote occurs after a word, which is followed by punctuation, the number appears after the punctuation (e.g., "as in his earlier paper.[1] It is...").

Quotations. The style for quotes varies according to size and use of quotes (see *Chicago Manual of Style* for more details). A line or two may be quoted within the text, within quotation marks. Anything more than a couple of lines should be a separate indented paragraph. Italics should not be used unless they are used to add emphasis or if they were used in the original text. If italics are used the quotes should be followed by the following statement in parentheses (emphasis added). Punctuation and capitalization of the text should be exactly as the original. All quotes should be properly referenced.

References. In the text all references should be cited as follows (Name, Year, Pages), for example, (Smith 1988, 255--266). Page numbers need only to be cited in the text if the author wishes to direct readers to a particular page(s) of the referenced work. If the name of the author has already been mentioned, the date, and the page numbers if applicable, alone may appear in parentheses, as shown by Smith (1988, 255--322). Semi-colons are used to separate multiple Citations.

Reference List. In the reference list at the end of the document, all references should appear in the style shown in the examples below. The style is based on the *Chicago Manual of Style*. Please be sure that all references are complete, including page numbers of journal articles. For example:

Smith, John J., Mary K. Doe, and Joseph Smoe. 1988. "How to Write References." *Journal of Reference Writing* 77: 100-121.

Smith, John J. and Mary K. Doe. 1988. "How to Write References." *Journal of Reference Writing* 77(10): 100-121.

Smith, John J. and Mary K. Doe. 1988. "How to Write References." *Journal of Reference Writing* 77(October): 100-121.

Smith, John J. and Mary K. Doe. 1988. "How to Write References." *Journal of Reference Writing* 77(no. 10, October): 100-121.

Smith, John J. (Ed) 1999. *How to Write References.* Boston, MA: Smith Publications.

Smith, John J., Mary K. Doe, and Joseph Smoe (Eds). *How to Write References.*Boston, MA: Smith Publications.

Smith, John J. "How to Write References." In *The Art of Reference Writing,* edited by Mary K. Doe and Joseph Smoe. Boston, MA: Smith Publications.

Spell Check. Spell Check should be run with the language set as English (U.S.), NOT BRITISH.

Questions Regarding Style Instructions. Any questions or comments regarding the style, formatting, of these instructions should be addressed to the Editor, Michael A. Crew, or his assistant, Jeremy T. Guenter, at CRRI@andromeda.rutgers.edu or 973-353-5761.

Further information about the *Journal of Regulatory Economics* and the Center for Research in Regulated Industries can be obtained at our website: http://www.crri.rutgers.edu.

ELECTRONIC DELIVERY OF ACCEPTED PAPERS
Important. After your paper has been ACCEPTED, please send the electronic version via disk (via electronic mail if created on a non-PC system). **Note**. In the event of minor discrepancies between the electronic version and hard copy, the electronic file will be used as the final version.

Kluwer accepts a wide range of file formats. For manuscripts: Word, WordPerfect, RTF, TXT, and LaTex. For figures: TIFF, GIF, EPS, PPT, and Postscript. PDF is not an acceptable format.

Via Disk
1. Label a disk with the names of the operating system and file types, along with the authors' names, manuscript title, and name of journal to which the paper has been accepted.

2. Mail disk to the Editor.

Via Electronic Mail (for non-PC operating systems)
1. Please e-mail electronic version to: CRRI@andromeda.rutgers.edu

2. Recommended formats for sending large files via e-mail:
   - Compression—.zip or .sit
   - Collecting files—.tar

3. The e-mail message should include the author's last name, the name of the journal to which the paper has been accepted, and the type of file. Our e-mail system can handle a maximum of 20 MB per e-mail. Please send larger files on CD-ROM.

Questions about the above procedures can be e-mailed to: CRRI@andromeda.rutgers.edu.

Proofing
Please be sure to include your e-mail address on your paper. If your paper is accepted, we will provide proofs electronically. Your cooperation is appreciated. The proofread copy should be returned to the Publisher within 72 hours.

Copyright
It is the policy of Kluwer Academic Publishers to own the copyright of all contributions it publishes. To comply with U.S. Copyright Law, authors are required to sign a copyright transfer form before publication. This form returns to authors and their employers full rights to reuse their material for their own purposes. Authors must submit a signed copy of this form with their manuscript.

Offprints
Each group of authors is entitled to 50 free offprints of their paper. Additional offprints may be ordered through the offprint form provided with the proofs.

Journal of Restructuring Finance

ADDRESS FOR SUBMISSION:

Mamouda Mbemap, Editor-in-Chief
Journal of Restructuring Finance
Birkholweg 46
Frankfurt am Main, D-60433
Germany
Phone: +49 179 534 5772
Fax: +49 69 273 100 22
E-Mail: jrfeditor@gmx.de
Web: www.worldscinet.com/jrf/jrf.shtml
Address May Change: 1/31/2008

PUBLICATION GUIDELINES:

Manuscript Length: 16-25
Copies Required: Three
Computer Submission: Yes Disk, Email
Format: MS Word
Fees to Review: 0.00 US$

Manuscript Style:
, World Scientific, Harvard System,
Webster's Dictionary

CIRCULATION DATA:

Reader: Academics, Business Persons,
Regulators & Standards Setters
Frequency of Issue: Quarterly
Copies per Issue: 5,001 - 10,000
Sponsor/Publisher: World Scientific
Publishing Co.
Subscribe Price: 95.00 US$ Individual
150.00 US$ Association
314.00 US$ Instn - Print+Electronic

REVIEW INFORMATION:

Type of Review: Blind Review
No. of External Reviewers: 1-2
No. of In House Reviewers: 1-2
Acceptance Rate: 6-10%
Time to Review: 1 Month or Less
Reviewers Comments: Yes
Invited Articles: 6-10%
Fees to Publish: 0.00 US$

MANUSCRIPT TOPICS:

Bankruptcy; Business Reorganization Plans; Chapter 11; Contracts; Corporate Finance;
Corporate Governance; Corporate Recovery & Renewal; Credit Rating; Default; Distressed
Firms & Securities; Econometrics; Economic Policies; Economic Reform;
Economics/Financial Laws & Regulations; Financial Institutions & Markets; Financial
Markets; Financial Restructuring; Financial Services; Industrial Organization; Insolvency;
International Economics & Trade; International Finance; International Finance; Investing;
Law & Regulation; Liquidation & Claims; Macro Economics; Mezzanine Finance; Micro
Economics; Models; Monetary Policy; Portfolio & Security Analysis; Private Equity;
Privatization; Public Policy Economics; Real Estate; Turnaround; Venture Capital; Workout

MANUSCRIPT GUIDELINES/COMMENTS:

Aims & Scope

The *Journal of Restructuring Finance* (*JRF*) is an international refereed journal that supports
an interdisciplinary approach to restructuring research. It is published quarterly and is devoted
to the study of business reorganization processes, turnaround and reinvention, and also to
research on economic reform and transformation.

Guidelines for Authors

1. The initial manuscript should be sent to the Editor-In-Chief preferably via email (see: email address above or in the *Journal of Restructuring Finance*).

2. Submission of a manuscript indicates a tacit understanding that the paper is not under consideration for publication with other journals.

3. Once the paper is accepted, authors are assumed to cede copyrights of the paper over to the *Journal of Restructuring Finance*.

4. The authors should ensure that all materials in the paper are original and abide by all copyright rules. In order to facilitate the review process, authors should also ensure that Internet access and access through other outlets to submitted papers, draft of papers and backup data cited in the papers is blocked or simply removed during the review.

5. All papers will be acknowledged and refereed. They will not be returned.

6. For reviewing purposes, the papers have to be prepared in the following manner:

- Apply double spacing and a 12-point font size for text.
- Supply diagrams at the back of the manuscript.
- Tables and figures should be numbered using Arabic numerals, with one table or figure to a page. All tables and figures should be self-contained.
- Headings and legends should be understandable without reference to the text.
- Refer to the *Webster's New Collegiate Dictionary* for spelling and *The Chicago Manual of Style* for punctuation and other points of style.
- Include the author's full titles, phone numbers, complete mailing and e-mail addresses.
- Provide a short concise executive summary of no more than 150 words, and between 5 and 10 keywords (eg, Workout, Turnaround, Distressed Debt etc.).
- Refer to the Harvard System [name (year)] for bibliographic reference. (Harvard System)
- Provide a text or prose description of all mathematical and statistical symbols. Preference should be given to text over Greek symbols.
- In order to facilitate editing and prompt publication, manuscripts accepted for publication will be prepared according to the Instructions for Typesetting Manuscripts of the publisher (on the web page of the *Journal*).

7. The first-named authors will be provided with 25 free reprints.

Journal of Risk & Insurance

ADDRESS FOR SUBMISSION:

P.L. Brockett & R.D. MacMinn, Editors
Journal of Risk & Insurance
University of Texas at Austin
College of Business Administration
Dept of Mgmt Sciences & Info Systems
CBA 5.202
Austin, TX 78712
USA
Phone: 512-471-0018
Fax: 305-768-0522
E-Mail: jri1@uts.cc.utexas.edu
Web: www.blackwellpublishing.com
Address May Change:

PUBLICATION GUIDELINES:

Manuscript Length: 16-20+
Copies Required:
Computer Submission: Yes - Preferred
Format: Wd, WdPerfect, Scien. Wd, PDF
Fees to Review:
   35.00 US$ Non-Member ARIA

Manuscript Style:
   See Manuscript Guidelines

CIRCULATION DATA:

Reader: Academics
Frequency of Issue: Quarterly
Copies per Issue: 1,001 - 2,000
Sponsor/Publisher: ARIA / Blackwell
  Publishing
Subscribe Price:
   See Web Site

REVIEW INFORMATION:

Type of Review: Blind Review
No. of External Reviewers: 2
No. of In House Reviewers: 2
Acceptance Rate: 10-20%
Time to Review: 3-4 Months
Reviewers Comments: Yes
Invited Articles: 0-5%
Fees to Publish: 0.00 US$

MANUSCRIPT TOPICS:
Financial Institutions & Markets; Insurance; International Finance; Public Policy Economics;
Real Estate; Risk Management in Public Policy; Weather

MANUSCRIPT GUIDELINES/COMMENTS:

Subscription prices can be found at:
   http://www.blackwellpublishing.com/journals/JRI/member.htm.

Editors. Richard D. MacMinn, Patrick L. Brockett

Editorial Policy
The *Journal of Risk and Insurance* publishes rigorous, original research in insurance
economics and risk management. This includes the following areas of specialization: (1)
industrial organization of insurance markets; (2) management of pure risks in the private and
public sectors; (3) insurance finance, financial pricing, and financial management; (4)
economics of employee benefits, pension plans, and social insurance; (5) utility theory,

demand for insurance, moral hazard and adverse selection; (6) insurance regulation; (7) actuarial and statistical methodology; and (8) economics of insurance institutions. Both theoretical and empirical submissions are encouraged. Empirical work should provide tests of hypotheses based on sound theoretical foundations.

Style Guide

The submission fee for those who are not members of the American Risk and Insurance Association is US$35. Electronic submissions are preferred—send as attachment to an email message.

Manuscripts should be typed, double-spaced, with 1" margins, on only one side of 8½" x 11" white bond paper. An abstract of 100 words or less appears on a separate page, beginning with the title of the manuscript and followed by the word Abstract. Quotes of 30 words or more are single-spaced and indented without quotation marks. Comments and notes are typically four to six pages. Submission of a manuscript implies that it is original, unpublished work. The *JRI* does not accept simultaneous submissions.

Names of authors should not appear in or on the manuscript. The anonymous referee process is facilitated by attaching, to only one copy, a cover page that includes the title, author(s)' name(s), title(s), and affiliation(s). The manuscript begins with its title at the top of the first page.

Titles and Headings

Titles are no longer than 85 letters and spaces, headings no longer than 44. Titles are bold-faced, centered, and capitalized. Headings are bold-faced and centered, but not underlined or numbered, and only the first letter of each main word is capitalized. Subheadings are flush with the left margin and underlined or italicized. The first letter of each main word is capitalized in first-level subheadings. Text begins on the next line. Sub-subheadings are indented five spaces, underlined, and followed by a period, two spaces, and text. Only the first word is capitalized. One double-space separates titles and headings from their corresponding text. For example:

TITLE

Text text text text text text text text text text text text text text
text text text text text text text text text text text text

Heading

Text text text text text text text text text text text text text text text text text text text
text text text text text text

Subheading

Text text text text text text text text text text text text text text text text text text text
text text text text text text

Sub-subheading: Text text text text text text text text text text text text text text text
text text text text text text text text

Footnotes
Footnotes are used sparingly for clarification and appear at the bottom of the page.

References
References are used to cite sources and appear in the text as the author's last name followed by the year of publication. Sources are listed alphabetically without numbers at the end of the manuscript. All works referred to in the text must have complete citations in the reference list. Examples follow.

Textual Citations
Harrington and Nelson (1986) reported that...

Although 39 states had adequate unemployment reserve accounts... (U.S. General Accounting Office, 1988, p. 3).

The hypothesis has been examined by a number of researchers (see Hogan, 1970; Schott, 1971; Pesando, 1974; Cummins, 1975).

Citations for direct quotations appear in parentheses and include page numbers. For example:

"A primary purpose of property-liability insurance regulation is to protect policyholders from losses due to in insurer insolvency" (Harrington and Nelson, 1986, p. 583).

Include page numbers in other instances when it would be helpful to readers to refer to a specific place in a publication.

Reference List at the End of the Article

Books and Monographs are referenced using authors' full names (last name first for the initial author) as they appear on the title page; year; title, italicized or underlined; and place and publisher in parentheses. For example:

Black, Kenneth, Jr., and Harold D. Skipper, Jr., 1987, Life Insurance, Eleventh edition (Englewood Cliff, N.J.: Prentice-HAII).

For Journals, author's name as it appears on the title page beginning with last name first; year; title of article; name of journal, italicized or underlined; volume number; a colon; and page numbers. Include the issue number or month only if pages are not consecutively numbered throughout the volume. For example:

Harrington, Scott E. and Jack M. Nelson, 1986, A Regression-Based Methodology for Solvency Surveillance in the Property-Liability Insurance Industry, Journal of Risk and Insurance, 53: 583-605

For Contributions to Collective Works, contributing author's last name, given name, and initials as they appear on the byline; year of publication; title of chapter or reading; the word "in" followed by a colon; editor's name as it appears on the title page, followed by "ed.," title of book, italicized or underlined; place and publisher in parentheses; and page numbers. For example:

> Marcus, Alan J., 1987, Corporate Pension Policy and the Value of PBGC Insurance, in Zvi Bodie, John B. Shoven, and David A. Wise, eds., Issues In Pension Economics (Chicago: Univerity of Chicago Press), 49-76.

For Government Documents, name of governmental unit authoring document or bearing testimony; year; title of document, italicized or underlined; followed by place and publisher in parentheses. For example:

> U.S. General Accounting Office, 1988, Unemployment Insurance: Trust Fund Reserves Inadequate (Washington, D.C.: U.S. Government Printing Office).

Figures
Figures should be in any commonly-used software.

Equations
Identifying numbers for equations appear in parentheses to the flush right of the equation. Algebraic equations should be followed by a clear prose explanation of all variables and abbreviations. Derivations and proofs are placed in an appendix. All steps of algebraic derivations should appear on supplemental sheets so that reviewers do not have to regenerate them.

Final Manuscript
After a manuscript has been through the referee process and is considered acceptable for publication subject to revisions (sometimes these are limited to minor changes in style), the author is asked to have the manuscript retyped. The preferred word processing programs are WordPerfect and Microsoft Word for Windows. Authors who do not have access to a word processor should notify the editor.

Tables
Tables should appear on separate pages at the end of the manuscript, with their approximate placement in the text indicated in brackets.

Tabular material should be single-spaced. Columns and other groupings should be separated by minimal white space. All-important words in the title, column headings, and stubs are capitalized.

The table number should be centered and bold. The title of the table should follow one blank line and be centered but not bold.

There should be no rules above or below the table title. There should be no vertical rules at all. Rules should appear only under column headings and at the bottom of the table.

Avoid using abbreviations. If abbreviations must be used, they must all be defined in the general table notes.

Footnotes should appear below the bottom rule in the following order:
1. Source notes
2. Other general notes that apply to the table as a whole, such as an explanation of all abbreviations used
3. Notes on specific parts of the table, denoted with superscript lowercase letters
4. Notes on level of probability (*p < .05, ** p < .01, etc.)

Table 1

Involuntary Market Deficit as a Proportion of Total Market
Incurred Losses: 1979-81

Involuntary Market Deficit/
Total Market Incurred Losses

State	Liability	Physical Damage	Combined	Involuntary Market Share	$\bar{P}_1/\bar{P}_r$
Massachusetts	.392	.326	.364	.419	.958
New Jersey	.351	.226	.317	.348	1.033
North Carolina, etc.	.172		.109	.245	1.342
Other Regulated					
Mean	-.002	.004	.001	.024	1.790
Maximum	. 022	.036	.027	.113	3.077
Minimum	-.029	-.022	-.026	.001	1.160
All Competitive					
Mean	.004	.003	.004	.015	1.896
Maximum	.043	.048	.044	.088	2.797
Minimum	-.005	-.004	-.004	.000	.506

Note: All values are means for the 1979-81 period. $\bar{P}_1$ and $\bar{P}_r$ denote estimated average liability premium per exposure for the involuntary and total market, respectively. The value of .506 for P_1/P_r was for Hawaii, which provides free involuntary market coverage to welfare recipients.

Miscellaneous
Avoid gender bias—use "his or her" or, when appropriate, plural pronouns.

Do not use the first person—use the third.

Do not confuse "policyowner," "insured," and "policyholder."

Do not use "property and casualty"—current usage is "property-liability."

Avoid weak sentence openings, such as "There is," "There are" or "It is."

Do not refer to a published manuscript or to your own manuscript, after it has been accepted for publication, as a paper. It is an article or a study.

Always spell out percent in the text. The percent sign (%) is acceptable only in tables and figures.

Spell out numbers one through ten unless they identify a visual aid (Table 2, Figure 1, etc.) or modify the word percent. Numbers 11 and above are always written in Arabic numerals unless they begin a sentence, in which case they are spelled out.

Fractions written as words are hyphenated (one-fifth, two-thirds, etc.).

Italicize non-English terms.

Do not use a hyphen for "through" in dates; instead of writing "during the period 1979-1988"—write "from 1979 through 1988."

Do not use italics, underlining or quotation marks for emphasis.

Use leading zeros for decimal fractions and percents less than 1, except for levels for probability (0.6, $p < .05$, for example).

Do not refer to variables in the text by their data abbreviations. For example, if you have an equation with an item of data called DB and it stands for death benefit, say death benefit in the text rather than DB.

Copyright
All material in the *Journal of Risk and Insurance* is copyrighted by the American Risk and Insurance Association. The written permission of the editor is required for reproduction of *JRI* material. Unless specified otherwise in a particular article, blank permission is granted for free classroom use (reproduction).

Journal of Risk and Uncertainty

ADDRESS FOR SUBMISSION:

W. Kip Viscusi, Editor-in-Chief
Journal of Risk and Uncertainty
Harvard University
Harvard Law School
Hauser Hall 302
Cambridge, MA 02138
USA
Phone: 617-496-0019
Fax: 617-495-3010
E-Mail: kip@law.harvard.edu
Web: www.kluweronline.com/
Address May Change:

PUBLICATION GUIDELINES:

Manuscript Length: 26-30
Copies Required: Three
Computer Submission: No
Format: N/A
Fees to Review: 0.00 US$

Manuscript Style:
   See Manuscript Guidelines

CIRCULATION DATA:

Reader: Academics,
   Psychologists/Behaviorists
Frequency of Issue: Bi-Monthly
Copies per Issue: Less than 1,000
Sponsor/Publisher: Profit Oriented Group/
   Kluwer Academic Publishers
Subscribe Price: 255.00 US$ Individual
   644.00 US$ Institution
      Paper or Online

REVIEW INFORMATION:

Type of Review: Blind Review
No. of External Reviewers: 2
No. of In House Reviewers: 2
Acceptance Rate: 21-30%
Time to Review: 4 - 6 Months
Reviewers Comments: Yes
Invited Articles: 11-20%
Fees to Publish: 0.00 US$

MANUSCRIPT TOPICS:
Behavioral Economics; Econometrics; Insurance; Micro Economics; Risk & Uncertainty

MANUSCRIPT GUIDELINES/COMMENTS:

Aims & Scope
The *Journal of Risk and Uncertainty* publishes original contributions, both theoretical and empirical, dealing with the analysis of risk-bearing behavior and decision-making under uncertainty. An important aim of the *Journal* is the encouragement of interdisciplinary communication and interaction between researchers in the areas of risk and uncertainty. The level of scientific sophistication of the papers is high, but they are accompanied by an introductory discussion setting out the nature of the work and the implications of the findings in a manner that makes them accessible to workers in other disciplines. The papers published in the *Journal* are mainly drawn from the areas of decision theory, economics of uncertainty, risk and public policy, experimental economics, and psychological models of choice.

Address for Contributors
Submissions (with cover letters) and three copies of the paper should be sent to the Editor at the above address.

Electronic Delivery of Accepted Papers
Please send only the electronic version (of ACCEPTED papers) via one of the methods listed below.

Kluwer can accept almost any file format (e.g., WordPerfect or Microsoft Word) as well as ASCII (text only) files.
Note: it is also helpful to supply both the source and the ASCII files of a paper. Please submit encapsulated PostScript files for figures. An encapsulated PostScript figure should be named after its figure number, e.g., fig 1.eps or circle 1.eps.

Via Electronic Mail
1. Please e-mail electronic version to KAPfileswkap.com.
2. Recommended formals for sending files via e-mail
   - Binary files—uuencode or binhex
   - Compressing files—compress, pkzip, or gzip
   - Collecting files—tar
3. The e-mail message should include the author's last name, the name of the journal to which the paper has been accepted, and the type of file (e.g., LaTex or ASCII).

Via Anonymous FTP
- ftp:/ftp.wkap.com
- cd:/incoming/production
Send e-mail to KAPfils@wkap.com to inform Kluwer the electronic version is at this FTP site.

Via Disk
1. Label a 3.5" floppy disk with the operating system and word processing program (e.g., DOS/WordPerfect) along with the authors' names, manuscript title, and name of journal to which the paper has been accepted.
2. Mail disk to Kluwer Academic Publishers, Desktop Department, 101 Philip Drive, Assinippi Park, Norwell, MA 02061, USA.

Any questions about the above procedures please send e-mail to: dthelp@wkap.com.

Manuscript Preparation
Final versions of accepted manuscripts, including notes, references, tables, and legends, should be typed double-spaced, on 8.5" x 11" (22cm x 29cm) white paper, with 1" (2.5cm) margins on all sides. Sections should appear in the following order: title page, abstract, text, notes, references, tables, figure legends, and figures. Comments or replies to previously published articles should also follow this format with the exception of abstracts, which are not required.

Title Page. The title page should include the article title, authors' names and permanent affiliations, and the name, current address, and telephone number of the person to whom page proofs and reprints should be sent.

Abstract. The following page should include an abstract of not more than 100 words and a list of two to six keywords. Also include JEL subject category number.

Text. The text of the article should begin on a new page. The introduction should have no heading or number. Subsequent headings (including appendices) should be designated by Arabic numerals (1, 2, etc.), and subsection headings should be numbered 1.1, 1.2, etc. Figures, tables, and displayed equations should be numbered consecutively throughout the text (1, 2, etc.). Equation numbers should appear flush right in parentheses and running variables for equations (e.g., $i = 1$,..., n) flush right in parentheses.

Notes. Acknowledgments and related information should appear in a note designated by an asterisk after the last author's name, and subsequent notes should be numbered consecutively and designated by superscripts [1], [2], etc.) in the text. All notes should be typed double-spaced, beginning on a separate page following the text.

Reference. References in the text should follow the author-date format (e.g., Brown (1986), Jones (1978a, 1978b), Smith and Johnson (1983)). References should be typed double-spaced, beginning on a separate page following the notes, according to the following samples (journal and book titles may be underlined rather than italicized). References with up to three authors should include the names of each author; references with four or more authors should cite the first author and add "et al." It is the responsibility of the authors to verify all references.

Sample References
Backer, Gordon, Morris DeGroot, and Jacob Marschak. (1964). "Measuring Utility by a Single-Response Sequential Method", Behavioral Science 9, 226-232.

Schoemaker, Paul. (1980). Experiments on Decisions Under Risk: The Expected Utility Hypothesis. Boston: Kluwer-Nijhoff Publishing.

Smith, V. Kerry. (1986). "A Conceptual Overview of the Foundations of Benefit-Cost Analysis". In Judith Bentkover, Vincent Covello, and Jeryl Mumpower (eds.), Benefits Assessment: The State of the Art. Dordrecht: D. Reidel Publishing Co.

Tables. Tables should be titled and typed double-spaced, each on a separate sheet, following the references. Notes to tables should be designated by superscripted letters (a, b, etc.) within each table and typed double-spaced on the same page as the table. Use descriptive labels rather than computer acronyms, and explain all abbreviations. When tables are typed on oversized paper, please submit both the original and a reduced copy.

Figures. Figures for accepted manuscripts should be submitted in camera-ready form, i.e., clear glossy prints or drawn in India ink on drafting paper or high quality white paper. Lettering in figures should be large enough to be legible after half-size reduction. Authors should submit one 5" x 7" (13cm x 18cm) original and two photocopies of each figure, with authors' names, manuscript title, and figure number on the back of each original and copy (use gummed labels if necessary to avoid damaging originals). Figures should be enclosed in a separate envelope backed by cardboard and without staples or paper clips. Figure legends should be typed double-spaced on a separate sheet following the tables.

Page Proofs and Reprints

Corrected page proofs must be returned within three days of receipt, and alterations other than corrections may be charged to the authors. Authors will receive 50 free reprints, and may order additional copies when returning the corrected proofs.

Journal of Risk Finance (The)

ADDRESS FOR SUBMISSION:

David K. A. Mordecai, Editor
Journal of Risk Finance (The)
Attn: Samantha Kappagoda, Mng Editor
Caxton Associates, LLC
667 Madison Avenue
New York, NY 10021
USA
Phone: 917-402-1422
Fax: 212-541-7060
E-Mail: iijrf@aol.com
Web: www.iijrf.com
Address May Change:

PUBLICATION GUIDELINES:

Manuscript Length: 16-25
Copies Required: Two
Computer Submission: Yes
Format: MS Word
Fees to Review: 0.00 US$

Manuscript Style:
    No Reply

CIRCULATION DATA:

Reader: Academics, Business Persons
Frequency of Issue: Quarterly
Copies per Issue: Less than 1,000
Sponsor/Publisher: Institutional Investor,
    Inc.
Subscribe Price: 500.00 US$

REVIEW INFORMATION:

Type of Review: Editorial Review
No. of External Reviewers: 2-3
No. of In House Reviewers: 0
Acceptance Rate: 11-20%
Time to Review: 2 - 3 Months
Reviewers Comments: Yes
Invited Articles: 11-20%
Fees to Publish: 0.00 US$

MANUSCRIPT TOPICS:

Alternative Risk Transfer; Corporate Finance; Financial Institutions & Markets; Financial Services; Insurance & Capital Structure/Credit Arbitrage; Modeling for Risk Intermediation; Portfolio & Security Analysis; Securitization; Tax Accounting

MANUSCRIPT GUIDELINES/COMMENTS:

Managing Editor: Samantha Kappagoda

Please follow the guidelines below when you prepare a manuscript for submission. The editors will edit and copyedit articles for clarity and consistency. *Please note that we reserve the right to return to an author any paper accepted for publication that is not prepared according to these instructions.*

1. **Article Submission**. Please submit 2 copies double-spaced sized on an 8.5"x11" page with 1.5"-2" margins and numbered pages. Include on the title page the authors' names and titles as they are to appear, including affiliation, mailing address, telephone and fax numbers, and e-mail address. Also submit an electronic file. Text should be formatted in 12 point type. If

submitting a pdf file, please prepare with all fonts embedded and, if possible, include an accompanying Word file which would include the running text. We do not support articles submitted in WordPerfect. Please save any WordPerfect files as a text document and please provide separate eps files for any graphic elements. **All manuscripts are expected to be submitted in final form.** We reserve the right to limit any changes following article formatting based upon content, not style.

2. **Abstract**. On the page after the title page, please provide a brief article summary or abstract suitable for the table of contents. Do not begin the paper with a heading such as "introduction." Do not number section or subsection headings.

3. Do not asterisk or footnote any authors' names listed as bylines. Footnoting should only begin in the body of the article.

4. **Exhibits**. Please put tables and graphs on separate individual pages at the end of the paper. Do not integrate them with the text; do not call them table 1 and figure 1. Please call any tabular or graphical material Exhibits, numbered in Arabic numbers consecutively in order of appearance in the text. We reserve the right to return to an author for reformatting any paper accepted for publication that does not conform to this style.

5. **Exhibit Presentation**. Please organize and present tables consistently throughout a paper, because we will print them the way they are presented to us. **Exhibits should be created as grayscale, as opposed to color, since the journal is printed in black and white. Please make sure that all categories in an exhibit can be distinguished from each other.** Align numbers correctly by decimal points; use the same number of decimal points for the same sorts of numbers; center headings, columns, and numbers correctly; use the exact same language in successive appearances; identify any bold-faced or italicized entries in exhibits; and provide any source notes necessary.

6. **Graphs**. Please submit graphs for accepted papers in electronic form. We cannot produce graphs for authors. Graphs will appear the way you submit them. Please be consistent as to fonts, capitalization, and abbreviations in graphs throughout the paper, and label all axes and lines in graphs clearly and absolutely consistently. When pasting graphs into Word, paste as an object, not as a picture, so we will be able to have access to original graph.

7. **Equations**. Please display called-out equations on separate lines, aligned on the exact same indents as the text paragraphs and with no punctuation following. Number equations consecutively throughout the paper in Arabic numbers at the right-hand margin. Clarify in handwriting any operations signs or Greek letters or any notation that may be unclear. Leave space around operations signs like plus and minus everywhere. We reserve the right to return for resubmission any accepted article that prepares equations in any other way. It would be preferable if manuscripts containing mathematical equations be submitted in Microsoft Word using either Equation Editor or MathType.

8. **Reference Citations**. In the text, please refer to authors and works as: Smith [2000]. Use brackets for the year, not parentheses. The same is true for references within parentheses, such as: "(see also Smith [2000])."

9. Reference Styles

Brokerage house internal publications	Askin, D.J., and S.D. Meyer. "Dollar Rolls: A Low-Cost Financing Technique." Mortgage-Backed Securities Research, Drexel Burnham Lambert, 1986.
Journal articles	Batlin, C.A. "Hedging Mortgage-Backed Securities with Treasury Bond Futures." *Journal of Futures Markets,* 7 (1987), pp. 675-693.
———. "Trading Mortgage-Backed Securities with Treasury Bond Futures." Journal of Futures Markets, 7 (1987), pp. 675-693.	Same author, alphabetized by title, two em-dashes instead of repeating name
Working papers	Boudoukh, J., M. Richardson, R. Stanton, and R.F. Whitelaw. "Pricing Mortgage-Backed Securities in a Multifactor Interest Rate Environment: A Multivariate Density Estimation Approach." Working Paper, New York University, 1995.
Sections of books	Breeden, D.T., and M.J. Giarla. "Hedging Interest Rate Risk with Futures, Swaps, and Options." In F. Fabozzi, ed., *The Handbook of Mortgage-Backed Securities.* Chicago: Probus Publishing, 1992, 3rd edition, pp. 847-960.
Books	Hull, J., ed. *Options, Futures and Other Derivative Securities.* Englewood Cliffs, NJ: Prentice-Hall, 1993, 2nd edition.

10. **Endnotes**. Please put in endnotes only material that is not essential to the understanding of an article. If it is essential, it belongs in the text. Do not place a footnote by the authors' names. Any biographical information can be indicated in a separate section and will not be footnoted. Authors' bio information appearing in the article will be limited to their titles, current affiliations, and locations. Do not include in endnotes full reference details; these belong in a separate references list; see below. We will delete non-essential endnotes in the interest of minimizing distraction and enhancing clarity. We also reserve the right to return to an author any article accepted for publication that includes endnotes with embedded reference detail and no separate references list in exchange for preparation of a paper with the appropriate endnotes and a separate references list.

11. **References lists**. Please list only those articles cited in a separate alphabetical references list at the end of the paper. Please follow absolutely the style you see in this journal. We reserve the right to return any accepted article for preparation of a references list according to this style.

12. **Electronic Files**. Word documents are preferred for the articles themselves. Excel can be used for the preparation of graphic elements, making sure that they are embedded in the Word document prior to submission. <u>For those working with .tek or LaTeX files</u>: *pdf files of the articles must be submitted*, making sure to embed all fonts when the pdf file is prepared. Please also include a Word file which contains the text of the article.

13. **Copyright Agreement**: Institutional Investor Inc.'s copyright agreement form - giving us non-exclusive rights to publish the material in all media - must be signed prior to publication.

14. Upon acceptance of the article, no further changes are allowed, except with the permission of the editor. If the article has already been forwarded to our production department, any changes must be made on the hard copy of the original submitted manuscript and faxed to them.

Journal of Risk Research

ADDRESS FOR SUBMISSION:

Ragnar E. Lofstedt, Editor
Journal of Risk Research
King's College London
School of Social Science & Public Policy
King's Centre for Risk Management
Strand Building
London, WC2R 2LS
UK
Phone: +44 (0)20 7848-1404
Fax: +44 (0)20 7848-2748
E-Mail: ragnar.lofstedt@ucl.ac.uk
Web: www.tandf.co.uk/journals
Address May Change:

PUBLICATION GUIDELINES:

Manuscript Length: 4,000-6,000 Words
Copies Required: Three
Computer Submission: Yes
Format: WordPerfect, Word 6.0
Fees to Review: 0.00 US$

Manuscript Style:
      See Manuscript Guidelines

CIRCULATION DATA:

Reader: Academics
Frequency of Issue: 8 Times/Year
Copies per Issue: Less than 1,000
Sponsor/Publisher: Society for Risk
    Analysis-Europe & Japan/Carfax
    Publishing-Taylor & Francis
Subscribe Price: 152.00 US$ Individual
      822.00 US$ Institution
      92.00 Pounds Indv, 498 Pounds Inst

REVIEW INFORMATION:

Type of Review: Blind Review
No. of External Reviewers: 2 2-3
No. of In House Reviewers: 1
Acceptance Rate: 21-30%
Time to Review: 4 - 6 Months
Reviewers Comments: Yes
Invited Articles: 21-30%
Fees to Publish: 0.00 US$

MANUSCRIPT TOPICS:
Insurance; Risk Management

MANUSCRIPT GUIDELINES/COMMENTS:

Aims & Scope
The *Journal of Risk Research* is the official journal of the Society for Risk Analysis Europe
and the Society for Risk Analysis Japan. It is a quarterly international journal which publishes
peer reviewed theoretical and empirical research articles within the risk field from the areas of
engineering, physical, health and social sciences, as well as articles related to decision
making, regulation and policy issues in all disciplines. Articles will be published in English.
The main aims of the *Journal of Risk Research* are to stimulate intellectual debate on risk
within Europe, Japan and elsewhere, to promote better risk management practices and to
contribute to the development of risk management methodologies.

The *Journal* serves the growing diversity of the risk community, addressing issues outside the current focus of the North American literature, providing the reader with a variety of interesting research results.

The *Journal* consists of letters to the Editor, viewpoints, theoretical and empirical research articles, commentaries, research notes, book reviews and news of upcoming risk conferences and SRA membership news.

1. Submission of Manuscripts

Manuscripts must be submitted in English, and must be original, unpublished work not under consideration for publication elsewhere. Three copies of the manuscript together with all original figures and tables should be submitted to the Editor or one of the Associate Editors at the addresses given in the Editorial Board list on the second page of the *Journal* issue. The manuscript will be subjected to blind review by one or two referees. Revisions may be required before a decision is made to accept or reject the paper. When a paper has been accepted, please send two copies of the manuscript in its final form to the Editor, together with a disc. Please use a standard word processing package and label the disc clearly. Please send books for review and book reviews to the Book Review Editor at the address given on the second page of the *Journal* issue.

2. Preparation of the Manuscript

The manuscript must be typed, double-spaced on A4 paper, with a least 3 cm margins (approximately 21 x 30cm) and between 4,000 and 6,000 words. Low quality dot-matrix printers should not be used. Clearly written, concise manuscripts should comprise:

2.1 Title page (page 1)

Including (a) a concise and informative title, (b) the full names and affiliations of all authors, and (c) the full mailing address, telephone and fax numbers of the corresponding author

2.2 Abstract (page 2)

Including a concise and informative abstract of 200 words maximum, summarizing the significant points of the paper.

2.3 Introduction (page 3)

The introduction should clearly state the purpose (aims and objectives) of the paper. It should include key references to appropriate work but should not be an historical or literature review.

2.4 Discussion

The discussion should emphasize the implications and practical significance of research findings, their limitations, and relevance to previous studies.

2.5 References

References in the text should be cited as follows:

One author	Smith (1993) or (Smith, 1993)
Two authors	Smith and Brown (1993) or (Smith and Brown, 1993)
Three or more authors	Smith *et al.* (1993) or (Smith *et al.,* 1993)

Papers by the same author(s) in the same year should be distinguished by the letters a, b, etc.

References should be listed at the end of the paper giving the year of publication, title of paper, journal titles in full, volume number, and first and last page numbers. References to books should include their edition, editors(s), publisher, and place of publication. Examples:

Book

Eiser, J.R. (1994) *Attitudes, Chaos and the Connectionist Mind,* Oxford: Blackwell.

Edited Book

Kaplan, R.S. (1986) Advances in experimental social psychology, in K. Clark and C. Lorenze (eds) *The Psychology of Attitudes,* pp. 165-98. Oxford: Pergamon.

Journal

Heberlein, T.A. (1982) Some social psychological explanations for changing environmental attitudes, *Risk Analysis* **2**, 81-90.

It is the authors' responsibility to check the accuracy of references.

3. Tables

Each table must be typed, double spaced on a separate page. They must be consecutively numbered and should have a brief informative title. Tables should be understandable without reference to the text. Explanatory footnotes should be brief, placed beneath the table and indicated by lower case letters. When using percentages state the absolute value that corresponds to 100%. Identify all statistical methods.

4. Figures

All illustrations of any kind must be submitted as sequentially numbered figures, one to a page. If photographs are included, please supply high-quality, glossy photographs. Line figures, graphs etc., must be supplied as high-quality laser printouts (not photocopies). If it is necessary to submit drawings, then these must be of the highest quality and clarity.

The author(s) name and the figure number should be written on the reverse of the figure in pencil. When symbols, arrows, numbers or letters are used to identify parts of illustrations, they must be clearly identified by a key in the figure legend, rather than in the figure itself. Similarly, internal scales, staining or processing of the figure must be explained where appropriate. Figure legends should be listed sequentially on a separate page.

Colour illustrations are acceptable; however, the cost of color production will be charged to the author.

8. Conventions

Use only recommended SI units. Numerals should be used for all numbers of two or more digits, and for single digits when attached to units of measure. Abbreviations should be defined in brackets after their first mention in the text in accordance with internationally agreed rules.

6. Proofs

Proofs will be sent to the designated corresponding author and should be returned directly to the publisher within 3 days of receipt. Alterations in proofs other than the correction of typesetter's error may cause delay and extra charges that may be made to the author(s).

7. **Offprints**

The corresponding author will be sent 25 free offprints as well as a bound copy of the *Journal*.

8. **Copyright**

Submission of a paper to *Journal of Risk Research* will be taken to imply that it presents original unpublished work, not under consideration for publication elsewhere. By submitting a manuscript authors agree that the copyright for their article is transferred to Taylor & Francis Ltd, if and when the article is accepted for publication. The copyright covers the exclusive rights to reproduce and distribute the article, including reprints, photographic reproductions, microfilm or any other reproduction or similar or any nature including translations.

Journal of Socio-Economics

ADDRESS FOR SUBMISSION:

Morris Altman, Editor
Journal of Socio-Economics
University of Saskatchesan
College of Economics
Arts 820
9 Campus Drive
Saskatoon, SK S7N 5A5
Canada
Phone: 306-966-5198
Fax: 306-966-5232
E-Mail: altman@sask.usask.ca
Web: www.elsevier.com
Address May Change:

CIRCULATION DATA:

Reader: Academics
Frequency of Issue: Bi-Monthly
Copies per Issue: 1,200
Sponsor/Publisher: Elsevier Science
   Publishing Co.
Subscribe Price: 95.00 US$ Personal
   369.00 US$ Institution

PUBLICATION GUIDELINES:

Manuscript Length: 16-20
Copies Required: Three
Computer Submission: Yes
Format: IBM, MS Word, WordPerfect,
   ASCII
Fees to Review: 0.00 US$

Manuscript Style:
   American Psychological Association

REVIEW INFORMATION:

Type of Review: Blind Review
No. of External Reviewers: 3
No. of In House Reviewers: 1
Acceptance Rate: 20-25%
Time to Review: 2 - 3 Months
Reviewers Comments: Yes
Invited Articles: 10%
Fees to Publish: 0.00 US$

MANUSCRIPT TOPICS:

Accounting Information Systems; Accounting Theory & Practice; Auditing; Behavioral
Economics; Consumer Behavior; Corporate Finance; Cost Accounting; Econometrics;
Economic Development; Economic History; Economics; Ethics; Financial Institutions &
Markets; Financial Services; Fiscal Policy; Global Business; Government & Non-Profit
Accounting; Health Care Administration; Industrial Organization; Insurance; International
Economics & Trade; International Finance; Labor Relations & Human Resource Mgt.; Macro
Economics; Marketing Theory & Application; Micro Economics; Monetary Policy;
Organizational Behavior &Theory; Organizational Development; Portfolio & Security
Analysis; Public Policy Economics; Real Estate; Regional Economics; Strategic Management
Policy; Tax Accounting

MANUSCRIPT GUIDELINES/COMMENTS:

Description
Journal of Socio-Economics is a general economics journal whose calling card is its
methodological open-mindedness and a strong commitment to economic rigor and economic

or analytical significance as opposed to the simple use of mathematical proofs and statistical significance.

The *JSE* welcomes the traditional, more focused, economics research as well as interdisciplinary discourses that serve to enhance our understanding of the world in which we live, recognizing that the economy is an interactive part of a larger socio-economic structure. With this in mind, the *JSE* also welcomes survey articles and suggestions for special topic issues. The objective of the *JSE* is to be a forum for theoretical and empirical research (inclusive of case studies, experiments and simulation based analyses) irrespective of its methodological orientation, that improves our knowledge of the state of the world past and present as well as enriches our causal understanding of the economy. In light of these objectives, research with a public policy orientation and literature reviews are also welcome. Articles should be written in a manner that is intelligible to our generalist readership.

The *Journal of Socio-Economics* welcomes submissions that are empirical in orientation. However, authors should carefully distinguish in their analysis between the use of statistical and substantive significance. We are most interested in the substantive or analytical significance of estimated coefficients. As Deirdre McCloskey often asks, how big is your coefficient in terms the scientific conversation at hand? Statistical significance only provides us with some information on the probability that coefficients estimated from a sample are a matter of chance. It provides us with no information on the analytical importance of the coefficient. With respect to samples, we are interested in how the sample is constructed and the probable representation of the sample. When the population of a data set is used in ones analysis, tests of statistical significance provide us with no useful information. Overall, please play particular attention to the substantive or analytical significance of your statistical analyses. For further information on this matter see, D.N. McCloskey, "The Loss Function Has Been Mislaid," *American Economic Review* 75: 201-205 and D.N. McCloskey and S.T Ziliak, "The Standard Error of Regressions," *Journal of Economic Literature* 34: 97-114.

Guide for Authors
1. Papers must be in English.
2. Papers for publication should be sent electronically along with 4 paper copies to the Editor.

Please send book reviews to Manhattan College, New York, New York, USA— jtomer@juno.com

Submission of a paper will be held to imply that it contains original unpublished work and is not being submitted for publication elsewhere. The Editor does not accept responsibility for damage or loss of papers submitted. Upon acceptance of an article, author(s) will be asked to transfer copyright of the article to the publisher. This transfer will ensure the widest possible dissemination of information.

3. Submission of accepted papers as electronic manuscripts, i.e., on disk with accompanying manuscript, is encouraged. Electronic manuscripts have the advantage that there is no need for rekeying of text, thereby avoiding the possibility of introducing errors and resulting in reliable and fast delivery of proofs. The preferred storage medium is a 5.25 or 3.5-inch disk in MS-

DOS format, although other systems are welcome, e.g., Macintosh (in this case, save your file in the usual manner; do not use the option 'save in MS-DOS format"). Do not submit your original paper as electronic manuscript but hold on to disk until asked for this by the Editor (in case your paper is accepted without revisions). Do submit the accepted version of your paper as electronic manuscript. Make absolutely sure that the file on the disk and the printout are identical. Please use a new and correctly formatted disk and label this with your name; also specify the software and hardware used as well as the title of the file to be processed. Do not convert the file to plain ASCII. Ensure that the letter 'l' and digit '1', and also the letter 'O' and digit '0' are used properly, and format your article (tabs, indents, etc.) consistently. Characters not available on your word processor (Greek letters mathematical symbols, etc.) should not be left open but indicated by a unique code (e.g. gralpha, <alpha>, etc., for the Greek letter α). Such codes should be used consistently throughout the entire text; a list of codes used should accompany the electronic manuscript. Do not allow your word processor to introduce word breaks and do not use a justified layout. Please adhere strictly to the general instructions below on style, arrangement and, in particular, the reference style of the journal.

4. Manuscripts should be double spaced, with wide margins, and printed on one side of the paper only. All pages should be numbered consequently. Titles and subtitles should be short. References, tables, and legends for the figures should be printed on separate pages.

5. The first page of the manuscript should contain the following information:
i)   The title
ii)   The name(s) and institutional affiliation(s) of the author(s)
iii) An abstract of not more than 100 words
iv)   At least one classification code according to the Classification System for Journal Articles as used by the *Journal of Economic Literature*; in addition, up to five key words should be supplied.

A footnote on the same sheet should give the name, address, and telephone and fax numbers of the corresponding author [as well as an e-mail address].

6. Acknowledgements and information on grants received can be given in a first footnote, which should not be included in the consecutive numbering of footnotes.

7. Footnotes should be kept to a minimum and numbered consecutively throughout the text with superscript Arabic numerals. They should be double spaced and not include displayed formulae or tables.

8. Displayed formulae should be numbered consecutively throughout the manuscript as (1), (2), etc. against the right-hand margin of the page. In cases where the derivation of formulae has been abbreviated, it is of great help to the referees if the full derivation can be presented on a separate sheet (not to be published).

9. References to publications should be as follows:
'Smith (1992) reported that...' or 'This problem has been studied previously (e.g., Smith et al., 1969)'.

The author should make sure that there is a strict one-to-one correspondence between the names and years in the text and those on the list. The list of references should appear at the end of the main text (after any appendices, but before tables and legends for figures). It should be double spaced and listed in alphabetical order by author's name.

For Monographs
Hawawini, G., Swary, I., 1990. Mergers and Acquisitions in the U.S. Banking Industry: Evidence from the Capital Markets. North-Holland, Amsterdam.

For Contributions to Collective Works
Brunner, K., Meltzer, A.H., 1990. Money supply, in: Friedman, B.M., Hahn, F.H. (Eds.), *Handbook of Monetary Economics*, Vol. 1. North-Holland, Amsterdam, pp. 357–396.

For Periodicals
Griffiths, W., Judge, G., 1992. Testing and estimating location vectors when the error covariance matrix is unknown. *Journal of Econometrics* 54, 121–138.

Note that journal titles should not be abbreviated.

10. Illustrations will be reproduced photographically from originals supplied by the author; they will not be redrawn by the publisher. Please provide all illustrations in quadruplicate (one high-contrast original and three photocopies). Care should be taken that lettering and symbols are of a comparable size. The illustrations should not be inserted in the text, and should be marked on the back with figure number, title of paper, and author's name. All graphs and diagrams should be referred to as figures, and should be numbered consecutively in the text in Arabic numerals. Illustration for papers submitted as electronic manuscripts should be in traditional form.

11. Tables should be numbered consecutively in the text in Arabic numerals and printed on separate sheets.

Any manuscript which does not conform to the above instructions may be returned for the necessary revision before publication.

12. Page proofs will be sent to the corresponding author. Proofs should be corrected carefully; the responsibility for detecting errors lies with the author. Corrections should be restricted to instances in which the proof is at variance with the manuscript. Extensive alterations will be charged. Fifty reprints of each paper are supplied free of charge to the corresponding author; additional reprints are available at cost if they are ordered when the proof is returned.

Journal of Sports Economics

ADDRESS FOR SUBMISSION:

Leo H. Kahane, Co-Editor
Journal of Sports Economics
California State University-Hayward
Department of Economics
25800 Carlos Bee Boulevard
Hayward, CA 94542-3068
USA
Phone: 510-885-3369
Fax: 510-885-4699
E-Mail: lkahane@csuhayward.edu
Web: www.sagepub.co.uk
Address May Change:

PUBLICATION GUIDELINES:

Manuscript Length: 26-30
Copies Required: Four
Computer Submission: Yes
Format: MS Word, WordPerfect
Fees to Review: 0.00 US$

Manuscript Style:
American Psychological Association

CIRCULATION DATA:

Reader: Academics
Frequency of Issue: Quarterly
Copies per Issue: Less than 1,000
Sponsor/Publisher: Sage Publications, Inc.
Subscribe Price: 45.00 US$ Individual
225.00 US$ Institution

REVIEW INFORMATION:

Type of Review: Blind Review
No. of External Reviewers: 2
No. of In House Reviewers: 1
Acceptance Rate: 21-30%
Time to Review: 2 - 3 Months
Reviewers Comments: Yes
Invited Articles: 6-10%
Fees to Publish: 0.00 US$

MANUSCRIPT TOPICS:
All as Related to Sports; Econometrics; Industrial Organization; Public Policy Economics

MANUSCRIPT GUIDELINES/COMMENTS:

Description
Journal of Sports Economics publishes scholarly research in the field of sports economics. The aim of the journal is to further research in the area of sports economics by bringing together theoretical and empirical research in a single intellectual venue.

Relevant Topics
- Labor market research
- Labor-management relations
- Collective bargaining
- Wage determination
- Local public finance
- Plus other fields related to the economics of sports

Published quarterly, the *Journal of Sports Economics* is unique in that it is the only journal devoted specifically to this rapidly growing field. The Editorial Board is composed of some of the top academic economists in North America and Europe.

Aims and Scope

Journal of Sports Economics publishes scholarly research in the field of sports economics. The aim of the journal is to further research in the area of sports economics by bringing together theoretical and empirical research in a single intellectual venue. Relevant topics include: labor market research; labor-management relations; collective bargaining; wage determination; local public finance; and other fields related to the economics of sports. Published quarterly, the *Journal of Sports Economics* is unique in that it is the only journal devoted specifically to this rapidly growing field.

Submission Manuscript Guidelines

Manuscripts are invited on a variety of applied, theoretical, and empirical research topics related to the field of sports economics, including (but not limited to): labor economics and market research, labor management relations, collective bargaining, wage determination, and local public finance. The *Journal of Sports Economics* follows the *American Psychological Association* (APA) publication style. Notes and references should appear at the back of the manuscripts in separate sections. Manuscripts normally should not exceed 30 single-sided typewritten pages with 1-inch margins. All text should be double-spaced (including abstracts, references and notes). Authors should include an abstract of no more than 100 words on a separate page following the title page. The name(s) of authors should appear only on the title page. Contact information, including mailing address, phone and fax numbers, and e-mail address for each author must be provided on the title page. Manuscripts submitted to the *Journal of Sports Economics* should not be under review elsewhere. Authors of manuscripts accepted for publication in the *Journal of Sports Economics* will be sent a more comprehensive style sheet to which they must adhere. Authors should submit four (4) copies of their manuscript to: Leo Kahane, Co-Editor, Journal of Sports Economics, California State University, 25800 Carlos Bee Blvd., Hayward, CA 94542-3068, Phone: 510-885-3369, Fax: 510-885-4699, E-mail: Lkahane@csuhayward.edu.

Journal of Structured and Project Finance (The)

ADDRESS FOR SUBMISSION:

Henry A. Davis, Managing Editor
Journal of Structured and Project Finance
   (The)
3133 Connecticut Avenue, NW #624
Washington, DC 20008-5147
USA
Phone: 202-328-7074
Fax: 202-483-0828
E-Mail: hdresearch@aol.com
Web: www.iijspf.com
Address May Change:

PUBLICATION GUIDELINES:

Manuscript Length: 16-20
Copies Required: Two
Computer Submission: Yes
Format: MS Word
Fees to Review: 0.00 US$

Manuscript Style:
   No Reply

CIRCULATION DATA:

Reader: Academics, Business Persons
Frequency of Issue: Quarterly
Copies per Issue: Less than 1,000
Sponsor/Publisher: Institutional Investor,
   Inc.
Subscribe Price: 365.00 US$

REVIEW INFORMATION:

Type of Review: Editorial Review
No. of External Reviewers: 2
No. of In House Reviewers: No Reply
Acceptance Rate: 21-30%
Time to Review: 2 - 3 Months
Reviewers Comments: Yes
Invited Articles: 21-30%
Fees to Publish: 0.00 US$

MANUSCRIPT TOPICS:

Financial Institutions & Markets; Financial Services; International Finance; Private Financing
for Public Projects; Project Risk Mitigation & Risk-Related Insurance; Public Policy
Economics; Safety, Environment & Technology Factors

MANUSCRIPT GUIDELINES/COMMENTS:

Co-Editors. Christopher Dymond, Edwin F. Feo, Barry P. Gold, Jonathan S. Saiger

Please follow the guidelines below when you prepare a manuscript for submission. The
editors will edit and copyedit articles for clarity and consistency. *Please note that we reserve
the right to return to an author any paper accepted for publication that is not prepared
according to these instructions.*

1. **Article Submission**. Please submit 2 copies double-spaced sized on an 8.5" x 11" page
with 1.5"-2" margins and numbered pages. Include on the title page the authors' names and
titles as they are to appear, including affiliation, mailing address, telephone and fax numbers,
and e-mail address. Also submit an electronic file. Text should be formatted in 12-point type.
If submitting a PDF file, please prepare with all fonts embedded and, if possible, include an

accompanying Word file which would include the running text. We do not support articles submitted in WordPerfect. Please save any WordPerfect files as a text document and please provide separate EPS files for any graphic elements. **All manuscripts are expected to be submitted in final form.** We reserve the right to limit any changes following article formatting based upon content, not style.

2. **Abstract**. On the page after the title page, please provide a brief article summary or abstract suitable for the table of contents. Do not begin the paper with a heading such as "introduction." Do not number section or subsection headings.

3. Do not asterisk or footnote any authors' names listed as bylines. Footnoting should only begin in the body of the article.

4. **Exhibits**. Please put tables and graphs on separate individual pages at the end of the paper. Do not integrate them with the text; do not call them table 1 and figure 1. Please call any tabular or graphical material Exhibits, numbered in Arabic numbers consecutively in order of appearance in the text. We reserve the right to return to an author for reformatting any paper accepted for publication that does not conform to this style.

5. **Exhibit Presentation**. Please organize and present tables consistently throughout a paper, because we will print them the way they are presented to us. **Exhibits should be created as grayscale, as opposed to color, since the journal is printed in black and white. Please make sure that all categories in an exhibit can be distinguished from each other.** Align numbers correctly by decimal points; use the same number of decimal points for the same sorts of numbers; center headings, columns, and numbers correctly; use the exact same language in successive appearances; identify any bold-faced or italicized entries in exhibits; and provide any source notes necessary.

6. **Graphs**. Please submit graphs for accepted papers in electronic form. We cannot produce graphs for authors. Graphs will appear the way you submit them. Please be consistent as to fonts, capitalization, and abbreviations in graphs throughout the paper, and label all axes and lines in graphs clearly and absolutely consistently. When pasting graphs into Word, paste as an object, not as a picture, so we will be able to have access to original graph.

7. **Equations**. Please display called-out equations on separate lines, aligned on the exact same indents as the text paragraphs and with no punctuation following. Number equations consecutively throughout the paper in Arabic numbers at the right-hand margin. Clarify in handwriting any operations signs or Greek letters or any notation that may be unclear. Leave space around operations signs like plus and minus everywhere. We reserve the right to return for resubmission any accepted article that prepares equations in any other way. It would be preferable if manuscripts containing mathematical equations be submitted in Microsoft Word using either Equation Editor or MathType.

8. **Reference Citations**. In the text, please refer to authors and works as: Smith [2000]. Use brackets for the year, not parentheses. The same is true for references within parentheses, such as: "(see also Smith [2000])."

9. Reference Styles

Brokerage house internal publications	Askin, D.J., and S.D. Meyer. "Dollar Rolls: A Low-Cost Financing Technique." Mortgage-Backed Securities Research, Drexel Burnham Lambert, 1986.
Journal articles	Batlin, C.A. "Hedging Mortgage-Backed Securities with Treasury Bond Futures." *Journal of Futures Markets,* 7 (1987), pp. 675-693.
——. "Trading Mortgage-Backed Securities with Treasury Bond Futures." Journal of Futures Markets, 7 (1987), pp. 675-693.	Same author, alphabetized by title, two em-dashes instead of repeating name
Working papers	Boudoukh, J., M. Richardson, R. Stanton, and R.F. Whitelaw. "Pricing Mortgage-Backed Securities in a Multifactor Interest Rate Environment: A Multivariate Density Estimation Approach." Working Paper, New York University, 1995.
Sections of books	Breeden, D.T., and M.J. Giarla. "Hedging Interest Rate Risk with Futures, Swaps, and Options." In F. Fabozzi, ed., *The Handbook of Mortgage-Backed Securities.* Chicago: Probus Publishing, 1992, 3rd edition, pp. 847-960.
Books	Hull, J., ed. *Options, Futures and Other Derivative Securities.* Englewood Cliffs, NJ: Prentice-Hall, 1993, 2nd edition.

10. **Endnotes.** Please put in endnotes only material that is not essential to the understanding of an article. If it is essential, it belongs in the text. Do not place a footnote by the authors' names. Any biographical information can be indicated in a separate section and will not be footnoted. Authors' bio information appearing in the article will be limited to their titles, current affiliations, and locations. Do not include in endnotes full reference details; these belong in a separate references list; see below. We will delete non-essential endnotes in the interest of minimizing distraction and enhancing clarity. We also reserve the right to return to an author any article accepted for publication that includes endnotes with embedded reference detail and no separate references list in exchange for preparation of a paper with the appropriate endnotes and a separate references list.

11. **References lists.** Please list only those articles cited in a separate alphabetical references list at the end of the paper. Please follow absolutely the style you see in this journal. We reserve the right to return any accepted article for preparation of a references list according to this style.

12. **Electronic Files**. Word documents are preferred for the articles themselves. Excel can be used for the preparation of graphic elements, making sure that they are embedded in the Word document prior to submission. <u>For those working with .tek or LaTeX files</u>: ***PDF files of the articles must be submitted***, making sure to embed all fonts when the PDF file is prepared. Please also include a Word file which contains the text of the article.

13. **Copyright Agreement**: Institutional Investor Inc.'s copyright agreement form—giving us non-exclusive rights to publish the material in all media—must be signed prior to publication.

14. Upon acceptance of the article, no further changes are allowed, except with the permission of the editor. If the article has already been forwarded to our production department, any changes must be made on the hard copy of the original submitted manuscript and faxed to them.

Journal of Technical Analysis

ADDRESS FOR SUBMISSION:

Charles D. Kirkpatrick, Editor
Journal of Technical Analysis
Market Technicians Assoc.
74 Main Street, 3rd Floor
Woodbridge, NJ 07095
USA
Phone: 970-884-0821
Fax: 970-884-0823
E-Mail: kirkco@capecod.net
Web: www.mta.org
Address May Change:

PUBLICATION GUIDELINES:

Manuscript Length: Any
Copies Required: Two
Computer Submission: Yes - Disk, Email
Format: MS Word, JPG
Fees to Review: 0.00 US$

Manuscript Style:
    American Psychological Association

CIRCULATION DATA:

Reader: , Business Persons 80%,
    Academics 20%
Frequency of Issue: 2 Times/Year
Copies per Issue: 2,001 - 3,000
Sponsor/Publisher: Market Techicians
    Association, Inc.
Subscribe Price: 50.00 US$ Individual
    Free - MTA Member

REVIEW INFORMATION:

Type of Review: Editorial Review
No. of External Reviewers: 1
No. of In House Reviewers: 1
Acceptance Rate: 21-30%
Time to Review: 2 - 3 Months
Reviewers Comments: Yes
Invited Articles: 11-20%
Fees to Publish: 0.00 US$

MANUSCRIPT TOPICS:
Portfolio & Security Analysis; Psychology of Financial Markets; Technical Analysis of Financial Markets; Trading Systems

MANUSCRIPT GUIDELINES/COMMENTS:

We want your article to be published and to be read. In the latter regard, we ask for active simple rather than passive sentences, minimal syllables per word, and brevity. Charts and graphs must be cited in the text, clearly marked, and limited in number. All equations should be explained in simple English, and introductions and summaries should be concise and informative.

1. Authors should submit, with a cover letter, their manuscripts and supporting material on a 1.44MB diskette or through email. The cover letter should include the authors' names, addresses, telephone numbers, email addresses, the article title, format of the manuscript and charts, and a brief description of the files submitted. We prefer Word for documents, and *.jpg for charts, graphs or illustrations.

2. As well as the manuscript, referees, endnotes, tables, charts, figures, or illustrations, each in separate files on the diskette, we request that the authors' submit a non-technical abstract of the paper as well as a short biography of each author, including educational background and special designations such as PhD., CFA or CMT.

3. References should be limited to works cited in the text and should follow the format standards of the *Journal of Finance*.

4. Upon acceptance of the article, to conform to the above style conventions, we maintain the right to make revisions or to return the manuscript to the author for revisions.

Please submit your non-CMT paper to Charles D. Kirkpatrick II, CMT, 7669 CR 502, Bayfield, CO 81122-9007—kirkco@capecod.net.

Journal of the Academy of Finance

ADDRESS FOR SUBMISSION:

Raj Kohli, Editor
Journal of the Academy of Finance
Indiana University at South Bend
Division of Business and Economics
1700 Mishawaka Avenue
South Bend, IN 46634
USA
Phone: 219-237-4144
Fax: 219-237-4599
E-Mail: rkohli@iusb.edu
Web:
Address May Change:

PUBLICATION GUIDELINES:

Manuscript Length: 10-14 Maximum
Copies Required: Four
Computer Submission: No
Format: None
Fees to Review: 0.00 US$

Manuscript Style:
No Reply

CIRCULATION DATA:

Reader: Academics
Frequency of Issue: Yearly
Copies per Issue: Less than 1,000
Sponsor/Publisher: Academy of Finance
Subscribe Price: 25.00 US$

REVIEW INFORMATION:

Type of Review: Blind Review
No. of External Reviewers: 2
No. of In House Reviewers: 0
Acceptance Rate: 50%
Time to Review: 4 - 6 Months
Reviewers Comments: Yes
Invited Articles: 0-5%
Fees to Publish: 0.00 US$ 1-10 Pages
5.00 US$ Per Page Over 10

MANUSCRIPT TOPICS:

Corporate Finance; Financial Institutions; Insurance & Risk Management; International Finance; Portfolio & Security Analysis; Real Estate

MANUSCRIPT GUIDELINES/COMMENTS:

Special Editor Guidelines

Submissions must be postmarked between July 1 and September 30. Any submissions mailed after September 30 of a year will not be considered for publication in the journal edition of the following year. Those papers will be returned to the authors with a recommendation to resubmit between July 1 and September 30 of the next year.

Submitters may be invited to participate in the review process and may be asked to present their papers at the annual meeting of the Academy of Finance. The Academy of Finance's national conference has traditionally been held in Chicago, over a three-day period, between the last week in February and mid-March. Only articles presented at the annual meeting will be considered for inclusion in the journal, which is published in April. Authors of accepted submissions will be asked to submit a camera-ready copy of their manuscript and an electronic copy, using either WordPerfect or Microsoft Word.

Style Sheet

Author's Name*

In order to publish a high quality publication and to keep the costs manageable, certain standards and criteria have been established. Thus, all authors must follow the following instructions.

Submission Deadline. Mail your paper directly to the editor no later than January 10, 2001. Please do not send your paper to the Program Chair.

Margins. Margins for the first page of manuscript should be 1½" from top, 1¼" from left, and 1" from right and bottom of the page. The margins for all other pages must be same as for the first page with the top margin reduced to 1" only. All pages must be numbered.

Author(s) Name(s). On the first page, the author's name should be a double-space below the title of the paper with an asterisk (*). At the bottom of the first page, please give your title, department name, university, telephone number and e-mail address (see Website). Please do not use cover sheet.

Table and Bibliography. All tables must be numbered in roman numerals and placed just before the bibliography. Place references in the paper inside parentheses, e.g., (Fama 1993; Balik 1991). Explanatory footnotes are discouraged, but necessary footnotes should be numbered and placed at the bottom of the page on which they appear. Bibliography containing all references should appear at the end of the paper.

Other Requirements. The manuscript should not exceed a maximum of 10 single-spaced typed pages (Times New Roman, 12 point font), including tables and bibliography. For any page over this limit, there will be a five-dollar ($5) additional charge for each page or any part thereof. (Make your check payable to the Academy of Finance.) If you do not follow the suggested format and guidelines for the Review of the Academy of Finance, your paper will not be published. Please mail your package containing a copy of the paper, on 3.5" high-density disk (WordPerfect 7.0 Windows or higher) to the editor. You can also email your paper as a WordPerfect.

* Title, Department, School, Telephone, Email

Journal of the Asia Pacific Economy

ADDRESS FOR SUBMISSION:

Maureen Todhunter, Editorial Assistant
Journal of the Asia Pacific Economy
Griffith University
School of International Business
and Asian Studies
Nathan, QLD 4111
Australia
Phone: +61 7 387-55368
Fax: +61 7 3875 5111
E-Mail: m.todhunter@griffith.gu.edu.au
Web: www.tandf.co.uk
Address May Change:

CIRCULATION DATA:

Reader: Academics
Frequency of Issue: 3 Times/Year
Copies per Issue: Less than 1,000
Sponsor/Publisher: Routledge Journals,
Taylor & Francis
Subscribe Price: 83.00 US$ Individual
380.00 US$ Institution
55.00 Pounds Indv, 233 Pounds Inst

PUBLICATION GUIDELINES:

Manuscript Length: 16-20
Copies Required: Three
Computer Submission: Yes
Format: MS Word or Text File
Fees to Review: 0.00 US$

Manuscript Style:
See Manuscript Guidelines

REVIEW INFORMATION:

Type of Review: Blind Review
No. of External Reviewers: 2
No. of In House Reviewers: 0
Acceptance Rate: 50%
Time to Review: 2 - 3 Months
Reviewers Comments: Yes
Invited Articles: 6-10%
Fees to Publish: 0.00 US$

MANUSCRIPT TOPICS:

Economic Development; Economic History; Fiscal Policy; International Economics & Trade; International Finance; Macro Economics; Micro Economics; Monetary Policy; Portfolio & Security Analysis; Public Policy Economics; Regional Economics

MANUSCRIPT GUIDELINES/COMMENTS:

Aims and Scope

Journal of the Asia Pacific Economy (*JAPE*) aims to promote greater understanding of the complex economic, historical, political, social and cultural factors that have influenced and continue to shape the transformation of the diverse economies that make up the Asia Pacific region. The *JAPE* editorial policy is to maintain a sound balance between theoretical and empirical works. *JAPE* publishes research papers written from the perspective of a single discipline such as economics, politics or sociology, and it particularly welcomes multi-disciplinary perspectives. Submissions can range from overview articles spanning the region, to papers with a detailed focus on particular issues facing individual countries.

Specifically, we ask authors to state clearly at the outset the research problem and motivation of their research. Papers should not be simply one more application of a formal model or statistical technique. Authors should note that discussion of results must make sense intuitively, and relate to the institutional and historical context of the geographic area under analysis. We particularly ask authors to spell out the practical policy implications of their work for governments and business.

In addition to articles, *JAPE* publishes short notes, comments and book reviews.

Submission of Manuscripts
Please send papers to be considered for publication in this journal to the address listed above.

Send the paper as an e-mail attachment, followed by regular mail of one paper copy with original illustrations, and a copy on computer disk, with details of the computer make and model and the name and version of software used (preferably Word 6 or 7). If you cannot send your paper electronically, please post one paper copy and computer disk. Authors need to ensure that all copies of the submission sent to us—e-mailed, computer disk and paper copy—are identical.

Authors should submit with all papers to be considered for publication: (1) an abstract of the paper, of up to 150 words; (2) a list of up to six keywords to be used for indexing and abstracting; (3) JEL classification/s for your paper. Access the classification on the American Economics Association's Website: http://www.aeaweb.org/journal/elclasjn.html. (4) a brief explanatory piece about all authors for Notes on Contributors. Also provide full postal and e-mail addresses and telephone and fax numbers for all authors.

Submissions should be typed with double-line spacing (including all notes and references), preferably A4 sized. English/Australian or American spelling can be used as long as it is used consistently, but English punctuation will be adopted by the Publishers. Permission to quote from or reproduce copyright material must be obtained by authors before submission. Acknowledgements should be included in the typescript, preferably in the form of an Acknowledgements section at the end of the paper. Source and copyright of photographs or figures should be acknowledged immediately below them if appropriate. Notes should be kept to a minimum as endnotes. Please indicate date of finalizing the manuscript, and if possible word count at the end of the text.

Submission of a paper to the journal will be taken to imply that the paper presents original, unpublished work that is not under consideration for publication elsewhere. By submitting a manuscript, the authors agree that the exclusive rights to produce and distribute the article have: been given to the Publishers.

Journal of the International Academy for Case Studies

ADDRESS FOR SUBMISSION:

Current Editor/Check Web Site
Journal of the International Academy for
  Case Studies
Digital Submission Through Web Site
Address other questions to:
  Jim or JoAnn Carland at #s below
USA
Phone: 828-293-9151
Fax: 828-293-9407
E-Mail: info@alliedacademies.org
Web: www.alliedacademies.org
Address May Change:

PUBLICATION GUIDELINES:

Manuscript Length: 16-20
Copies Required: Submit Through Web
Computer Submission: Yes
Format: MS Word, WordPerfect
Fees to Review: 0.00 US$

Manuscript Style:
  American Psychological Association

CIRCULATION DATA:

Reader: Academics
Frequency of Issue: Bi-Monthly
Copies per Issue: Less than 1,000
Sponsor/Publisher: Allied Academies, Inc.
Subscribe Price: 75.00 US$ Individual
  150.00 US$ Foreign

REVIEW INFORMATION:

Type of Review: Blind Review
No. of External Reviewers: 3
No. of In House Reviewers: 2
Acceptance Rate: 21-30%
Time to Review: 3-4 Months
Reviewers Comments: Yes
Invited Articles: 0-5%
Fees to Publish: 75.00 US$ Membership

MANUSCRIPT TOPICS:

Corporate Finance; Econometrics; Economic Development; Financial Institutions & Markets; Financial Services; Fiscal Policy; Government & Non-Profit Accounting; Industrial Organization; Insurance; International Economics & Trade; International Finance; Macro Economics; Micro Economics; Monetary Policy; Portfolio & Security Analysis; Public Policy Economics; Real Estate; Regional Economics; Teaching cases in any discipline or area.

MANUSCRIPT GUIDELINES/COMMENTS:

Editorial Comment on Manuscript Topics
Our scope is broader than the topics listed above. The journal publishes Teaching cases in any discipline or area. Cases must be accompanied by an Instructor's Note.

Comments. All authors of published manuscripts must be members of the appropriate academy affiliate of Allied Academies. The current membership fee is US$75.00.

Editorial Policy Guidelines

The primary criterion upon which cases are judged is whether the case, together with its instructor's note, can be an effective teaching tool.

Cases need not conform to any guideline and may be in any discipline. Narrative cases are acceptable as well as disguised field cases, library cases or illustrative cases. Each case must be accompanied by an instructor's note and the note MUST conform to the editorial policy. This policy may be found on the website.

Referees require a decision point in a case and pay particular attention to readability and potential for student interest and involvement. Consequently, cases which DESCRIBE action are NOT generally acceptable. The important point is the use of a case in classroom teaching.

Journal of Transport Economics and Policy

ADDRESS FOR SUBMISSION:

Steve Morrison, Managing Editor
Journal of Transport Economics and Policy
University of Bath
Claverton Down
Bath, BA2 7AY
England
Phone: +44 (0)1225 386-302
Fax: +44 (0)1225 386-767
E-Mail: jtep@management.bath.ac.uk
Web: www.jtep.com
Address May Change:

PUBLICATION GUIDELINES:

Manuscript Length: 20+
Copies Required: Two
Computer Submission: Yes
Format: MS Word, PDF
Fees to Review: 0.00 US$

Manuscript Style:
　See Manuscript Guidelines

CIRCULATION DATA:

Reader: Academics, Professionals
Frequency of Issue: 3 Times/Year
Copies per Issue: 1,001 - 2,000
Sponsor/Publisher: University of Bath,
　London School of Economics
Subscribe Price: 54.00 US$ Individual
　120.00 US$ Institution
　60.00 Pounds Indv., 120 Pounds Inst.

REVIEW INFORMATION:

Type of Review: Editorial Review
No. of External Reviewers: 2
No. of In House Reviewers: 2
Acceptance Rate: 21-30%
Time to Review: 4 - 6 Months
Reviewers Comments: Yes
Invited Articles: 0-5%
Fees to Publish: 0.00 US$

MANUSCRIPT TOPICS:

Econometrics; Economic Development; International Economics & Trade; Micro Economics; Public Policy Economics; Transport Economics & Policy

MANUSCRIPT GUIDELINES/COMMENTS:

Manuscript Guidelines/Comments

1. Articles range from fundamental studies making original contributions to analysis, to those exploring innovations in policy. All articles are refereed by appropriate experts, and editorial policy is assisted by a distinguished international Editorial Board. The *Journal* takes no sides on transport issues; the interest and academic merit of articles are the sole criteria for acceptance.

2. The *Journal* is distributed worldwide; it has subscribers from over 70 countries. This is reflected in its coverage, with transport practices in over 30 countries and every continent forming the basis for articles. Many aspects of urban traffic have been examined both in general and in the context of particular cites, though invariably with universal application. Topics include rail, air and motor vehicle modes, as well as shipping and infrastructure. There are regular notes on developments in government policy.

3. Contributors range from mathematicians and theoretical economists to practicing consultants, administrators and people involved in business. Their nationalities are varied as the countries about which they write.

4. Manuscripts should be submitted electronically in PDF or Word format, supported by two hard copies. If the articles are submitted in PDF format and accepted for publication, a non-PDF format will be required for typesetting.

An abstract of not more than 200 words, detailing the main points of the article, must be submitted with the article.

5. Articles should contain a final section in which the author sets out his or her main conclusions in a way which will be at least broadly intelligible to the non-specialist reader.

6. Camera-ready copy of diagrams must be provided with the manuscript; otherwise, if the article is accepted, a charge will be made to cover the cost of artwork. Diagrams should be clearly drawn and accompanied by the basic statistics that were required for their preparation; the axes must be clearly labelled; the reader must be able to understand the diagrams without hunting in the text for explanations.

7. Where mathematical arguments are used, the full working necessary for justifying each step of the argument should accompany the article, in order to assist the referee. The detailed workings will not be published. Care should be taken to ensure that all signs and symbols are clear and to avoid any possible confusion between, for example, figure 1 and letter 1.

8. Statistical tables should be clearly headed and the reader should be able to understand the meaning of each row or column without hunting in the text for explanations of symbols, etc. Units of measurement, base-dates for index numbers, geographical area covered and sources should be clearly stated. Authors are fully responsible for the accuracy of the data and for checking their proofs; whenever they feel that the referee would have difficulty in testing the derivation of their statistics, they should provide supplementary notes on the methods used, which will not be published.

9. Footnotes should be brief, as they are placed at the foot of the page. Any explanation requiring more than a very few lines should be either included in the text or placed in an appendix at the end of the article.

10. References should be carefully checked, and complete in respect of the place and year of publication. If a bibliographical list is given, it should follow the style used in the current issue. Only these works cited in the text should be included.

11. Authors are expected to read proofs expeditiously and to keep corrections down to a very low level. If alterations are made at the proof stage, the editors reserve the right either not to give effect to them or to make a charge.

12. Because of the heavy pressure on space, the editors will give preference to articles which deal succinctly with an issue which is both important and clearly defined. The editors will not consider articles which have been submitted elsewhere.

13. **Comments on published articles.** Anyone wanting to submit comments on a *Journal* article is asked first to send a copy to the author, inviting him to send the commentator his observations and in particular to explain any points on which the commentator has misunderstood what the author was saying. The commentator is asked to allow the author a reasonable time to reply before he sends anything to the editors, and to enclose any reply which he may have received, so that the convent and rejoinder may be published together.

Journal of Urban Economics

ADDRESS FOR SUBMISSION:

Jan K. Brueckner, Editor
Journal of Urban Economics
University of Illinois
Department of Economics
1206 South Sixth Street
Champaign, IL 61820
USA
Phone: 217-333-4557
Fax: 217-244-6678
E-Mail: jbrueckn@uiuc.edu
Web: www.elsevier.com
Address May Change:

PUBLICATION GUIDELINES:

Manuscript Length: 20-45 Pages
Copies Required: Three
Computer Submission: No
Format: N/A
Fees to Review: 0.00 US$

Manuscript Style:
, A Manual for Authors, 1980, published
by American Mathematical Society

CIRCULATION DATA:

Reader: Academics
Frequency of Issue: Bi-Monthly
Copies per Issue: 600
Sponsor/Publisher: Elsevier Science
    Publishing co.
Subscribe Price: 95.00 US$ Individual
    916.00 US$ Institution
    125.00 Euro Indv, 1,192 Euro Inst

REVIEW INFORMATION:

Type of Review: Editorial Review
No. of External Reviewers: 2
No. of In House Reviewers: 1
Acceptance Rate: 30-35%
Time to Review: 3 - 4 Months
Reviewers Comments: Yes
Invited Articles: 0-5%
Fees to Publish: 0.00 US$

MANUSCRIPT TOPICS:
Econometrics; Fiscal Policy; Micro Economics; Public Policy Economics; Real Estate;
Regional Economics

MANUSCRIPT GUIDELINES/COMMENTS:

Web Page. http://www.elsevier.com/homepage/sae/econworld/econbase/juec/frame.htm

The *Journal of Urban Economics* is the leading journal for articles that illustrate empirical, theoretical, positive, and normative approaches to urban economics. The journal also features brief notes that contain new information, provide commentary on published work, and make new theoretical suggestions about theory.

Information for Authors
The *Journal of Urban Economics* provides a focal point for the publication of research papers in the rapidly expanding field of urban economics. It publishes papers of great scholarly merit on a wide range of topics and employing a wide range of approaches to urban economics. The *Journal* welcomes papers that are theoretical or empirical, positive or normative. Although the

Journal is not intended to be multidisciplinary, papers by noneconomists are welcome if they are of interest to economists. Brief Notes are also published if they lie within the purview of the *Journal* and if they contain new information, comment on published work, or new theoretical suggestions.

Manuscripts should be prepared according to the following style rules (deviation from these rules causes publication delays).

Submission of Manuscripts. Manuscripts must be written in English and should be submitted in triplicate (one original and two photocopies), including three sets of good-quality figures, to: Professor Jan K. Brueckner Editor at the address listed above.

There are no submission fees or page charges. Each manuscript should be accompanied by a letter outlining the basic findings of the paper and their significance.

Original papers only will be considered. Manuscripts are accepted for review with the understanding that the same work has not been and will not be nor is presently submitted elsewhere, and that its submission for publication has been approved by all of the authors and by the institution where the work was carried out; further, that any person cited as a source of personal communications has approved such citation. Written authorization may be required at the Editor's discretion. Articles and any other material published in the *Journal of Urban Economics* represent the opinions of the author(s) and should not be construed to reflect the opinions of the Editor(s) and the Publisher.

Authors submitting a manuscript do so on the understanding that if it is accepted for publication, copyright in the article, including the right to reproduce the article in all forms and media, shall be assigned exclusively to the Publisher. The Copyright Transfer Agreement, which may be copied from the pages following the Information for Authors in the printed journal or found on the journal home page, should be signed by the appropriate person(s) and should accompany the original submission of a manuscript to this journal. The transfer of copyright does not take effect until the manuscript is accepted for publication.

Authors are responsible for obtaining permissions to reprint previously published figures, tables, and other material. Letters of permission should accompany the final submission.

Electronic Transmission of Accepted Manuscripts. Authors are requested to transmit the text and art of the manuscript in electronic form, via either computer disk, e-mail, or FTP, **after all revisions have been incorporated** and the manuscript has been accepted for publication. Submission as an e-mail attachment is acceptable provided that all files are included in a single archive the size of which does not exceed 2 megabytes (jue@acad.com). Manuscripts prepared using TeX or LaTeX are welcome; however, LaTeX(2e) is strongly preferred. Note that the use of other specialized versions of TeX or extensive use of custom macros may necessitate conventional typesetting from the hard-copy manuscript. Hard-copy printouts of the manuscript and art must also be supplied. The manuscript will be edited according to the style of the journal, and authors must read the proofs carefully. Complete instructions for electronic transmission can be found on the Electronic Submission Information page of Academic Press website.

Digital Object Identifier. Academic Press assigns a unique digital object identifier (DOI) to every article it publishes. The DOI appears on the title page of the article. It is assigned after the article has been accepted for publication and persists throughout the lifetime of the article. Because of its persistence, it can be used to query Academic Press for information on the article during the production process, to find the article on the Internet through various Web sites, including IDEAL, and to cite the article in academic references. When an Academic Press article is used in a reference section, authors may wish to include the article's DOI in the reference, as volume and page information is not always available for articles published online. The DOI may be found on the Table of Contents page on the IDEAL Web site. See **References** below for samples of DOIs included in references. Further information may be found at http://www.academicpress.com/doi.

Preparation of Manuscript. Manuscripts should be double-spaced throughout on one side of 8.5 x 11-inch or A4 white paper. Pages should be numbered consecutively and organized as follows:

The **Title Page** (p. 1) should contain the article title, authors' names and complete affiliations, footnotes to the title, a running title of fewer than 35 characters, and the address for manuscript correspondence (including e-mail address and telephone and fax numbers).

The **Abstract** (p. 2) must be a single paragraph that summarizes the main findings of the paper in fewer than 150 words. After the abstract a list of up to 10 key words that will be useful for indexing or searching should be included.

References should be cited in the text by Arabic numerals in brackets, e.g., [1, 2]. Journal titles should be spelled out in full. Personal communications should be cited as such in the text and should not be included in the reference list. Please note the following examples, the first of which shows an article available on IDEAL but not yet assigned to a printed issue.

1. D.W. Early, Rent control, rental housing supply, and the distribution of tenant benefits, *Journal of Urban Economics* (2000), doi:10.1006/juec.1999.2163.

2. D. Feenberg and E.S. Mills, "Measuring the Benefits of Water Pollution Abatement," Academic Press, New York (1980).

3. J. Henkel, K. Stahl, and U. Walz, Coalition building in a spatial economy, *Journal of Urban Economics*, 47, 136–163 (2000), doi:10.1006/juec.1999.2139.

4. G. Peterson and T. Mueller, Regional impact of federal tax and spending policies, in "Alternatives to Confrontation" (E. Arnold, Ed.), Heath, Lexington, MA (1980).

Figures should be in a finished form suitable for publication. Number figures consecutively with Arabic numerals, and indicate the top and the authors on the back of each figure. Lettering on drawings should be professional quality or generated by high-resolution computer graphics and must be large enough to withstand appropriate reduction for publication. **Color Figures**. Illustrations in color can be accepted only if the authors defray the cost.

Tables should be numbered consecutively with Arabic numerals in order of appearance in the text. Type each table double-spaced on a separate page, with a short descriptive title typed directly above and with essential footnotes below. Authors should submit complex tables as camera-ready copy.

Proofs will be sent to the corresponding author. To avoid delay in publication, only necessary changes should be made, and proofs should be returned promptly. Authors will be charged for alterations that exceed 10% of the total cost of composition.

Reprints. Fifty reprints will be provided to the corresponding author free of charge. Additional reprints may be ordered.

Journal of Wealth Management (The)

ADDRESS FOR SUBMISSION:

Jean L.P. Brunel, Editor
Journal of Wealth Management (The)
Brunel Associates
5600 Parkwood Lane
Edina, MN 55436
USA
Phone: 952-933-3580
Fax: 952-933-3590
E-Mail: jean.brunel@worldnet.att.net
Web: www.iijwm.com
Address May Change:

PUBLICATION GUIDELINES:

Manuscript Length: 16-25
Copies Required: Two
Computer Submission: Yes
Format: MS Word
Fees to Review: 0.00 US$

Manuscript Style:
See Manuscript Guidelines

CIRCULATION DATA:

Reader: Academics, Business Persons
Frequency of Issue: Quarterly
Copies per Issue: Less than 1,000
Sponsor/Publisher: Institutional Investor,
Inc.
Subscribe Price: 410.00 US$

REVIEW INFORMATION:

Type of Review: Editorial Review
No. of External Reviewers: 2-3
No. of In House Reviewers: 0
Acceptance Rate: 11-20%
Time to Review: 2 - 3 Months
Reviewers Comments: Yes
Invited Articles: 6-10%
Fees to Publish: 0.00 US$

MANUSCRIPT TOPICS:
Behavioral Economics; Financial Institutions & Markets; Interdisciplinary Issues;
International Finance; Investment Policy; Micro Economics; Performance Measurement;
Portfolio & Security Analysis; Tax Accounting

MANUSCRIPT GUIDELINES/COMMENTS:

Please follow the guidelines below when you prepare a manuscript for submission. The
editors will edit and copyedit articles for clarity and consistency. *Please note that we reserve
the right to return to an author any paper accepted for publication that is not prepared
according to these instructions.*

1. **Article Submission.** Please submit 2 copies double-spaced sized on an 8.5"x11" page with
1.5"-2" margins and numbered pages. Include on the title page the authors' names and titles as
they are to appear, including affiliation, mailing address, telephone and fax numbers, and e-
mail address. Also submit an electronic file. Text should be formatted in 12-point type. If
submitting a PDF file, please prepare with all fonts embedded and, if possible, include an
accompanying Word file which would include the running text. We do not support articles
submitted in WordPerfect. Please save any WordPerfect files as a text document and please

provide separate EPS files for any graphic elements. **All manuscripts are expected to be submitted in final form.** We reserve the right to limit any changes following article formatting based upon content, not style.

2. **Abstract.** On the page after the title page, please provide a brief article summary or abstract suitable for the table of contents. Do not begin the paper with a heading such as "introduction." Do not number section or subsection headings.

3. Do not asterisk or footnote any authors' names listed as bylines. Footnoting should only begin in the body of the article.

4. **Exhibits.** Please put tables and graphs on separate individual pages at the end of the paper. Do not integrate them with the text; do not call them table 1 and figure 1. Please call any tabular or graphical material Exhibits, numbered in Arabic numbers consecutively in order of appearance in the text. We reserve the right to return to an author for reformatting any paper accepted for publication that does not conform to this style.

5. **Exhibit Presentation.** Please organize and present tables consistently throughout a paper, because we will print them the way they are presented to us. **Exhibits should be created as grayscale, as opposed to color, since the journal is printed in black and white. Please make sure that all categories in an exhibit can be distinguished from eachother.** Align numbers correctly by decimal points; use the same number of decimal points for the same sorts of numbers; center headings, columns, and numbers correctly; use the exact same language in successive appearances; identify any bold-faced or italicized entries in exhibits; and provide any source notes necessary.

6. **Graphs.** Please submit graphs for accepted papers in electronic form. We cannot produce graphs for authors. Graphs will appear the way you submit them. Please be consistent as to fonts, capitalization, and abbreviations in graphs throughout the paper, and label all axes and lines in graphs clearly and absolutely consistently. When pasting graphs into Word, paste as an object, not as a picture, so we will be able to have access to original graph.

7. **Equations.** Please display called-out equations on separate lines, aligned on the exact same indents as the text paragraphs and with no punctuation following. Number equations consecutively throughout the paper in Arabic numbers at the right-hand margin. Clarify in handwriting any operations signs or Greek letters or any notation that may be unclear. Leave space around operations signs like plus and minus everywhere. We reserve the right to return for resubmission any accepted article that prepares equations in any other way. It would be preferable if manuscripts containing mathematical equations be submitted in Microsoft Word using either Equation Editor or MathType.

8. **Reference Citations.** In the text, please refer to authors and works as: Smith [2000]. Use brackets for the year, not parentheses. The same is true for references within parentheses, such as: "(see also Smith [2000])."

1024

9. Reference Styles

Brokerage house internal publications	Askin, D.J., and S.D. Meyer. "Dollar Rolls: A Low-Cost Financing Technique." Mortgage-Backed Securities Research, Drexel Burnham Lambert, 1986.
Journal articles	Batlin, C.A. "Hedging Mortgage-Backed Securities with Treasury Bond Futures." *Journal of Futures Markets,* 7 (1987), pp. 675-693.
——. "Trading Mortgage-Backed Securities with Treasury Bond Futures." Journal of Futures Markets, 7 (1987), pp. 675-693.	Same author, alphabetized by title, two em-dashes instead of repeating name
Working papers	Boudoukh, J., M. Richardson, R. Stanton, and R.F. Whitelaw. "Pricing Mortgage-Backed Securities in a Multifactor Interest Rate Environment: A Multivariate Density Estimation Approach." Working Paper, New York University, 1995.
Sections of books	Breeden, D.T., and M.J. Giarla. "Hedging Interest Rate Risk with Futures, Swaps, and Options." In F. Fabozzi, ed., *The Handbook of Mortgage-Backed Securities.* Chicago: Probus Publishing, 1992, 3rd edition, pp. 847-960.
Books	Hull, J., ed. *Options, Futures and Other Derivative Securities.* Englewood Cliffs, NJ: Prentice-Hall, 1993, 2nd edition.

10. **Endnotes.** Please put in endnotes only material that is not essential to the understanding of an article. If it is essential, it belongs in the text. Do not place a footnote by the authors' names. Any biographical information can be indicated in a separate section and will not be footnoted. Authors' bio information appearing in the article will be limited to their titles, current affiliations, and locations. Do not include in endnotes full reference details; these belong in a separate references list; see below. We will delete non-essential endnotes in the interest of minimizing distraction and enhancing clarity. We also reserve the right to return to an author any article accepted for publication that includes endnotes with embedded reference detail and no separate references list in exchange for preparation of a paper with the appropriate endnotes and a separate references list.

11. **References lists.** Please list only those articles cited in a separate alphabetical references list at the end of the paper. Please follow absolutely the style you see in this journal. We reserve the right to return any accepted article for preparation of a references list according to this style.

12. **Electronic Files.** Word documents are preferred for the articles themselves. Excel can be used for the preparation of graphic elements, making sure that they are embedded in the Word document prior to submission. For those working with .tek or LaTeX files: **PDF files of the articles must be submitted**, making sure to embed all fonts when the PDF file is prepared. Please also include a Word file which contains the text of the article.

13. **Copyright Agreement**: Institutional Investor Inc.'s copyright agreement form—giving us non-exclusive rights to publish the material in all media—must be signed prior to publication.

14. Upon acceptance of the article, no further changes are allowed, except with the permission of the editor. If the article has already been forwarded to our production department, any changes must be made on the hard copy of the original submitted manuscript and faxed to them.

Notes

Notes

Notes

Notes

Notes

Notes

Notes